A while ago, I went to West Izu for some hot springs and fishing.

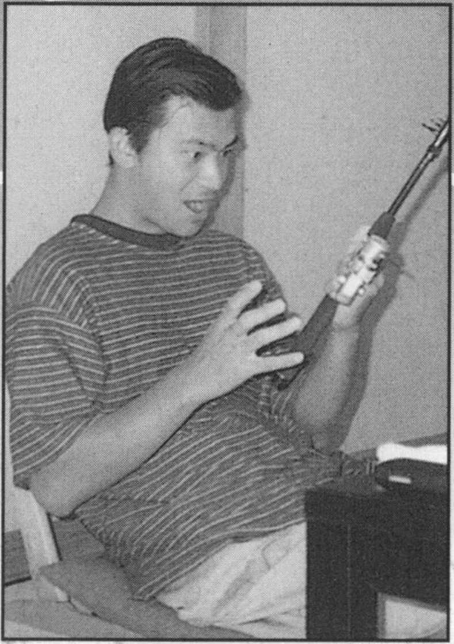

I hooked a cute shark about 20 cm long, but as soon as I shook my fishing rod, I heard a splash...

The reel was missing from the handle?!

Takeshi Konomi 2000

About Takeshi Konomi

Takeshi Konomi exploded onto the manga scene with the incredible **THE PRINCE OF TENNIS**. His refined art style and sleek character designs proved popular with **Weekly Shonen Jump** readers and **THE PRINCE OF TENNIS** became the No. 1 sports manga in Japan almost overnight. Its cast of fascinating male tennis players attracted legions of female readers even though it was originally intended to be a boys' comic. The manga continues to be a success in Japan. A hit anime series was created, as well as several video games and mountains of merchandise.

THE PRINCE OF TENNIS
VOL. 5
The SHONEN JUMP Graphic Novel

STORY AND ART BY
TAKESHI KONOMI

English Adaptation/Gerard Jones
Translation/Joe Yamazaki
Touch-up Art & Lettering/Andy Ristaino
Graphics & Cover Design/Sean Lee
Interior Design/Terry Bennett
Editor/Michelle Pangilinan

Editor in Chief, Books/Alvin Lu
Editor in Chief, Magazines/Marc Weidenbaum
VP, Publishing Licensing/Rika Inouye
VP, Sales & Product Marketing/Gonzalo Ferreyra
VP, Creative/Linda Espinosa
Publisher/Hyoe Narita

Printed in the U.S.A.

Published by VIZ Media, LLC
P.O. Box 77010
San Francisco, CA 94107

SHONEN JUMP Graphic Novel Edition
10 9 8 7 6 5 4
First printing, December 2004
Fourth printing, September 2008

PARENTAL ADVISORY
THE PRINCE OF TENNIS
is rated A and is suitable
for readers of all ages.
ratings.viz.com

THE WORLD'S
MOST POPULAR MANGA

www.shonenjump.com

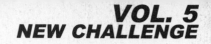

VOL. 5
NEW CHALLENGE

Story & Art by
Takeshi Konomi

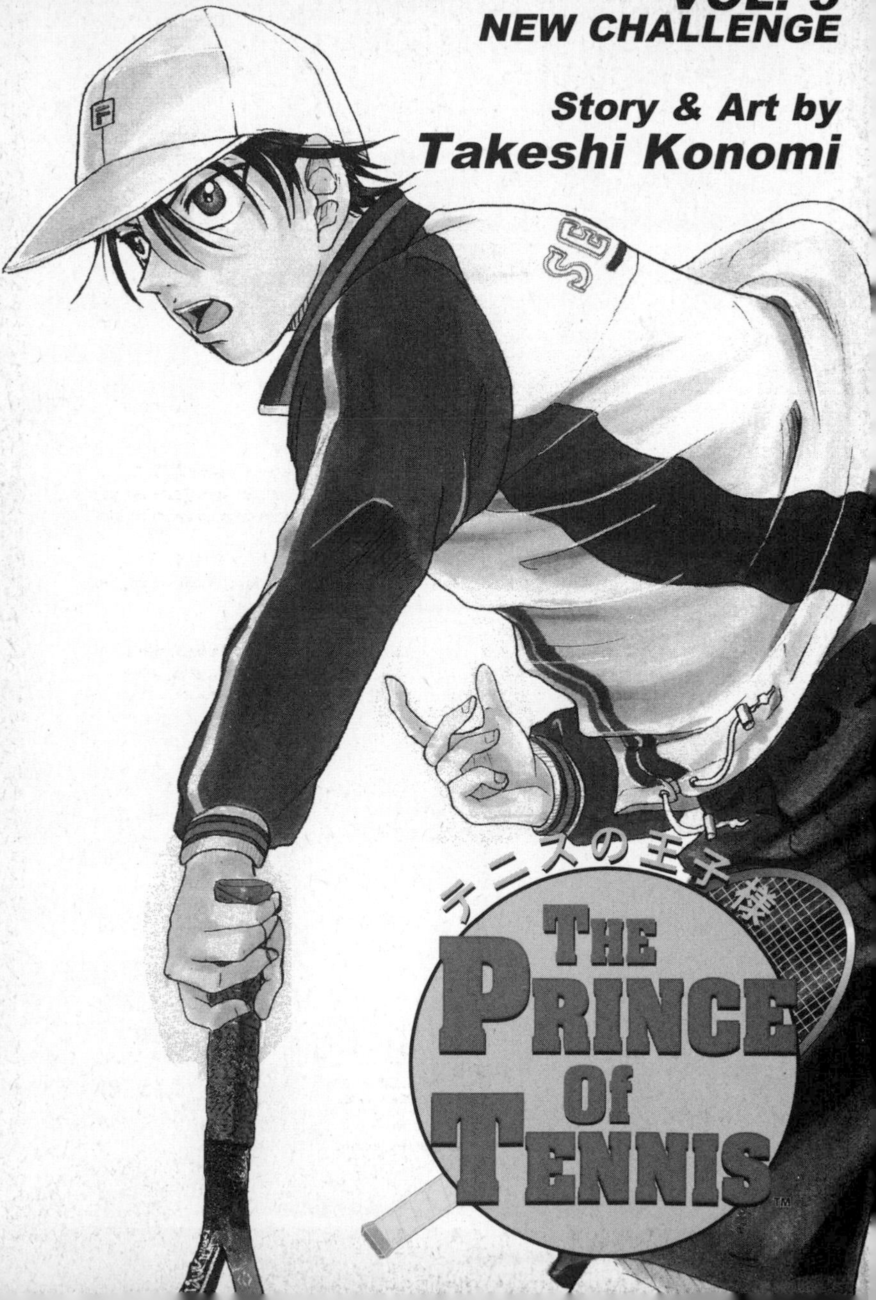

テニスの王子様
THE PRINCE OF TENNIS™

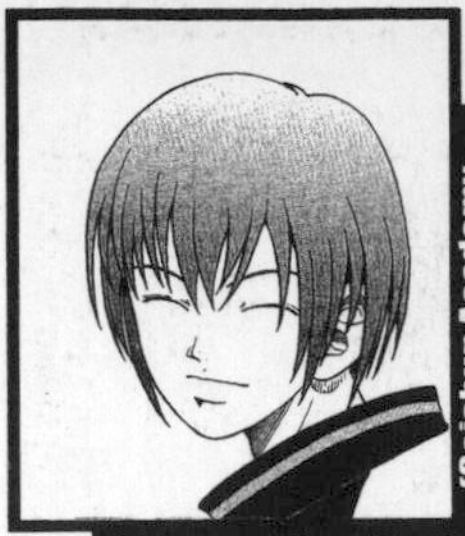

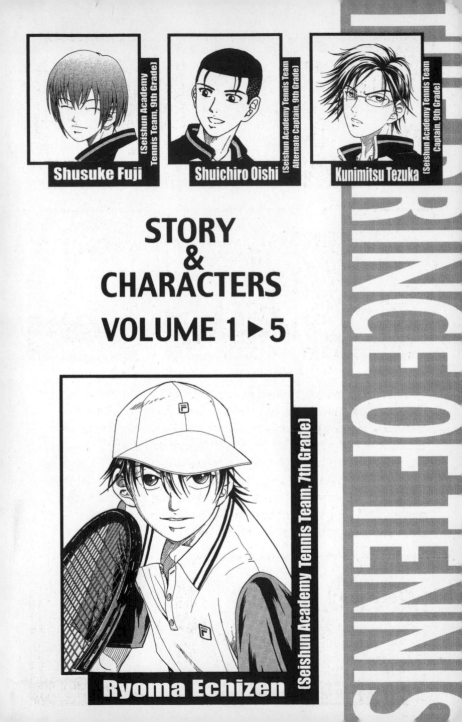

Shusuke Fuji

(Seishun Academy Tennis Team, 9th Grade)

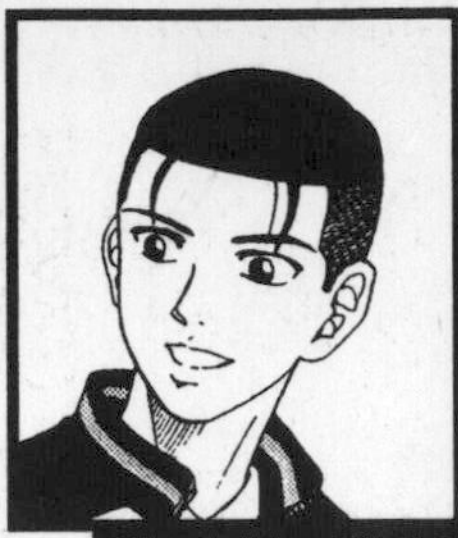

Shuichiro Oishi

(Seishun Academy Tennis Team Alternate Captain, 9th Grade)

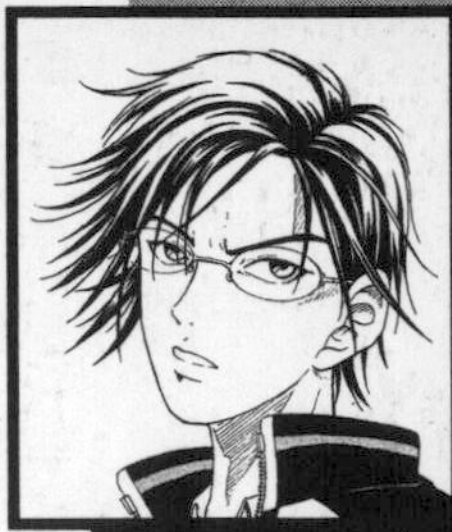

Kunimitsu Tezuka

(Seishun Academy Tennis Team Captain, 9th Grade)

STORY & CHARACTERS VOLUME 1 ▶ 5

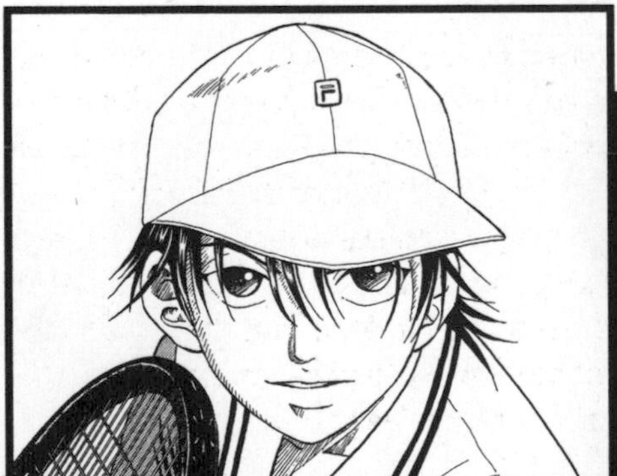

Ryoma Echizen

(Seishun Academy Tennis Team, 7th Grade)

THE PRINCE OF TENNIS

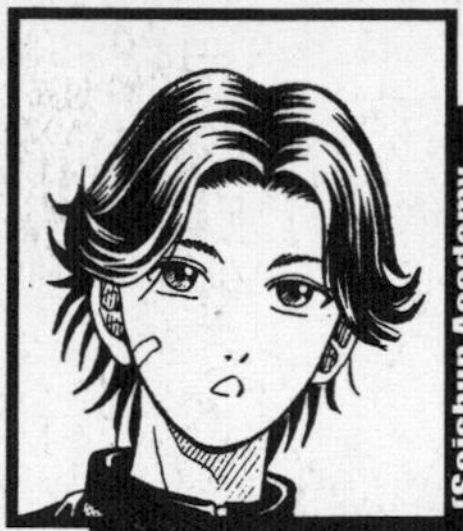

Eiji Kikumaru (Seishun Academy Tennis Team, 9th Grade)

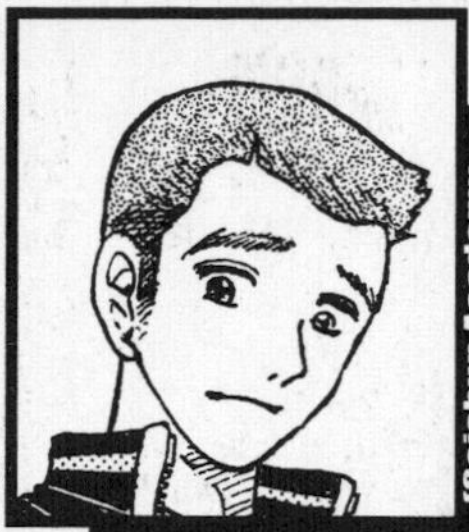

Takashi Kawamura (Seishun Academy Tennis Team, 9th Grade)

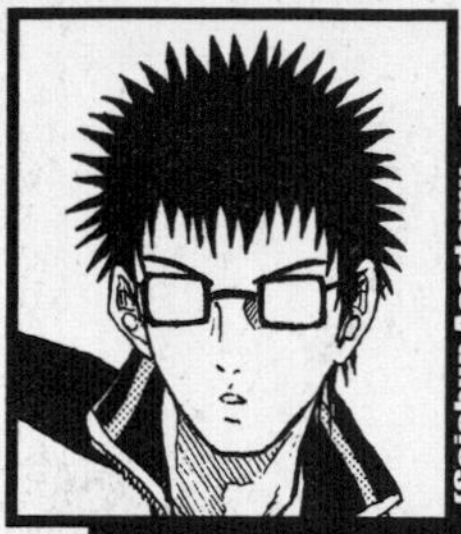

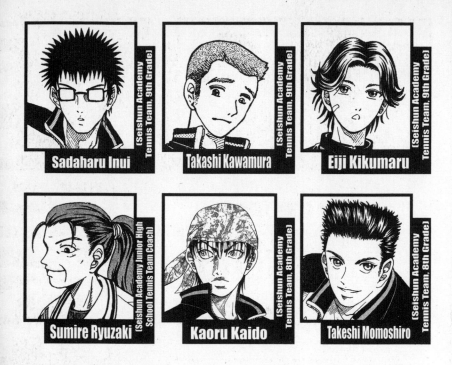

Sadaharu Inui (Seishun Academy Tennis Team, 9th Grade)

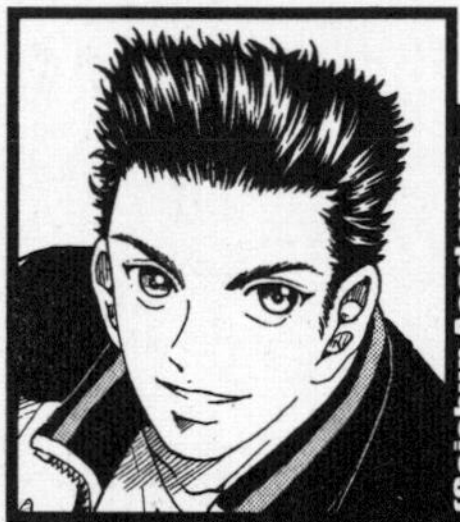

Takeshi Momoshiro (Seishun Academy Tennis Team, 8th Grade)

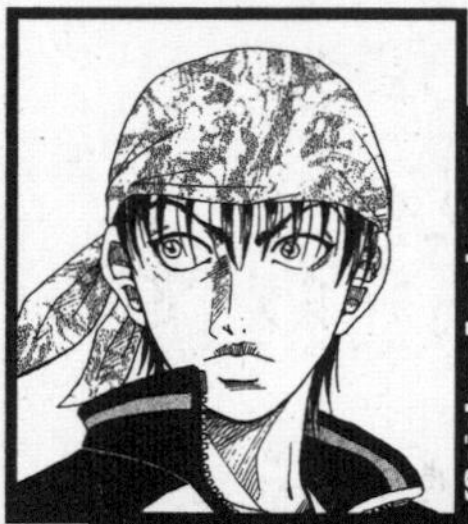

Kaoru Kaido (Seishun Academy Tennis Team, 8th Grade)

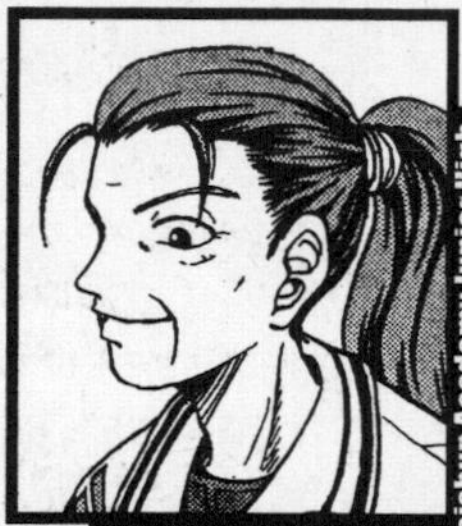

Sumire Ryuzaki (Seishun Academy Junior High School Tennis Team Coach)

Ryoma Echizen, a tennis prodigy and winner of four consecutive U.S. Junior tournaments, has returned to Japan and enrolled at Seishun Academy Junior High. Through his amazing talent, he has become a starter in the District Preliminaries even though he's still in 7th grade. In the first round, Ryoma plays doubles for the first time.

He struggles, but pulls off a win against Gyokurin. Ultimately, Seishun Academy advances to the finals, where they suffer a first-game forfeit loss, but win the second and third matches. Now Seishun's shot at the championship lies in Ryoma's hands...!

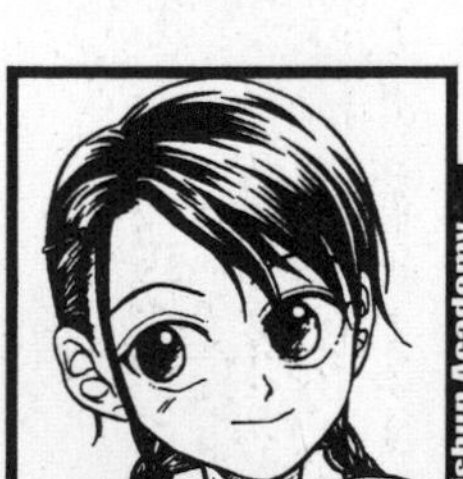

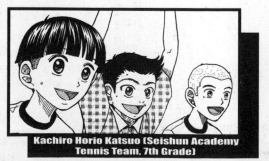

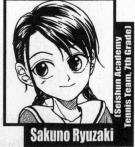

Sakuno Ryuzaki (Seishun Academy Tennis Team, 7th Grade)

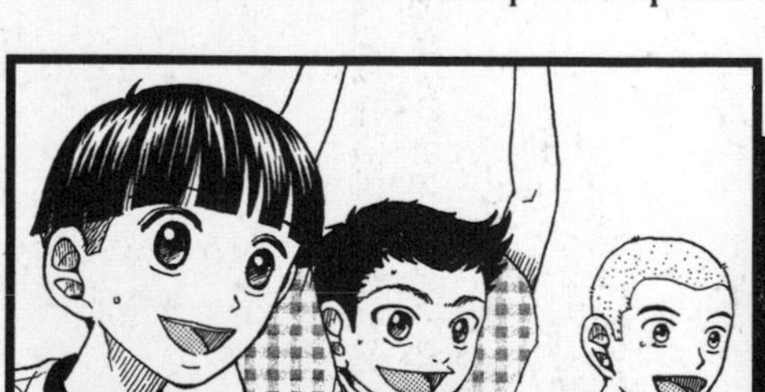

Kachiro Horio Katsuo (Seishun Academy Tennis Team, 7th Grade)

CONTENTS

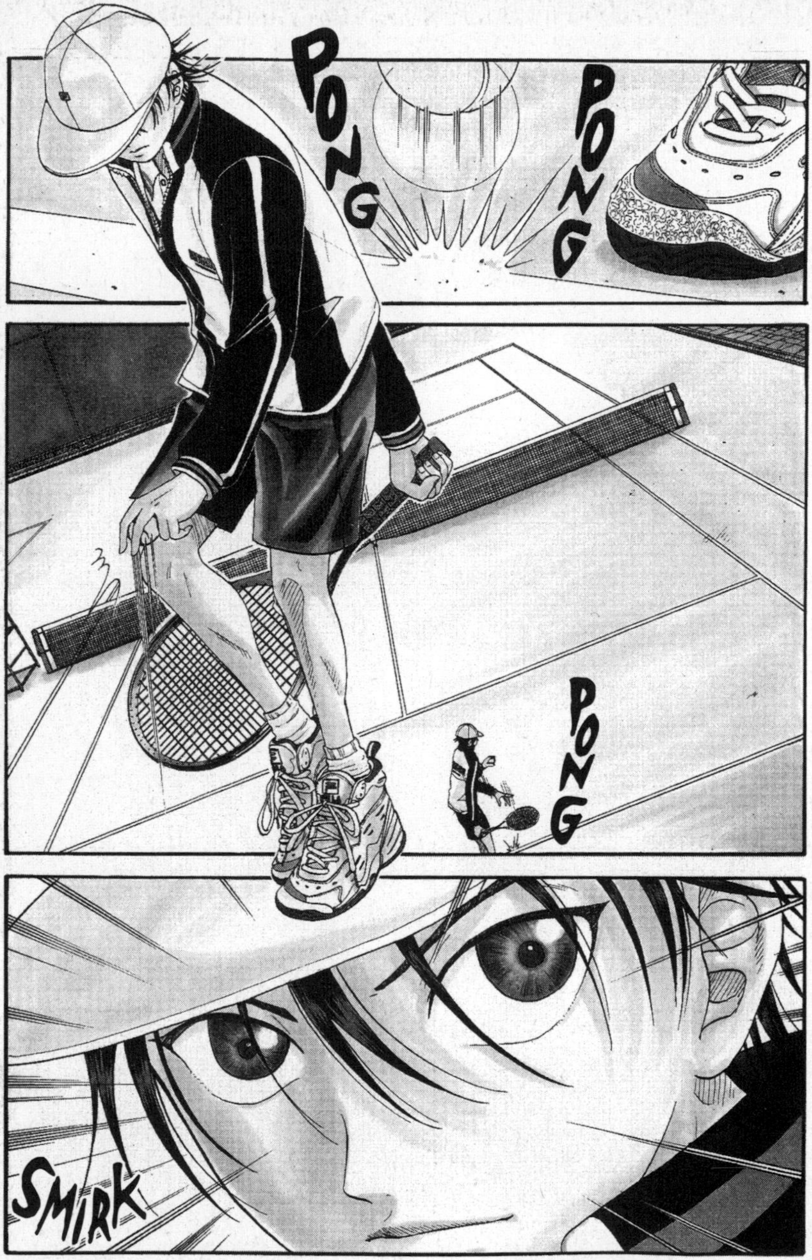
PONG
PONG
PONG
SMIRK

Genius 35: Shock The World!

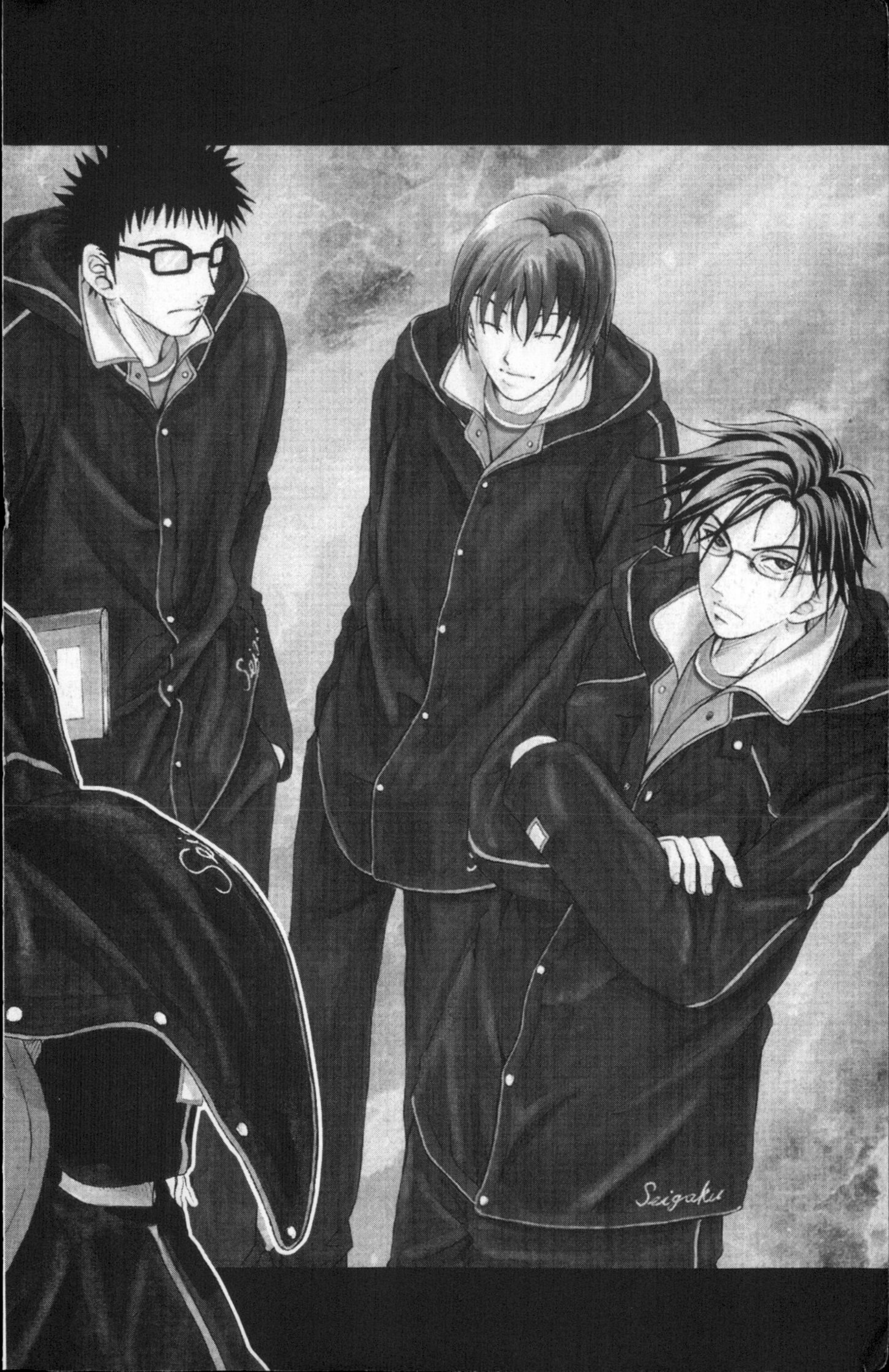
Seigaku

Genius 35:

Shock the World!

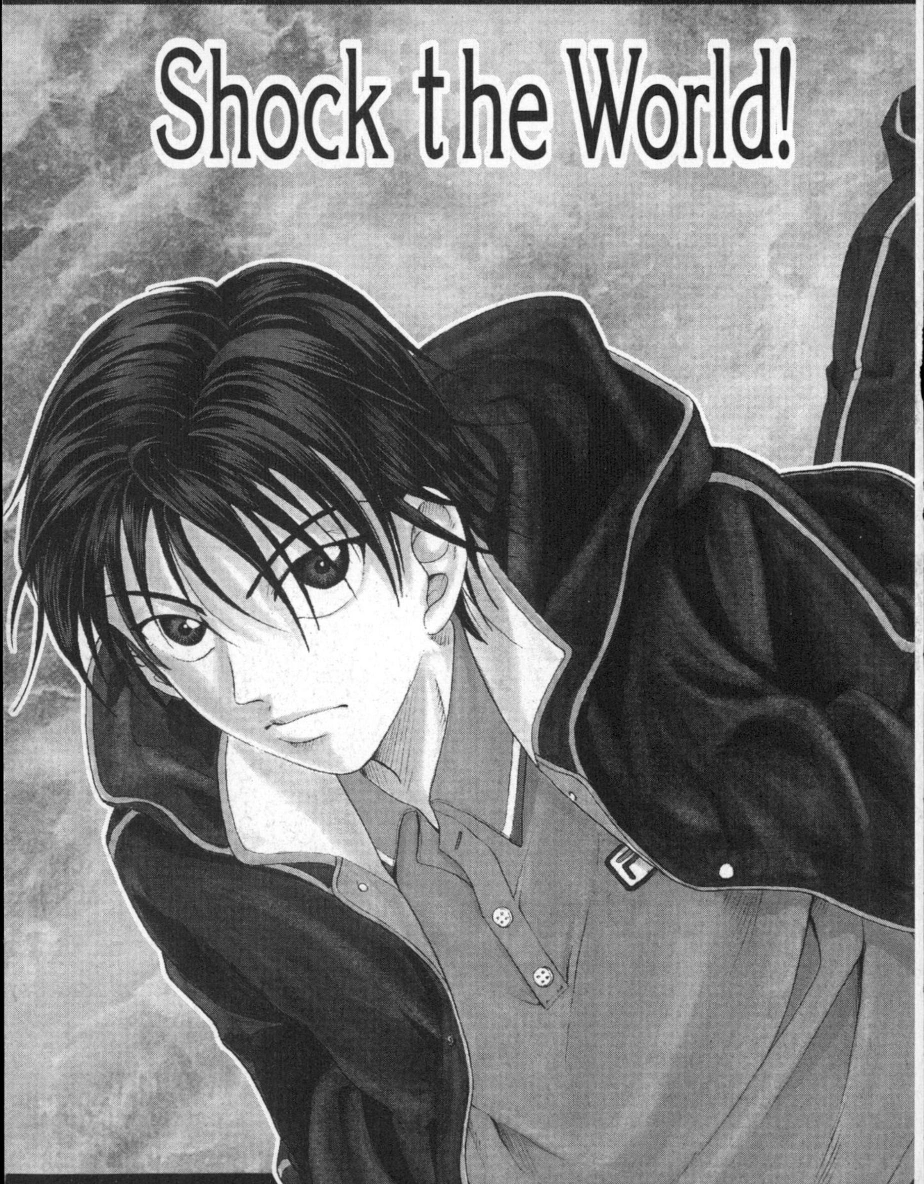

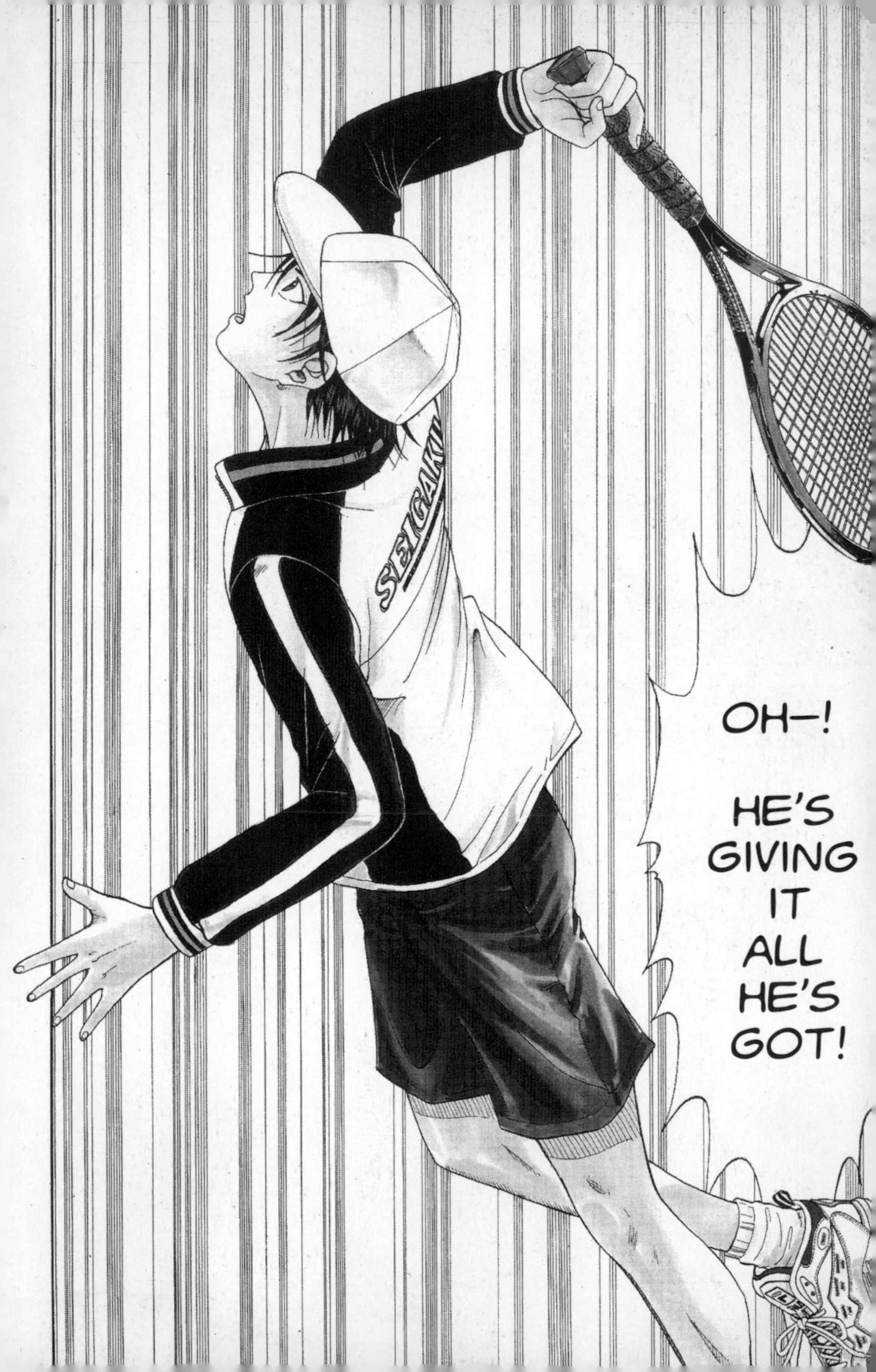
SEIGAKU
OH–!
HE'S GIVING IT ALL HE'S GOT!

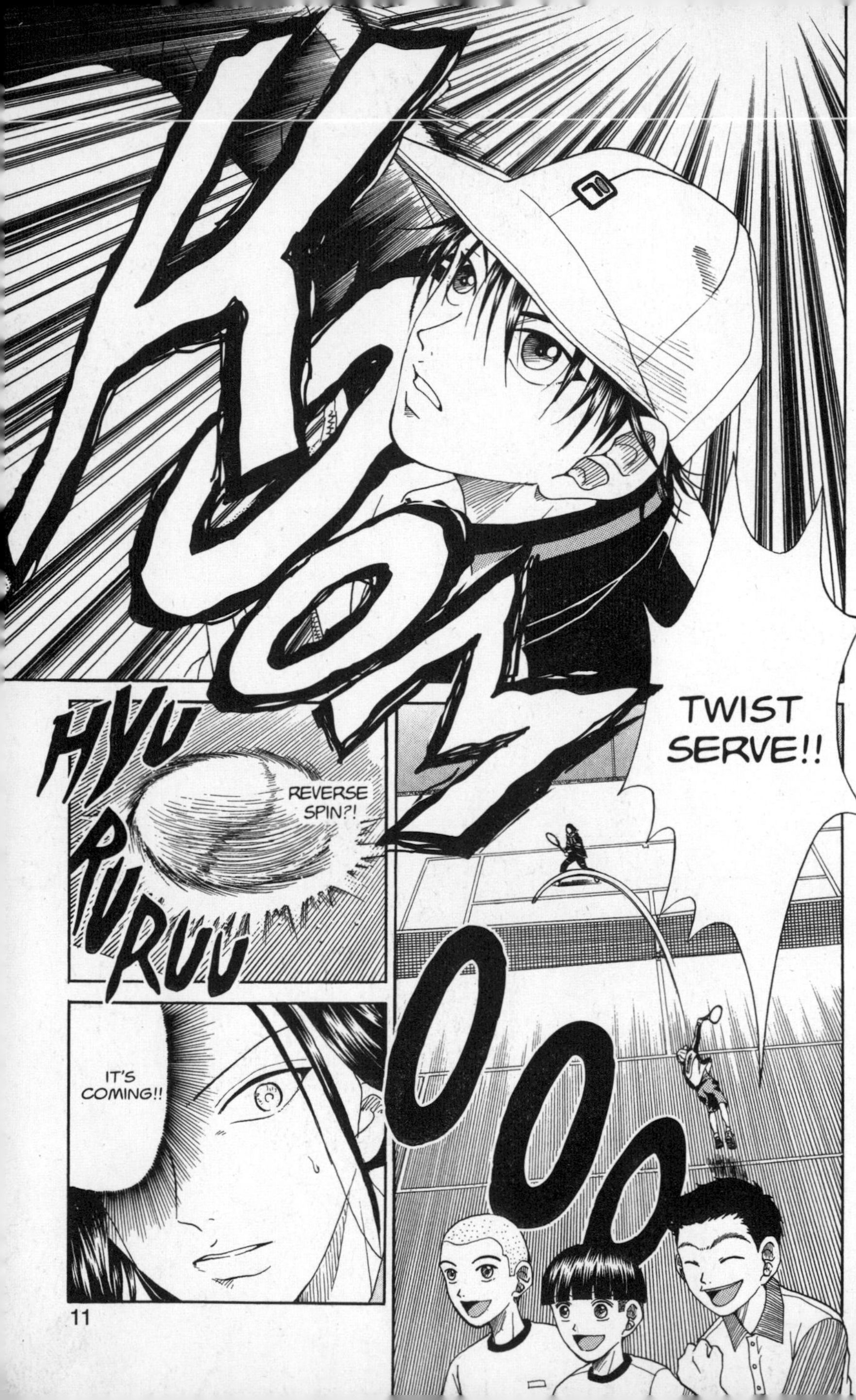
TWIST SERVE!!
REVERSE SPIN?!
IT'S COMING!!

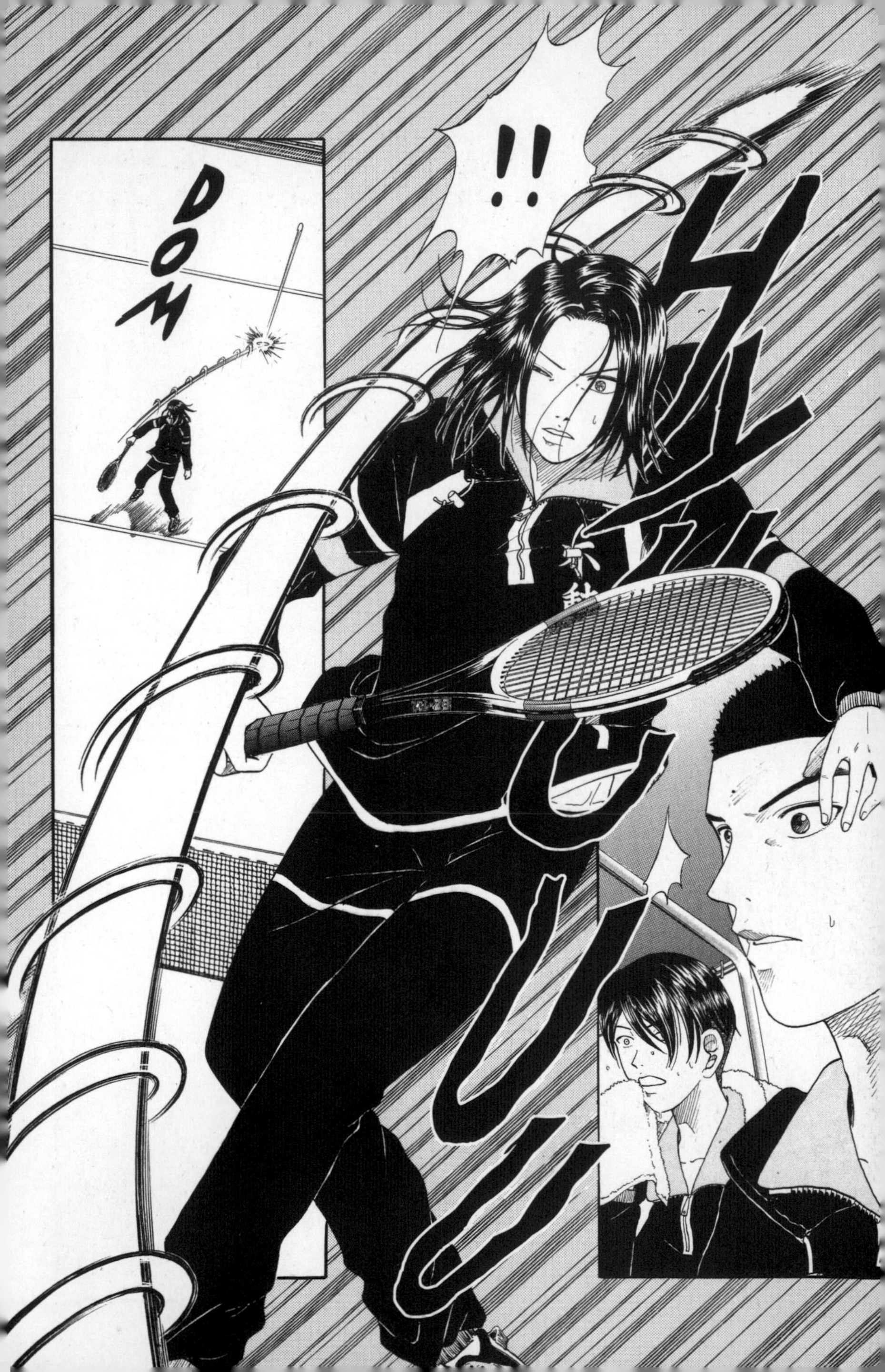
!!
DOM

READ THIS WAY

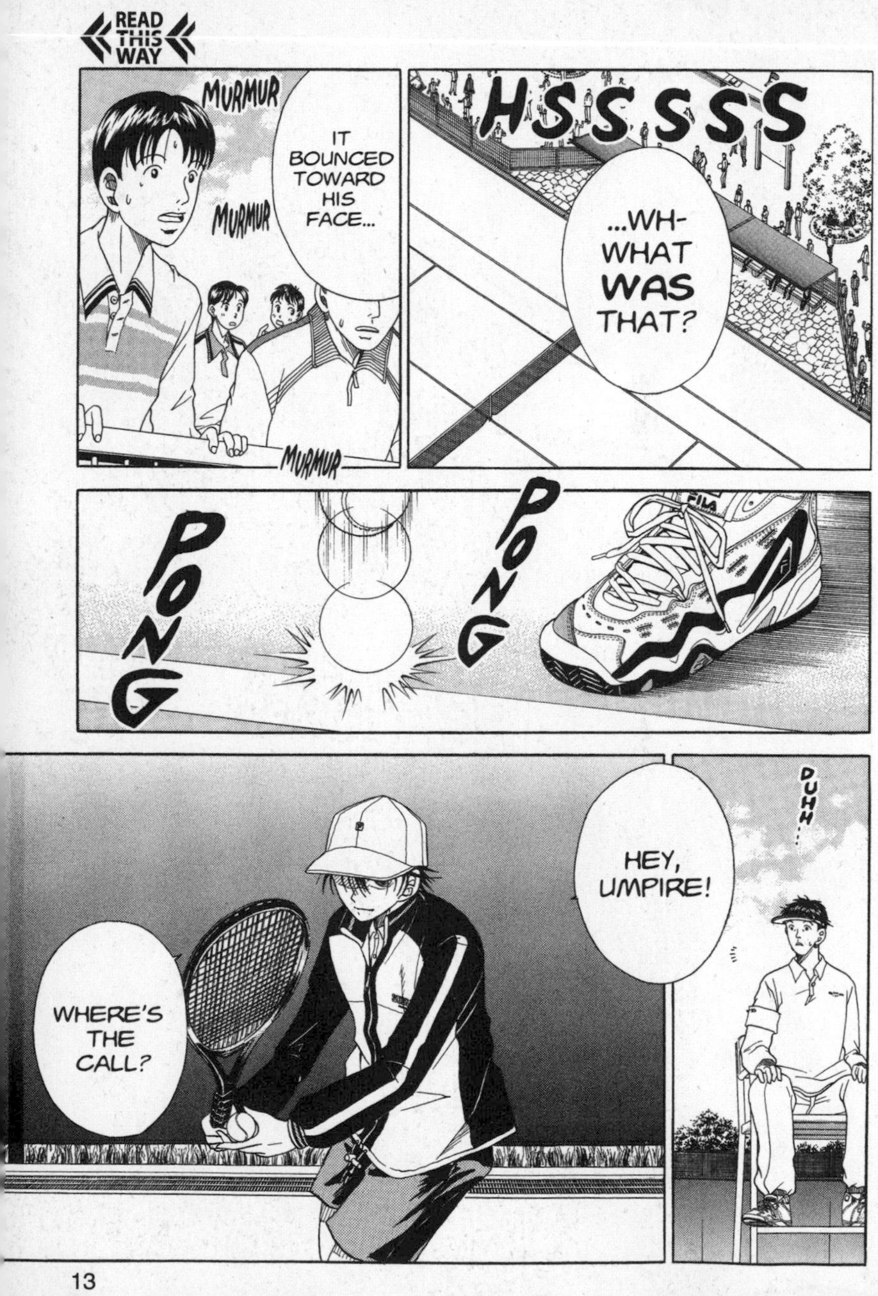
HSSSSS
...WH- WHAT WAS THAT?
MURMUR
IT BOUNCED TOWARD HIS FACE...
MURMUR
MURMUR
PONG
PONG
DUHH...
HEY, UMPIRE!
WHERE'S THE CALL?

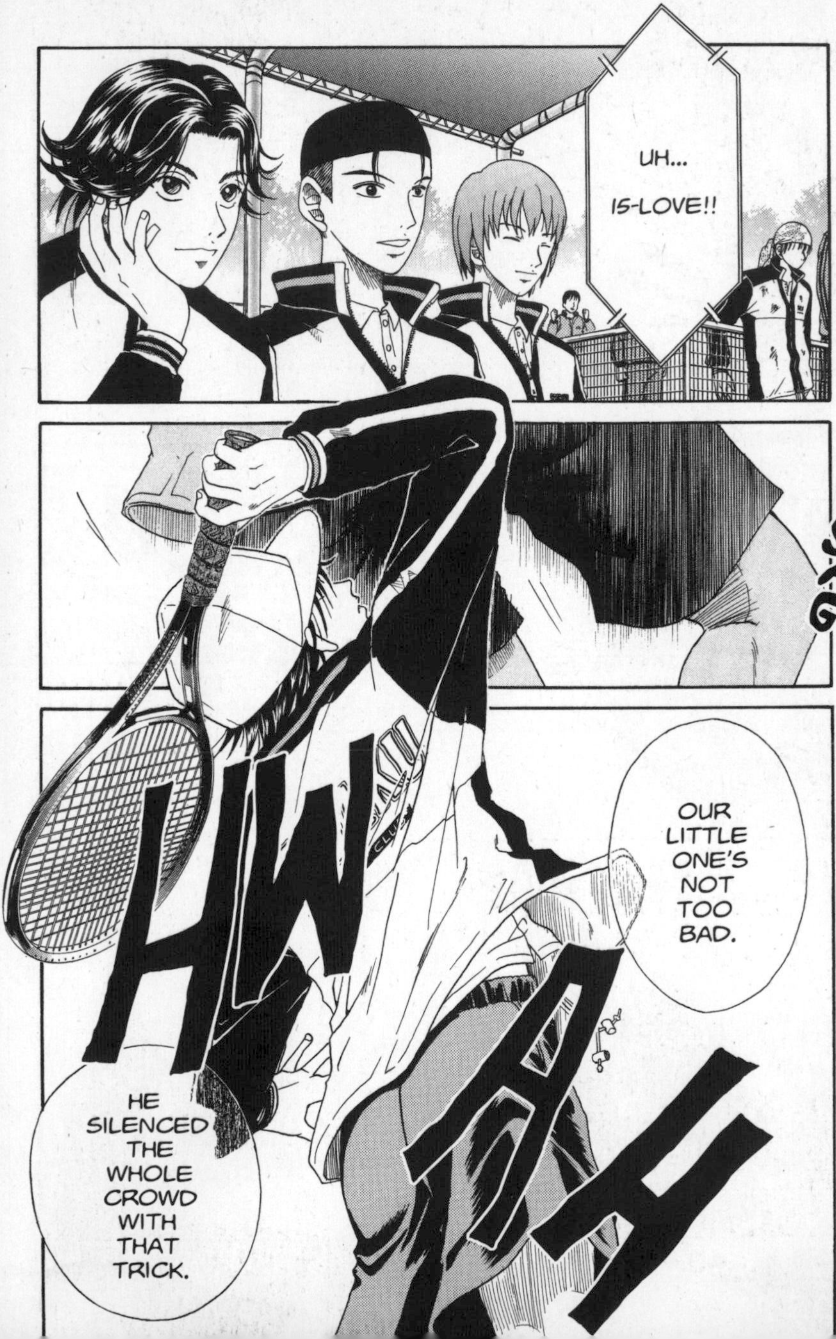
UH... IS-LOVE!!
S-A-G
OUR LITTLE ONE'S NOT TOO BAD.
HWAAH
HE SILENCED THE WHOLE CROWD WITH THAT TRICK.

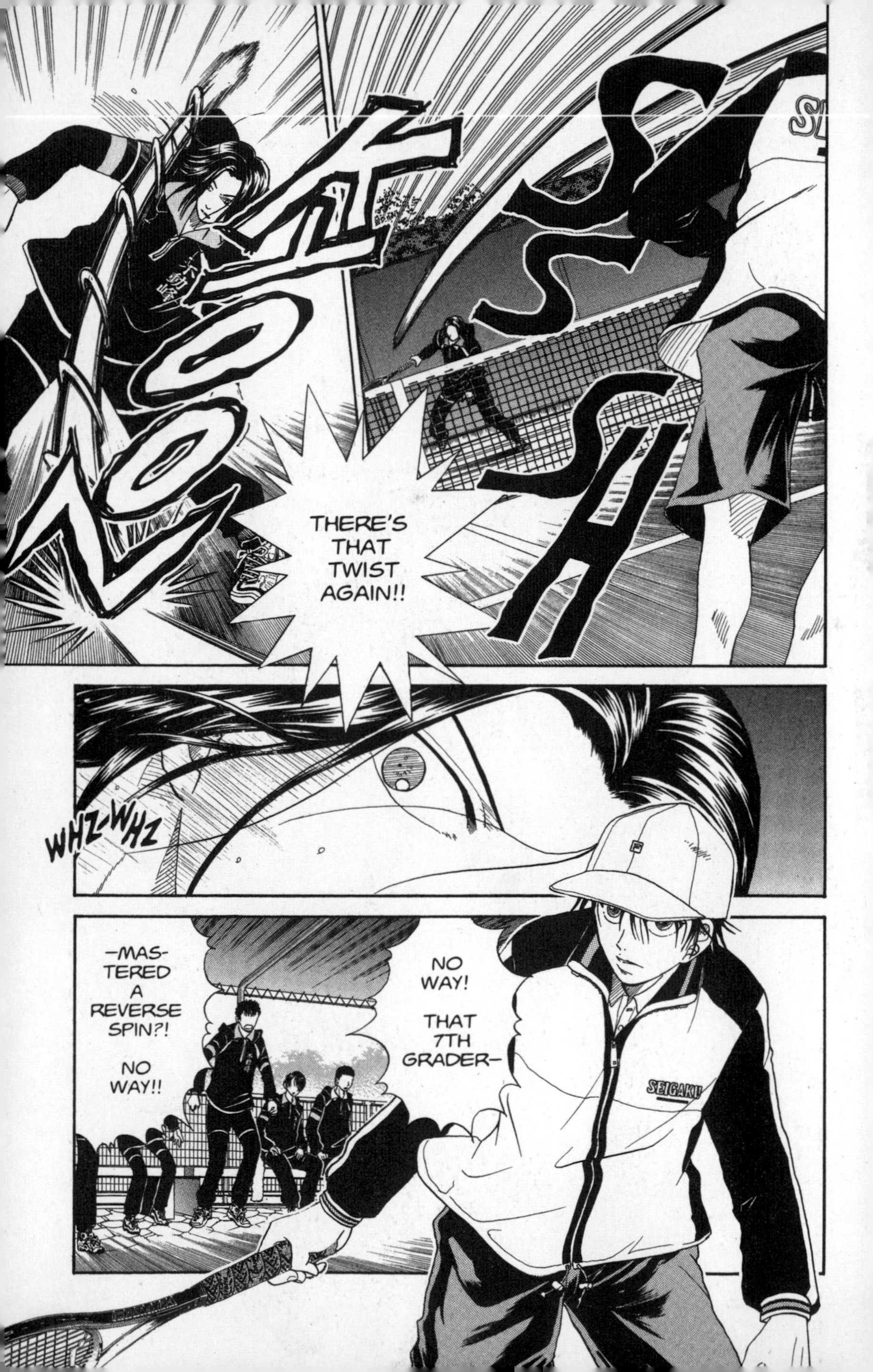
THERE'S THAT TWIST AGAIN!!
WHZ-WHZ
NO WAY! THAT 7TH GRADER—
—MAS-TERED A REVERSE SPIN?!
NO WAY!!

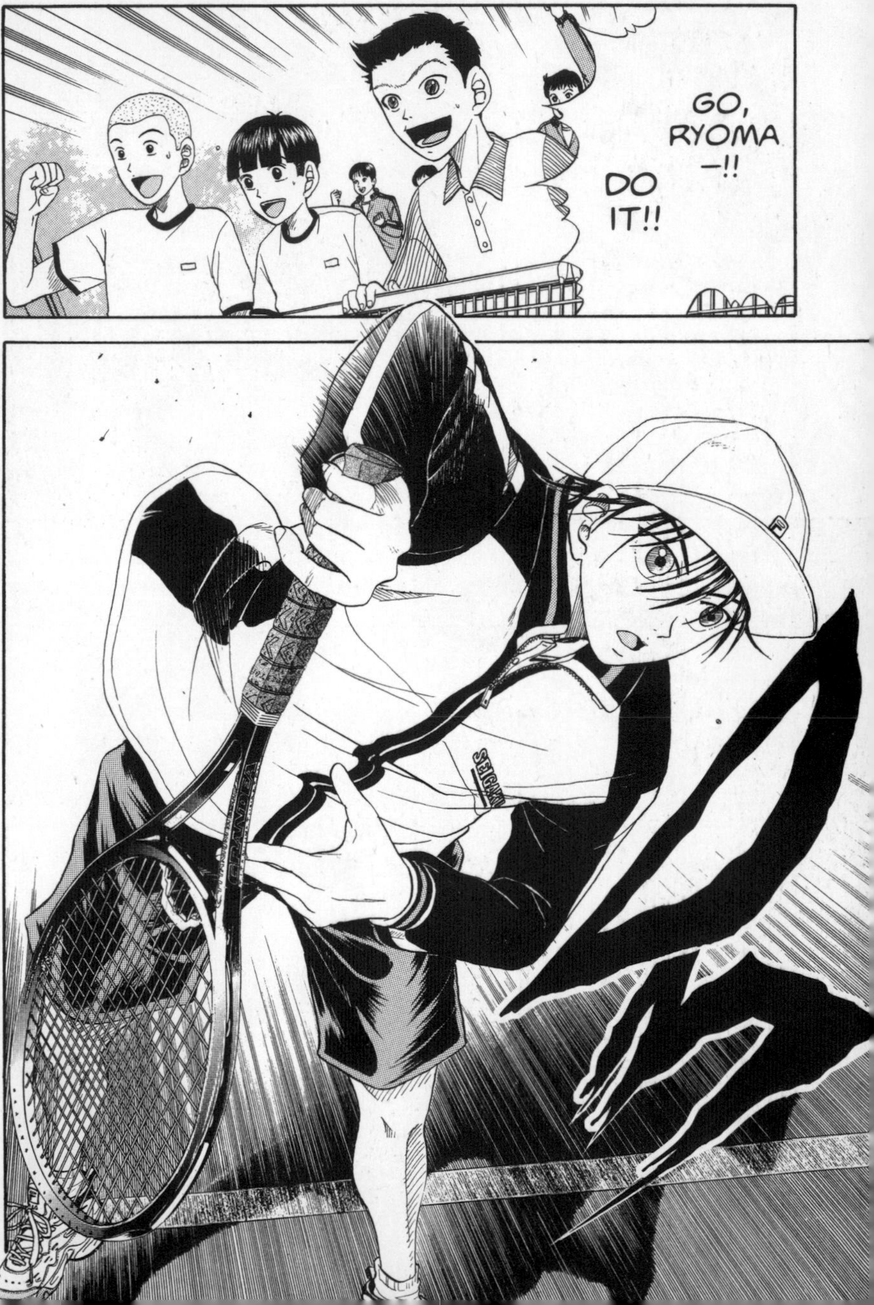
GO, RYOMA —!!
DO IT!!

READ THIS WAY

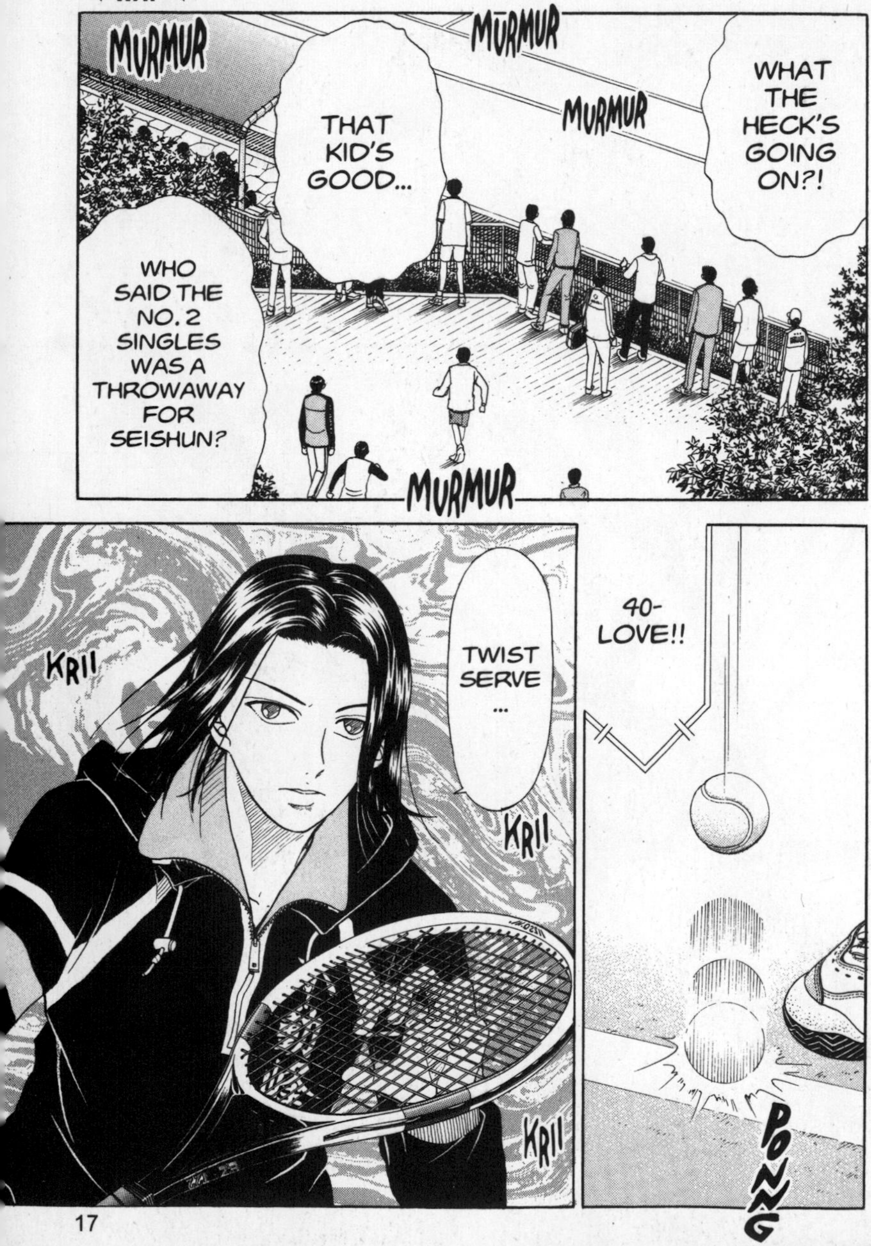

WHAT THE HECK'S GOING ON?!
MURMUR
MURMUR
THAT KID'S GOOD...
MURMUR
WHO SAID THE NO. 2 SINGLES WAS A THROWAWAY FOR SEISHUN?
MURMUR
40-LOVE!!
PONNG
TWIST SERVE ...
KRII
KRII
KRII

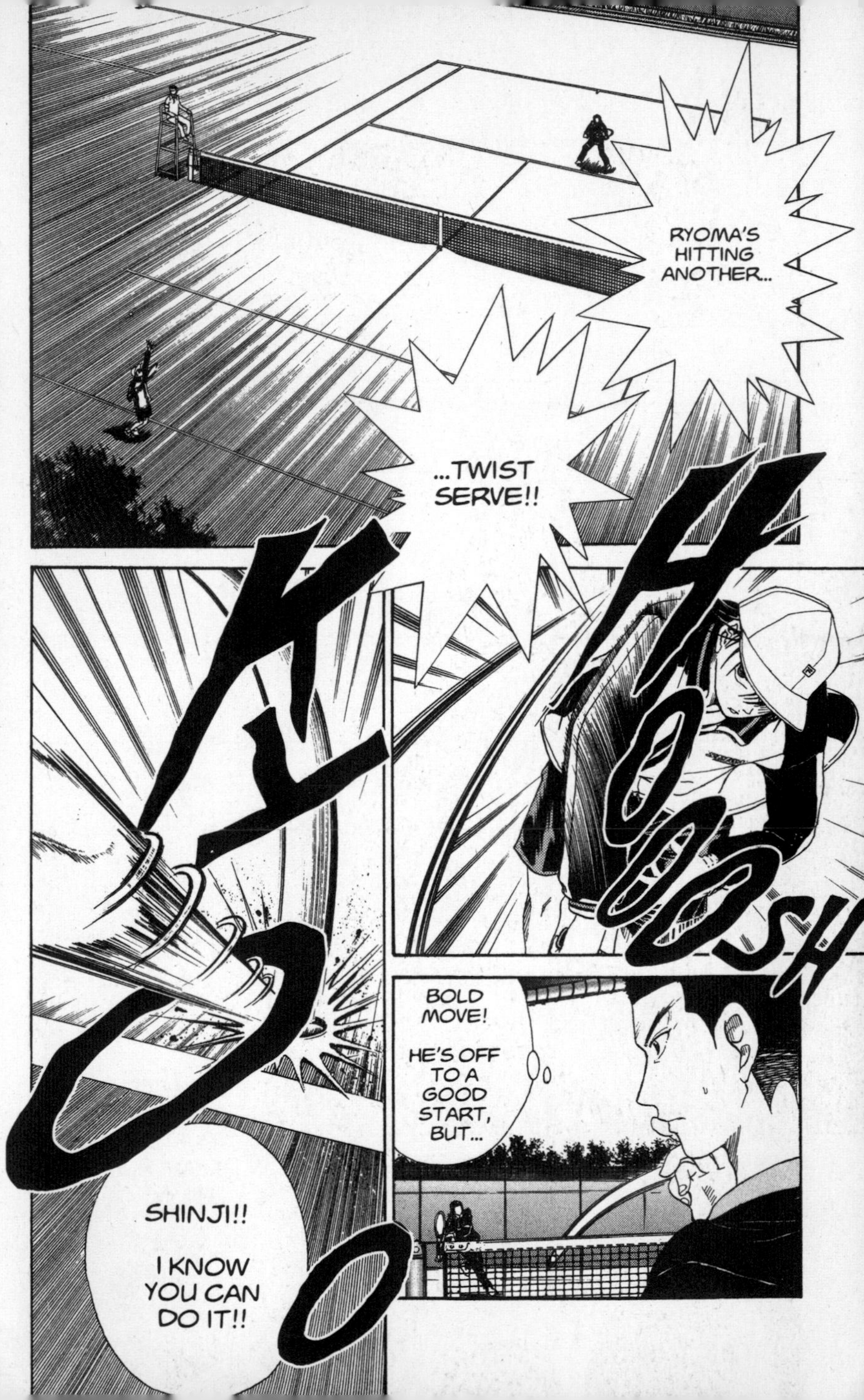
RYOMA'S HITTING ANOTHER...
...TWIST SERVE!!
BOLD MOVE!
HE'S OFF TO A GOOD START, BUT...
SHINJI!!
I KNOW YOU CAN DO IT!!

READ THIS WAY

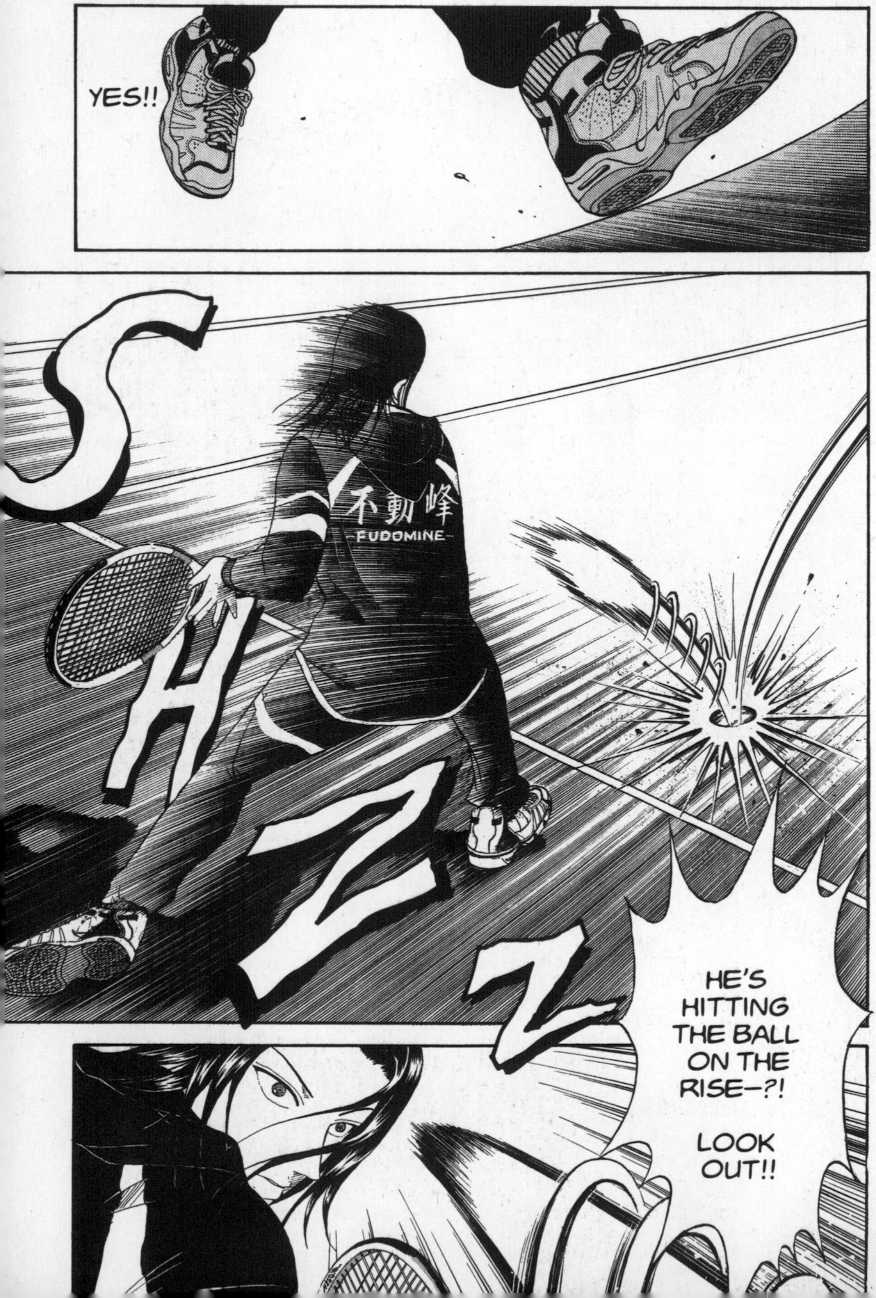
YES!!
SHZZ
不動峰
FUDOMINE
HE'S HITTING THE BALL ON THE RISE–?!
LOOK OUT!!

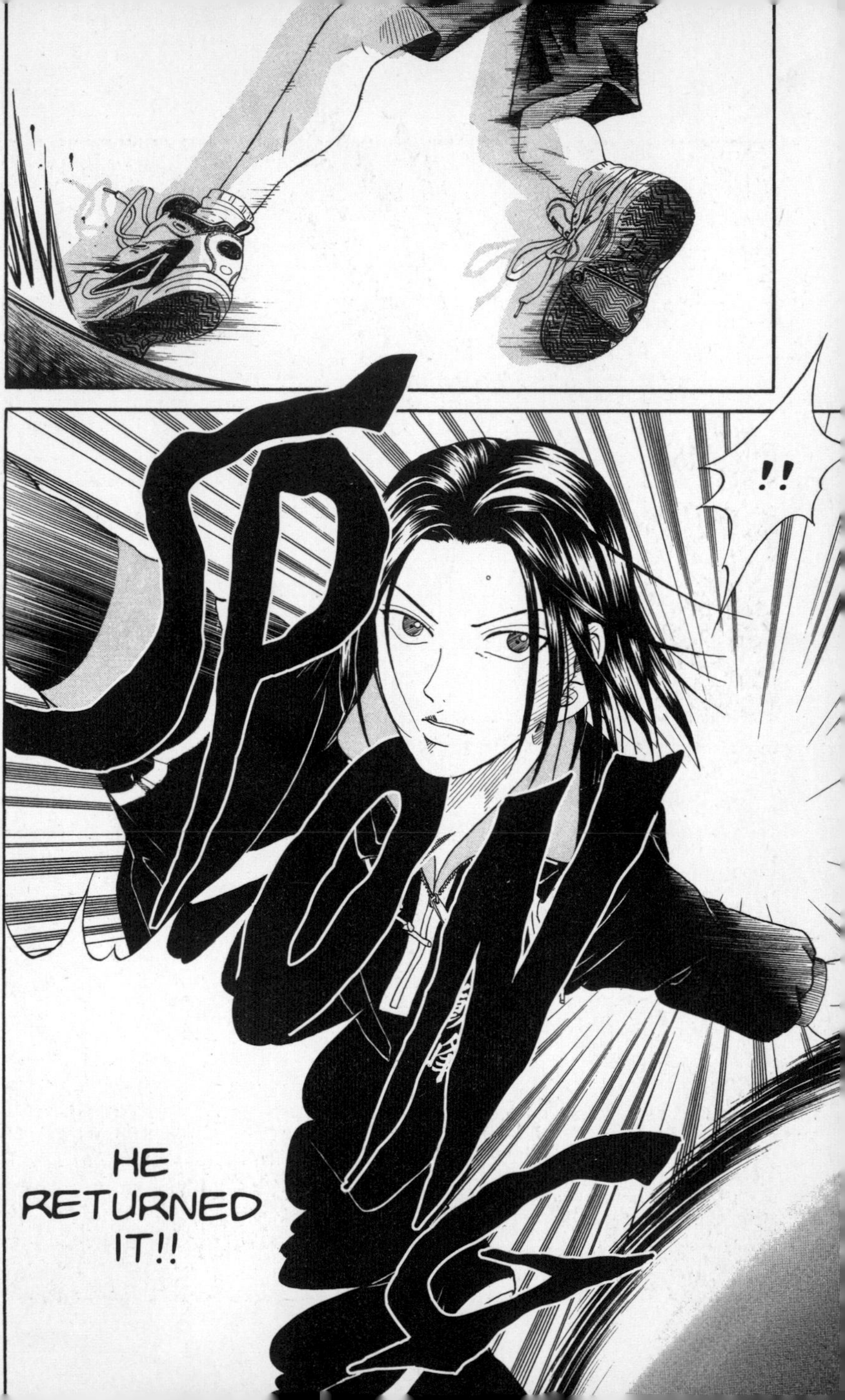
!!
HE RETURNED IT!!

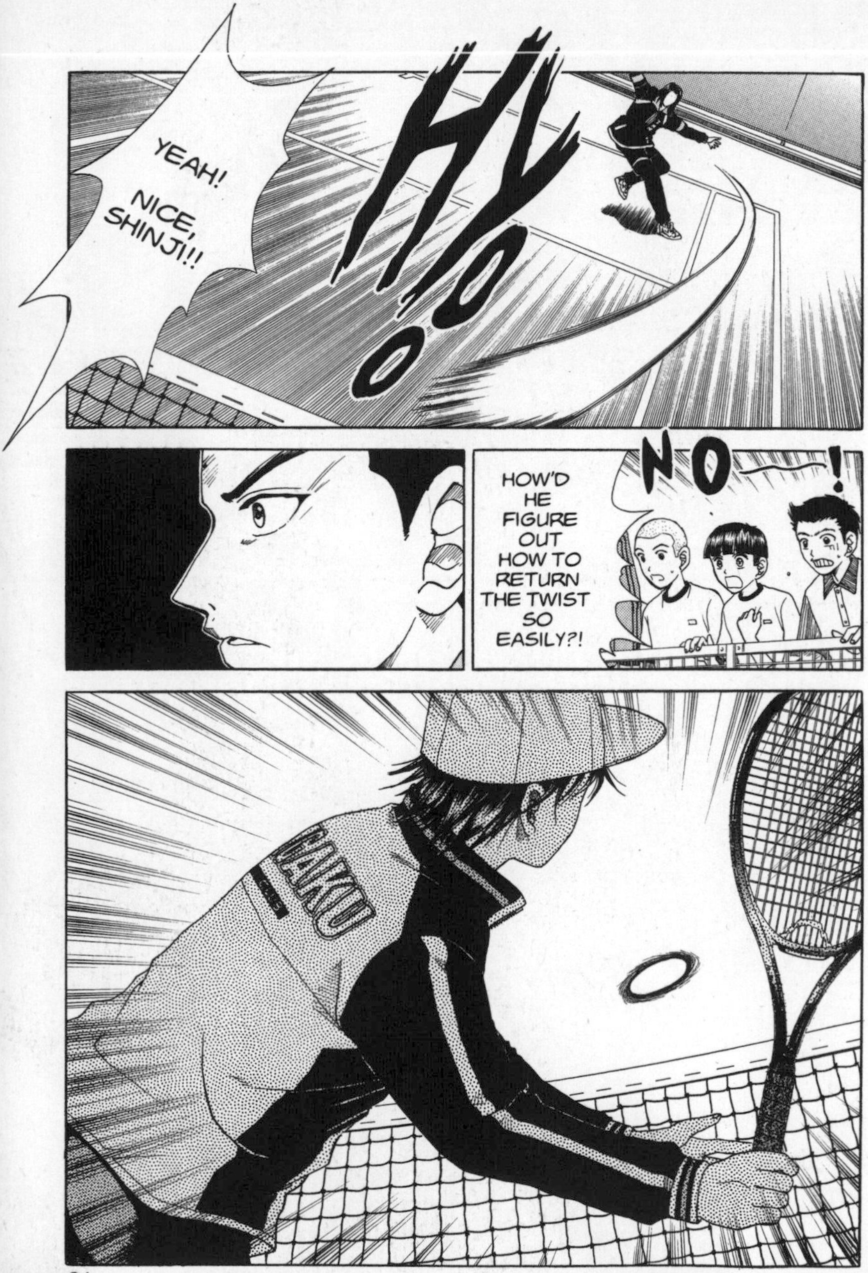
YEAH! NICE, SHINJI!!
HYOOO
NO—!
HOW'D HE FIGURE OUT HOW TO RETURN THE TWIST SO EASILY?!

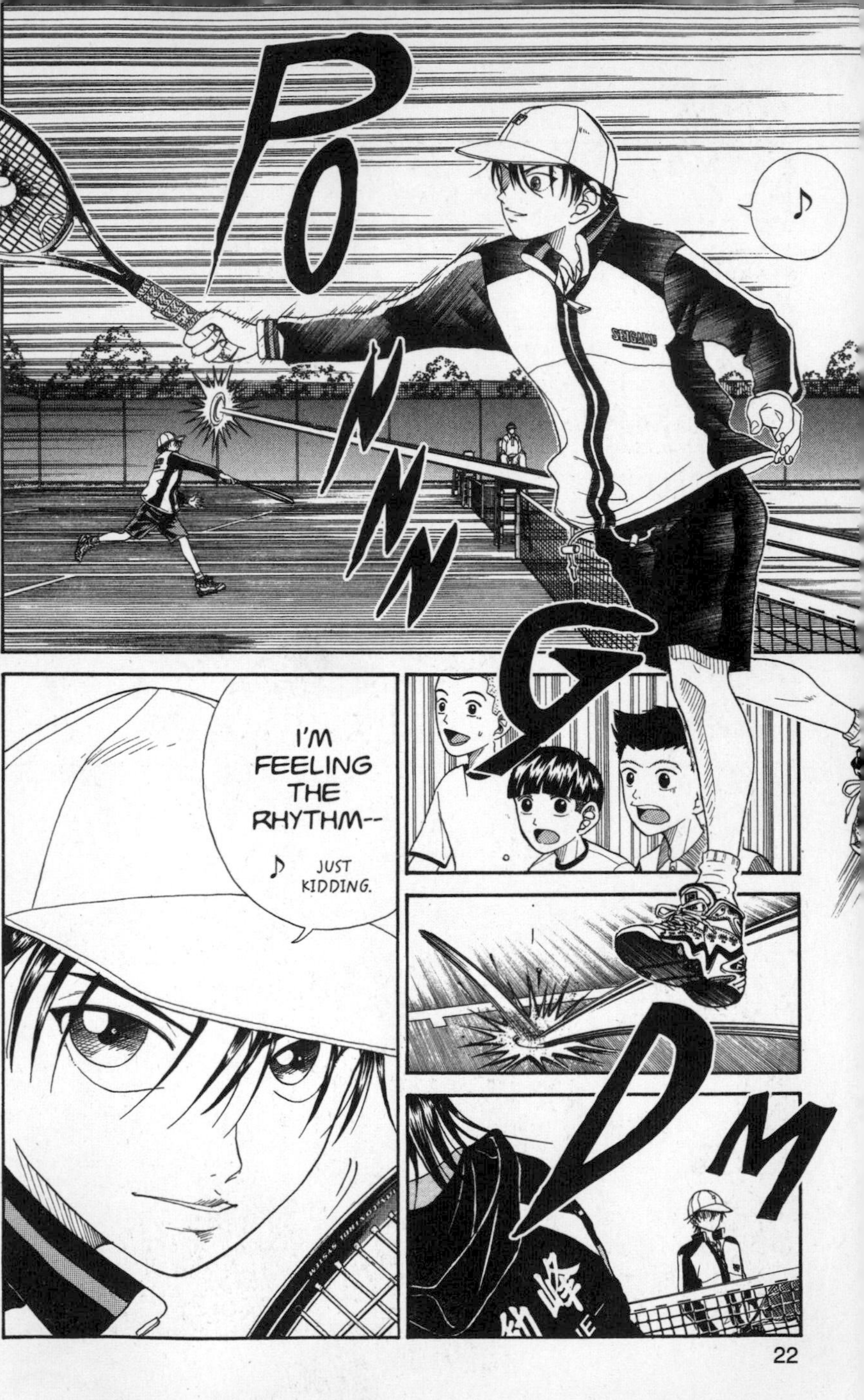
PONNNG
♪
DM
I'M FEELING THE RHYTHM--
♪ JUST KIDDING.

READ THIS WAY

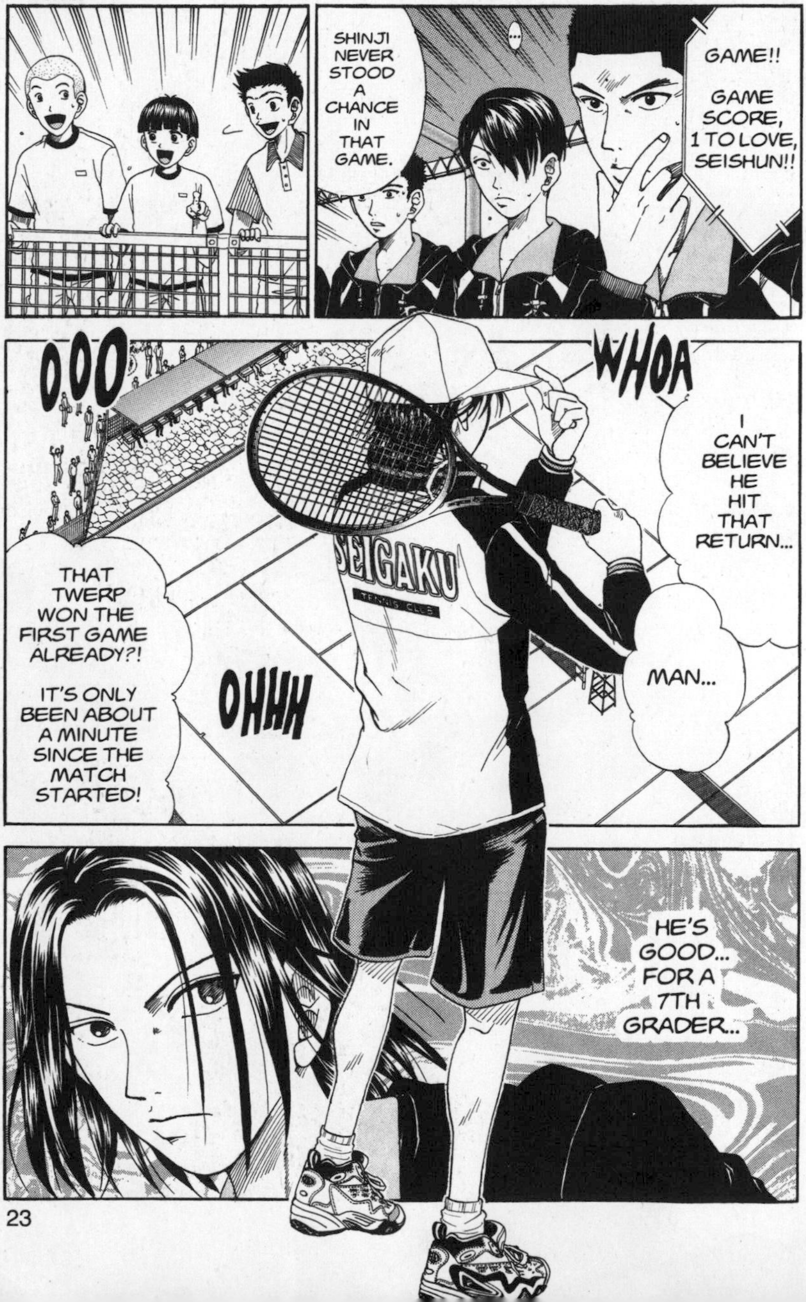
GAME!!
GAME SCORE, 1 TO LOVE, SEISHUN!!
...
SHINJI NEVER STOOD A CHANCE IN THAT GAME.
WHOA
I CAN'T BELIEVE HE HIT THAT RETURN...
MAN...
SEIGAKU
TENNIS CLUB
OHHH
O.OO
THAT TWERP WON THE FIRST GAME ALREADY?!
IT'S ONLY BEEN ABOUT A MINUTE SINCE THE MATCH STARTED!
HE'S GOOD... FOR A 7TH GRADER...

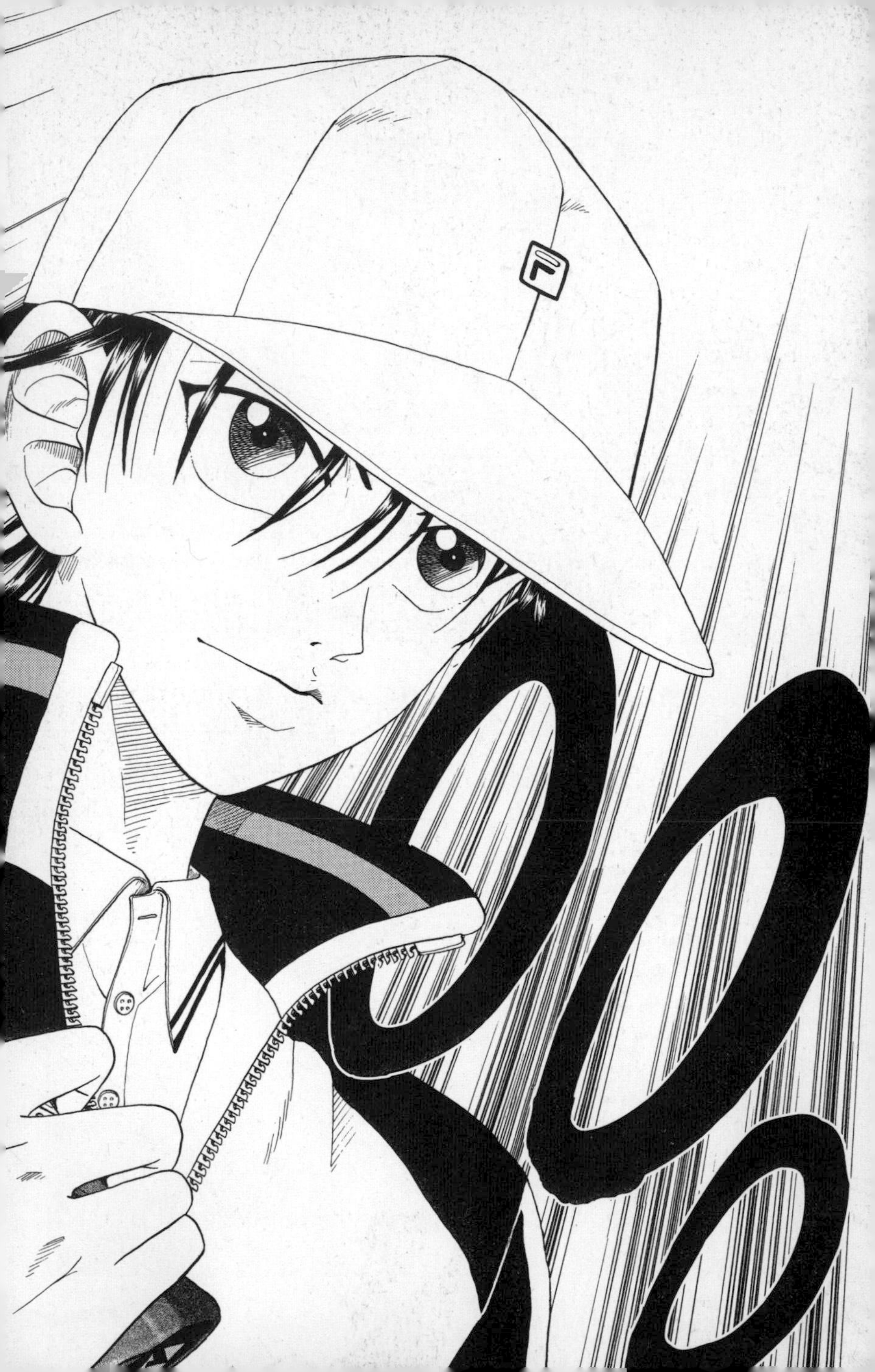

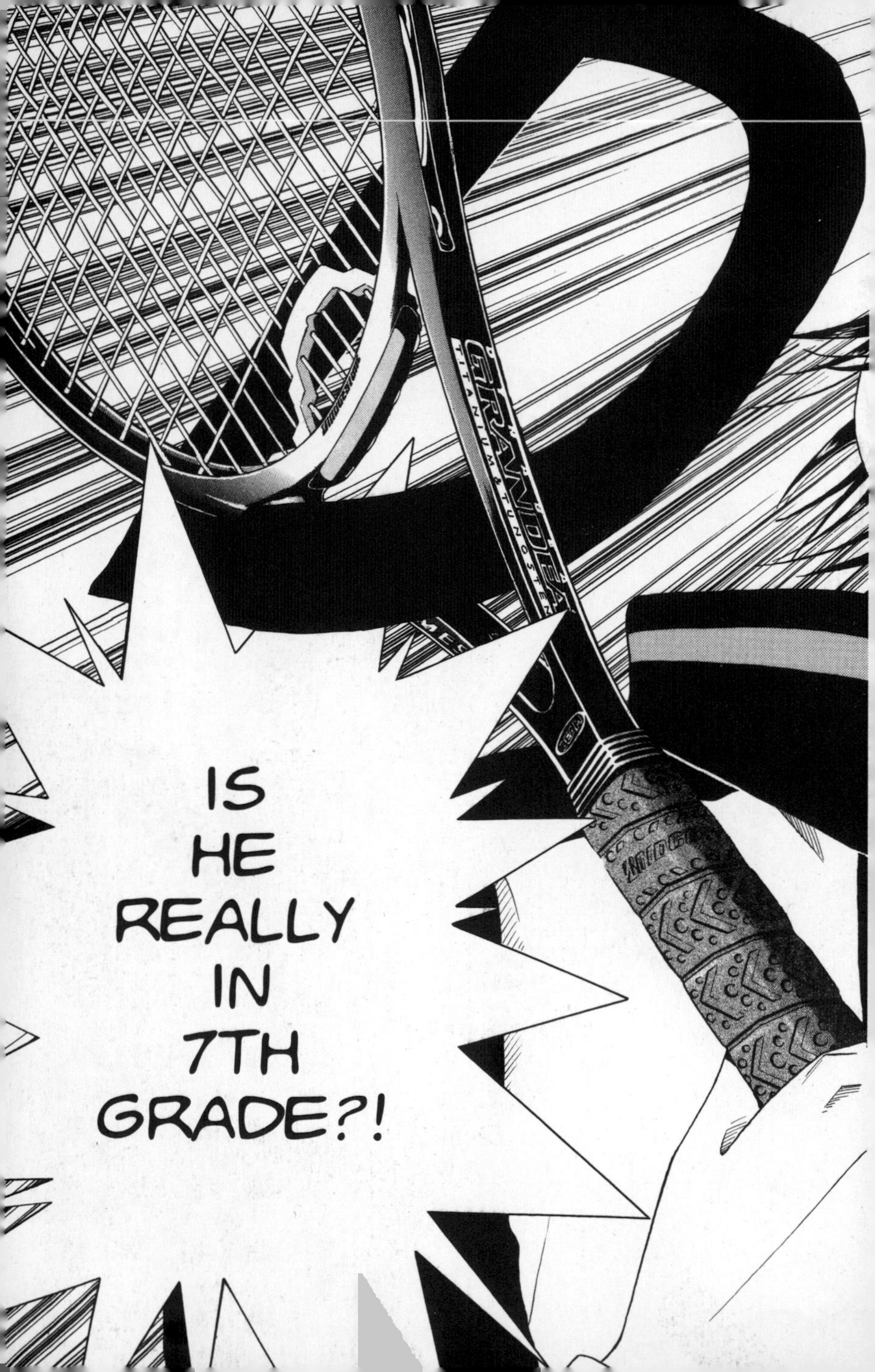
IS HE REALLY IN 7TH GRADE?!

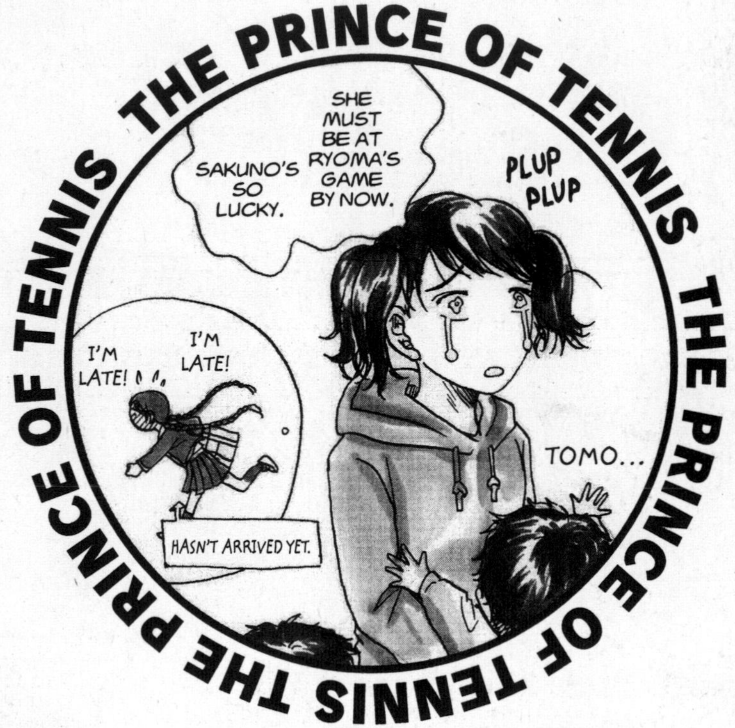
THE PRINCE OF TENNIS THE PRINCE OF TENNIS THE PRINCE OF TENNIS
PLUP PLUP
SHE MUST BE AT RYOMA'S GAME BY NOW.
SAKUNO'S SO LUCKY.
TOMO...
I'M LATE!
I'M LATE!
HASN'T ARRIVED YET.

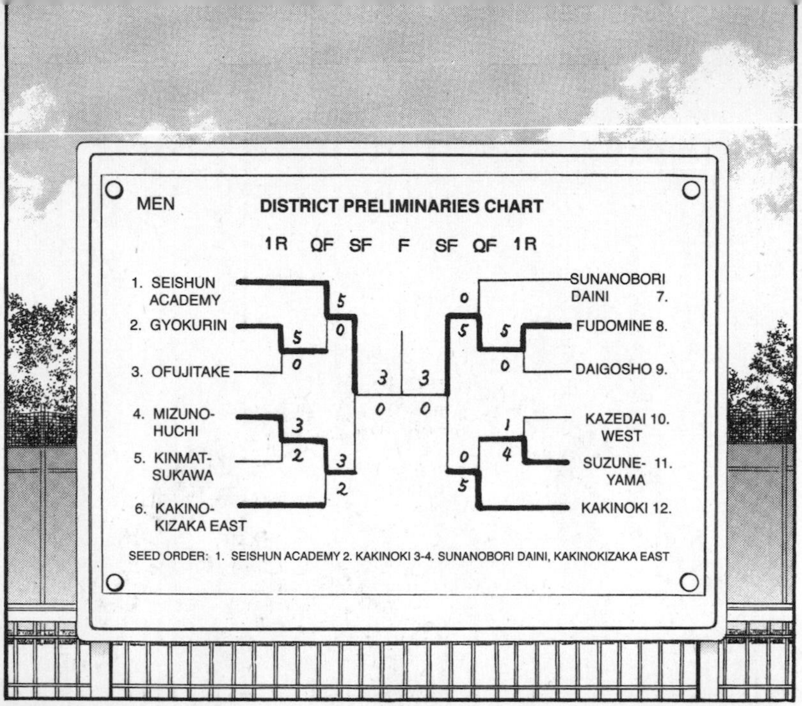
MEN
DISTRICT PRELIMINARIES CHART
1R QF SF F SF QF 1R
1. SEISHUN ACADEMY
2. GYOKURIN
3. OFUJITAKE
4. MIZUNO-HUCHI
5. KINMAT-SUKAWA
6. KAKINO-KIZAKA EAST
SUNANOBORI DAINI 7.
FUDOMINE 8.
DAIGOSHO 9.
KAZEDAI 10. WEST
SUZUNE- 11. YAMA
KAKINOKI 12.
5 0 5 0 3 0 3 2 3 2 3 0 3 0 0 5 5 0 1 4 0 5
SEED ORDER: 1. SEISHUN ACADEMY 2. KAKINOKI 3-4. SUNANOBORI DAINI, KAKINOKIZAKA EAST

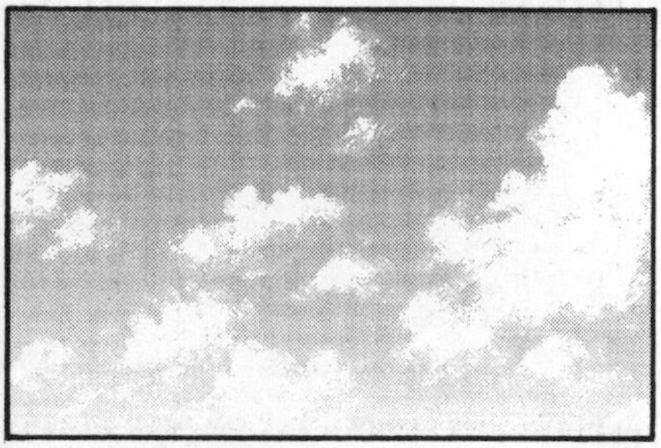

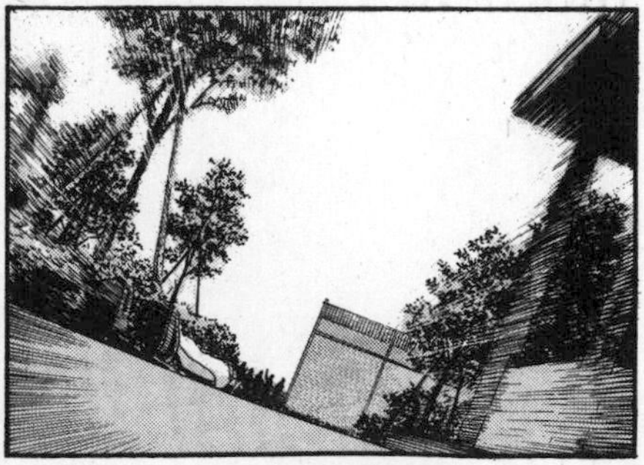

Genius 36: Mutter, Mutter

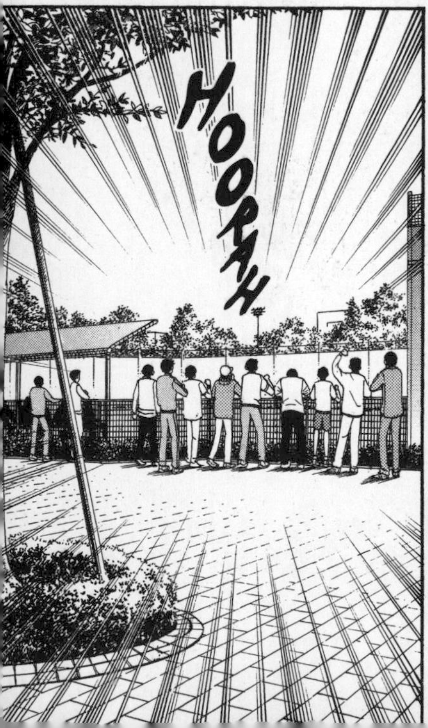
HOORAH

Genius 36: Mutter, Mutter

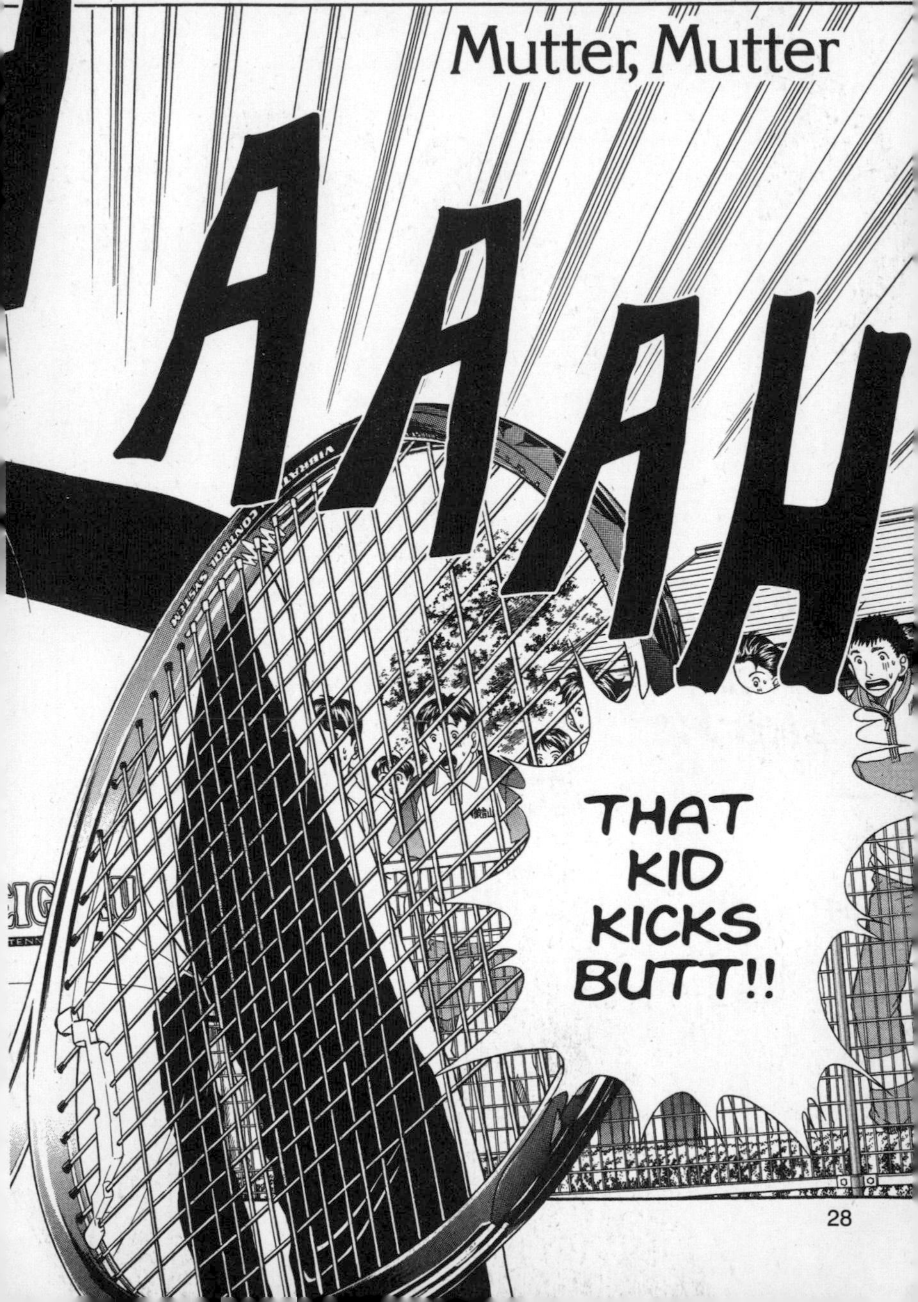
AAAH
THAT KID KICKS BUTT!!

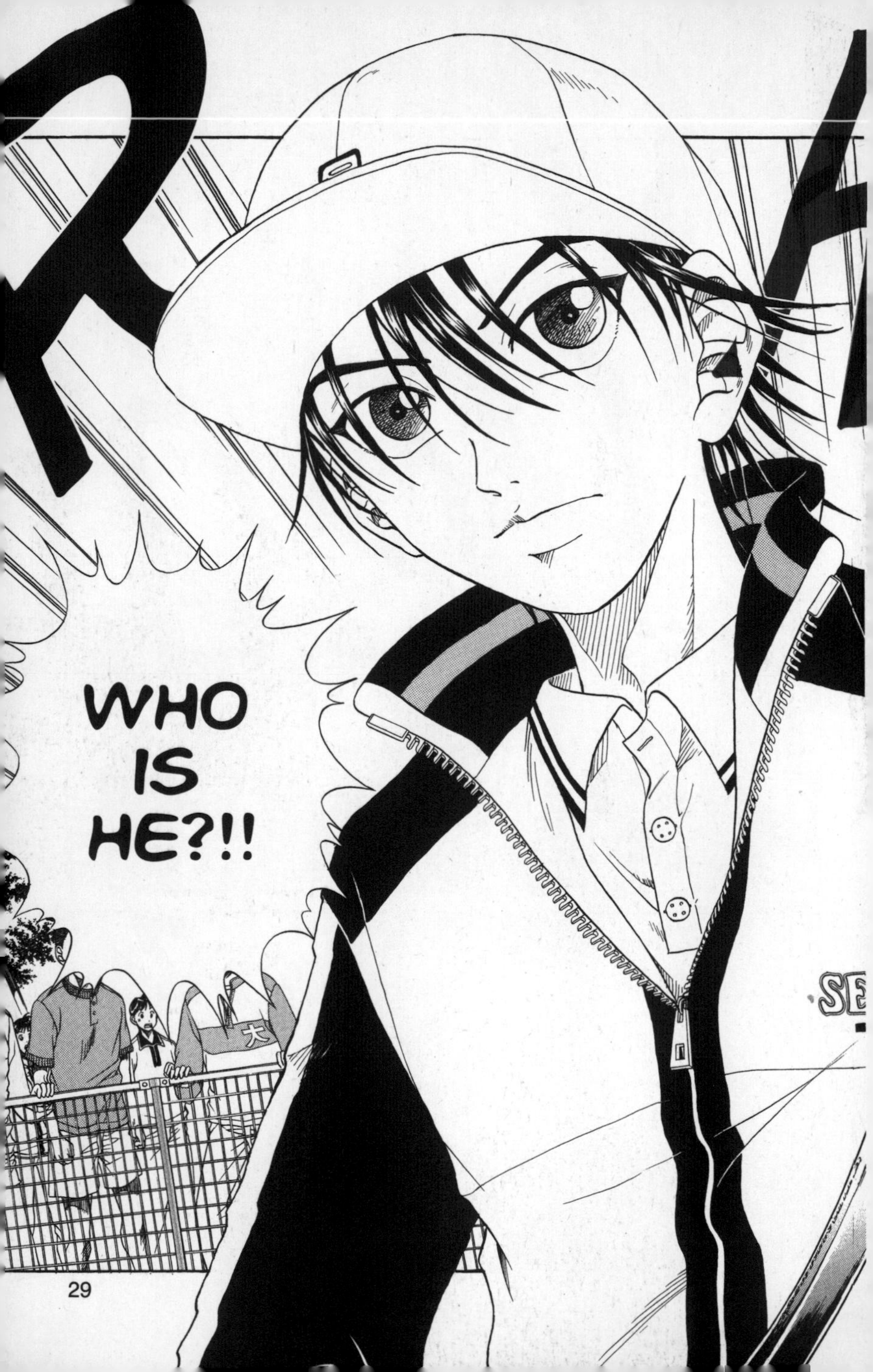
WHO IS HE?!!

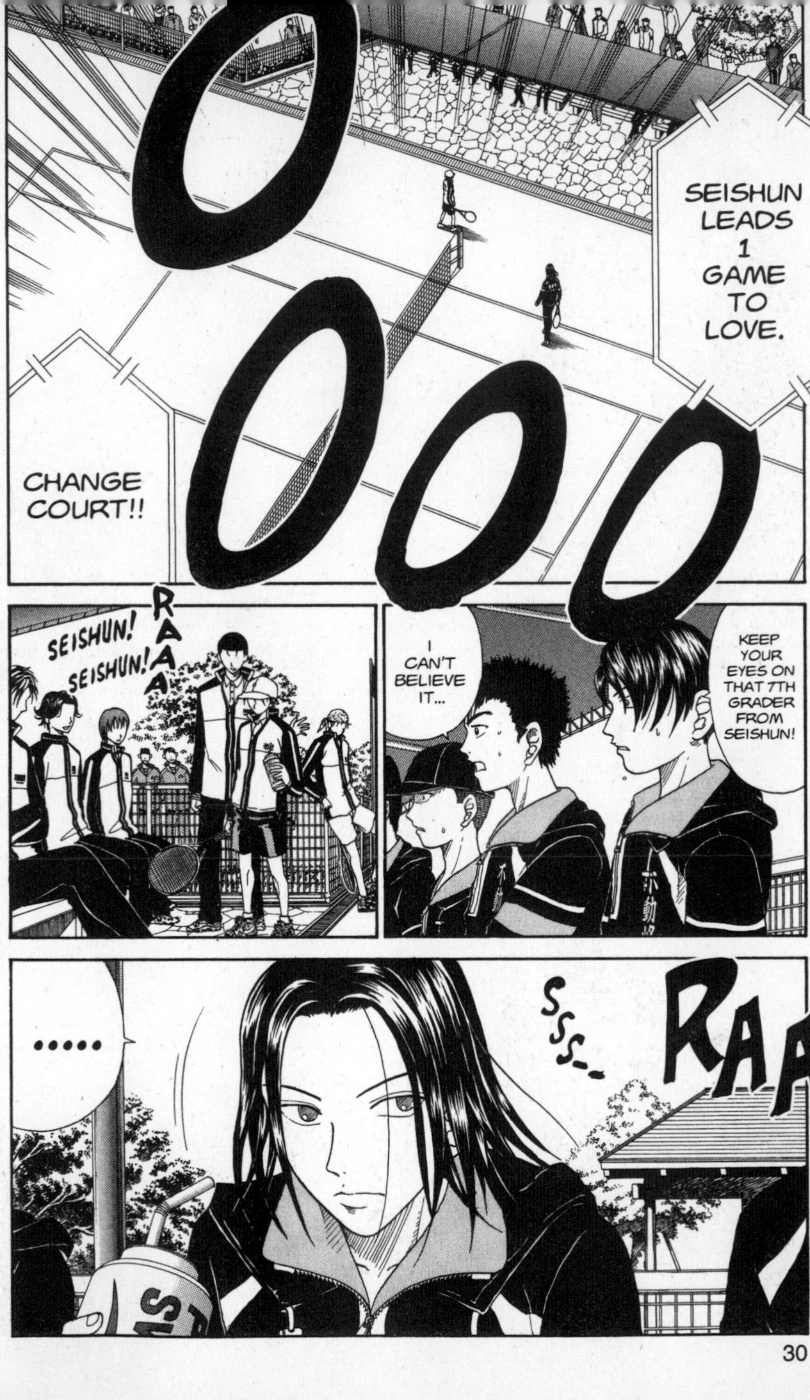
SEISHUN LEADS 1 GAME TO LOVE.
OOOO
CHANGE COURT!!
KEEP YOUR EYES ON THAT 7TH GRADER FROM SEISHUN!
I CAN'T BELIEVE IT...
RAAA
SEISHUN! SEISHUN!
SSS-- RAA
.....

READ THIS WAY

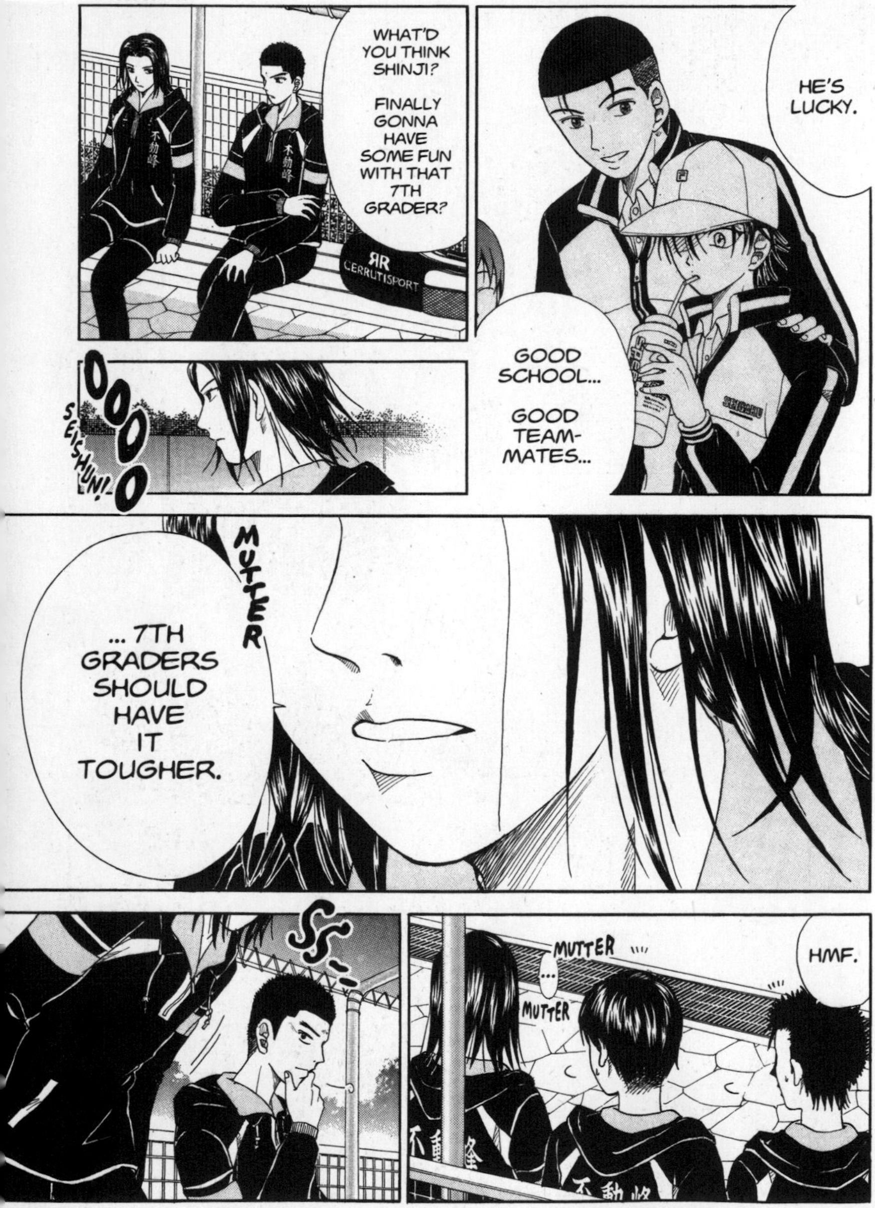

HE'S LUCKY.
GOOD SCHOOL... GOOD TEAM-MATES...
WHAT'D YOU THINK SHINJI? FINALLY GONNA HAVE SOME FUN WITH THAT 7TH GRADER?
CERRUTISPORT
SEISHUN!!
MUTTER
... 7TH GRADERS SHOULD HAVE IT TOUGHER.
HMF.
MUTTER
...
MUTTER

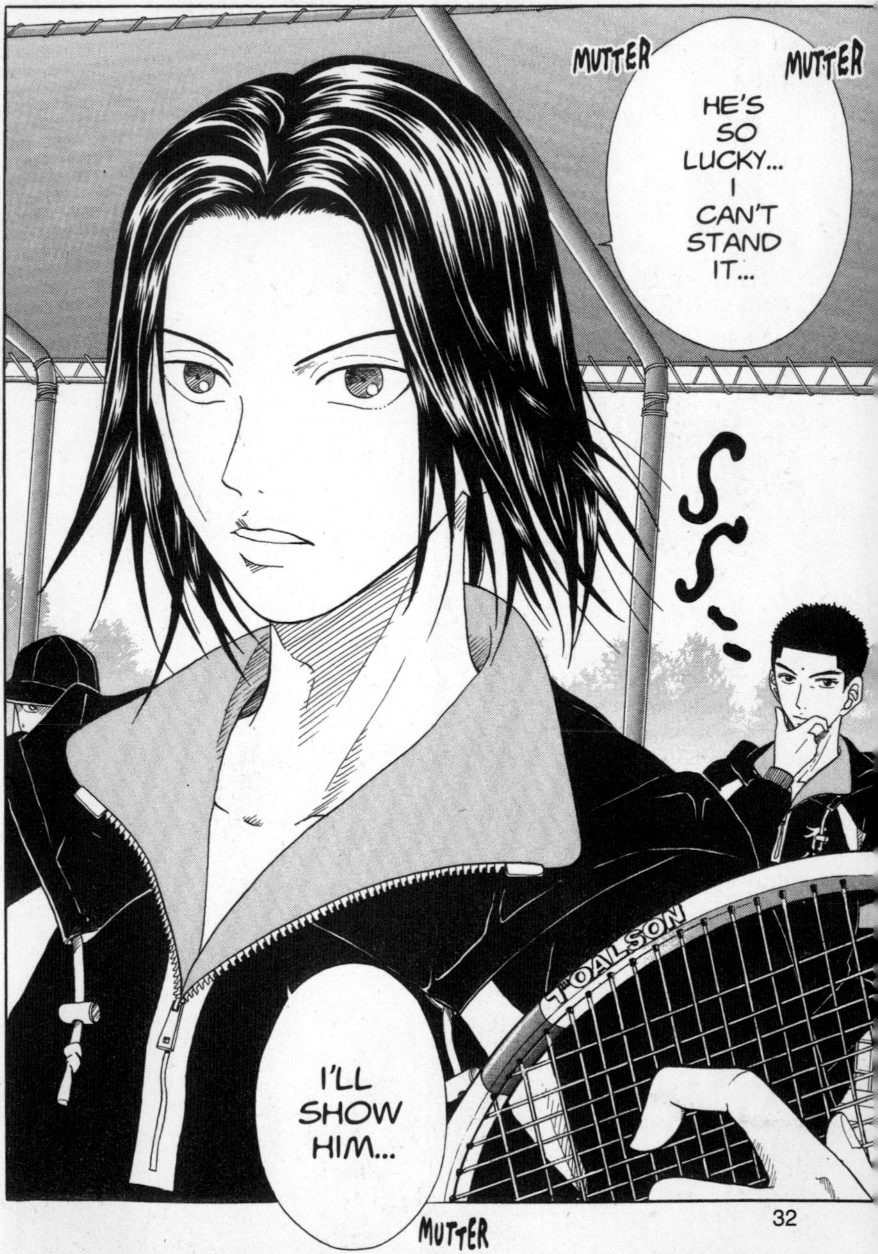
MUTTER
MUTTER
HE'S SO LUCKY... I CAN'T STAND IT...
TOALSON
I'LL SHOW HIM...
MUTTER

READ THIS WAY

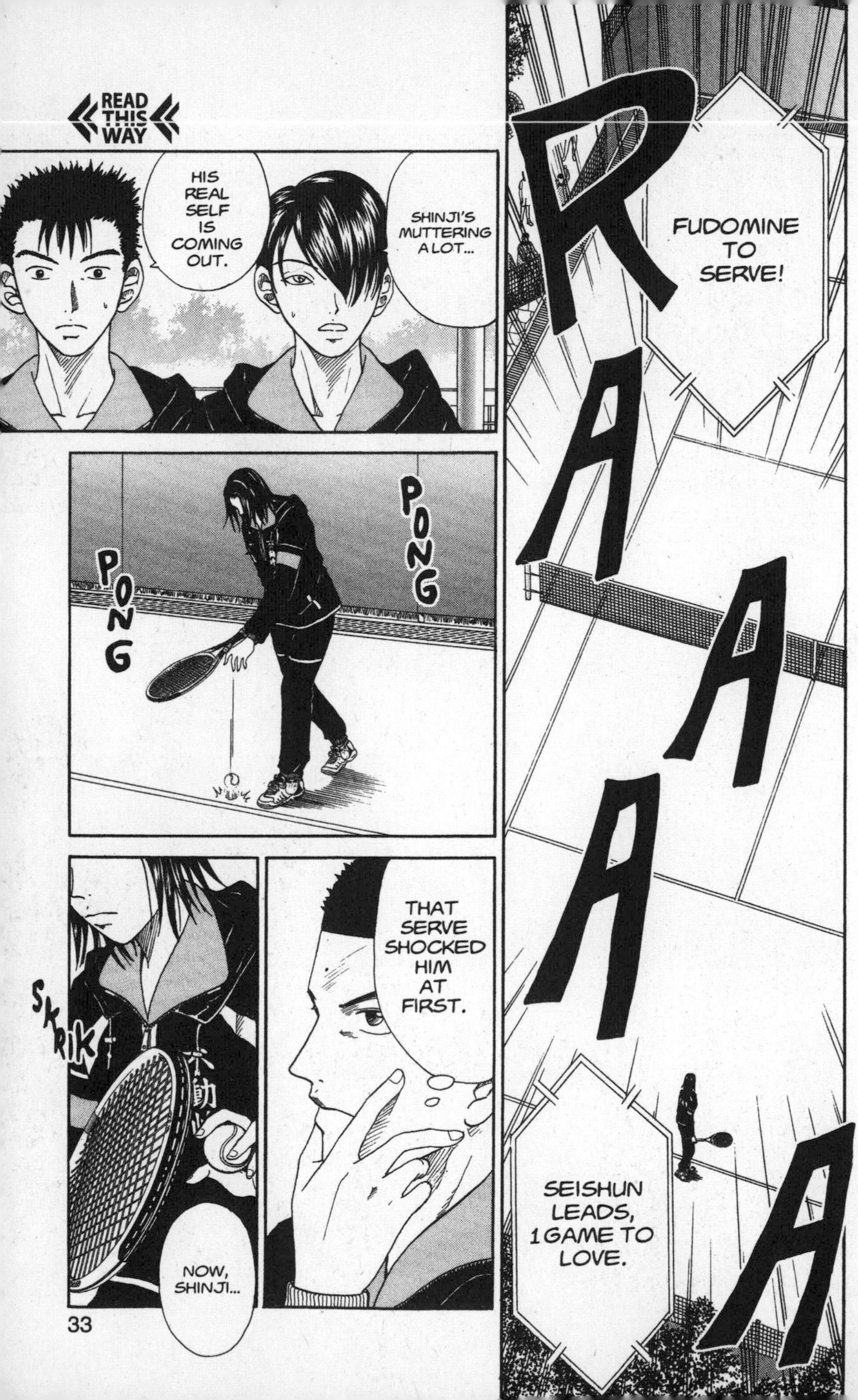

FUDOMINE TO SERVE!
RAAAAA
SEISHUN LEADS, 1 GAME TO LOVE.
SHINJI'S MUTTERING A LOT...
HIS REAL SELF IS COMING OUT.
PONG
PONG
PONG
THAT SERVE SHOCKED HIM AT FIRST.
SKRIK
NOW, SHINJI...

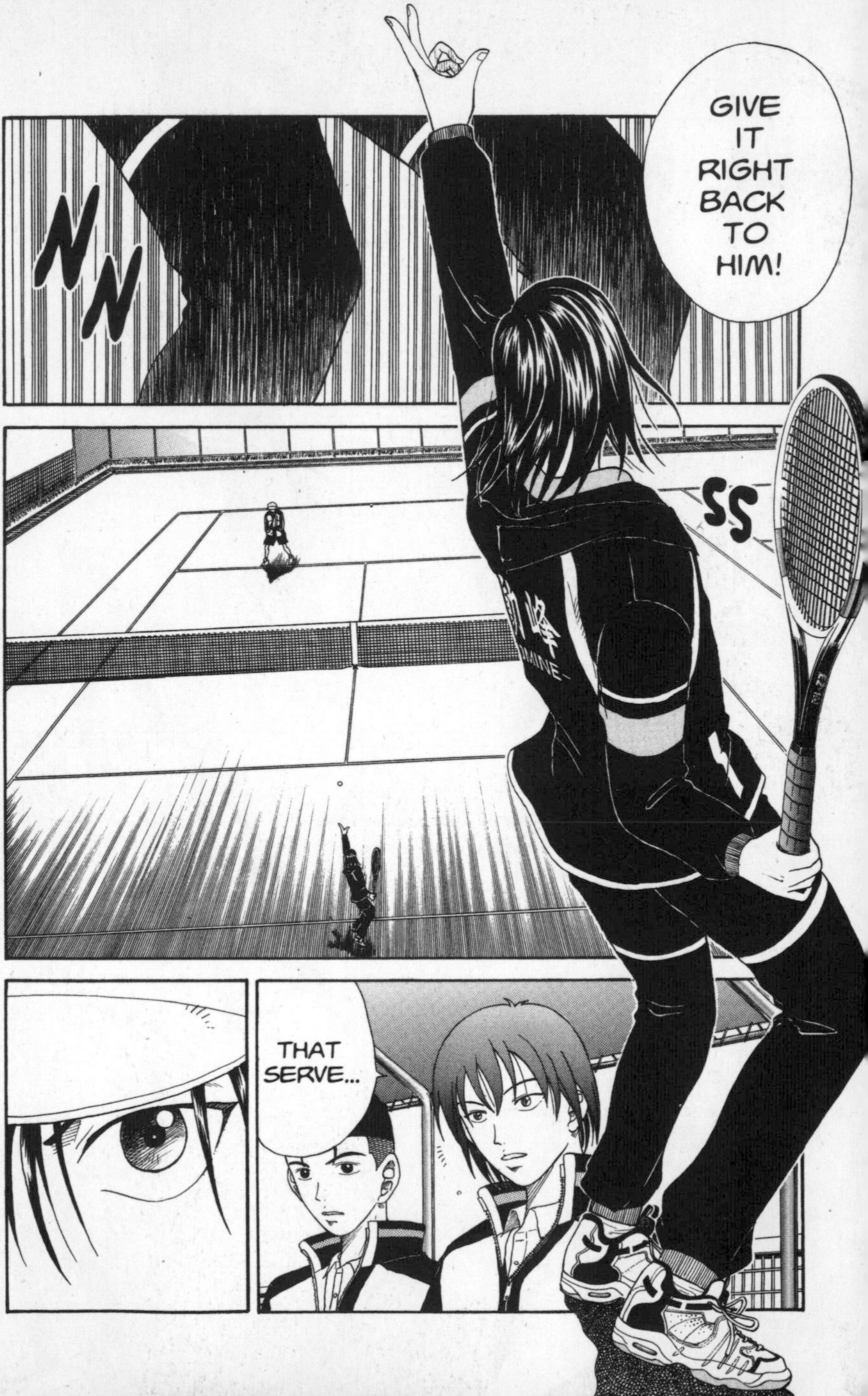
GIVE IT RIGHT BACK TO HIM!
NN
SS
THAT SERVE...

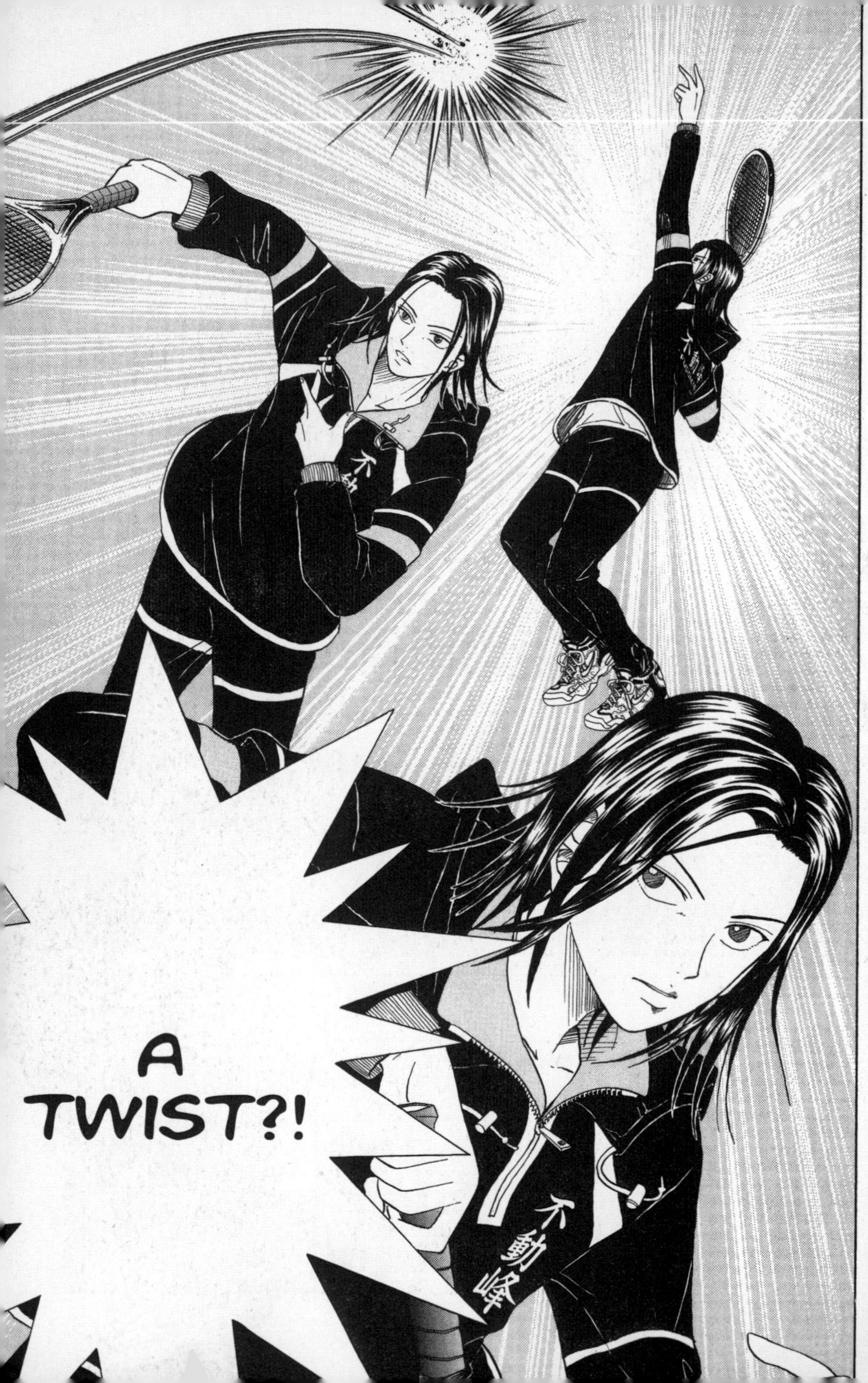
A TWIST?!
不動峰

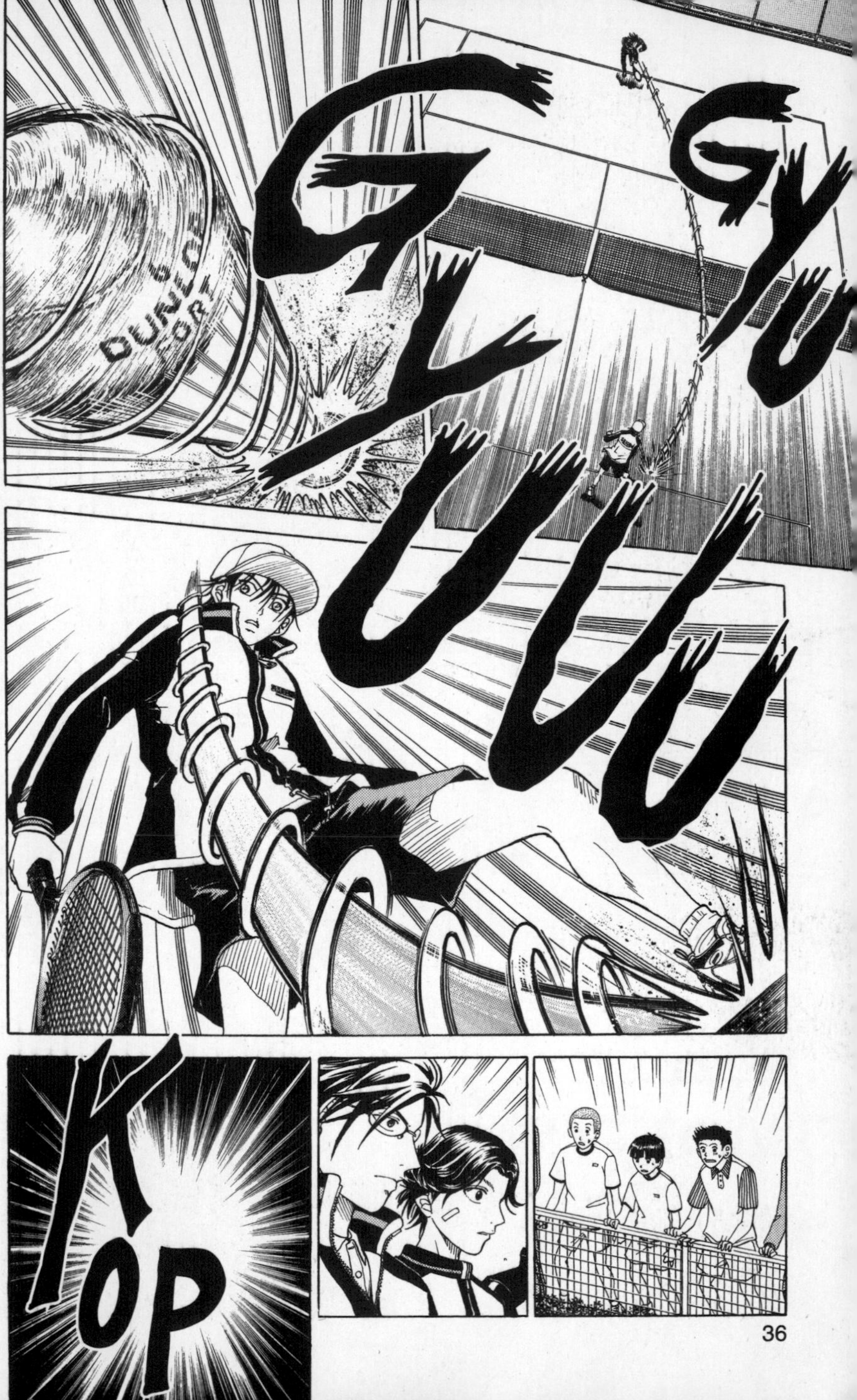
GYU
GYUUUU
KOP

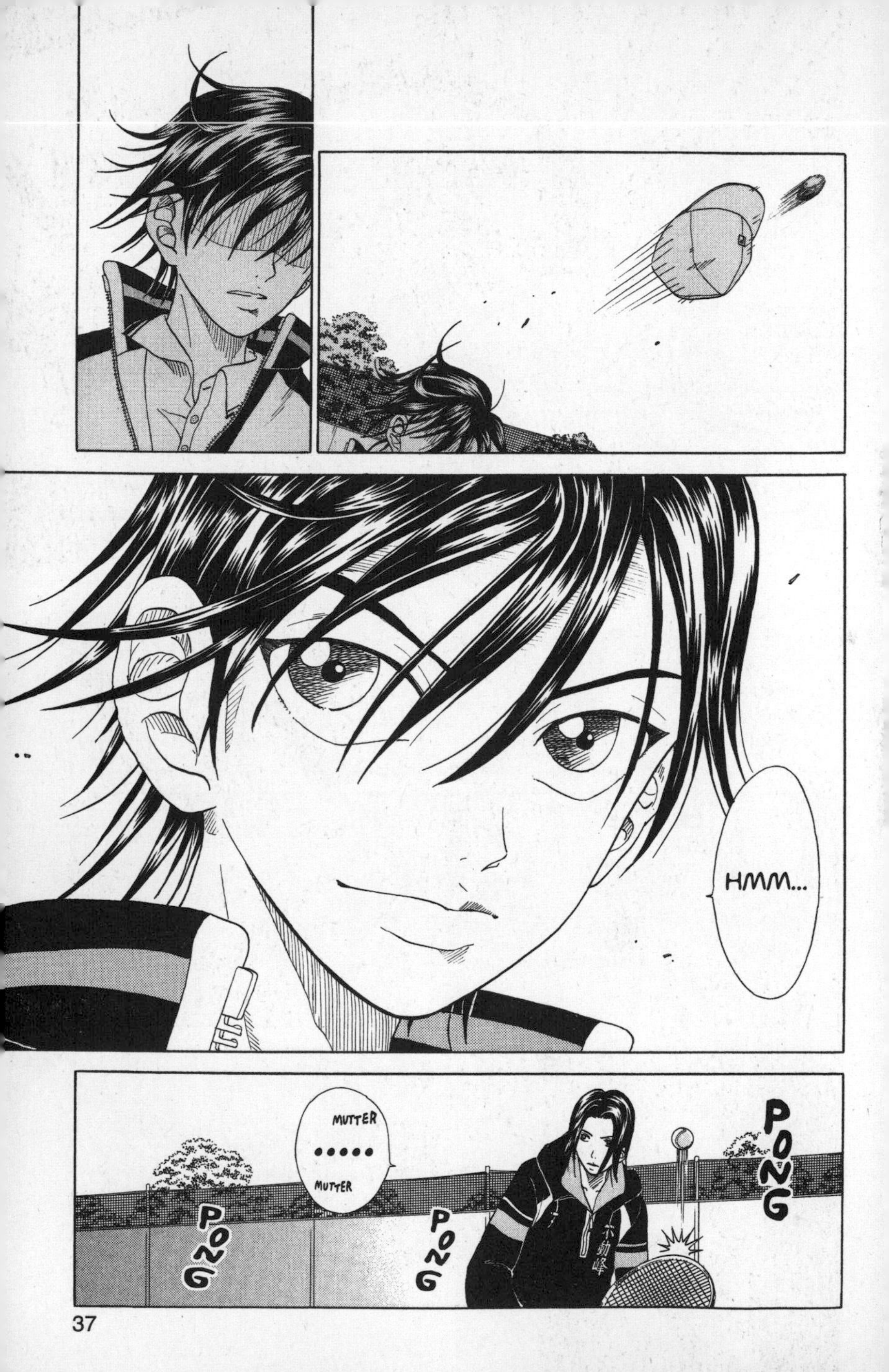
HMM...
MUTTER
.....
MUTTER
PONG
PONG
PONG
六角峰

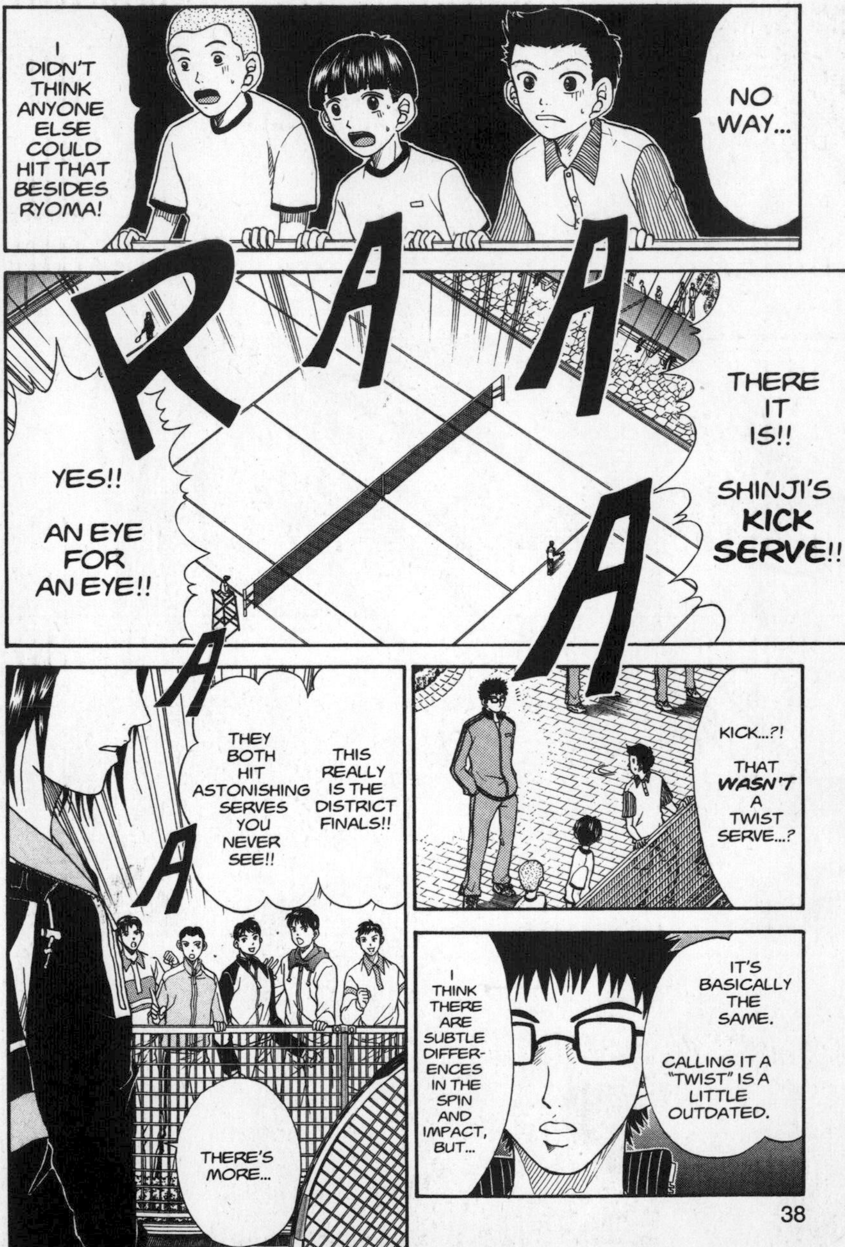
NO WAY...
I DIDN'T THINK ANYONE ELSE COULD HIT THAT BESIDES RYOMA!
THERE IT IS!!
SHINJI'S **KICK SERVE**!!
YES!!
AN EYE FOR AN EYE!!
RAAAAA
KICK...?!
THAT ***WASN'T*** A TWIST SERVE...?
IT'S BASICALLY THE SAME.
CALLING IT A "TWIST" IS A LITTLE OUTDATED.
I THINK THERE ARE SUBTLE DIFFERENCES IN THE SPIN AND IMPACT, BUT...
THIS REALLY IS THE DISTRICT FINALS!!
THEY BOTH HIT ASTONISHING SERVES YOU NEVER SEE!!
THERE'S MORE...

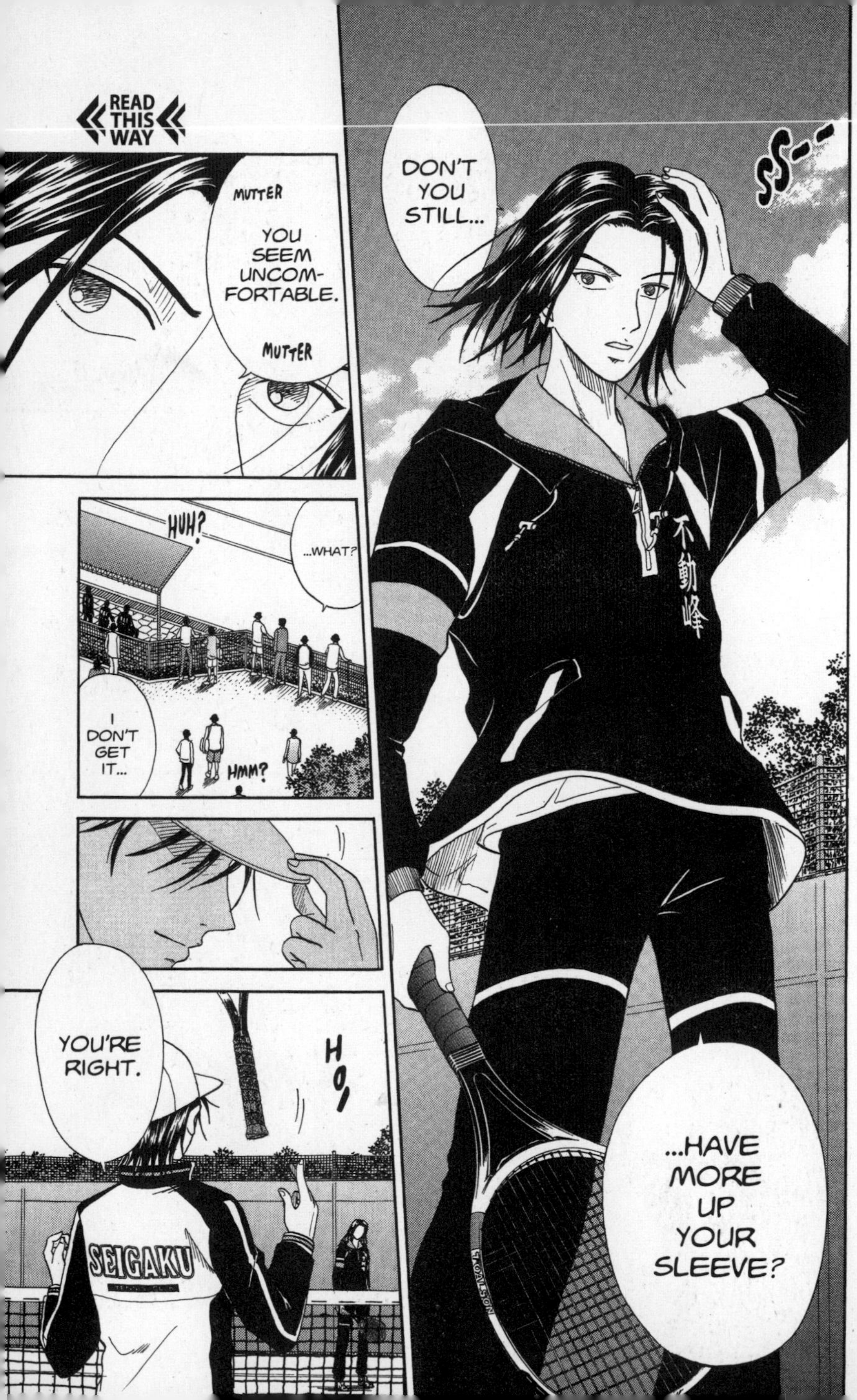
READ THIS WAY
SS--
DON'T YOU STILL...
...HAVE MORE UP YOUR SLEEVE?
MUTTER
YOU SEEM UNCOM- FORTABLE.
MUTTER
...WHAT?
HUH?
I DON'T GET IT...
HMM?
YOU'RE RIGHT.
HOI
SEIGAKU

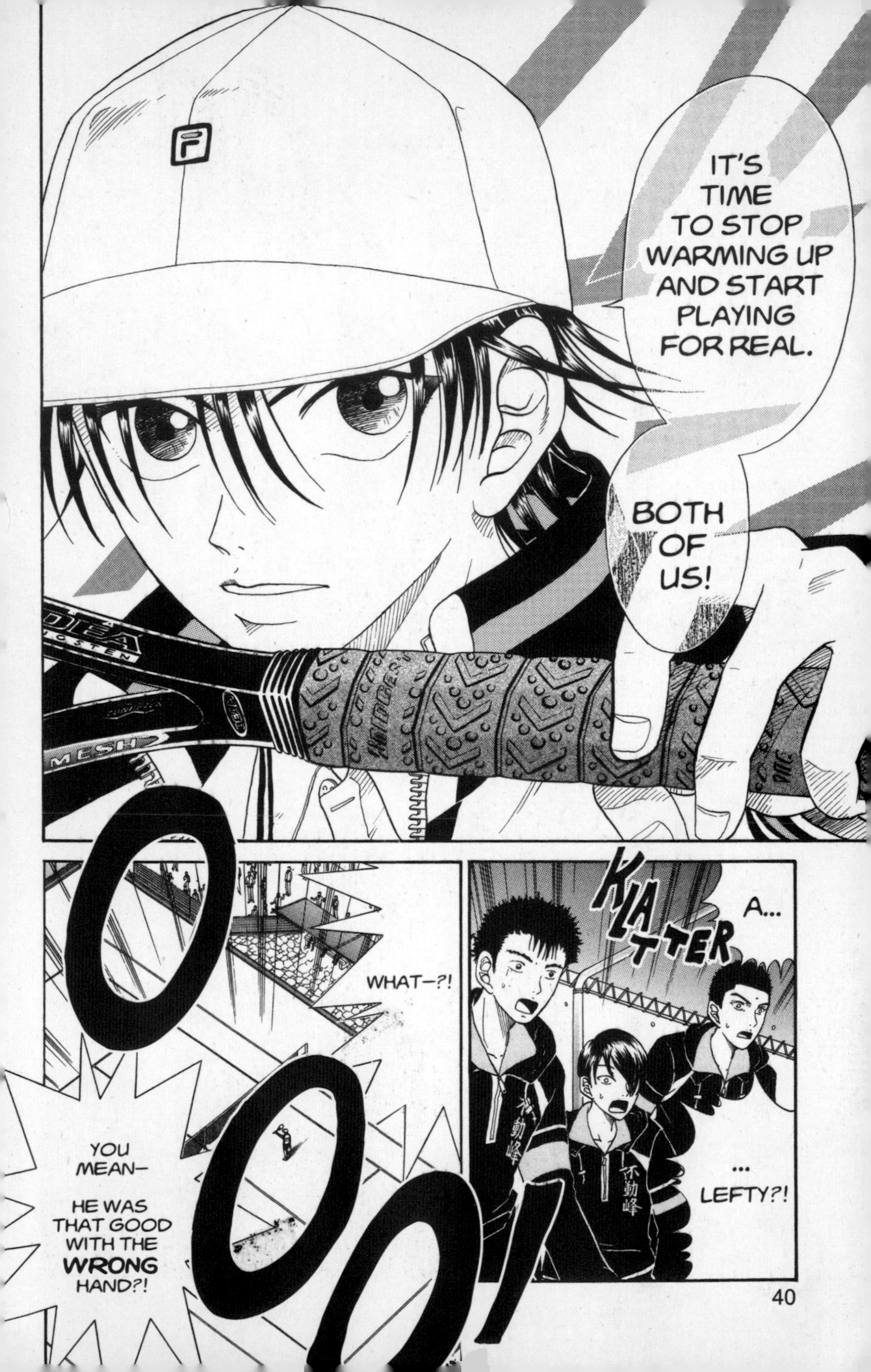
IT'S TIME TO STOP WARMING UP AND START PLAYING FOR REAL.
BOTH OF US!
KLATTER
A...
...LEFTY?!
WHAT—?!
OOO
YOU MEAN—
HE WAS THAT GOOD WITH THE **WRONG** HAND?!

READ THIS WAY

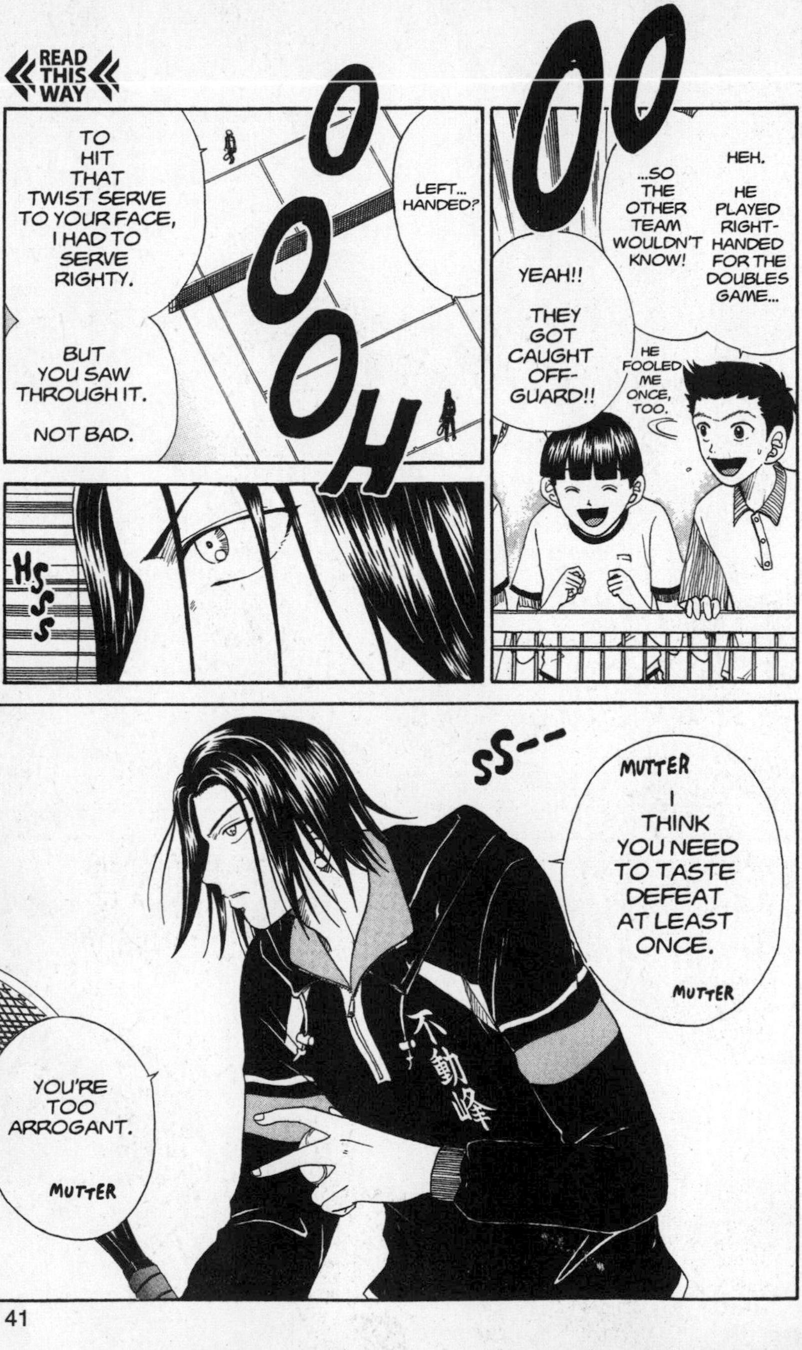
OOOOOH
HEH. HE PLAYED RIGHT-HANDED FOR THE DOUBLES GAME...
...SO THE OTHER TEAM WOULDN'T KNOW!
YEAH!! THEY GOT CAUGHT OFF-GUARD!!
HE FOOLED ME ONCE, TOO.
LEFT... HANDED?
TO HIT THAT TWIST SERVE TO YOUR FACE, I HAD TO SERVE RIGHTY.
BUT YOU SAW THROUGH IT. NOT BAD.
HSSS
SS--
MUTTER
I THINK YOU NEED TO TASTE DEFEAT AT LEAST ONCE.
MUTTER
YOU'RE TOO ARROGANT.
MUTTER

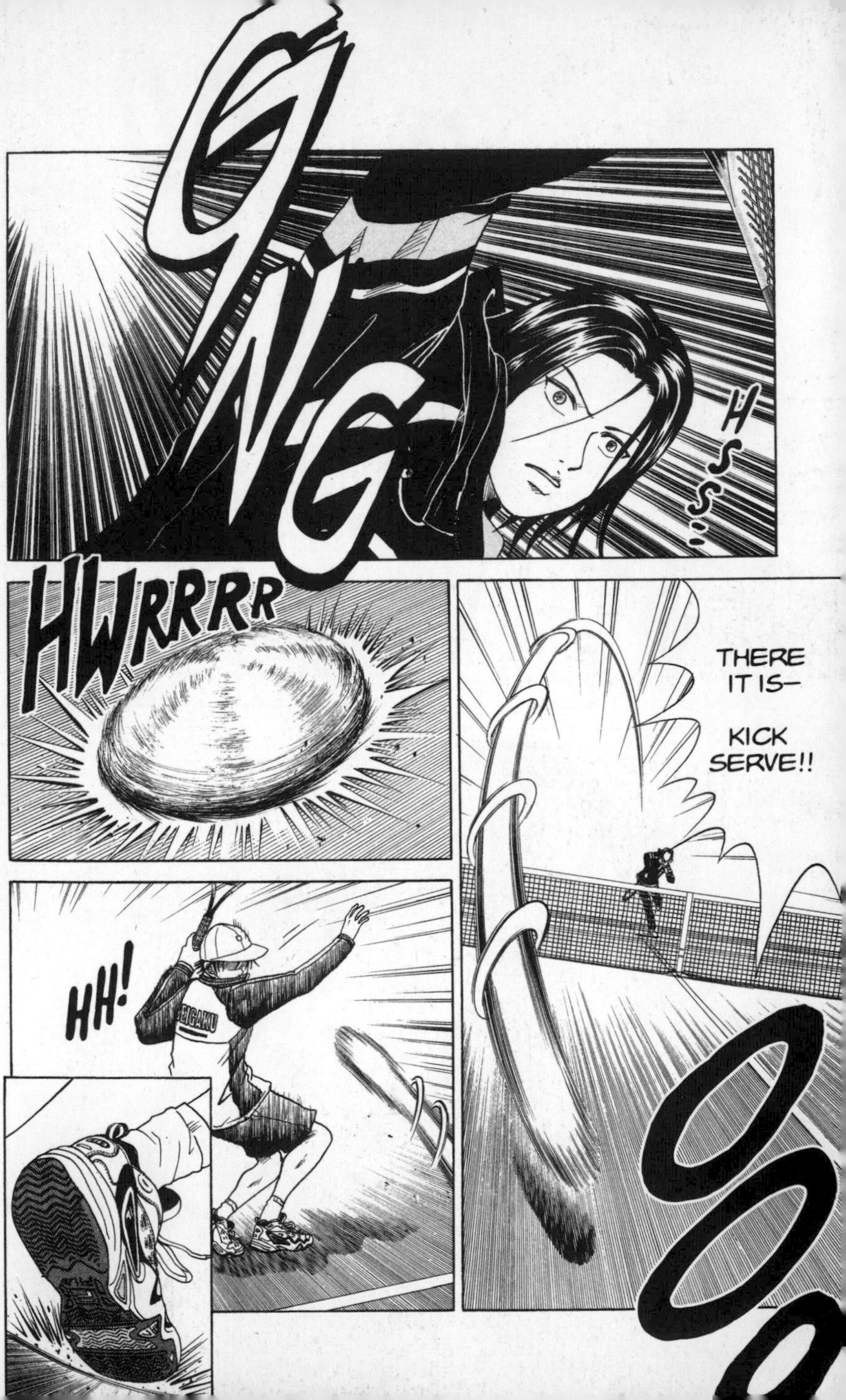
HSS..
THERE IT IS—
KICK SERVE!!
HWRRRR
HH!

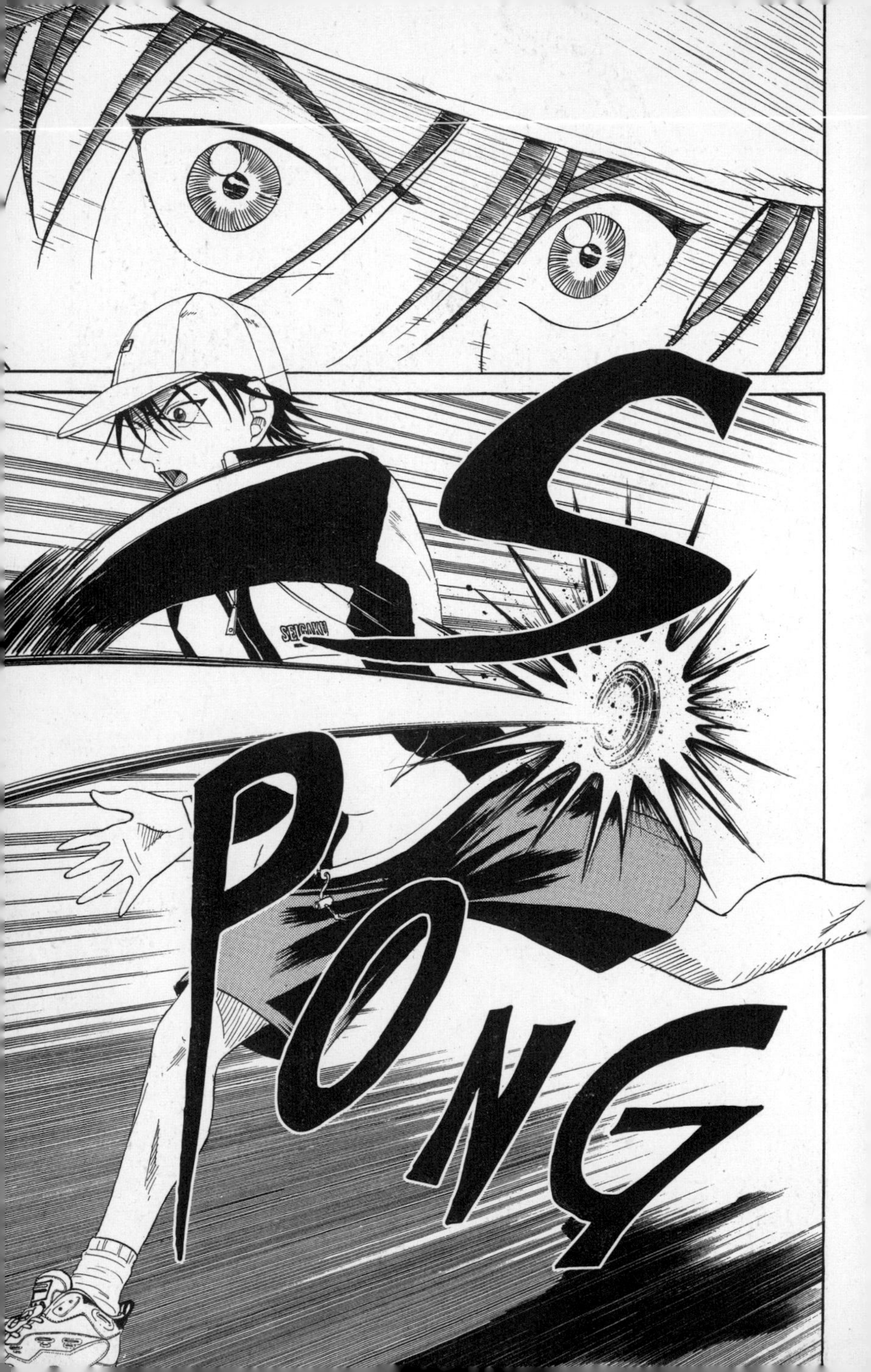
SPONG
SEIGAKU

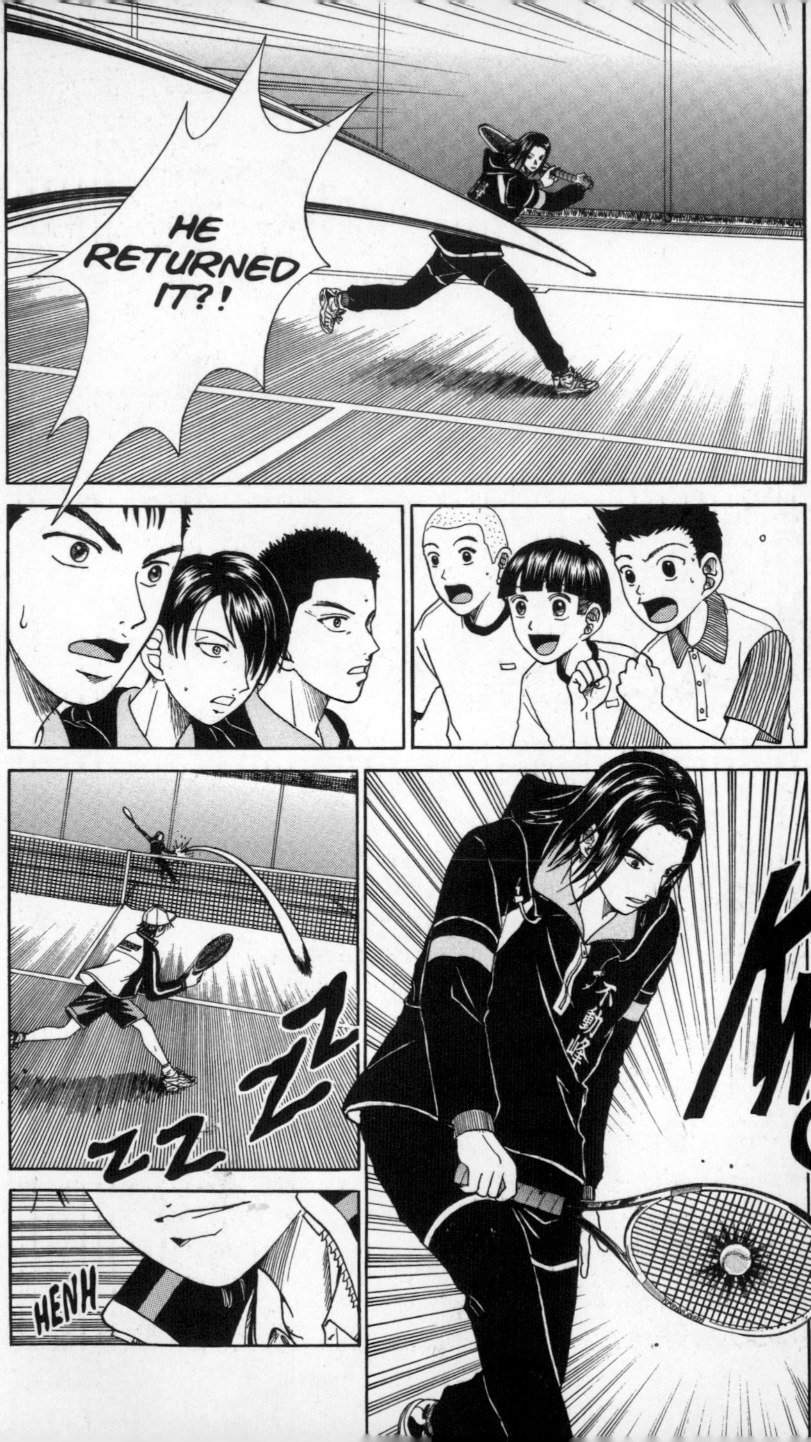
HE RETURNED IT?!
KNG
ZZZZ
HENH

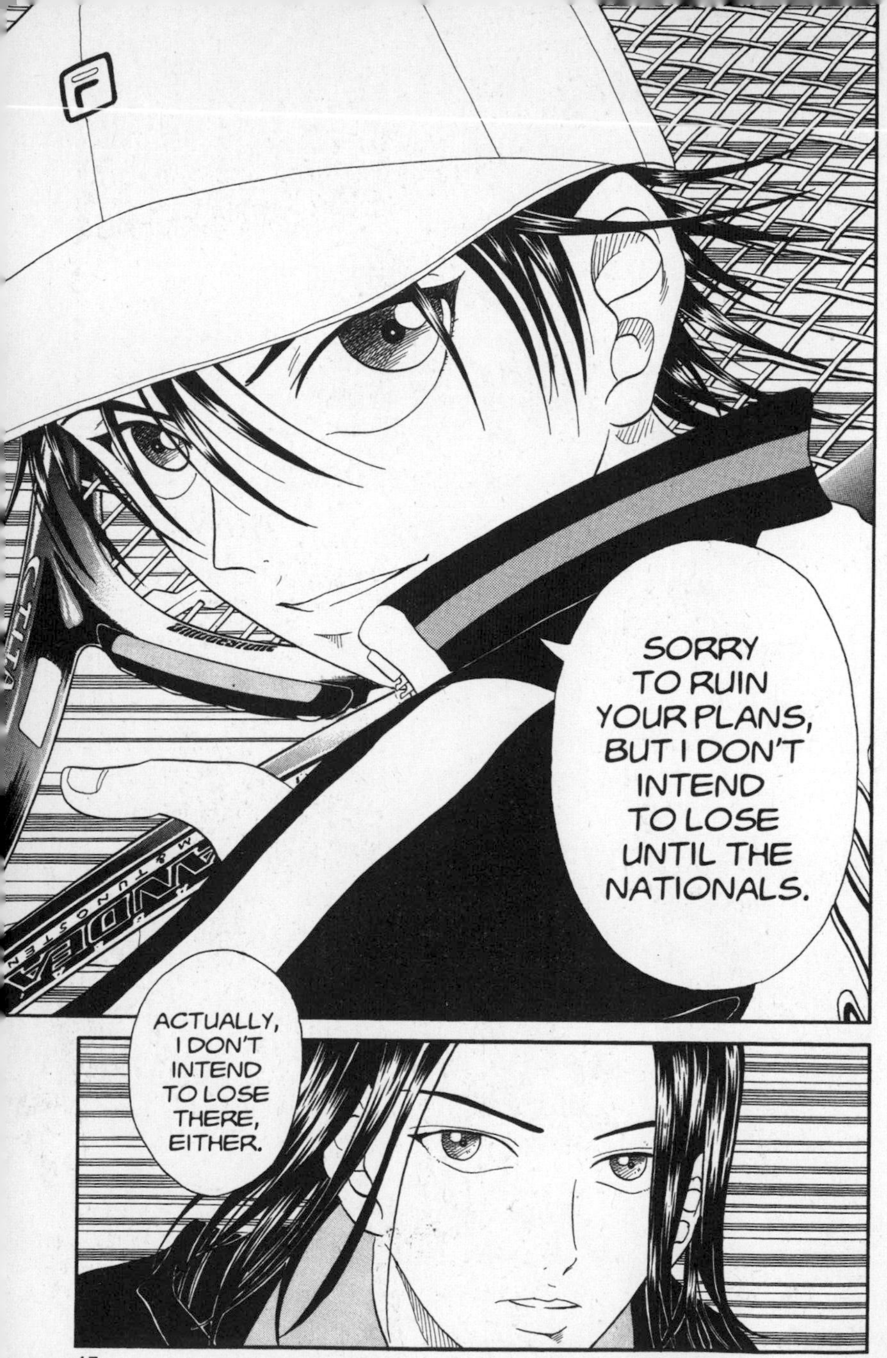
SORRY TO RUIN YOUR PLANS, BUT I DON'T INTEND TO LOSE UNTIL THE NATIONALS.
ACTUALLY, I DON'T INTEND TO LOSE THERE, EITHER.

Date . . No. 11

SHUICHIRO OISHI/RIGHT-HANDED

CHEERY TYPE!

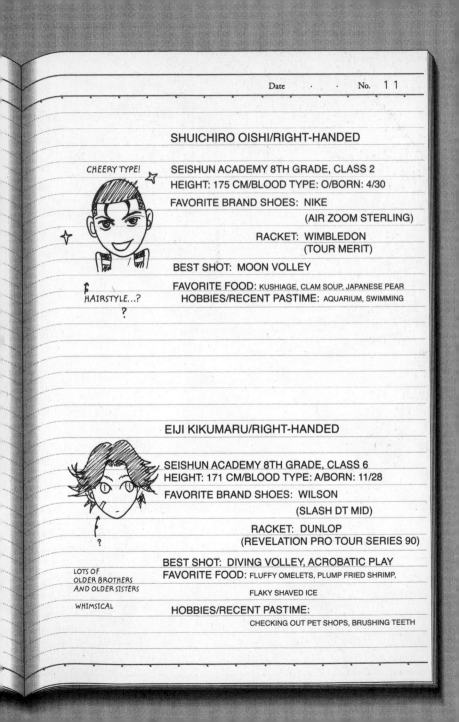

HAIRSTYLE...?
?

SEISHUN ACADEMY 8TH GRADE, CLASS 2
HEIGHT: 175 CM/BLOOD TYPE: O/BORN: 4/30
FAVORITE BRAND SHOES: NIKE
(AIR ZOOM STERLING)
RACKET: WIMBLEDON
(TOUR MERIT)
BEST SHOT: MOON VOLLEY
FAVORITE FOOD: KUSHIAGE, CLAM SOUP, JAPANESE PEAR
HOBBIES/RECENT PASTIME: AQUARIUM, SWIMMING

EIJI KIKUMARU/RIGHT-HANDED

?

SEISHUN ACADEMY 8TH GRADE, CLASS 6
HEIGHT: 171 CM/BLOOD TYPE: A/BORN: 11/28
FAVORITE BRAND SHOES: WILSON
(SLASH DT MID)
RACKET: DUNLOP
(REVELATION PRO TOUR SERIES 90)
BEST SHOT: DIVING VOLLEY, ACROBATIC PLAY
FAVORITE FOOD: FLUFFY OMELETS, PLUMP FRIED SHRIMP,
FLAKY SHAVED ICE
HOBBIES/RECENT PASTIME:
CHECKING OUT PET SHOPS, BRUSHING TEETH

LOTS OF
OLDER BROTHERS
AND OLDER SISTERS

WHIMSICAL

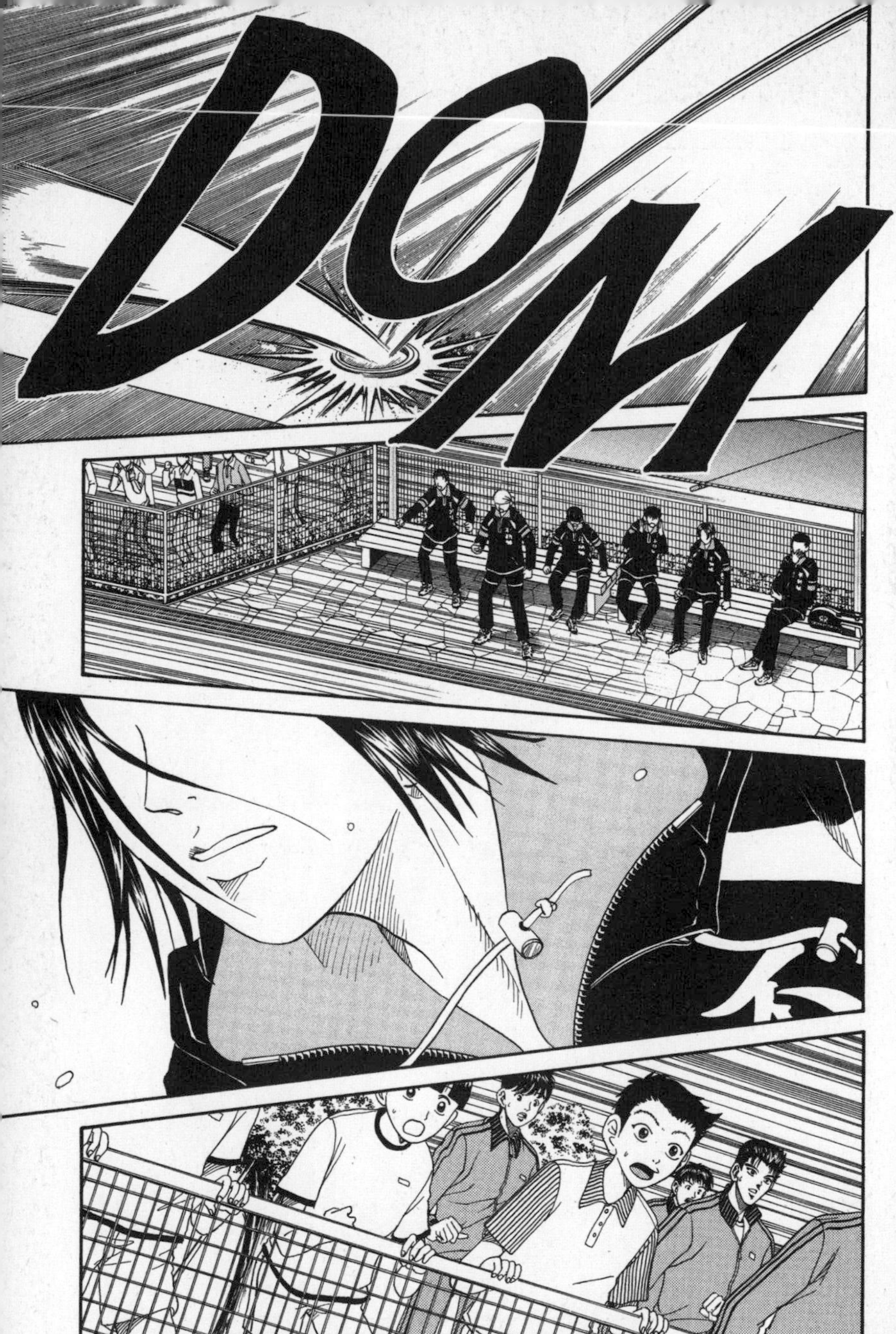
DOM

Genius 37: Spot

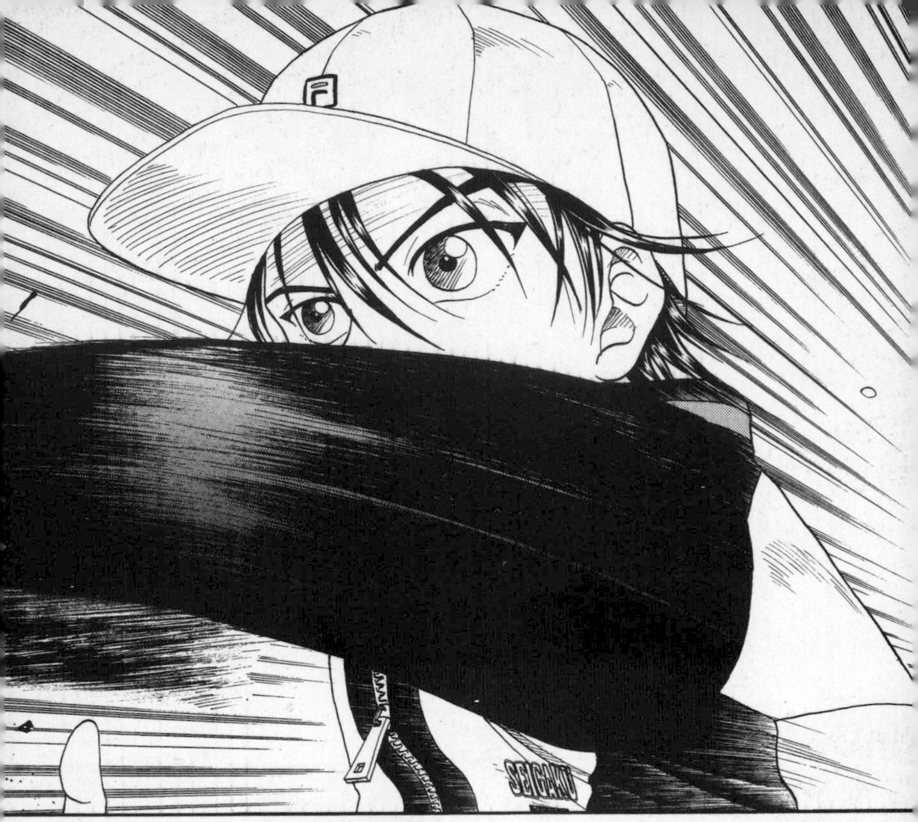
SEIGAKU
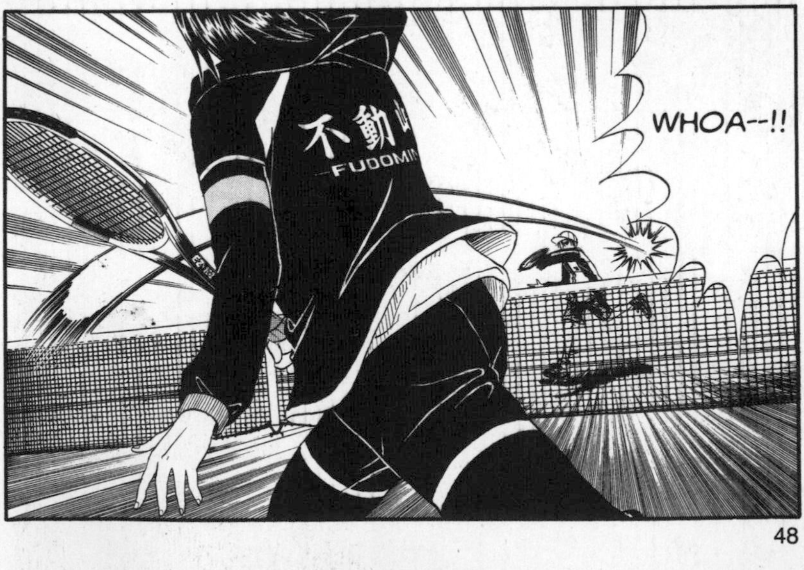
WHOA--!!
不動
FUDOMIN

Genius 37: Spot

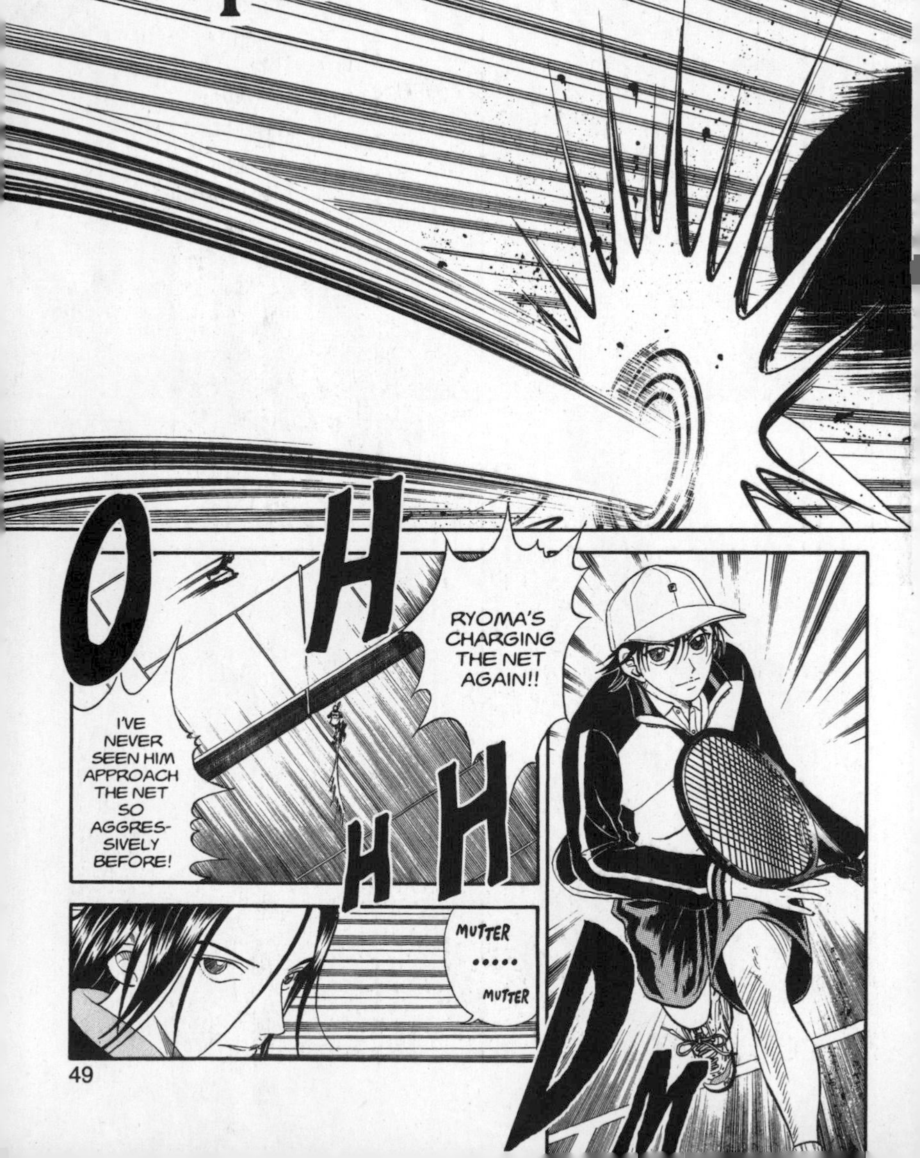

RYOMA'S CHARGING THE NET AGAIN!!
OHHH
I'VE NEVER SEEN HIM APPROACH THE NET SO AGGRES-SIVELY BEFORE!
MUTTER ..... MUTTER

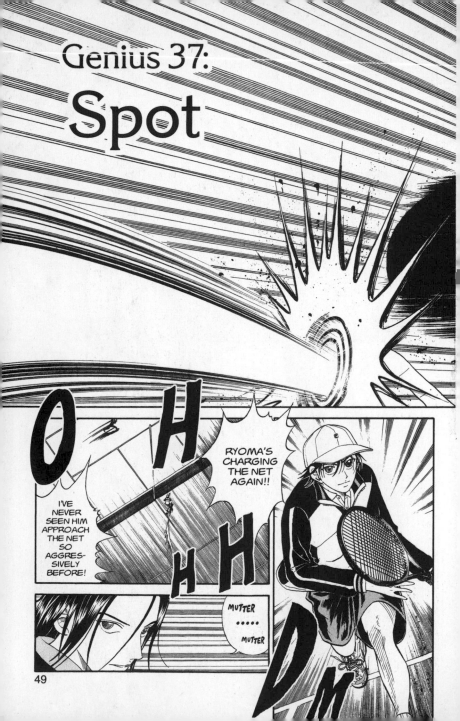

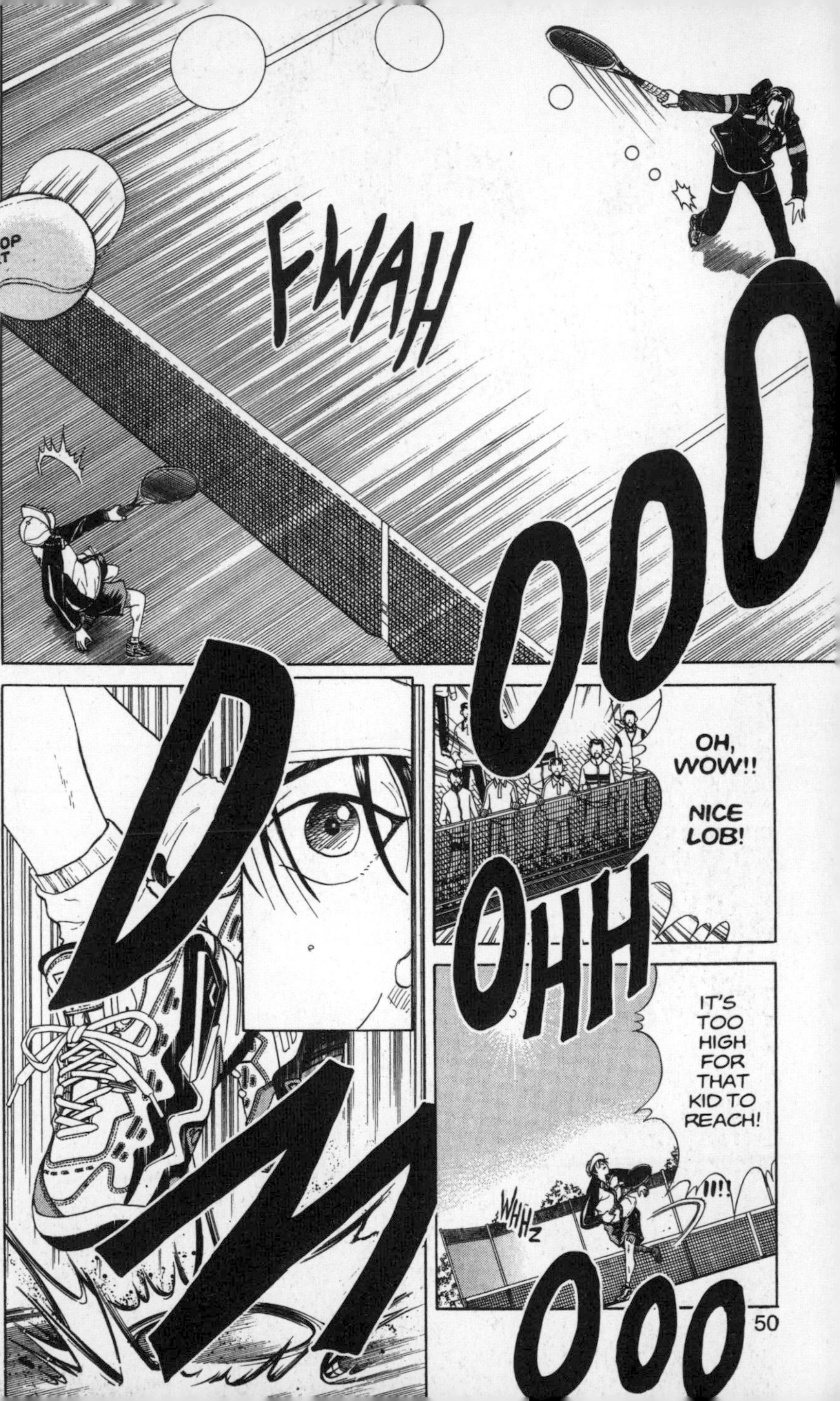
FWAH
OOOO
OHH
OOO
OH, WOW!!
NICE LOB!
IT'S TOO HIGH FOR THAT KID TO REACH!
WHHZ

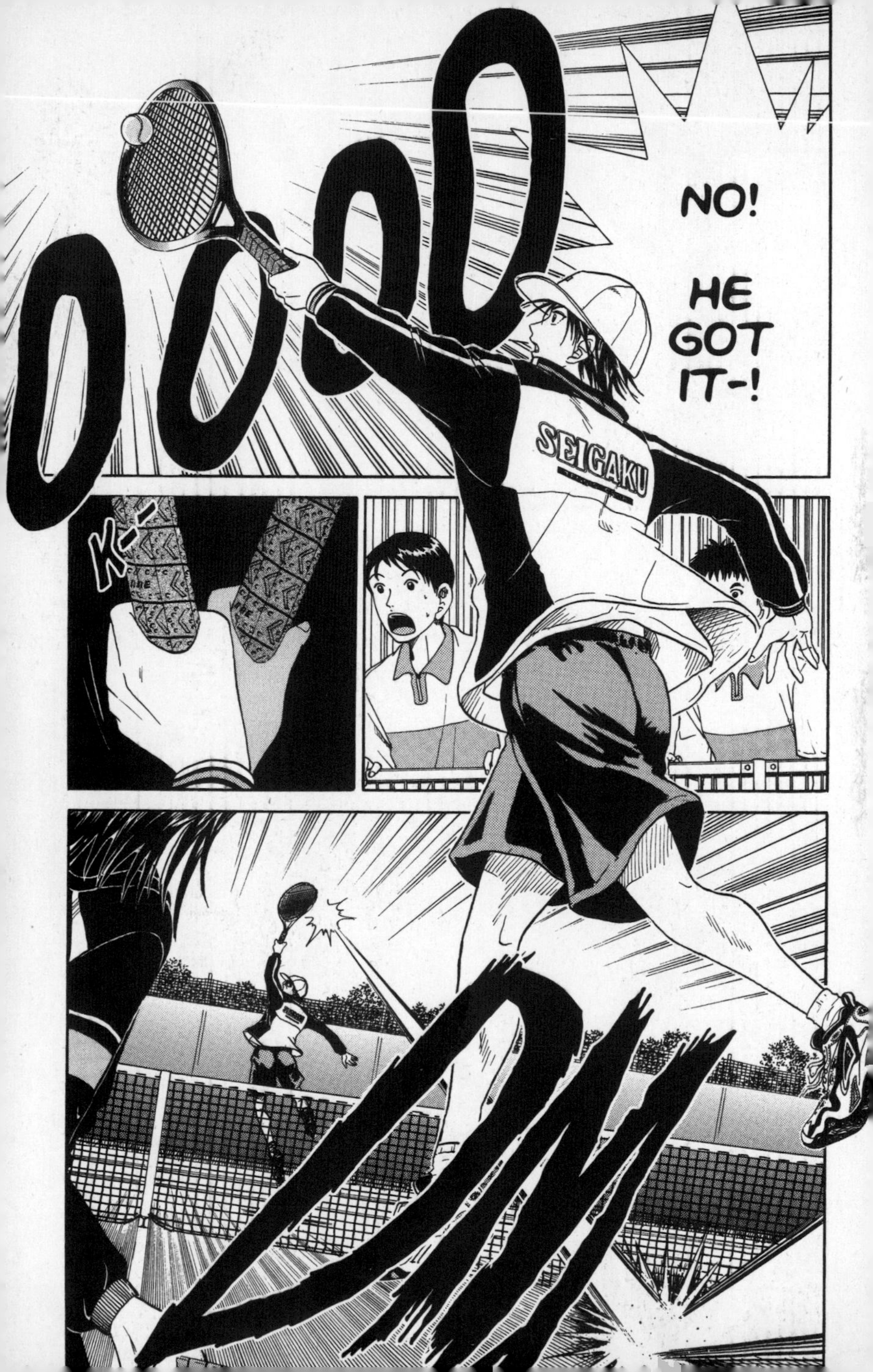

NO!
HE GOT IT-!
OOOO
SEIGAKU
K-

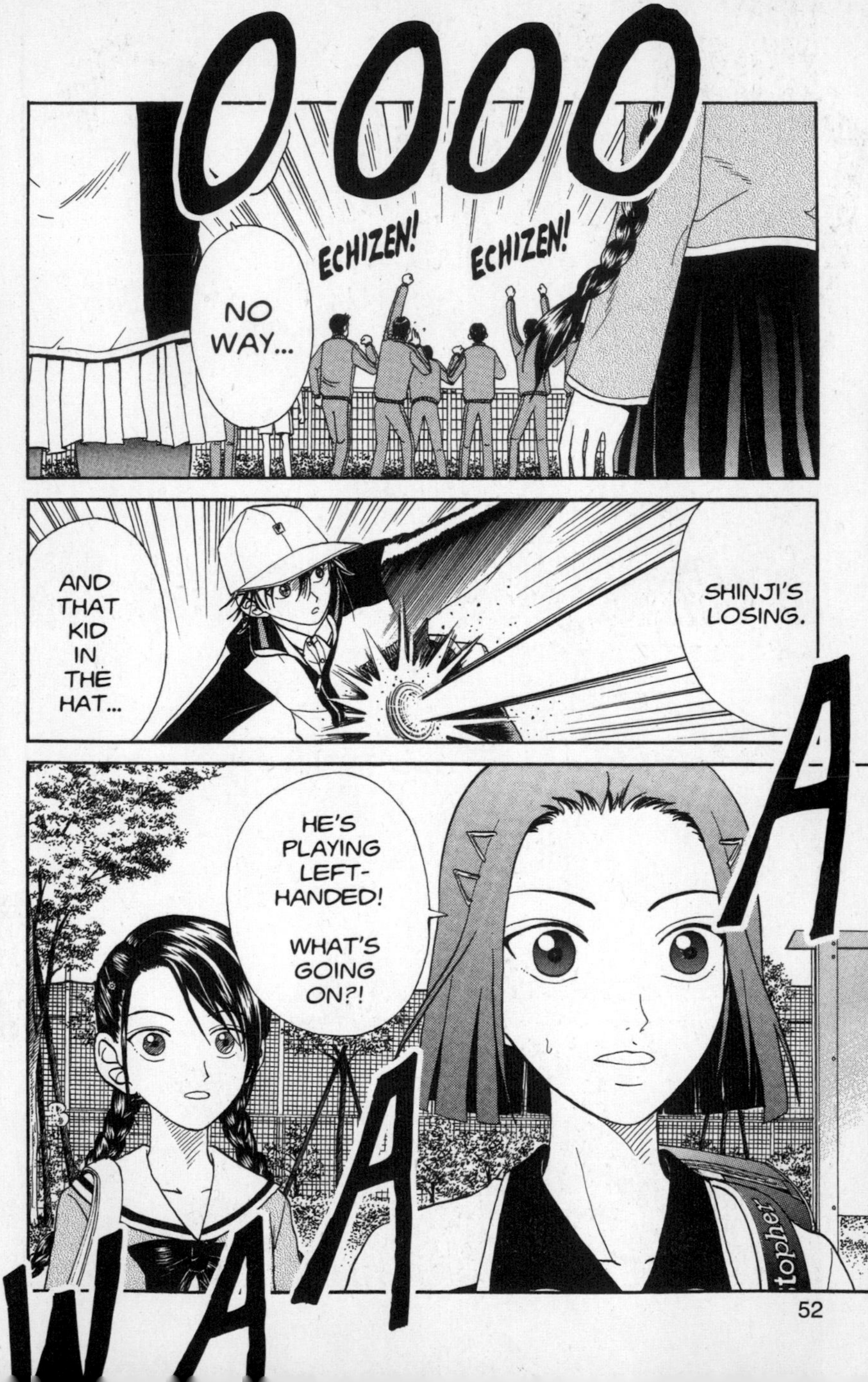
OOOO
ECHIZEN!
ECHIZEN!
NO WAY...
SHINJI'S LOSING.
AND THAT KID IN THE HAT...
HE'S PLAYING LEFT-HANDED!
WHAT'S GOING ON?!
WAAA

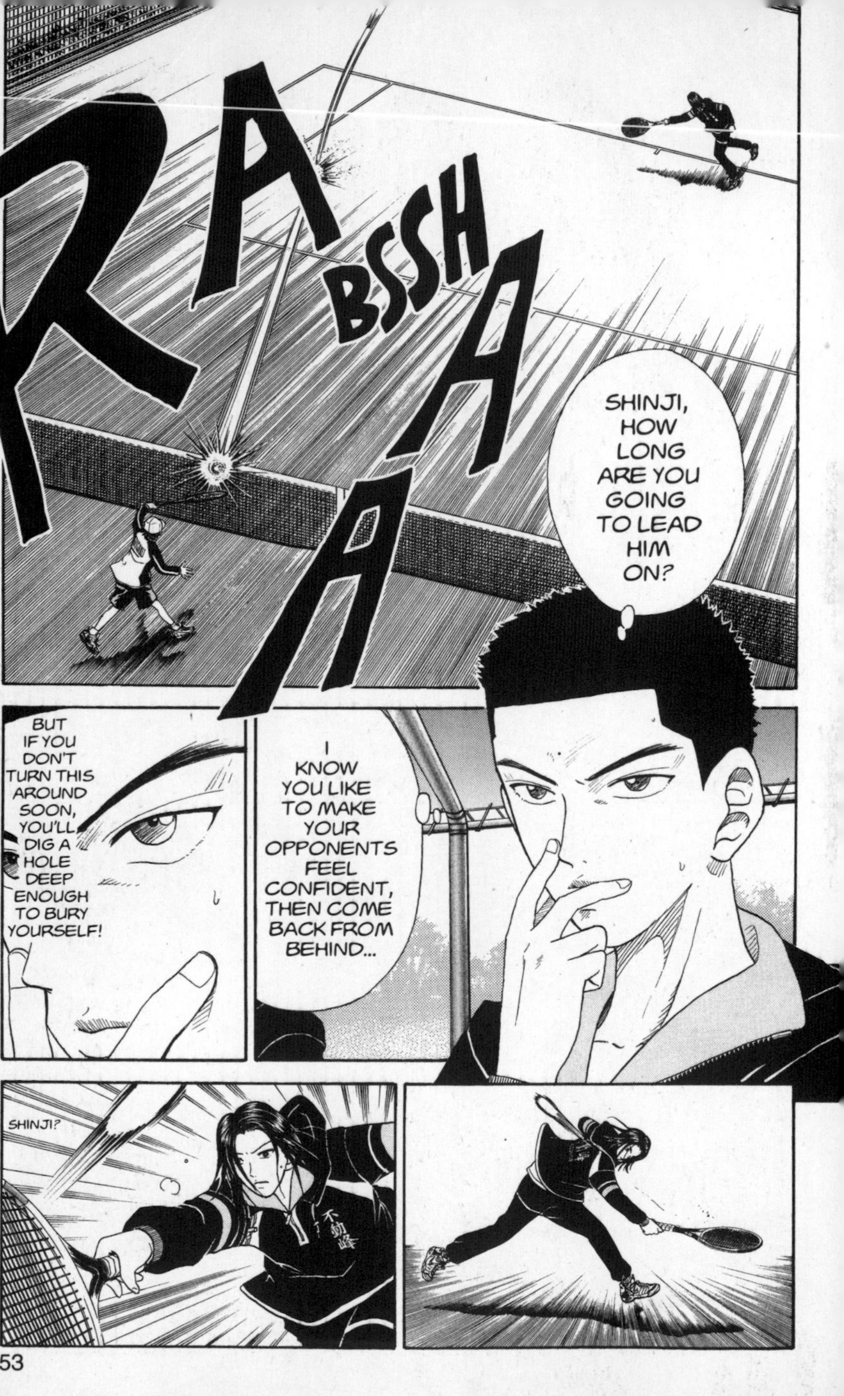

RAAA
BSSH
SHINJI, HOW LONG ARE YOU GOING TO LEAD HIM ON?
I KNOW YOU LIKE TO MAKE YOUR OPPONENTS FEEL CONFIDENT, THEN COME BACK FROM BEHIND...
BUT IF YOU DON'T TURN THIS AROUND SOON, YOU'LL DIG A HOLE DEEP ENOUGH TO BURY YOURSELF!
SHINJI?

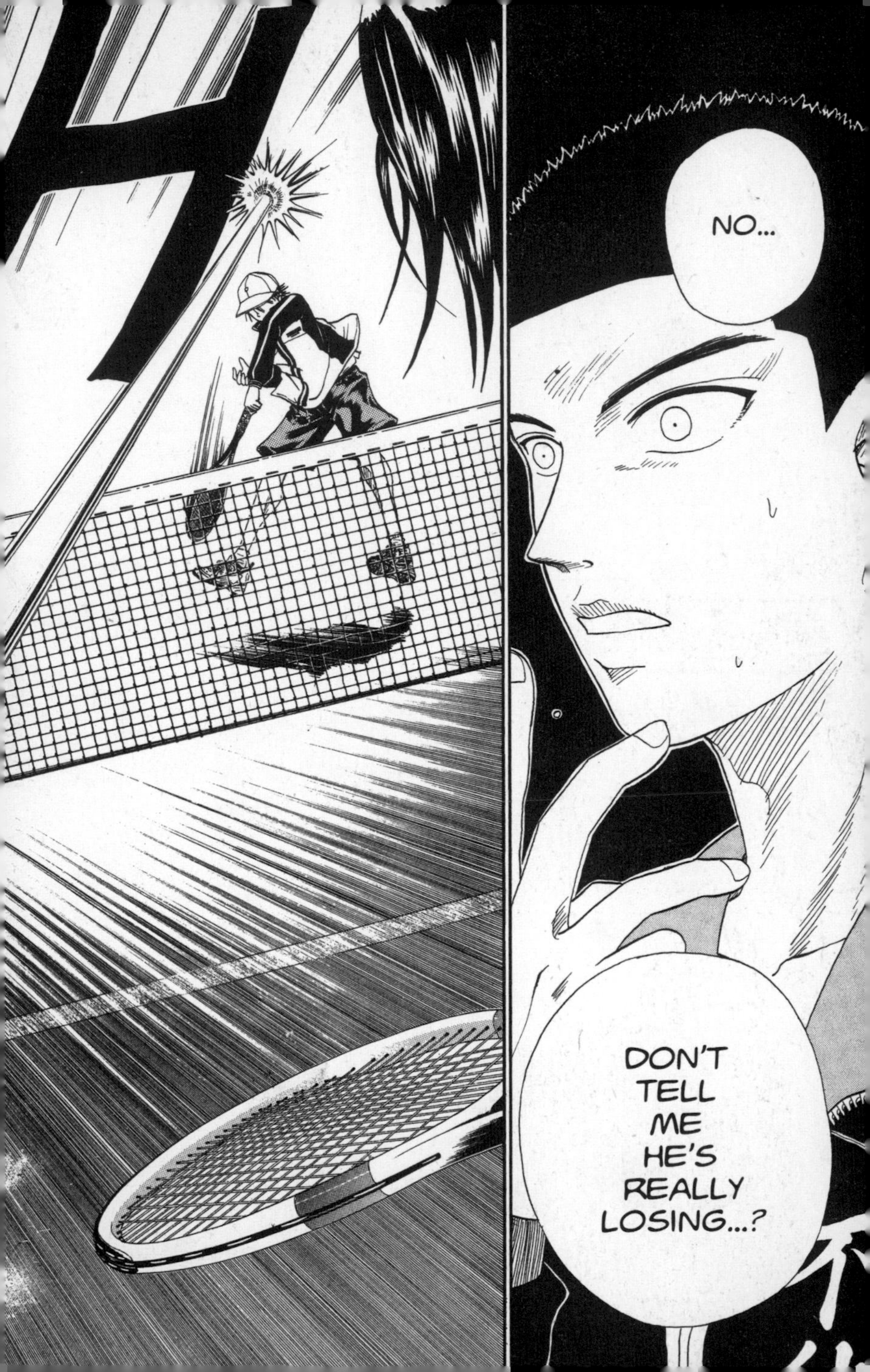
NO...
DON'T TELL ME HE'S REALLY LOSING...?

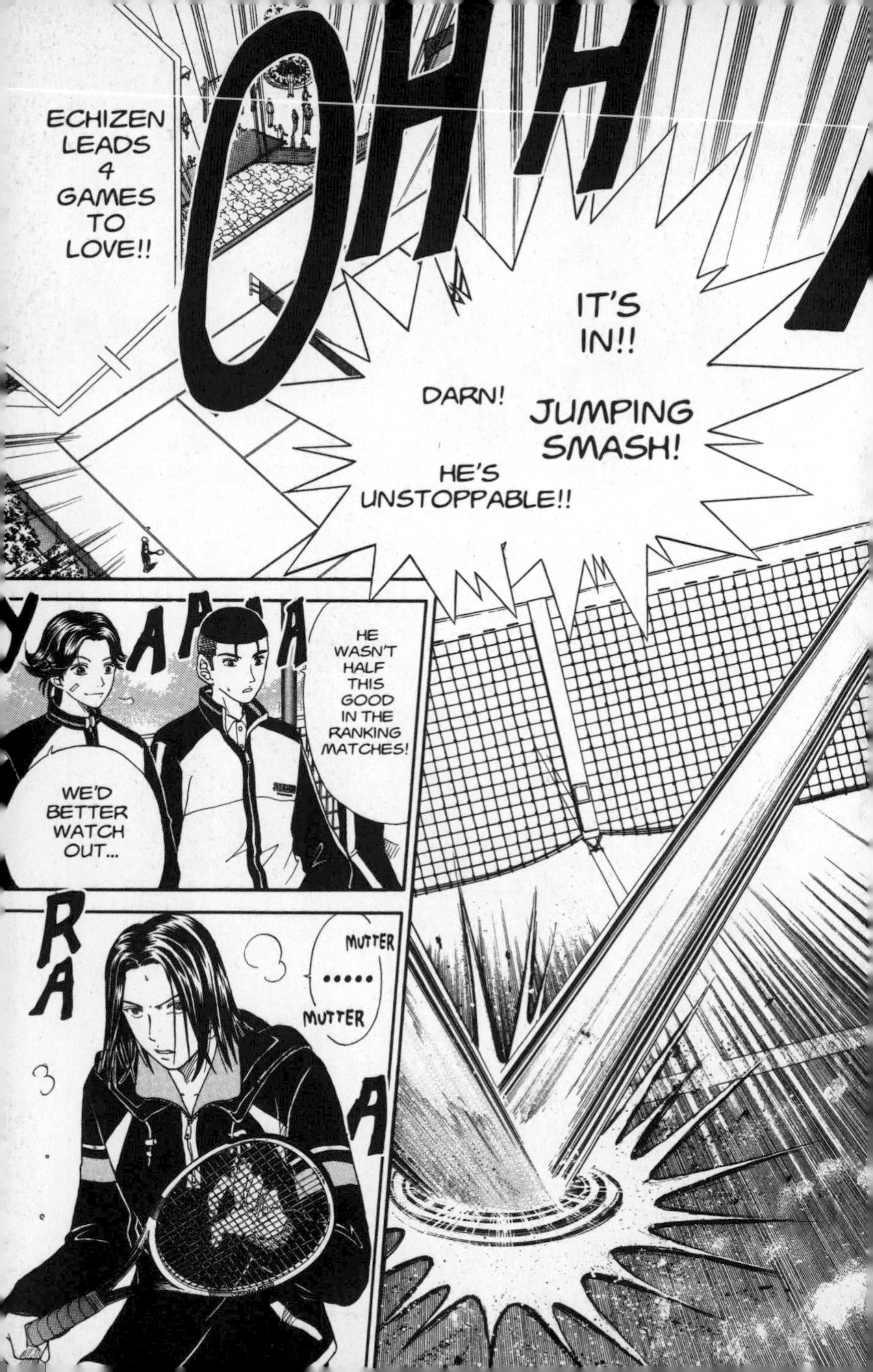
OHH
IT'S IN!!
JUMPING SMASH!
DARN!
HE'S UNSTOPPABLE!!
ECHIZEN LEADS 4 GAMES TO LOVE!!
HE WASN'T HALF THIS GOOD IN THE RANKING MATCHES!
WE'D BETTER WATCH OUT...
MUTTER ..... MUTTER

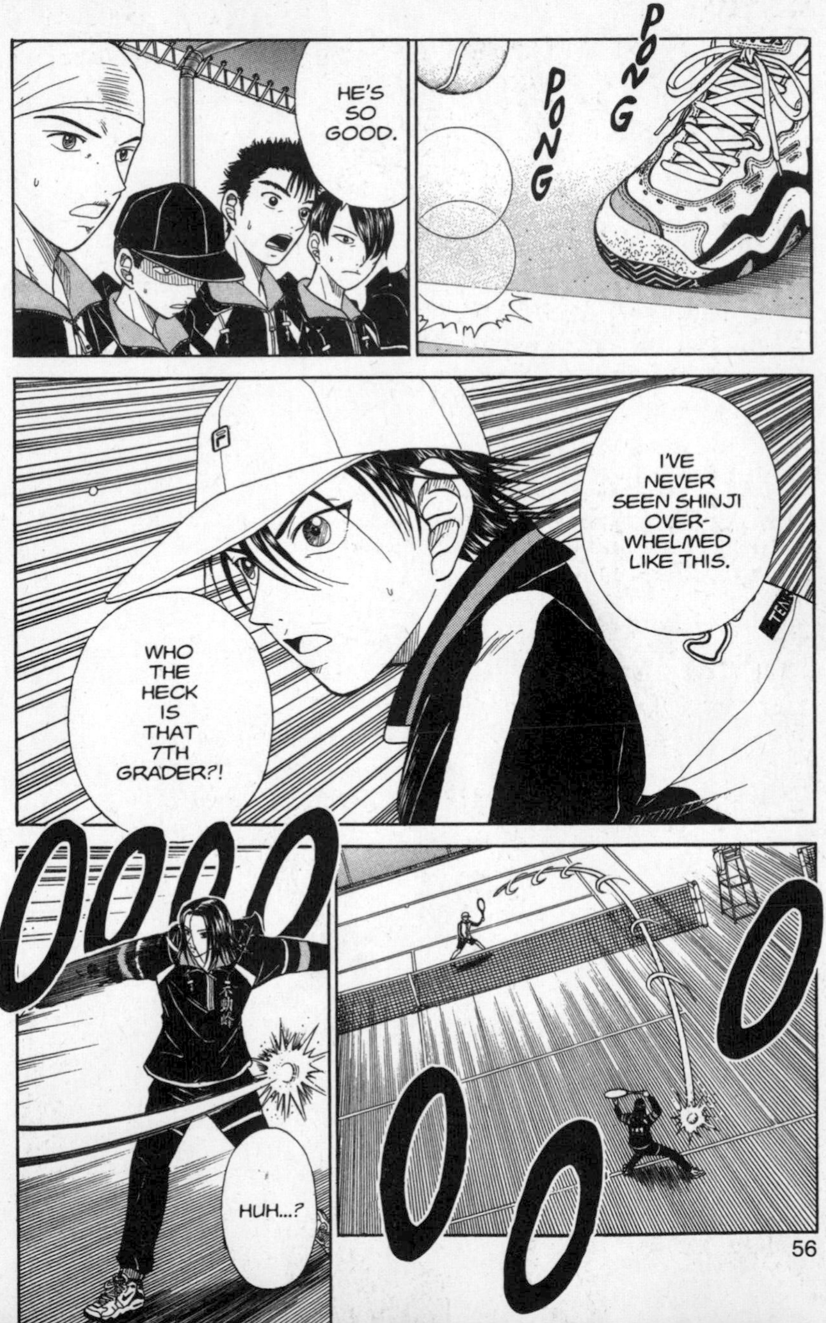
PONG
PONG
HE'S SO GOOD.
I'VE NEVER SEEN SHINJI OVER-WHELMED LIKE THIS.
WHO THE HECK IS THAT 7TH GRADER?!
HUH...?

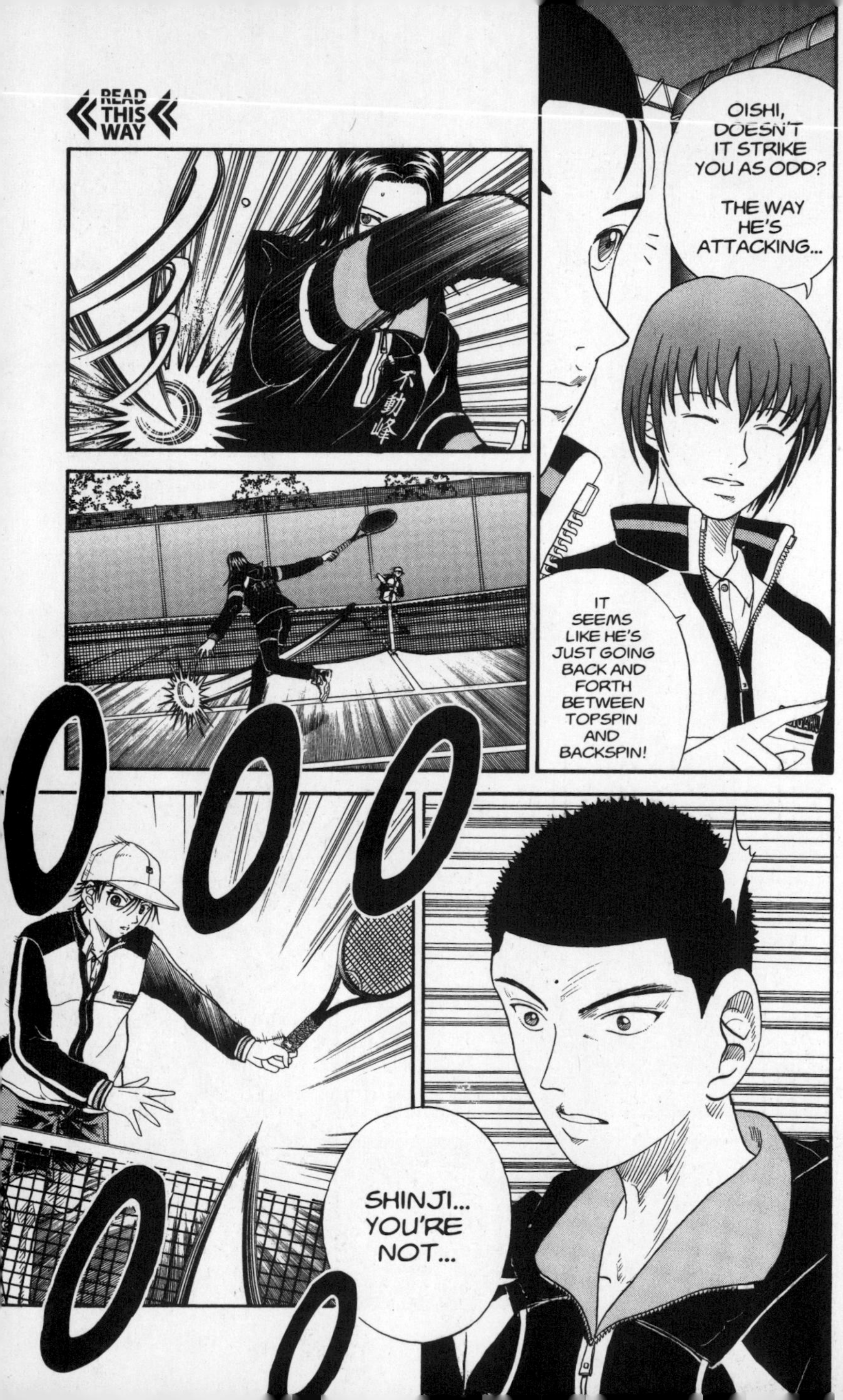
READ THIS WAY
OISHI, DOESN'T IT STRIKE YOU AS ODD? THE WAY HE'S ATTACKING...
IT SEEMS LIKE HE'S JUST GOING BACK AND FORTH BETWEEN TOPSPIN AND BACKSPIN!
不動峰
SHINJI... YOU'RE NOT...

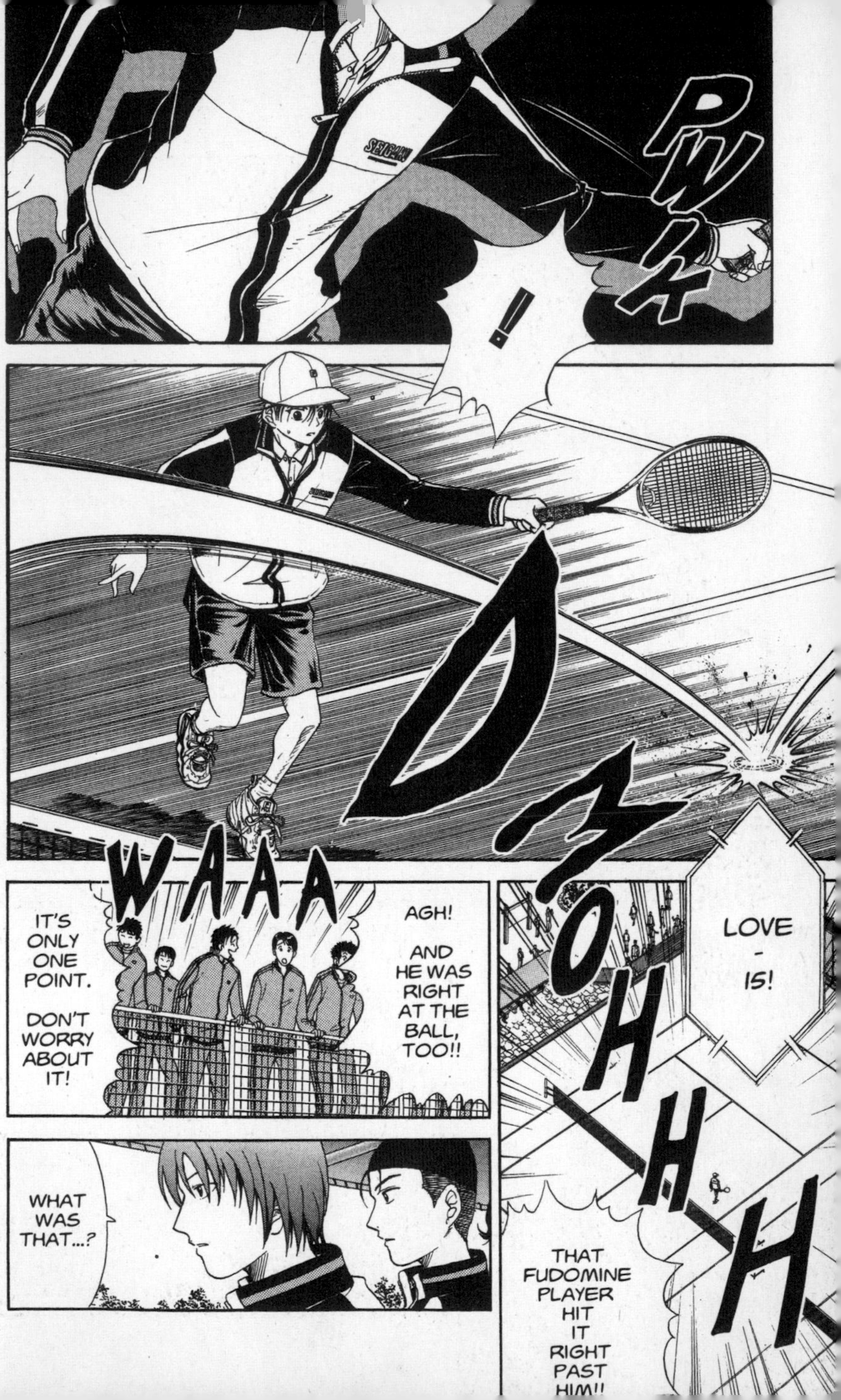
PWIK
!
LOVE - 15!
THAT FUDOMINE PLAYER HIT IT RIGHT PAST HIM!!
WAAA
AGH!
AND HE WAS RIGHT AT THE BALL, TOO!!
IT'S ONLY ONE POINT.
DON'T WORRY ABOUT IT!
WHAT WAS THAT...?

READ THIS WAY

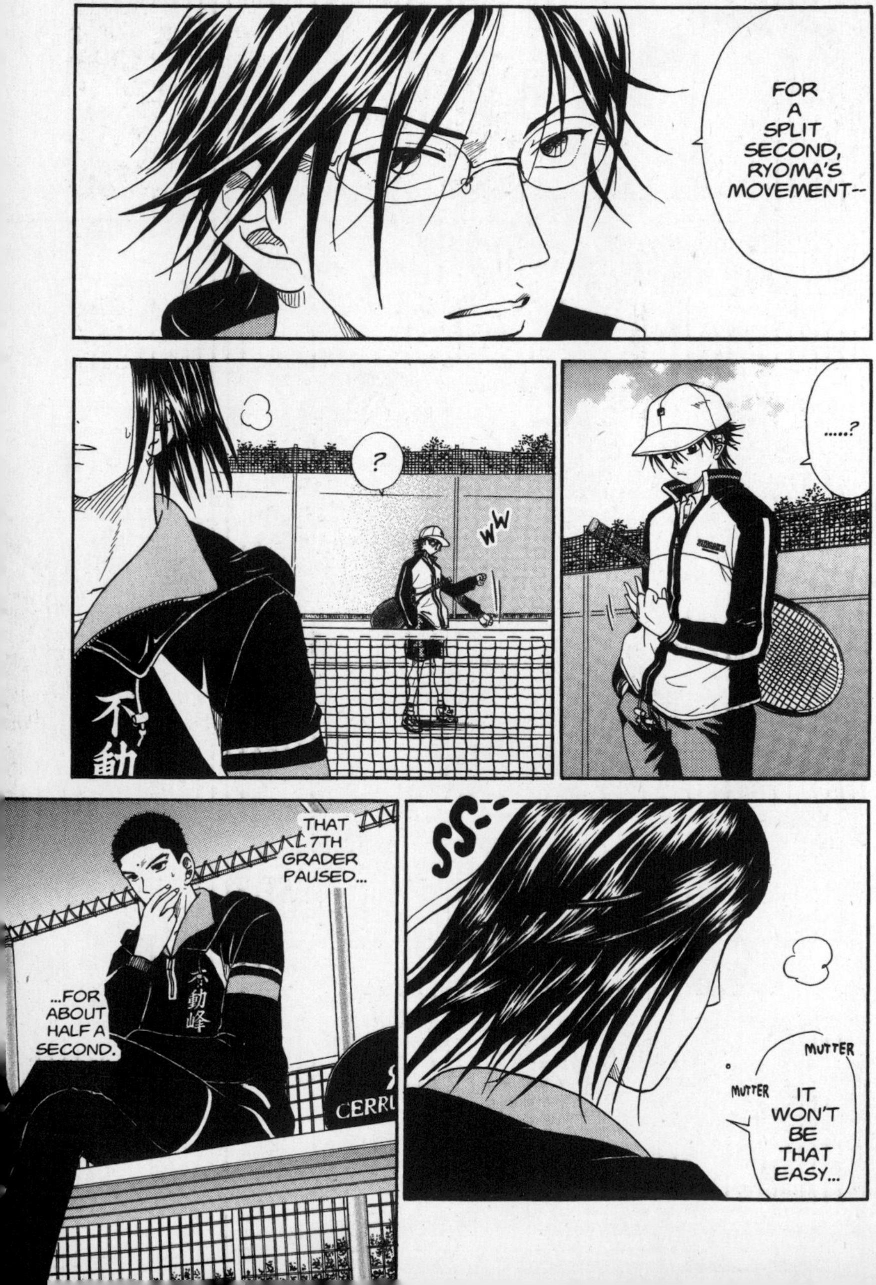
FOR A SPLIT SECOND, RYOMA'S MOVEMENT--
.....?
?
WW
SS--
MUTTER
MUTTER
IT WON'T BE THAT EASY...
THAT 7TH GRADER PAUSED...
...FOR ABOUT HALF A SECOND.

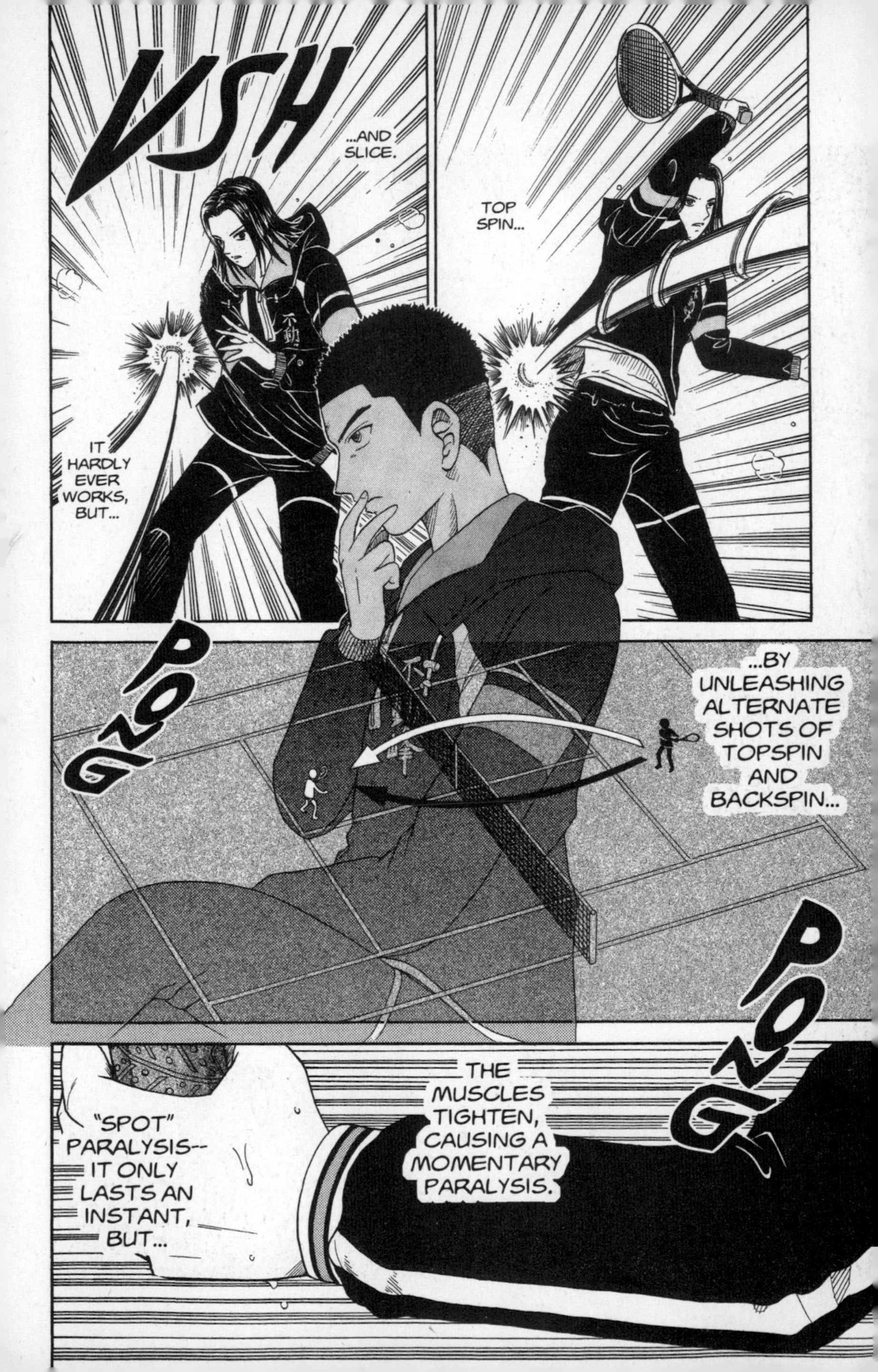

TOP SPIN...
...AND SLICE.
VSH
IT HARDLY EVER WORKS, BUT...
...BY UNLEASHING ALTERNATE SHOTS OF TOPSPIN AND BACKSPIN...
PONG
PONG
THE MUSCLES TIGHTEN, CAUSING A MOMENTARY PARALYSIS.
"SPOT" PARALYSIS--IT ONLY LASTS AN INSTANT, BUT...

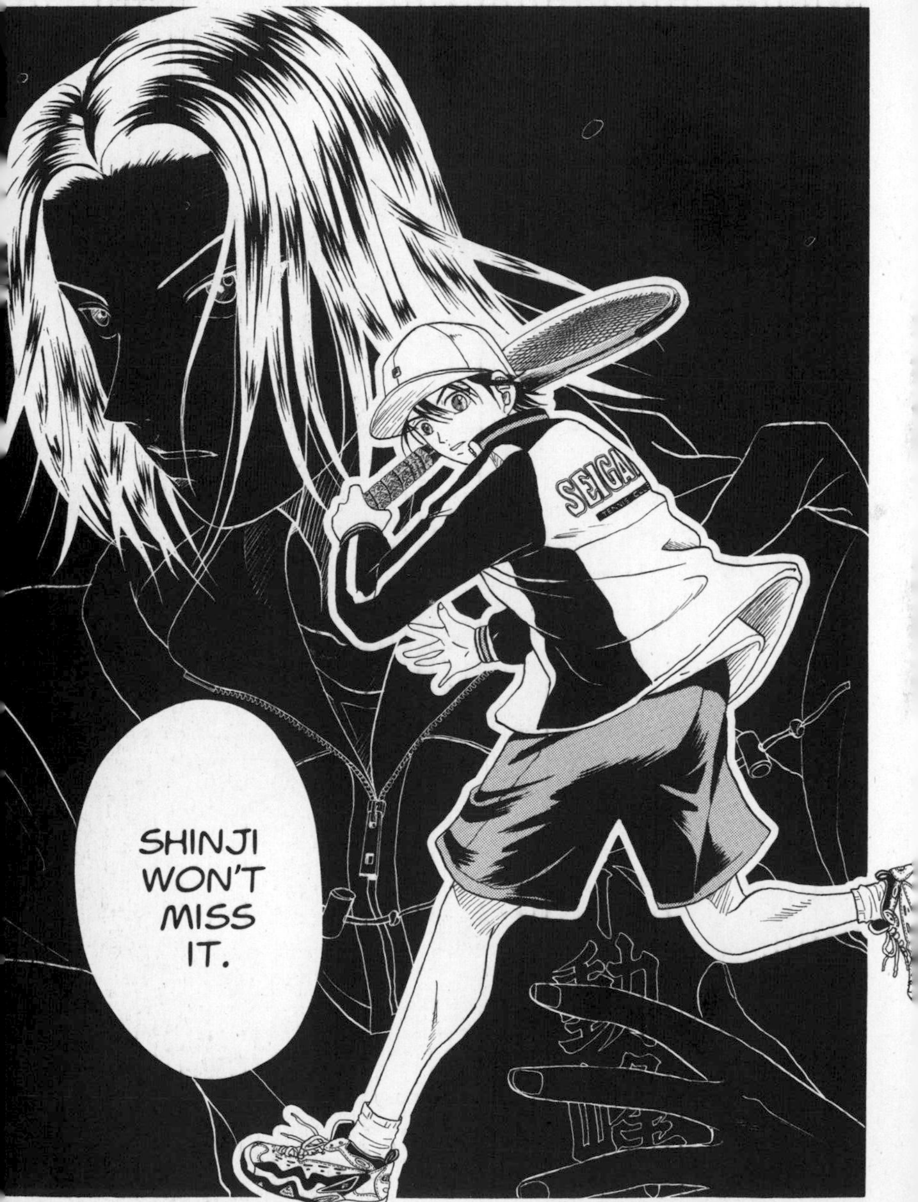
SEIGAKU
SHINJI WON'T MISS IT.

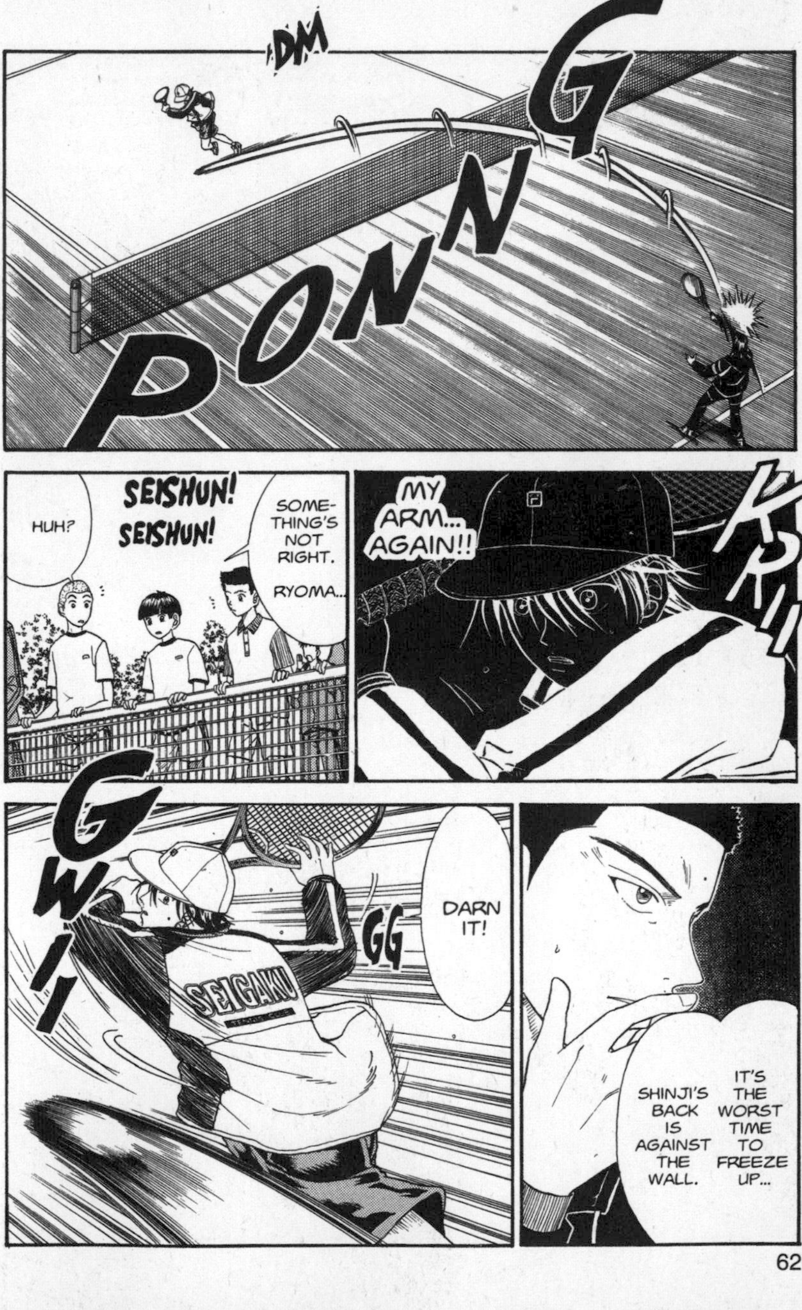
DM
PONNG
KRII
MY ARM... AGAIN!!
SOME-THING'S NOT RIGHT.
RYOMA...
SEISHUN! SEISHUN!
HUH?
IT'S THE WORST TIME TO FREEZE UP...
SHINJI'S BACK IS AGAINST THE WALL.
DARN IT!
GG
GWII
SEIGAKU

READ THIS WAY

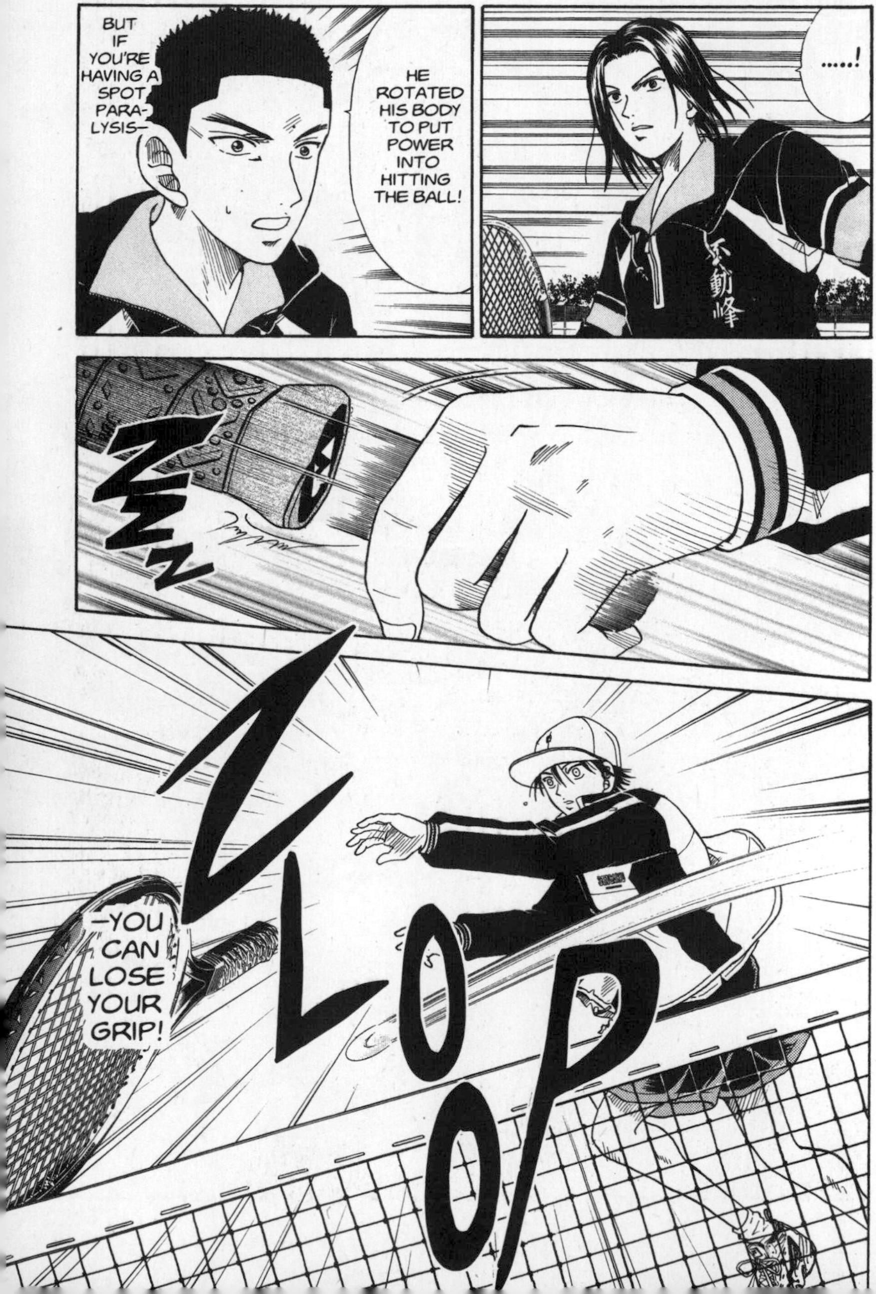
.....!
HE ROTATED HIS BODY TO PUT POWER INTO HITTING THE BALL!
BUT IF YOU'RE HAVING A SPOT PARA-LYSIS—
ZWWN
ZLOOP
—YOU CAN LOSE YOUR GRIP!

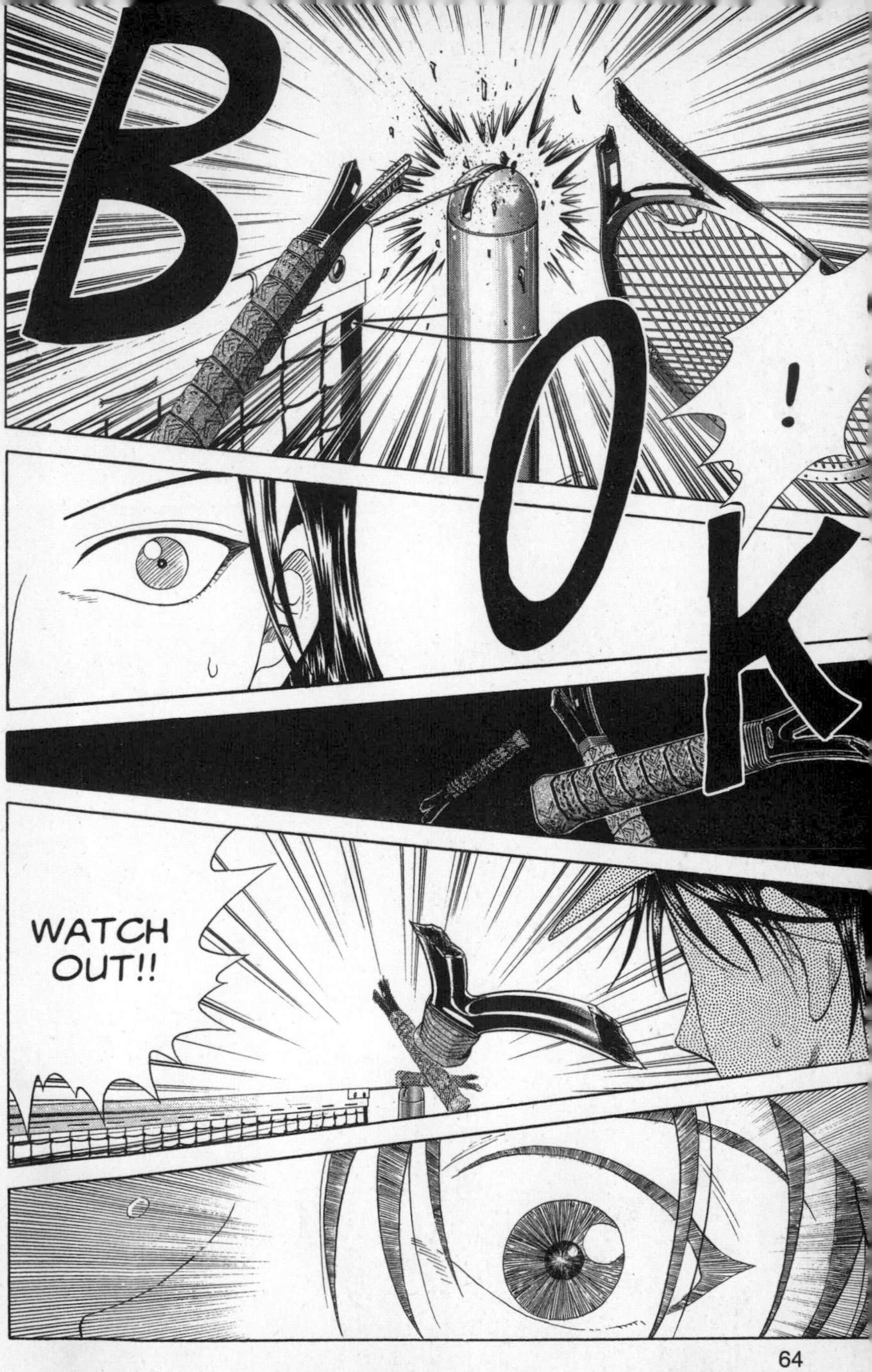
BOK
!
WATCH OUT!!

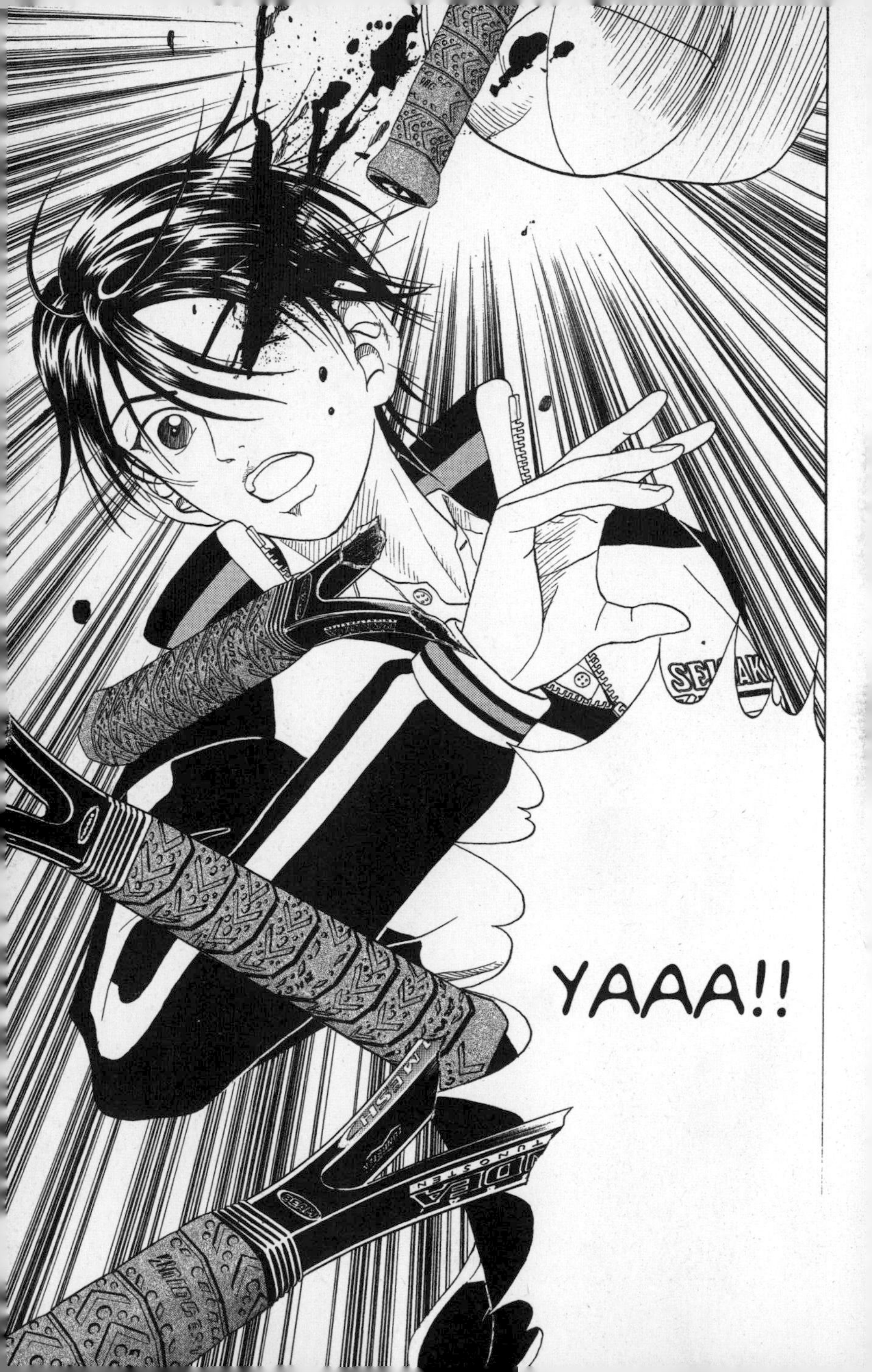
YAAA!!

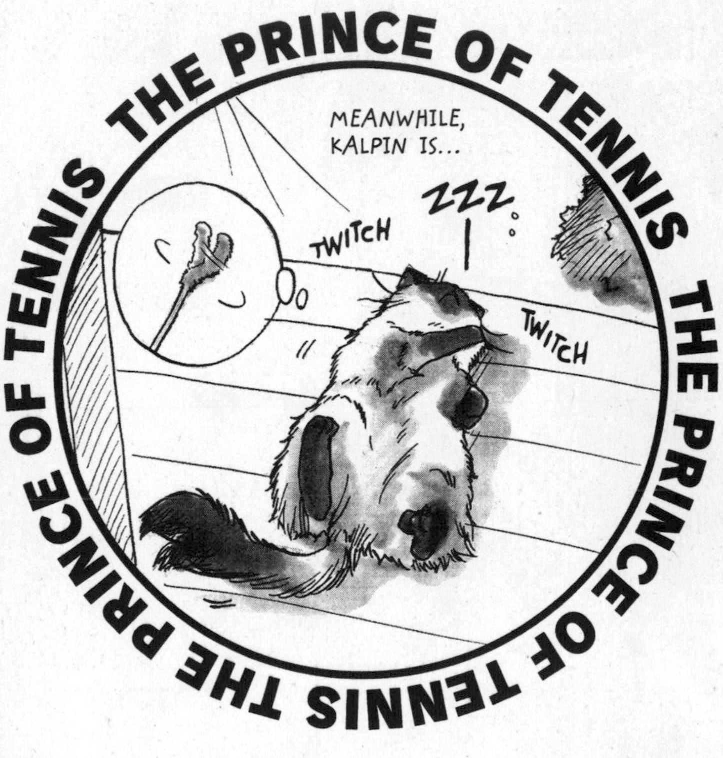
THE PRINCE OF TENNIS THE PRINCE OF TENNIS THE PRINCE OF TENNIS
MEANWHILE, KALPIN IS...
ZZZ
TWITCH
TWITCH

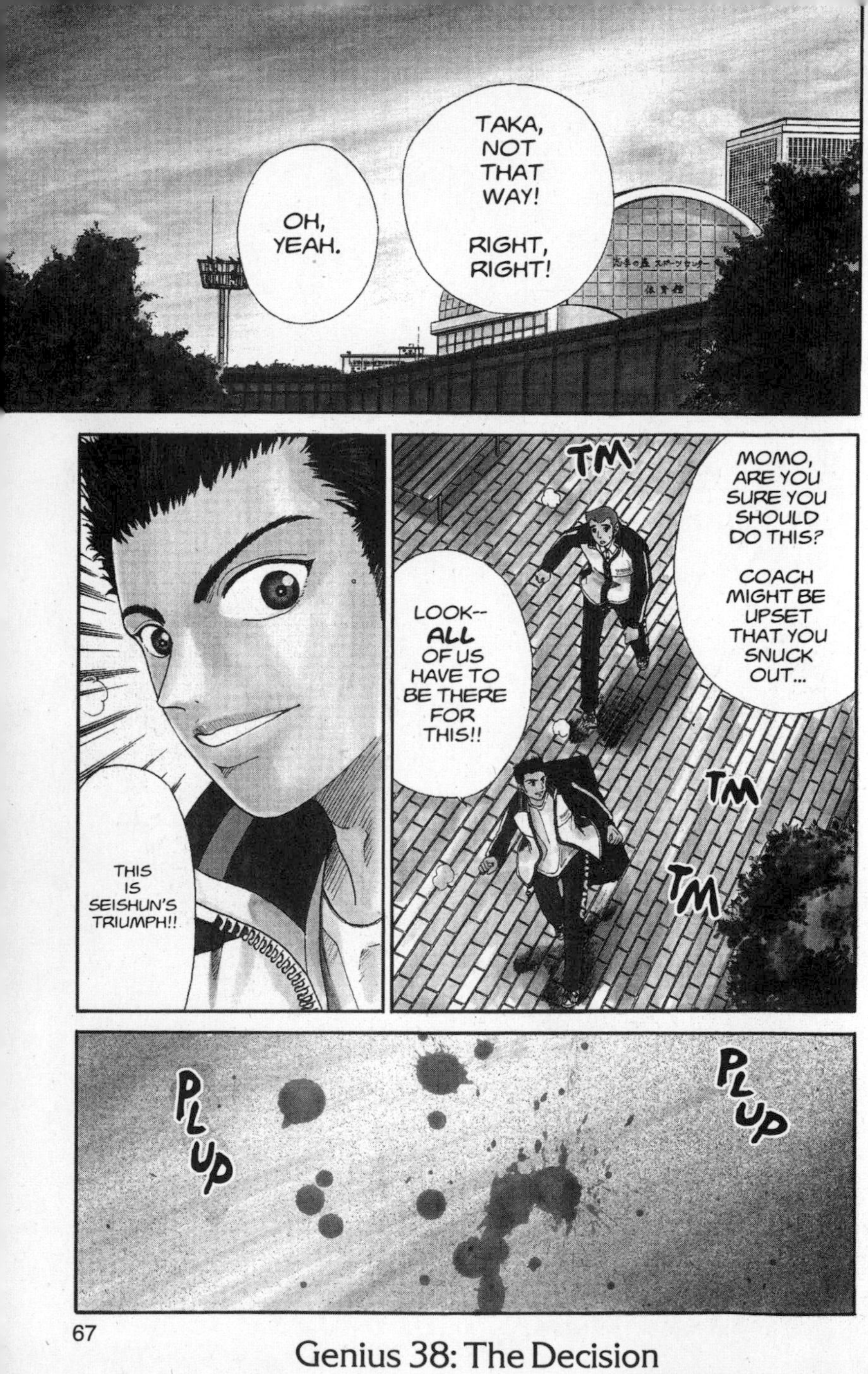
TAKA, NOT THAT WAY! RIGHT, RIGHT!
OH, YEAH.
TM
MOMO, ARE YOU SURE YOU SHOULD DO THIS? COACH MIGHT BE UPSET THAT YOU SNUCK OUT...
LOOK-- ALL OF US HAVE TO BE THERE FOR THIS!!
TM
TM
THIS IS SEISHUN'S TRIUMPH!!
PLUP
PLUP

Genius 38: The Decision

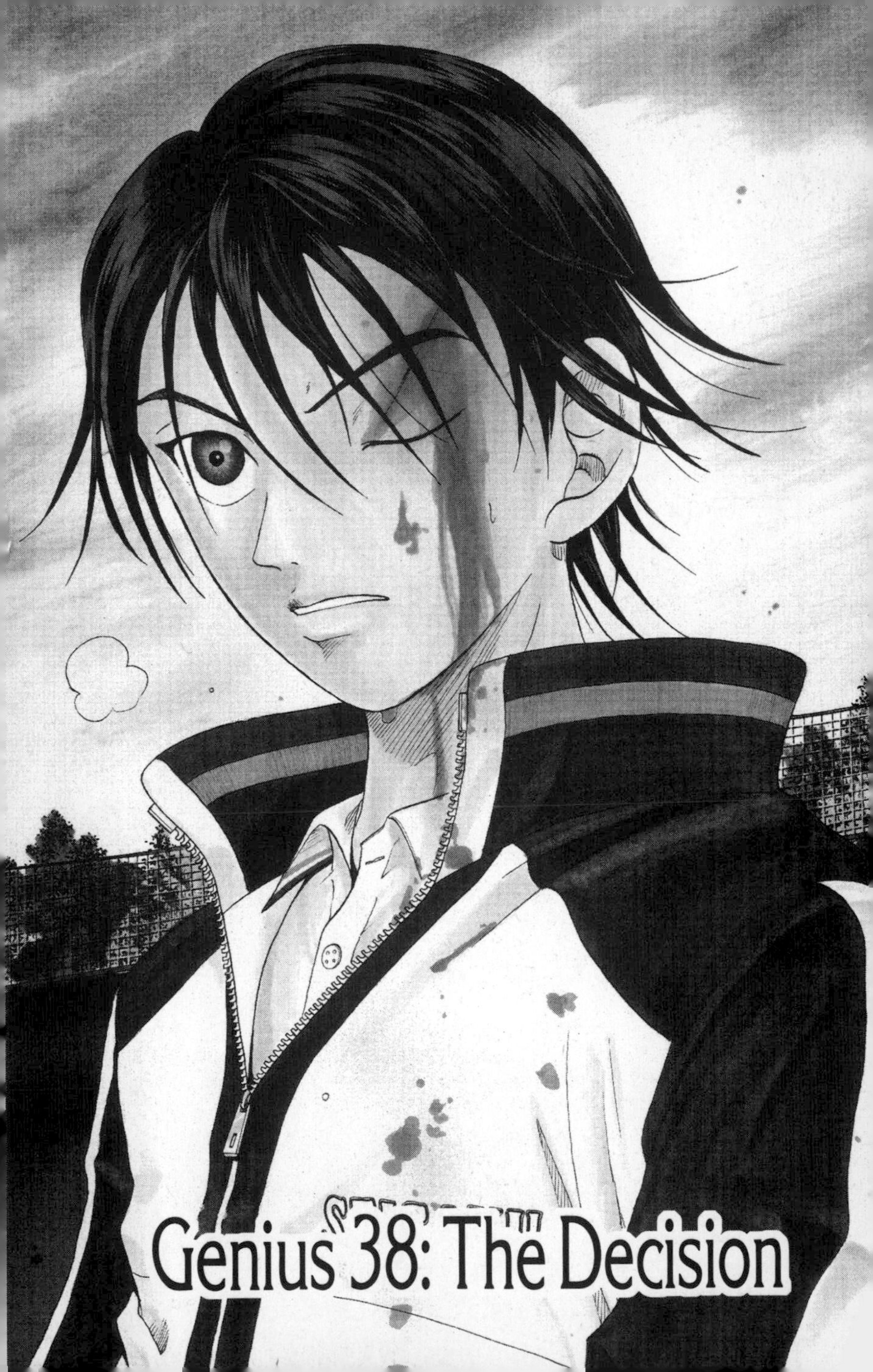

Genius 38: The Decision

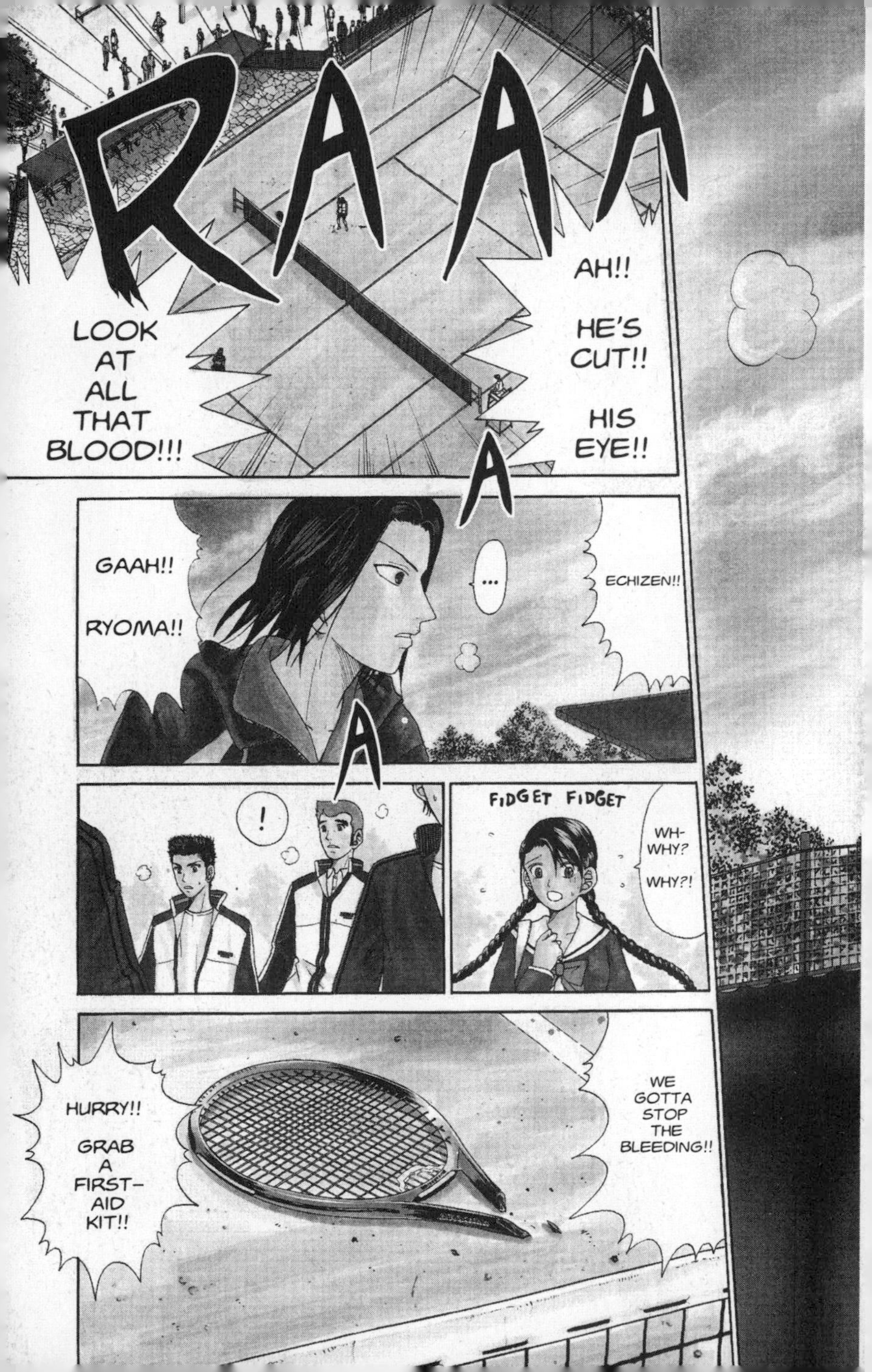
RAAAAAA
AH!! HE'S CUT!! HIS EYE!!
LOOK AT ALL THAT BLOOD!!!
ECHIZEN!!
...
GAAH!! RYOMA!!
FIDGET FIDGET
WH- WHY? WHY?!
!
WE GOTTA STOP THE BLEEDING!!
HURRY!! GRAB A FIRST-AID KIT!!

テニスの王子様

THE PRINCE OF TENNIS™

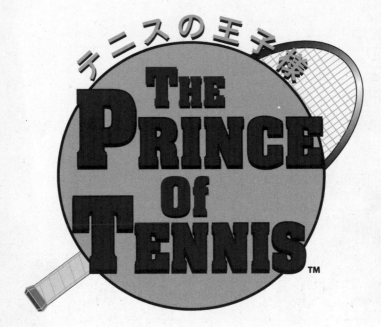

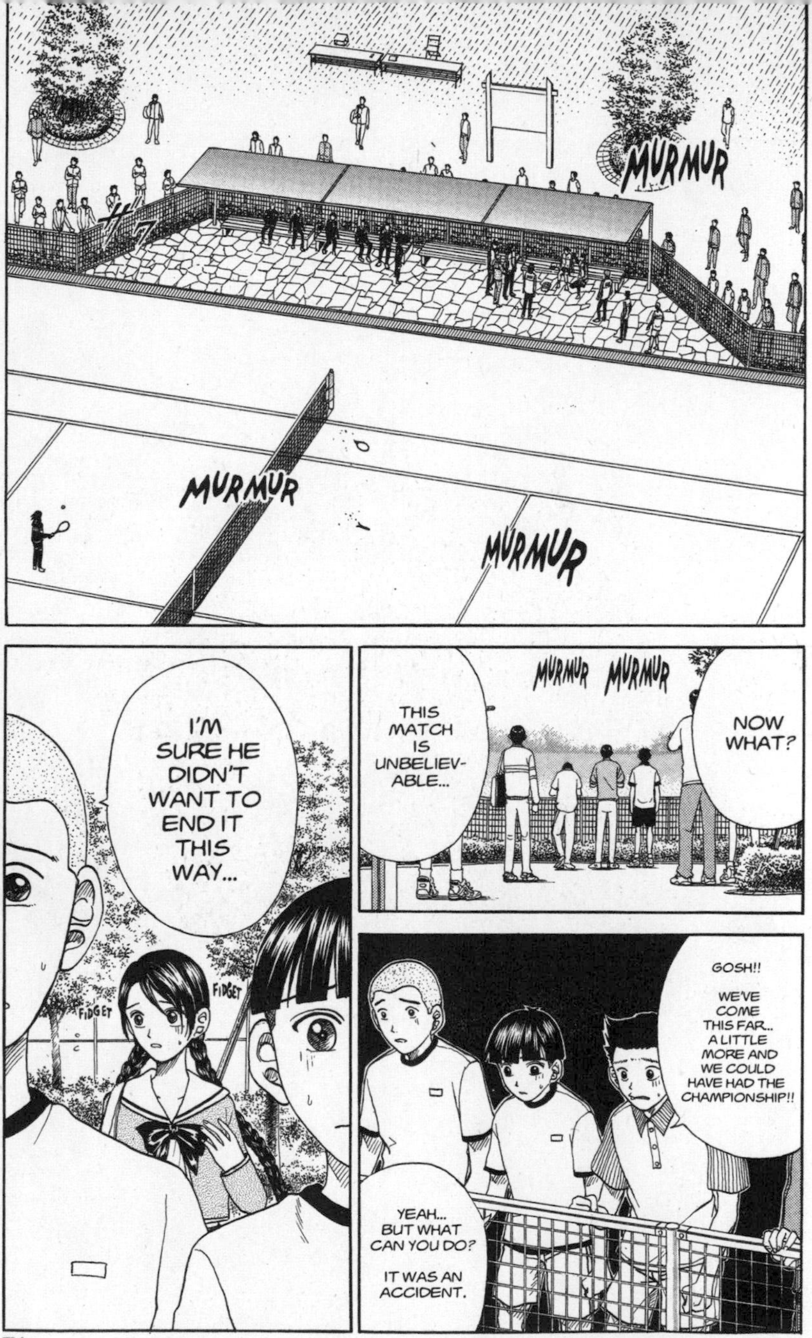
MURMUR
MURMUR
MURMUR
MURMUR MURMUR
NOW WHAT?
THIS MATCH IS UNBELIEV-ABLE...
GOSH!! WE'VE COME THIS FAR... A LITTLE MORE AND WE COULD HAVE HAD THE CHAMPIONSHIP!!
YEAH... BUT WHAT CAN YOU DO? IT WAS AN ACCIDENT.
I'M SURE HE DIDN'T WANT TO END IT THIS WAY...
FIDGET
FIDGET

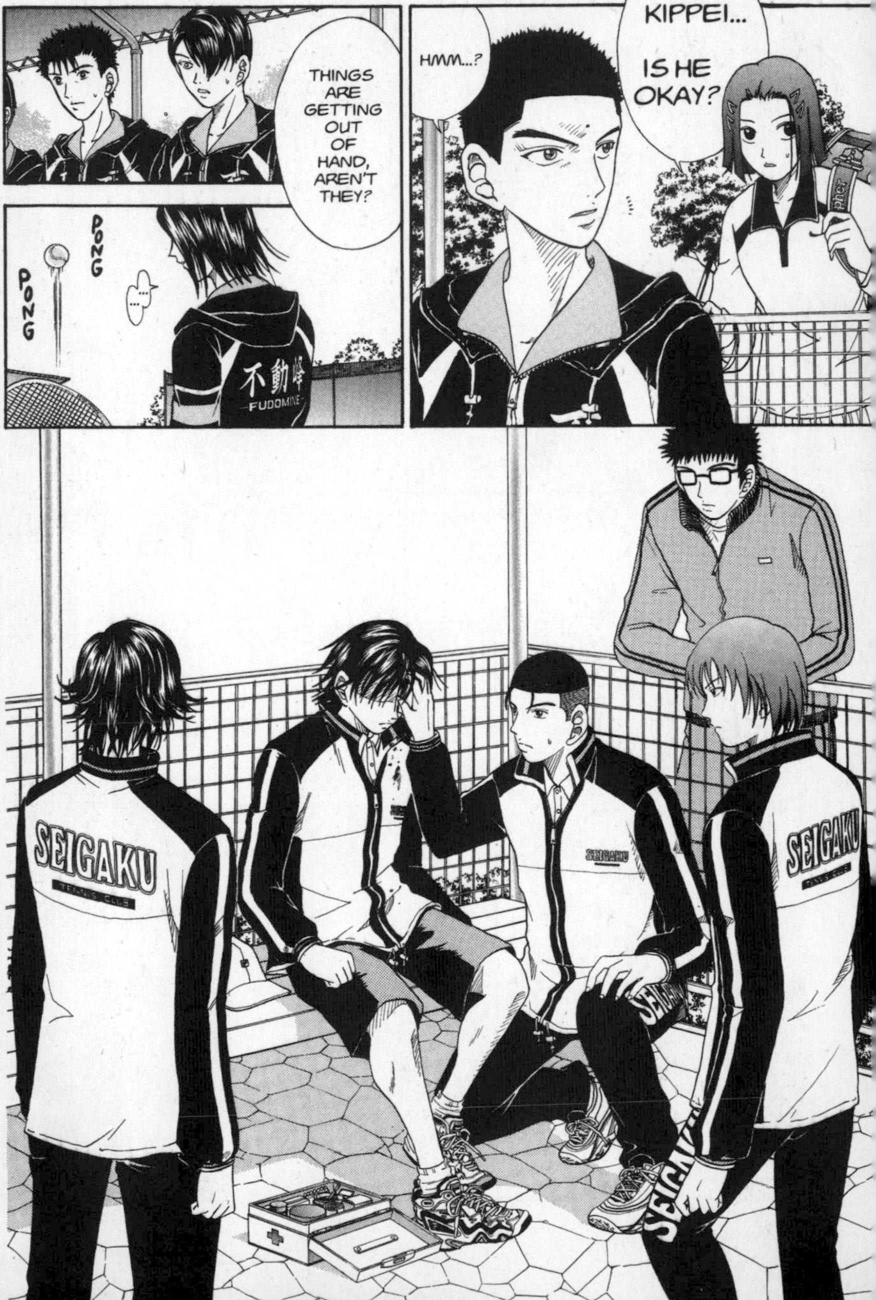
KIPPEI... IS HE OKAY?
HMM...?
THINGS ARE GETTING OUT OF HAND, AREN'T THEY?
PONG
PONG
......
不動峰
-FUDOMINE-
SEIGAKU
SEIGAKU
SEIGAKU
SEIGAKU

READ THIS WAY

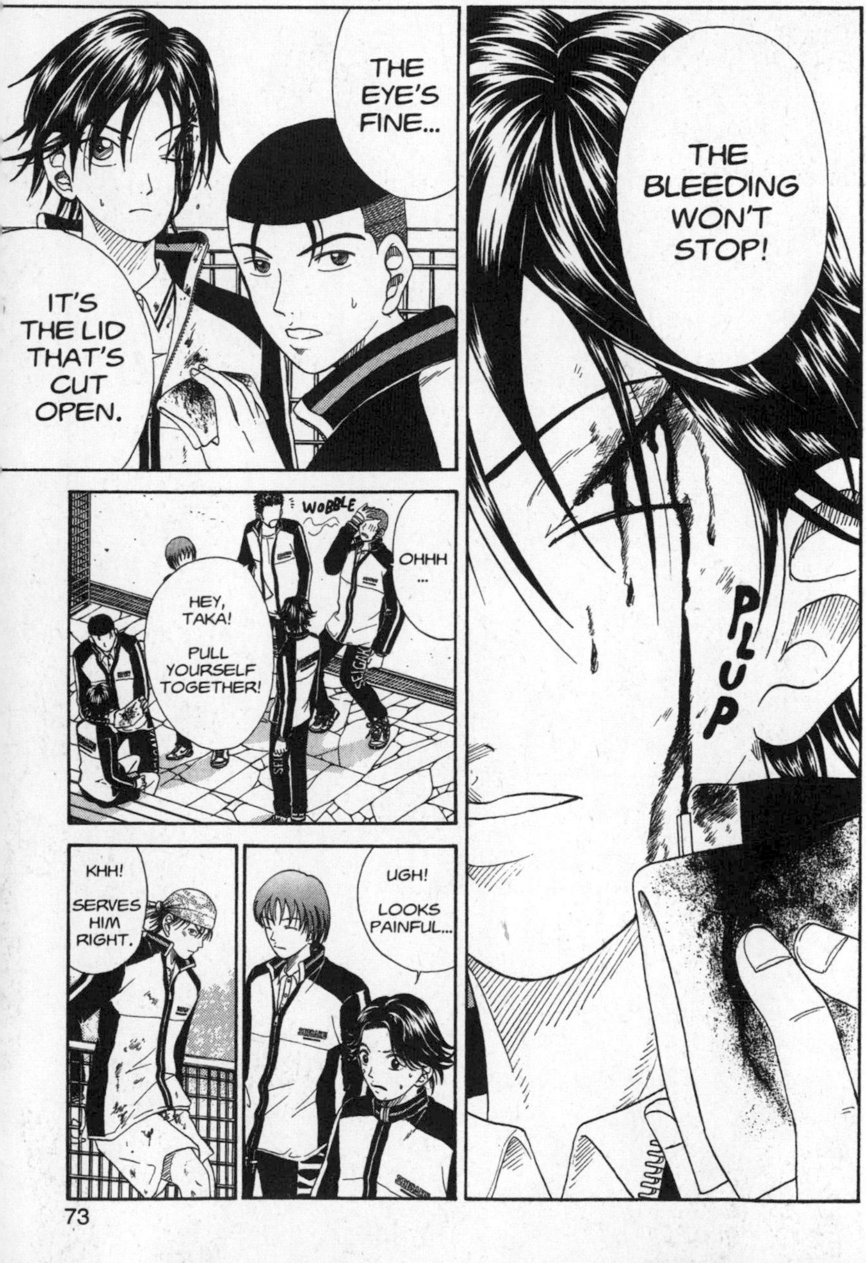
THE BLEEDING WON'T STOP!
PLUP
THE EYE'S FINE...
IT'S THE LID THAT'S CUT OPEN.
WOBBLE
OHHH...
HEY, TAKA! PULL YOURSELF TOGETHER!
UGH! LOOKS PAINFUL...
KHH! SERVES HIM RIGHT.

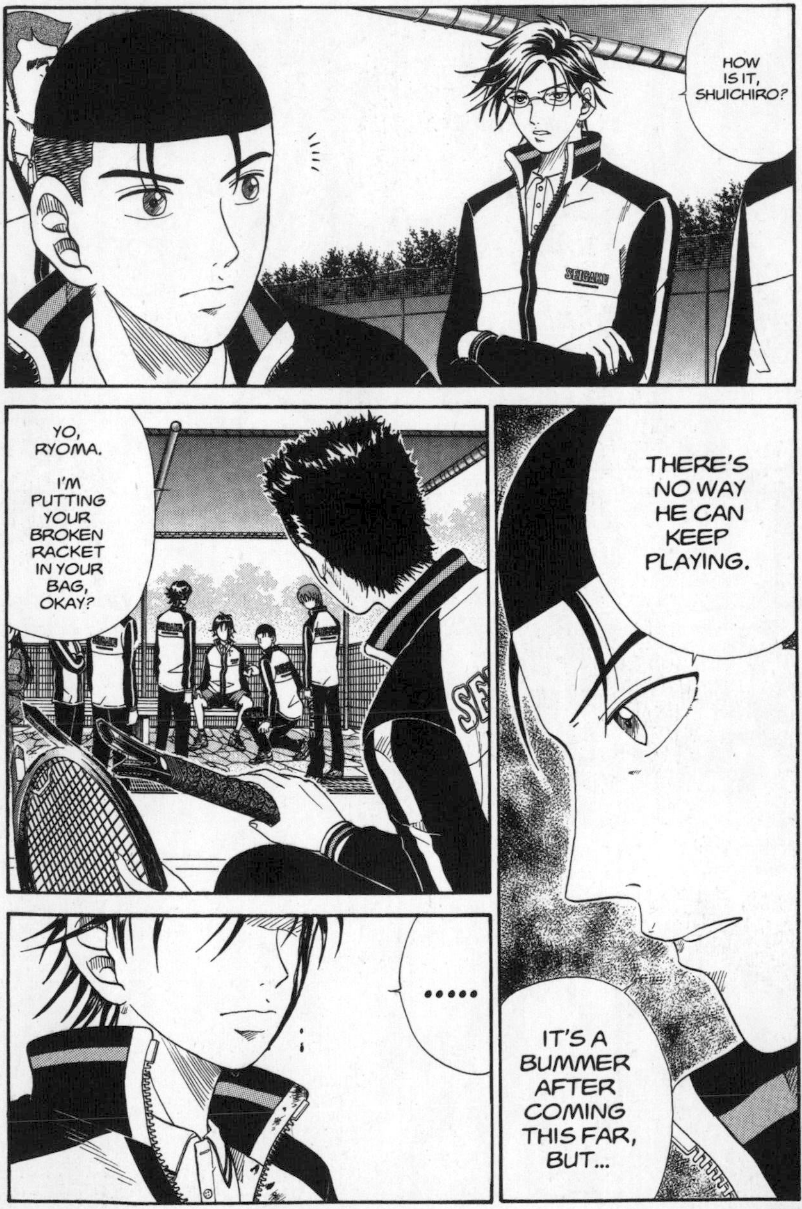
HOW IS IT, SHUICHIRO?
THERE'S NO WAY HE CAN KEEP PLAYING.
IT'S A BUMMER AFTER COMING THIS FAR, BUT...
YO, RYOMA.
I'M PUTTING YOUR BROKEN RACKET IN YOUR BAG, OKAY?
.....

READ THIS WAY

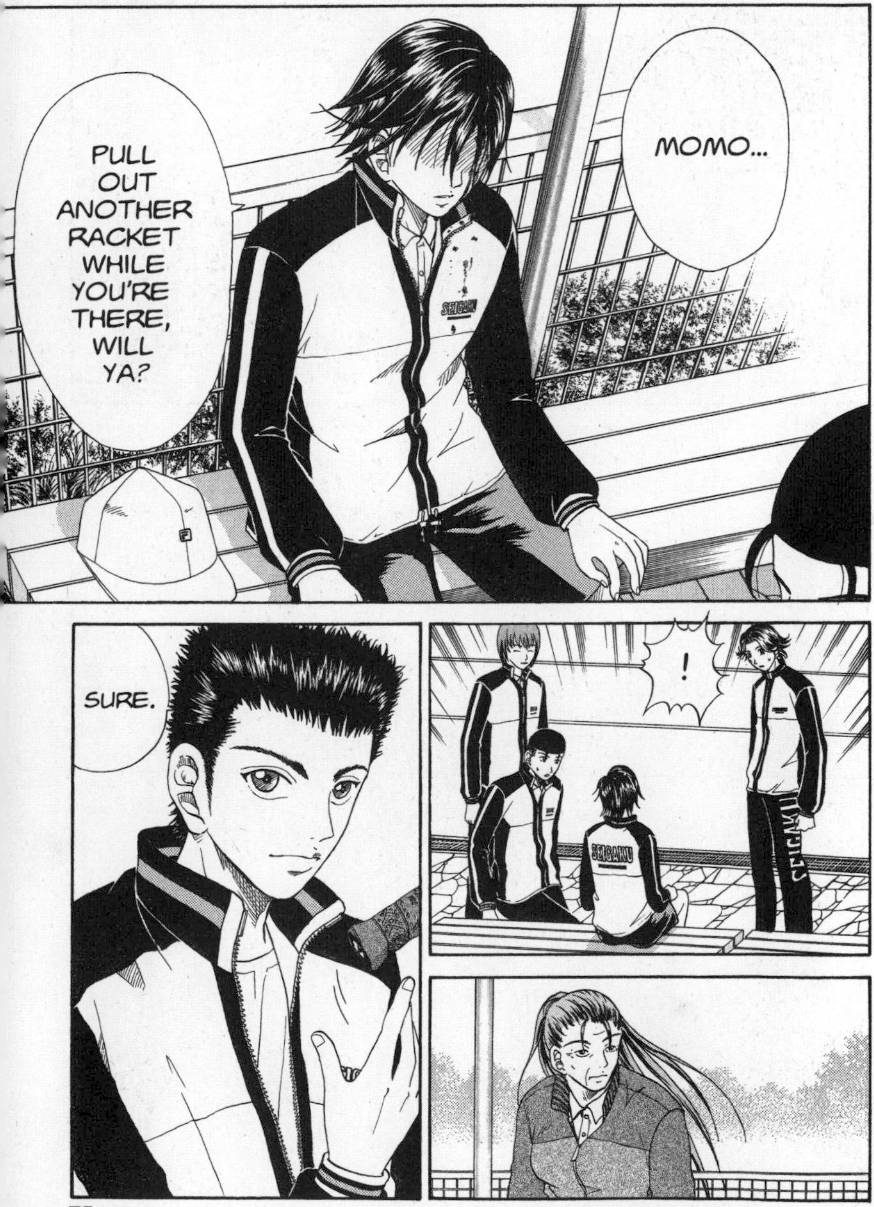
MOMO...
PULL OUT ANOTHER RACKET WHILE YOU'RE THERE, WILL YA?
!
SURE.

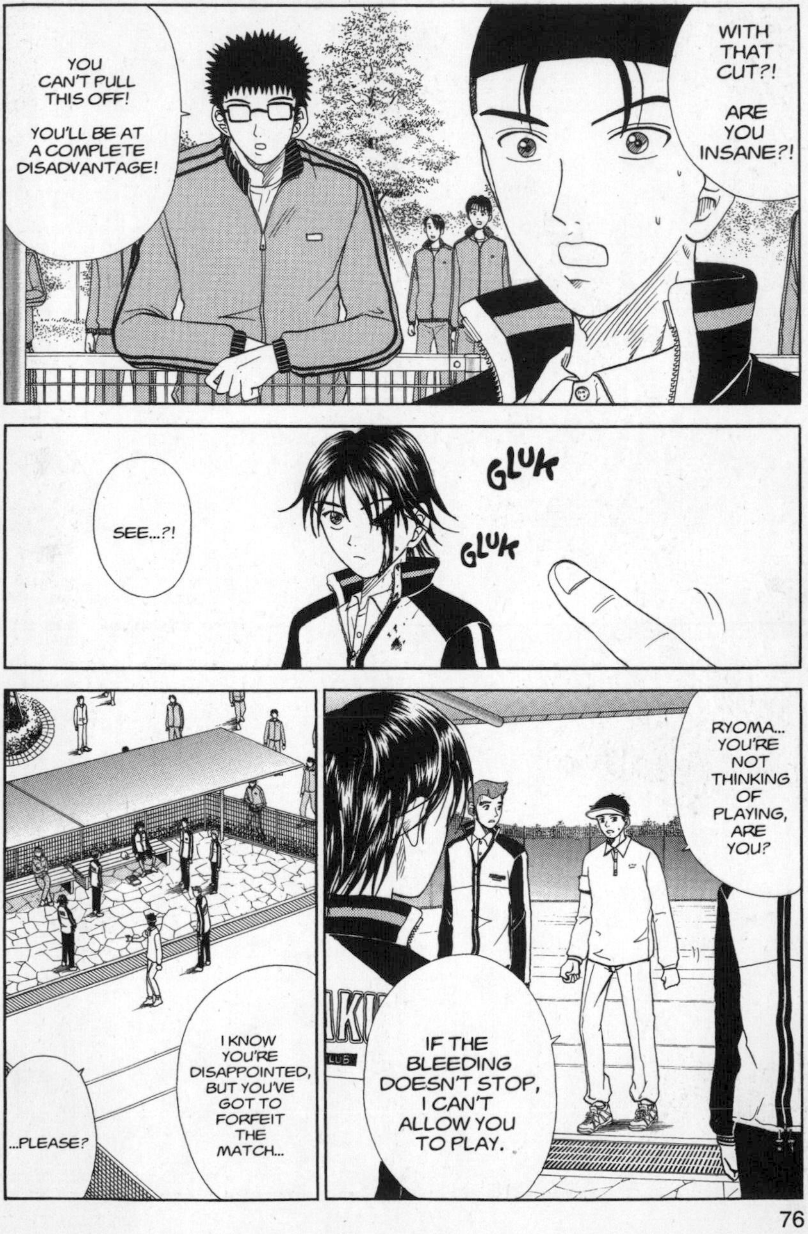
WITH THAT CUT?! ARE YOU INSANE?!
YOU CAN'T PULL THIS OFF! YOU'LL BE AT A COMPLETE DISADVANTAGE!
GLUK
GLUK
SEE...?!
RYOMA... YOU'RE NOT THINKING OF PLAYING, ARE YOU?
IF THE BLEEDING DOESN'T STOP, I CAN'T ALLOW YOU TO PLAY.
I KNOW YOU'RE DISAPPOINTED, BUT YOU'VE GOT TO FORFEIT THE MATCH...
...PLEASE?

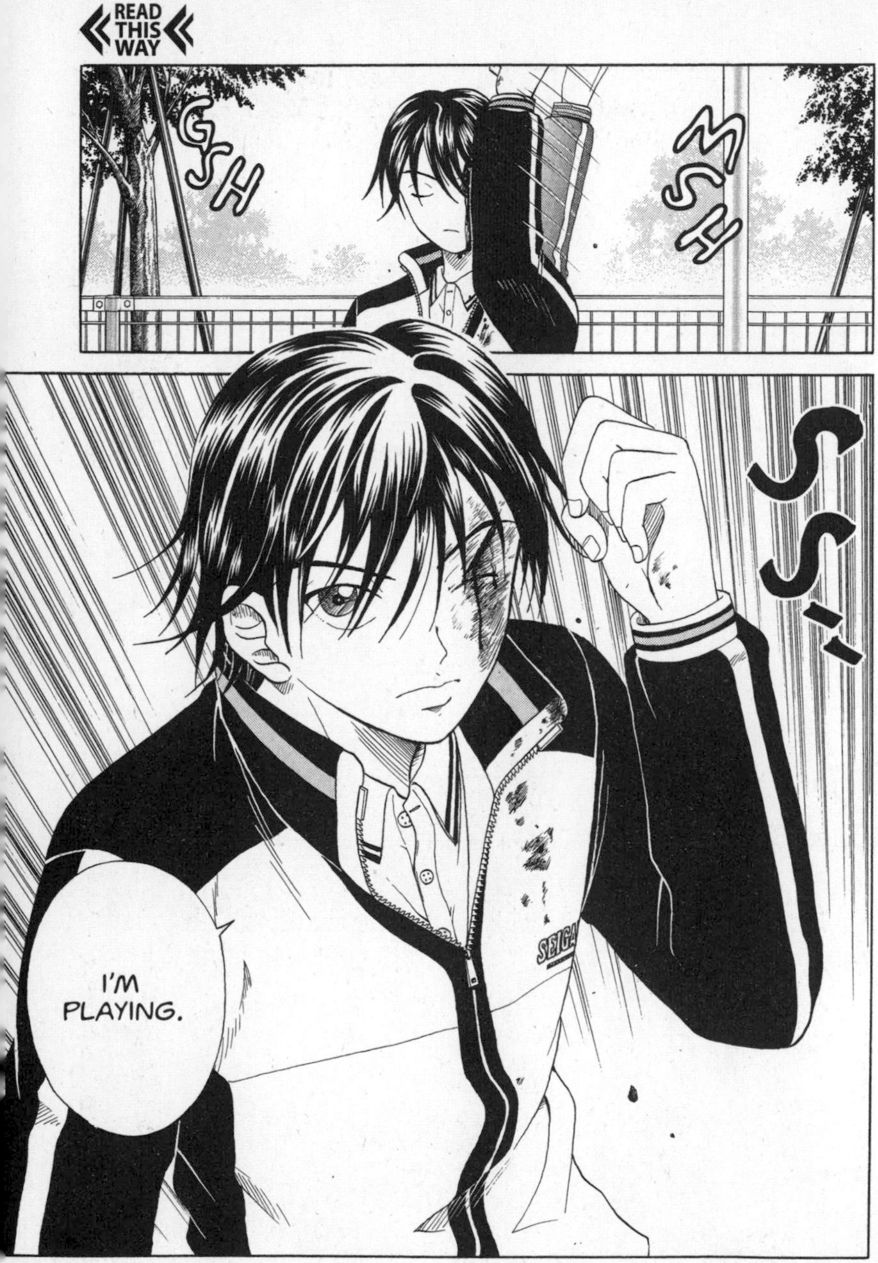
READ THIS WAY
MSH
GSH
SSS
I'M PLAYING.

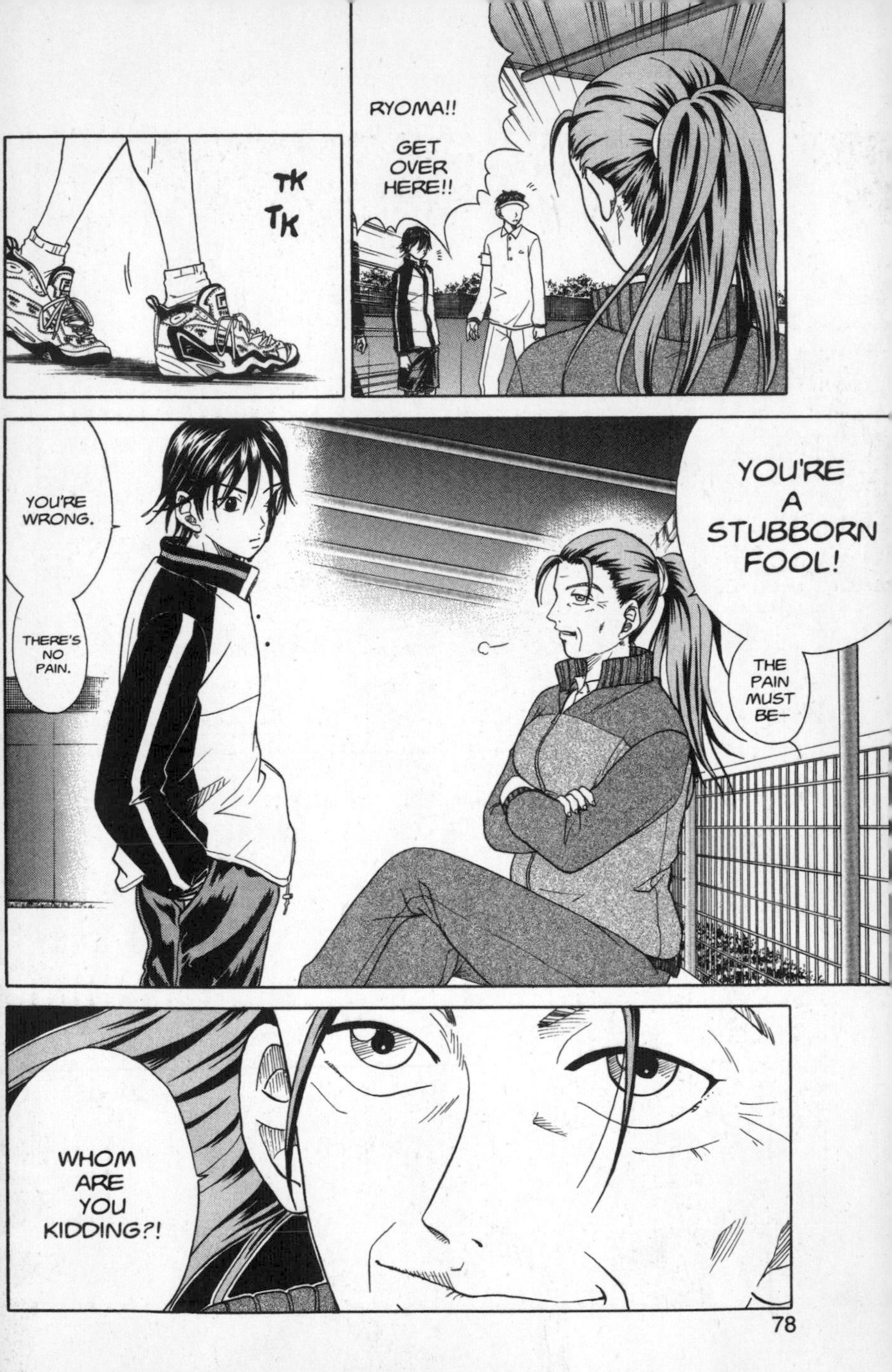
RYOMA!!
GET OVER HERE!!
TK TK
YOU'RE A STUBBORN FOOL!
THE PAIN MUST BE–
YOU'RE WRONG.
THERE'S NO PAIN.
WHOM ARE YOU KIDDING?!

READ THIS WAY

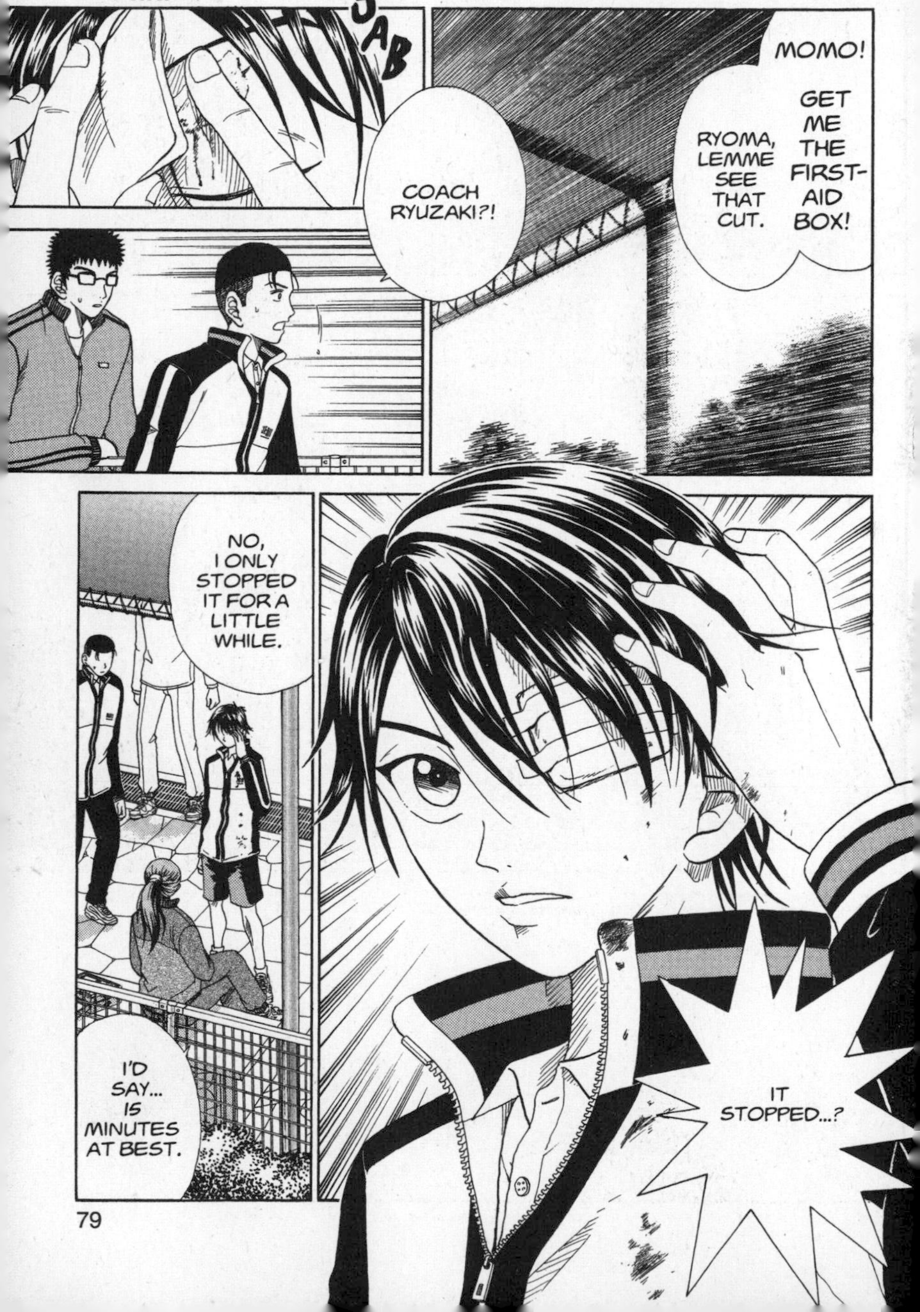

MOMO!
GET ME THE FIRST-AID BOX!
RYOMA, LEMME SEE THAT CUT.
JAB
COACH RYUZAKI?!
IT STOPPED...?
NO, I ONLY STOPPED IT FOR A LITTLE WHILE.
I'D SAY... 15 MINUTES AT BEST.

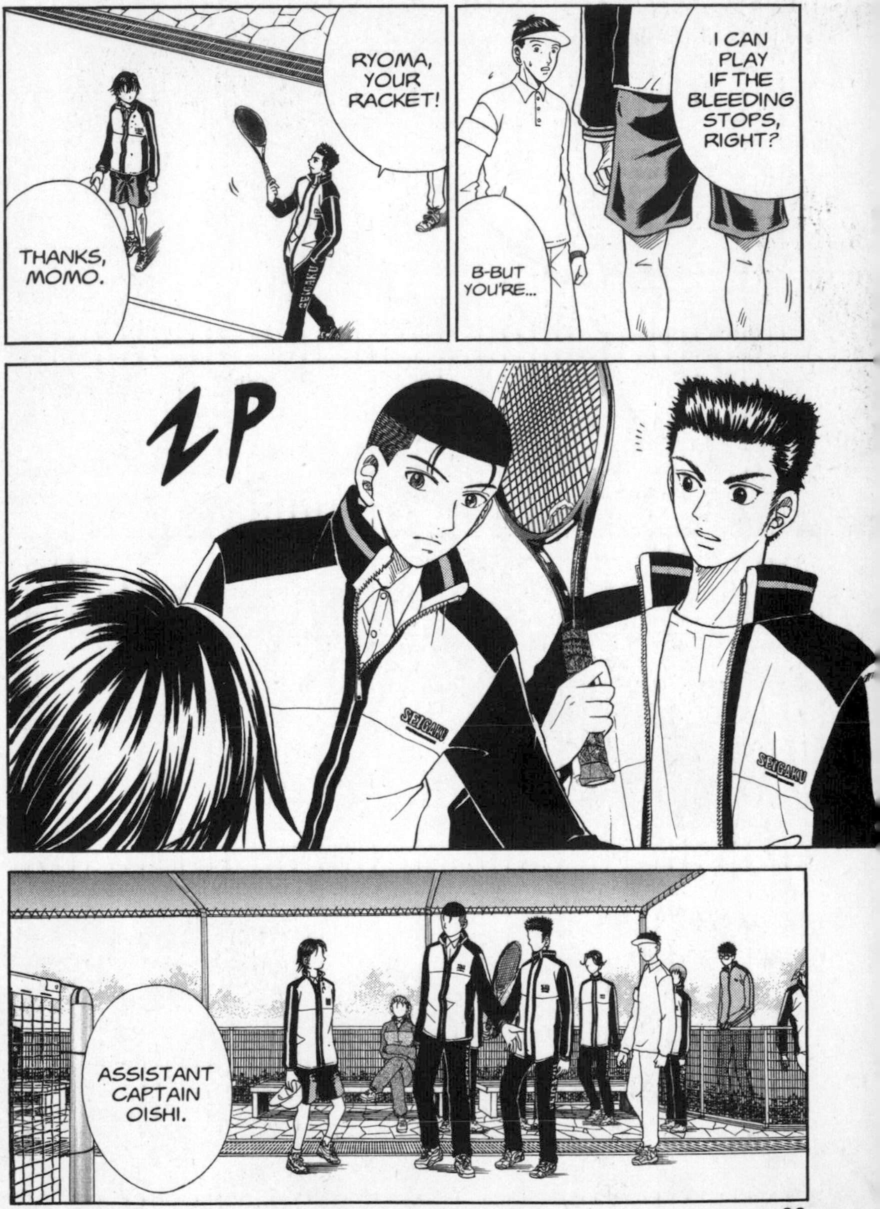
I CAN PLAY IF THE BLEEDING STOPS, RIGHT?
B-BUT YOU'RE...
RYOMA, YOUR RACKET!
THANKS, MOMO.
ZP
ASSISTANT CAPTAIN OISHI.

READ THIS WAY

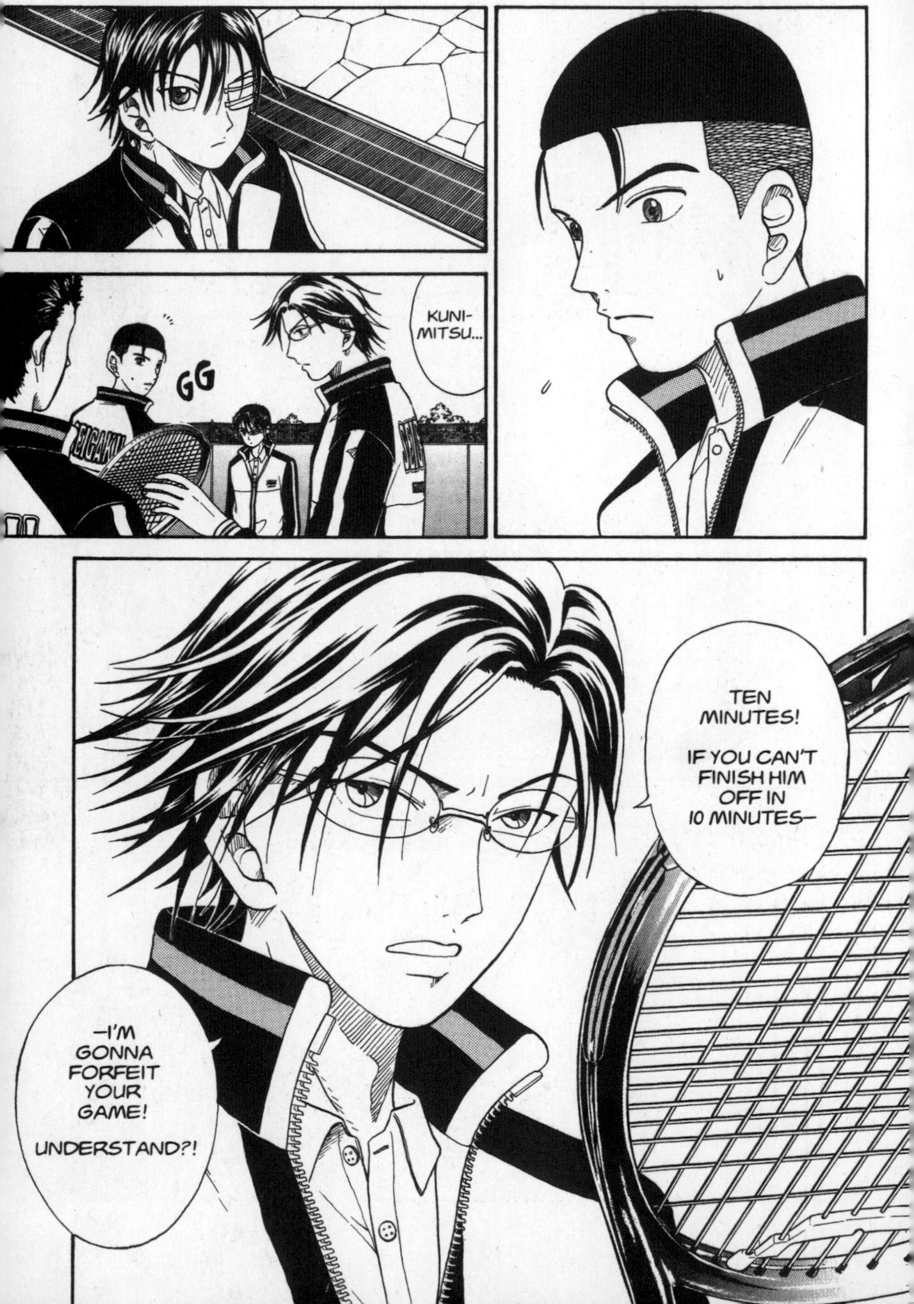
KUNI-MITSU...
GG
TEN MINUTES!
IF YOU CAN'T FINISH HIM OFF IN 10 MINUTES—
—I'M GONNA FORFEIT YOUR GAME!
UNDERSTAND?!

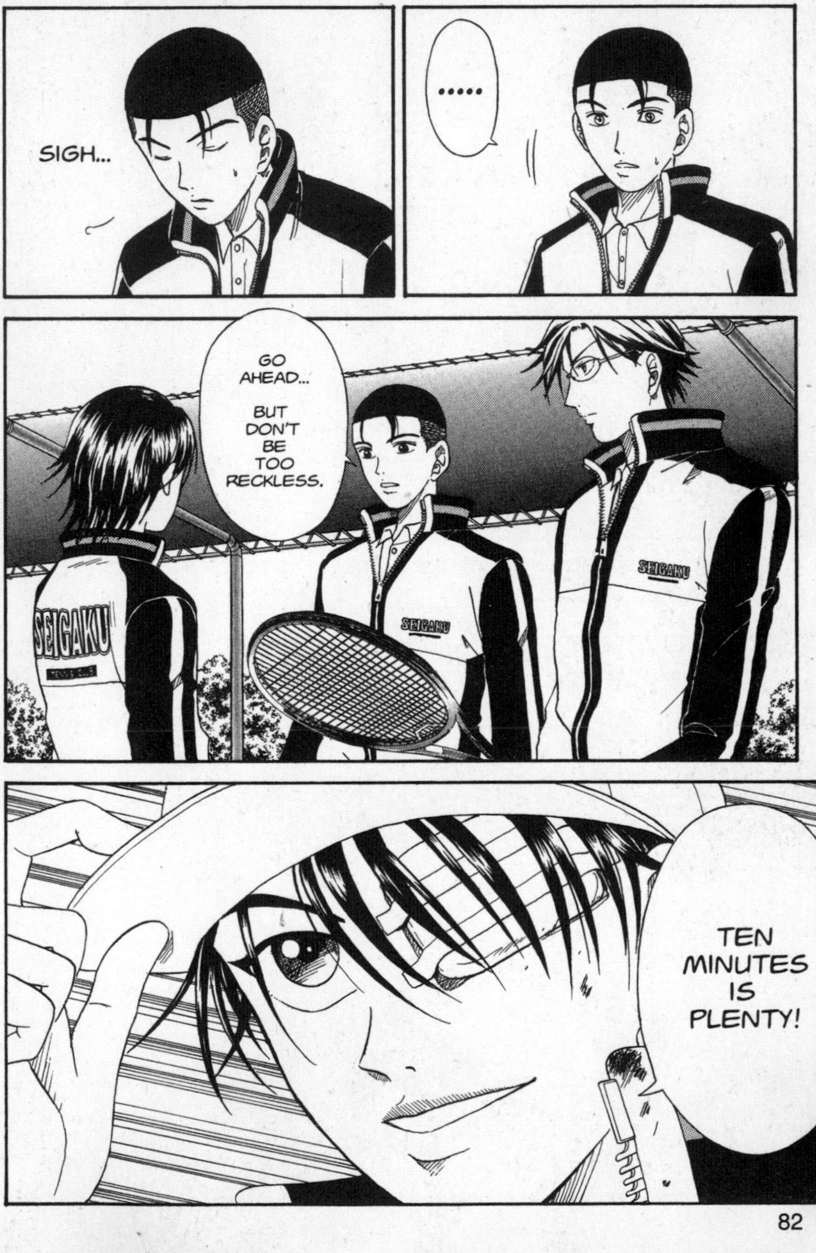
......
SIGH...
GO AHEAD... BUT DON'T BE TOO RECKLESS.
TEN MINUTES IS PLENTY!

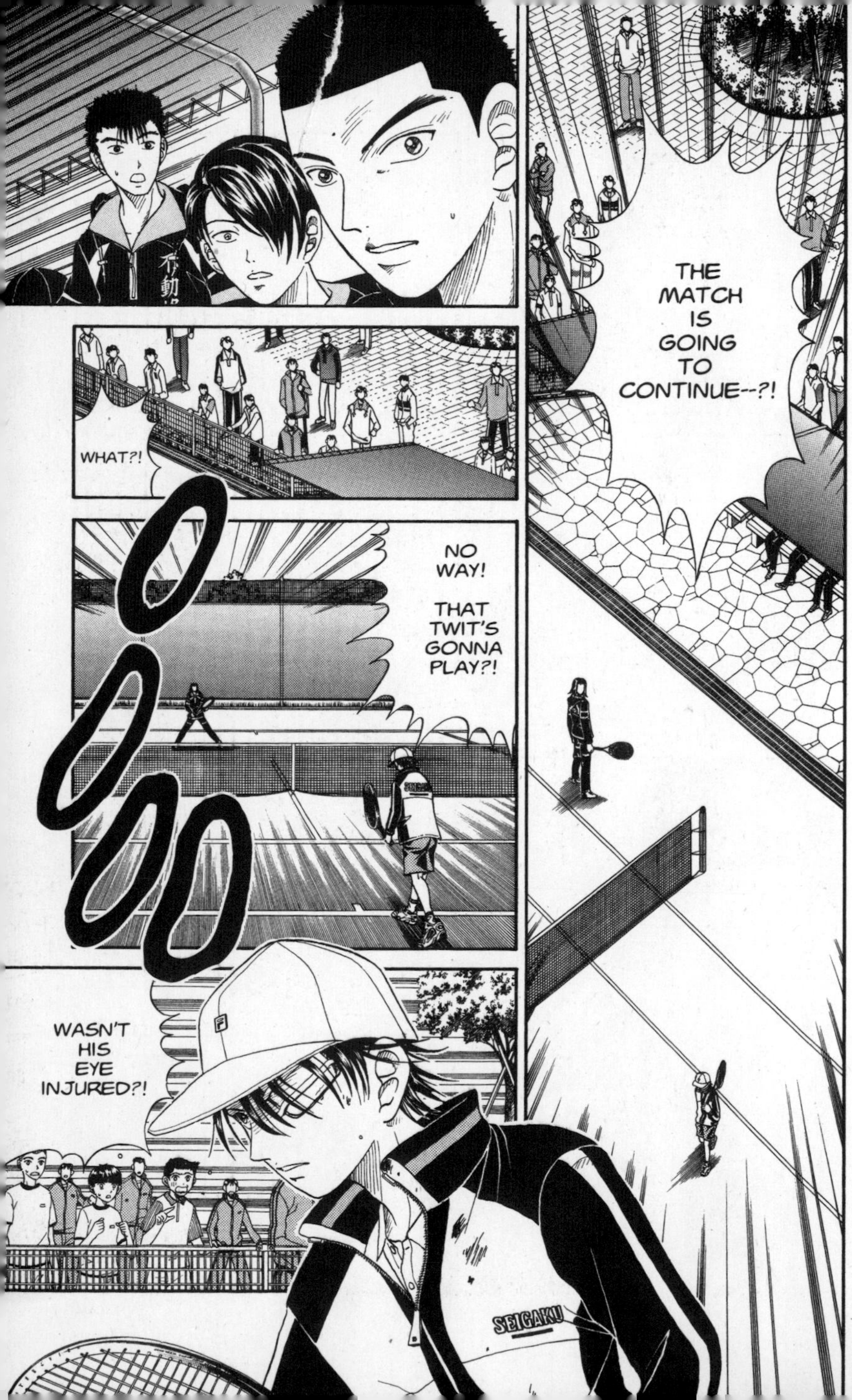
THE MATCH IS GOING TO CONTINUE--?!
WHAT?!
NO WAY!
THAT TWIT'S GONNA PLAY?!
WASN'T HIS EYE INJURED?!
SEIGAKU

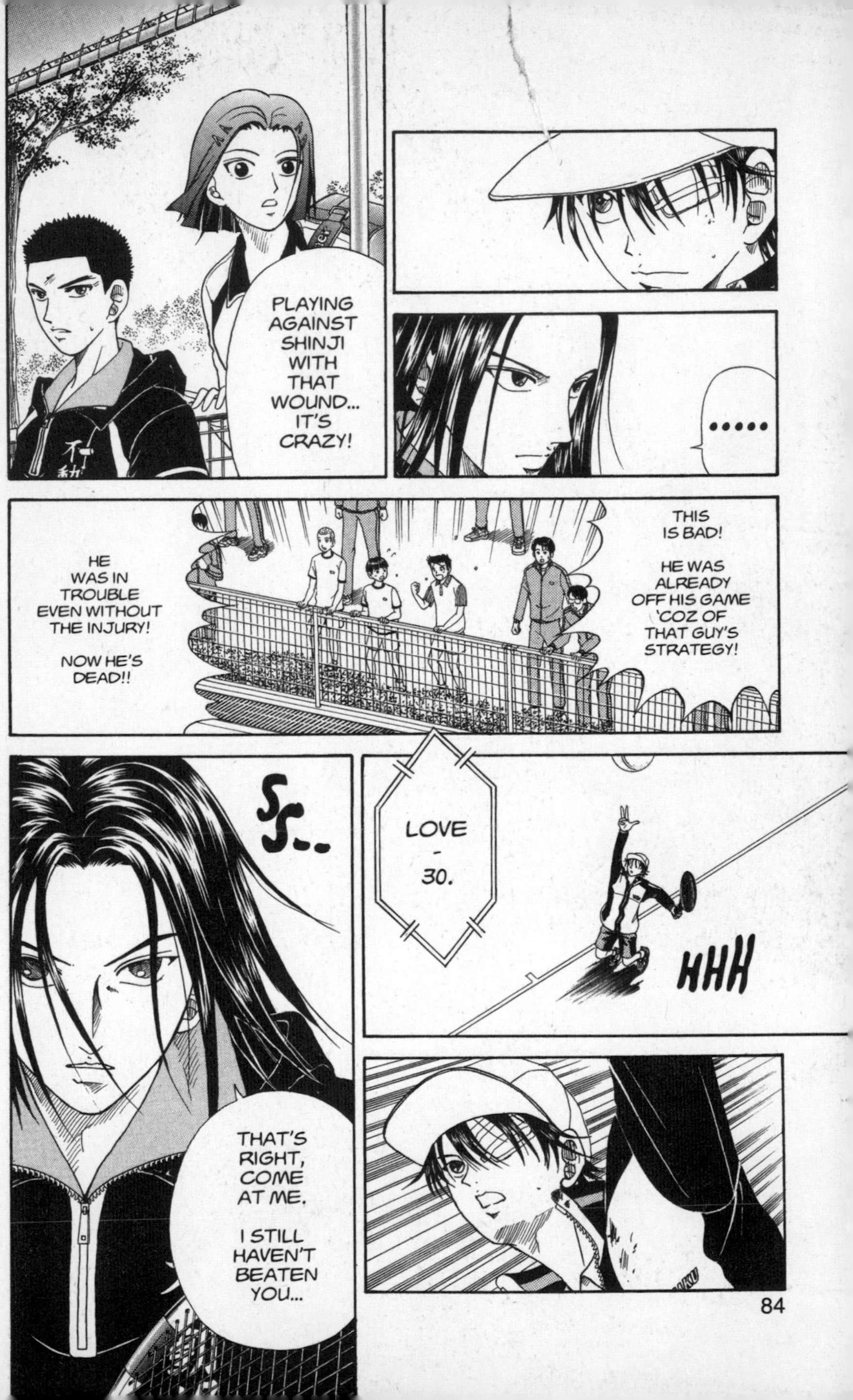
.....
PLAYING AGAINST SHINJI WITH THAT WOUND... IT'S CRAZY!
THIS IS BAD!
HE WAS ALREADY OFF HIS GAME 'COZ OF THAT GUY'S STRATEGY!
HE WAS IN TROUBLE EVEN WITHOUT THE INJURY!
NOW HE'S DEAD!!
LOVE - 30.
HHH
SS..
THAT'S RIGHT, COME AT ME.
I STILL HAVEN'T BEATEN YOU...

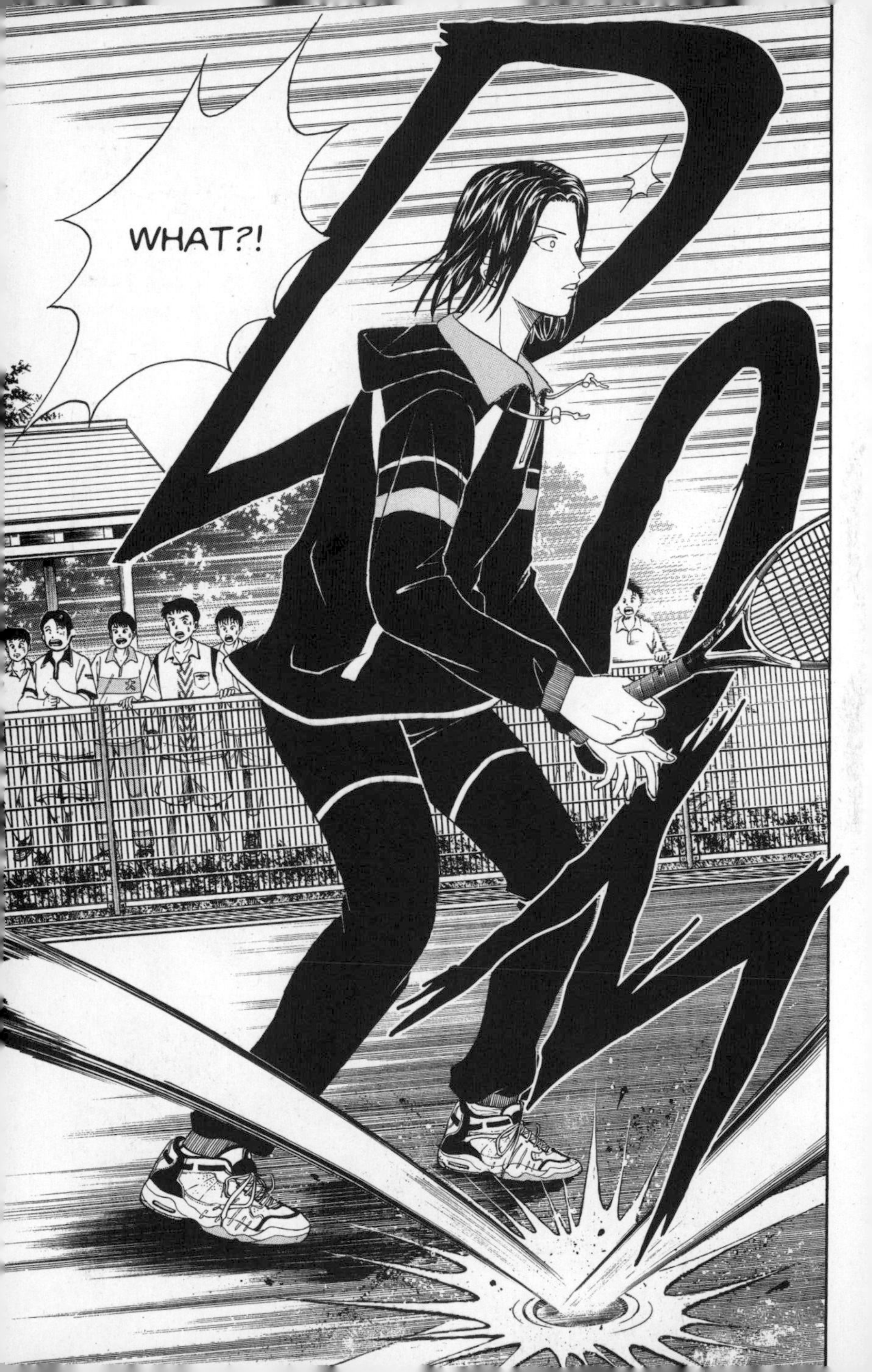
WHAT?!

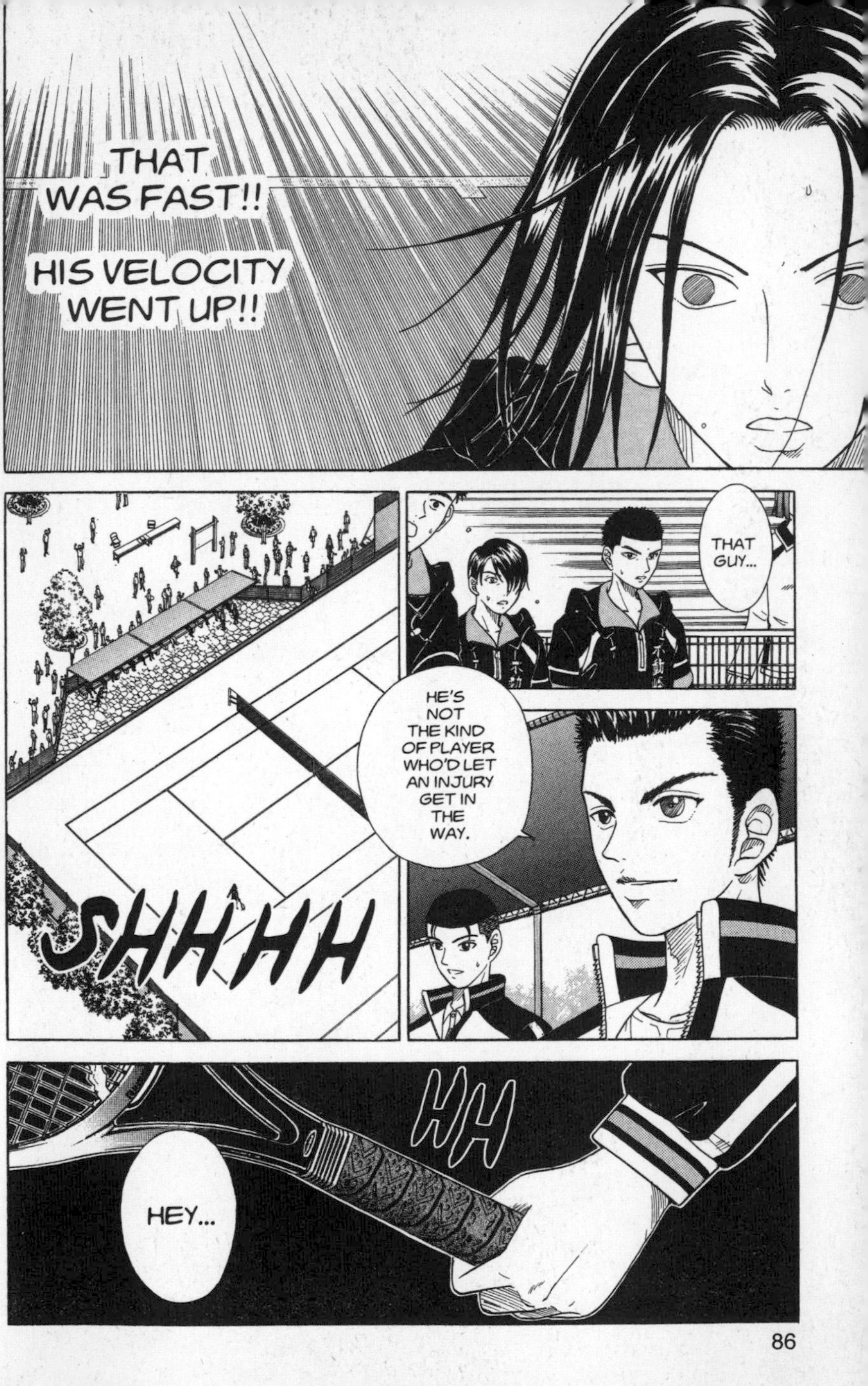
THAT WAS FAST!!
HIS VELOCITY WENT UP!!
THAT GUY...
HE'S NOT THE KIND OF PLAYER WHO'D LET AN INJURY GET IN THE WAY.
SHHHH
HH
HEY...

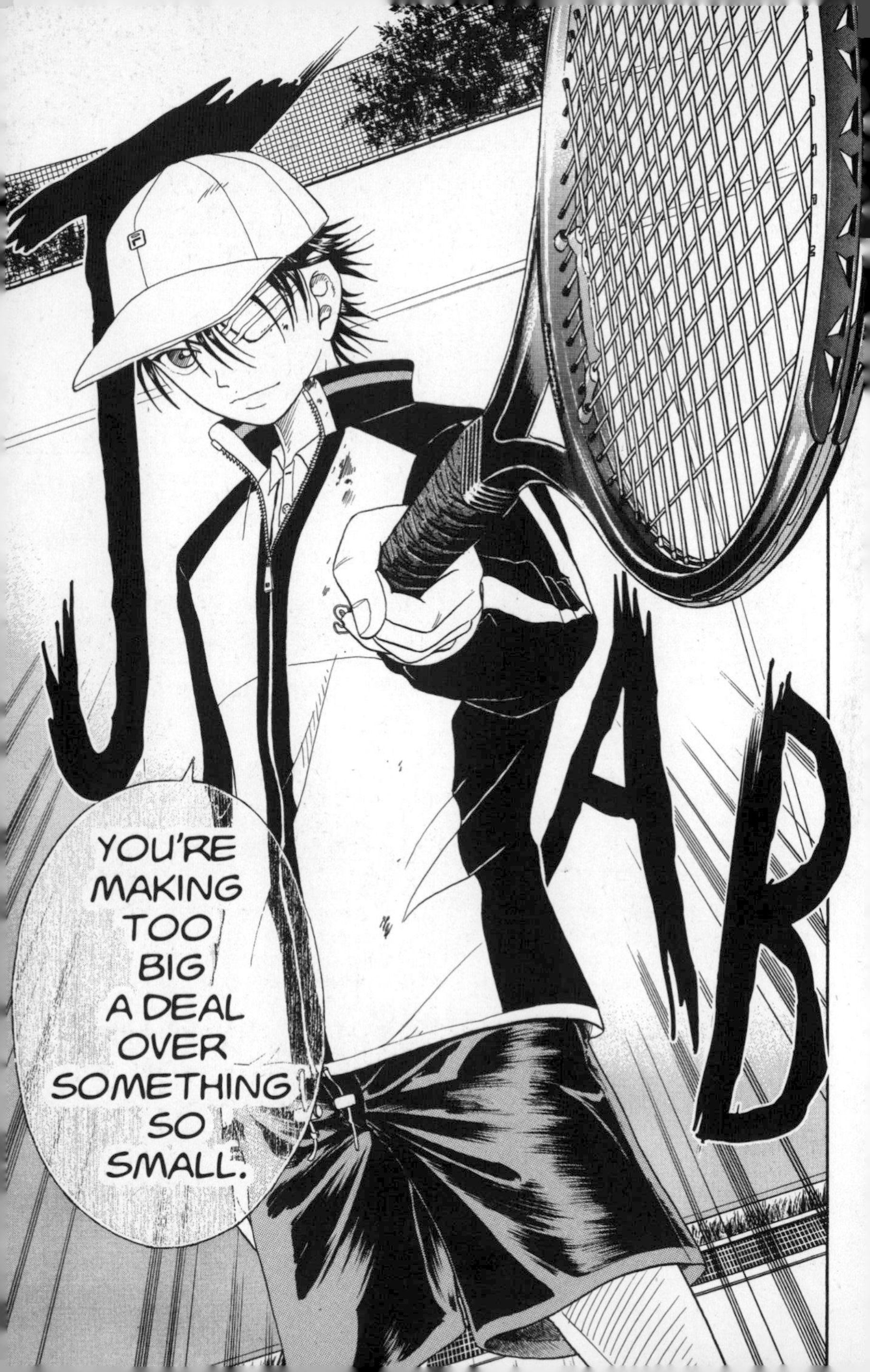
JAB
YOU'RE MAKING TOO BIG A DEAL OVER SOMETHING SO SMALL.

RYOMA'S CLASS (7TH GRADE CLASS 2) STUDENT LIST!!

WE GOT TONS AND TONS OF SUBMISSIONS OF NAMES FOR RYOMA'S CLASSMATES WHEN WE ASKED

FOR THEM IN WEEKLY SHONEN JUMP ISSUE 38!! THERE WERE NEW FACES, REGULARS, AND THOSE

WHO MISSED OUT ON THE PREVIOUS 9TH GRADE CLASS 6—AND I WAS WORRIED ABOUT THE SHORT

DEADLINE THIS ISSUE! THANKS FOR ALL YOUR SUBMISSIONS!! I LOOKED AT EACH AND EVERY ONE

OF THEM. I NOTICED THIS TIME THAT A LOT OF YOU HAVE STARTED PLAYING TENNIS. MANY OF YOU

SAID IT WAS FUN. I'M PLEASED THAT MY COMIC GAVE YOU A REASON TO START PLAYING. AND,

SAME AS ALWAYS, TO THOSE OF YOU WHO MISSED THE CUT—I'M REALLY SORRY! THIS "CLASSMATE

PROJECT" BRINGS ME JOY AND HEARTBREAK. I CAN'T CHOOSE!! I CAN'T NARROW IT DOWN!!

I TOLD MYSELF, "THIS IS THE FINAL CUT," BUT WENT THROUGH THE SUBMISSIONS AGAIN AND AGAIN.

BELOW ARE THE PEOPLE WHO MADE IT THROUGH THE SELECTION PROCESS—WHICH WAS EVEN TOUGHER

THAN THE PREVIOUS TIME. ONCE AGAIN, THANKS TO ALL OF YOU WHO SENT IN SUBMISSIONS!!

7TH GRADE CLASS 2 ATTENDANCE NUMBER

(BOYS)	(GIRLS)
1 KAZUTERU ISHIDO	1 HITOMI ABE
2 KOTARO ICHINO	2 AKANE ITO
3 RYOMA ECHIZEN	3 SATOE OKA
4 MAKOTO OHBA	4 MEGUMI KOHNO
5 DAINEN MOMISHIMA	5 NATSUKA SAGAMIHARA
6 AKIHIRO KOBAYASHI	6 RIE SHIRAI
7 YASUTETSU KONDO	7 MATSURI SUZUKI
8 YUKI KONDO	8 MARIKO SUZUKI
9 AKIMITSU KONDO	9 SHIHO TAKAO
10 KEISUKE SHISHIDO	10 MIKI NAKAHACHI
11 SUGURU DAIDA	11 YUKI NAKAYA
12 SHOKO ARATE	12 NORIKO NAKAYAMA
13 YUMA TANAKA	13 SHOKO HATTORI
14 NAOKI HASUNUMA	14 TOMO HIRANO
15 HIROKI HAMAZAKI	15 AYAKA HUKUMI
16 SATOSHI HORIO	16 SACHIKO YOSHIKAWA
17 HIROKI MATSUSHIMA	17 AYUE YOSHIDA
18 KEISUKE MIYATA	18 MAI YOSHINO
19 KENTA YAZAWA	
20 TAKU YOSHIMURA	

TOTAL: 38 (TITLES OMITTED FROM NAMES)

Genius 39: Ten-Minute Limit

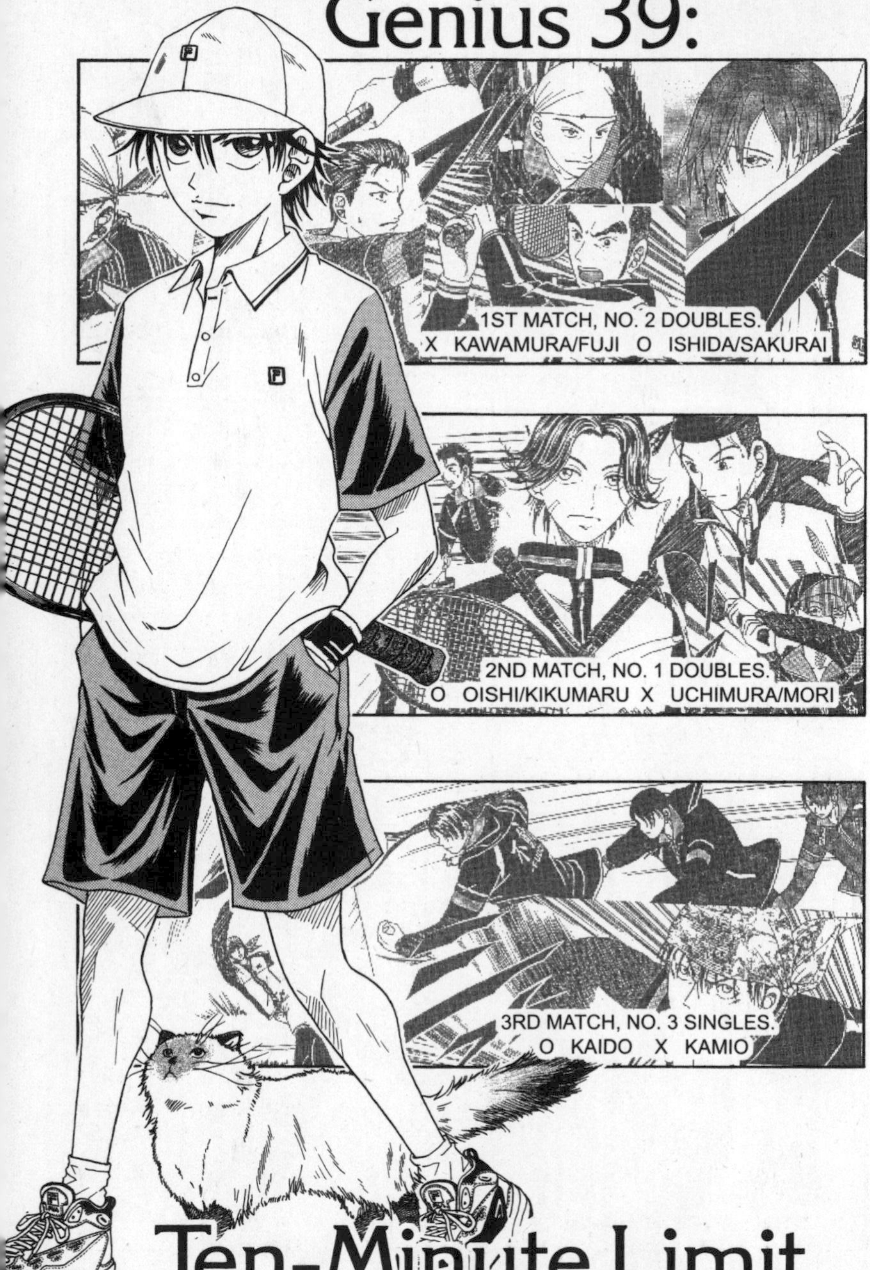
1ST MATCH, NO. 2 DOUBLES.
X KAWAMURA/FUJI O ISHIDA/SAKURAI
2ND MATCH, NO. 1 DOUBLES.
O OISHI/KIKUMARU X UCHIMURA/MORI
3RD MATCH, NO. 3 SINGLES.
O KAIDO X KAMIO

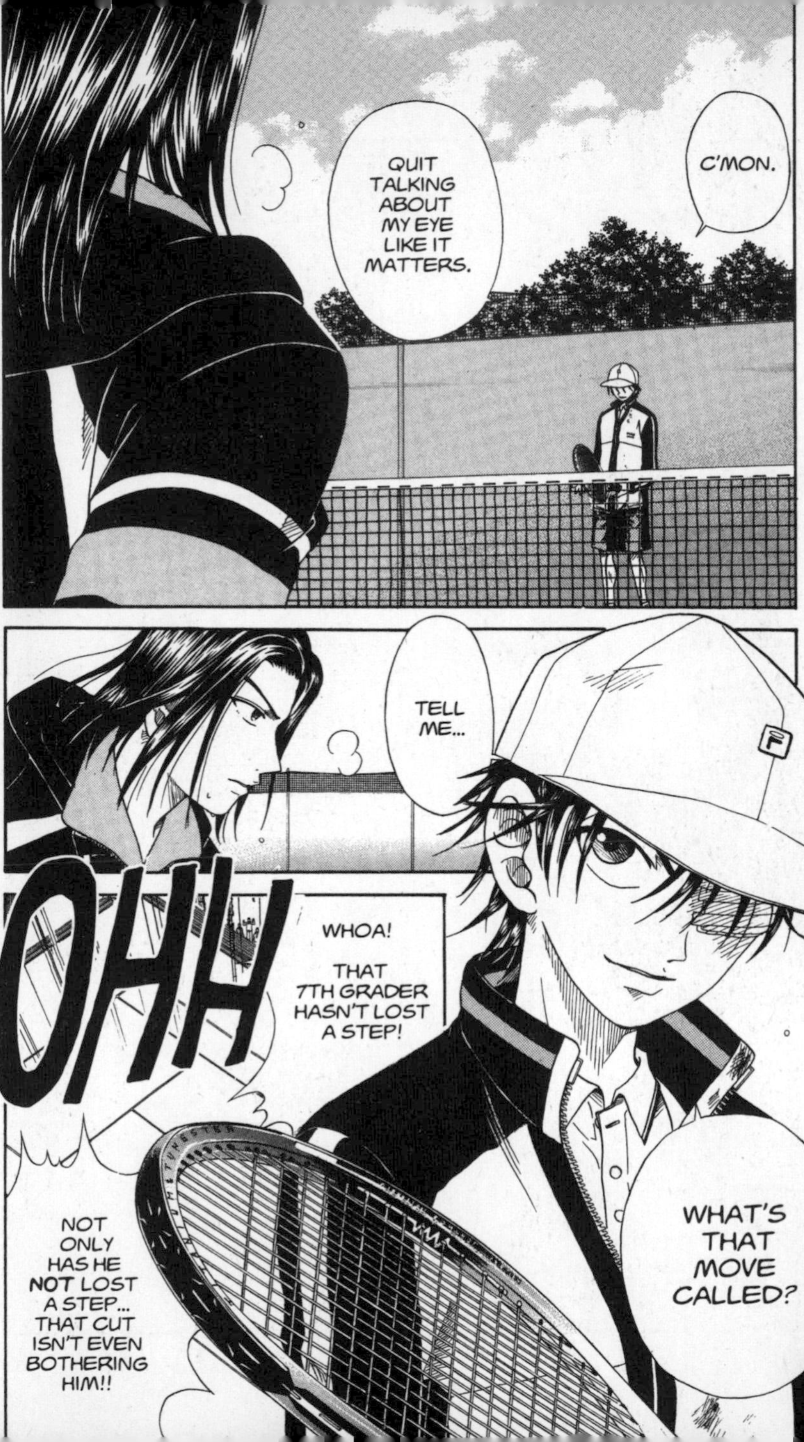
C'MON.
QUIT TALKING ABOUT MY EYE LIKE IT MATTERS.
TELL ME...
WHAT'S THAT MOVE CALLED?
OHH
WHOA!
THAT 7TH GRADER HASN'T LOST A STEP!
NOT ONLY HAS HE **NOT** LOST A STEP... THAT CUT ISN'T EVEN BOTHERING HIM!!

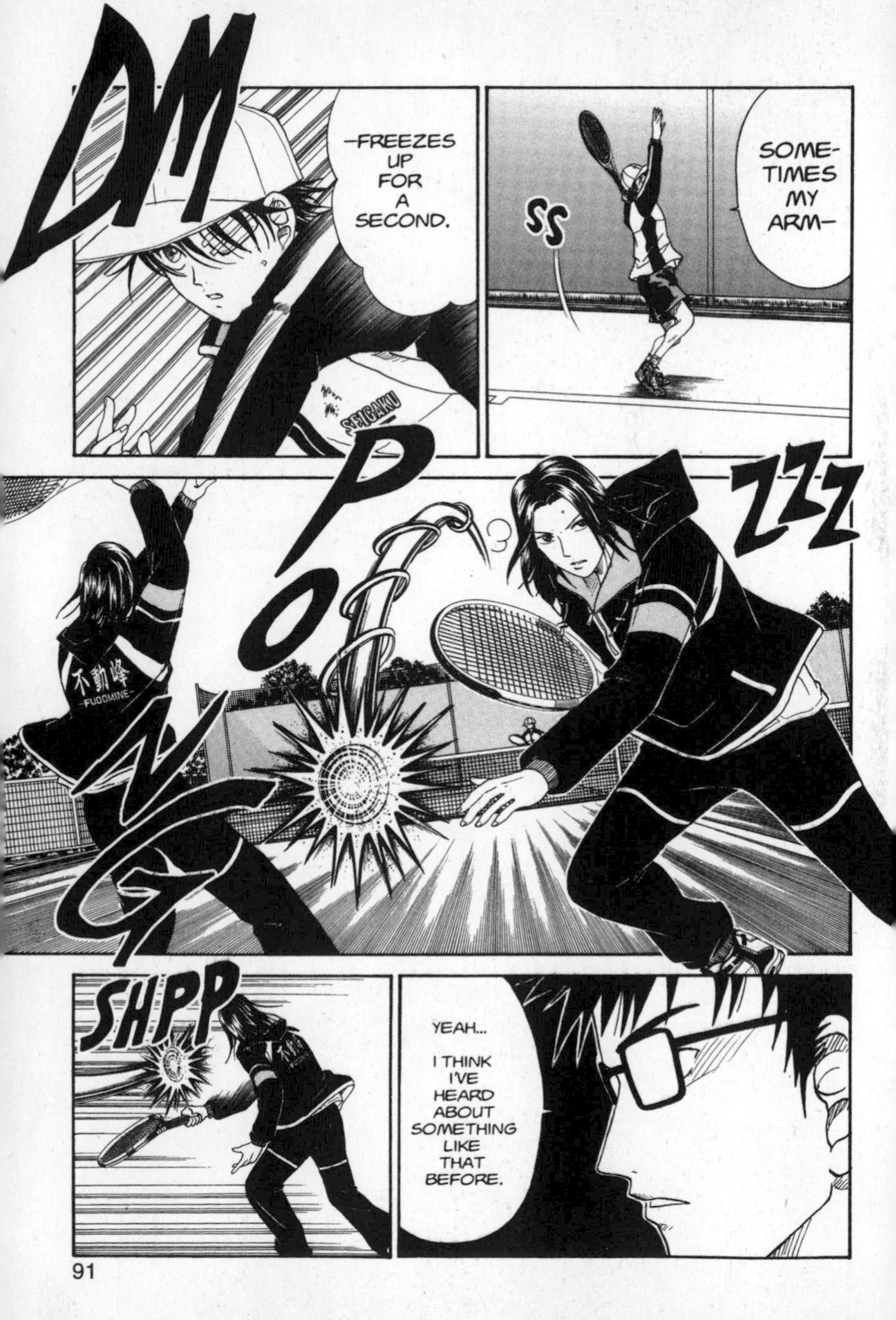
SOME-TIMES MY ARM—
SS
—FREEZES UP FOR A SECOND.
DM
SEIGAKU
ZZZ
PONG
不動峰 -FUDOMINE-
YEAH... I THINK I'VE HEARD ABOUT SOMETHING LIKE THAT BEFORE.
SHPP

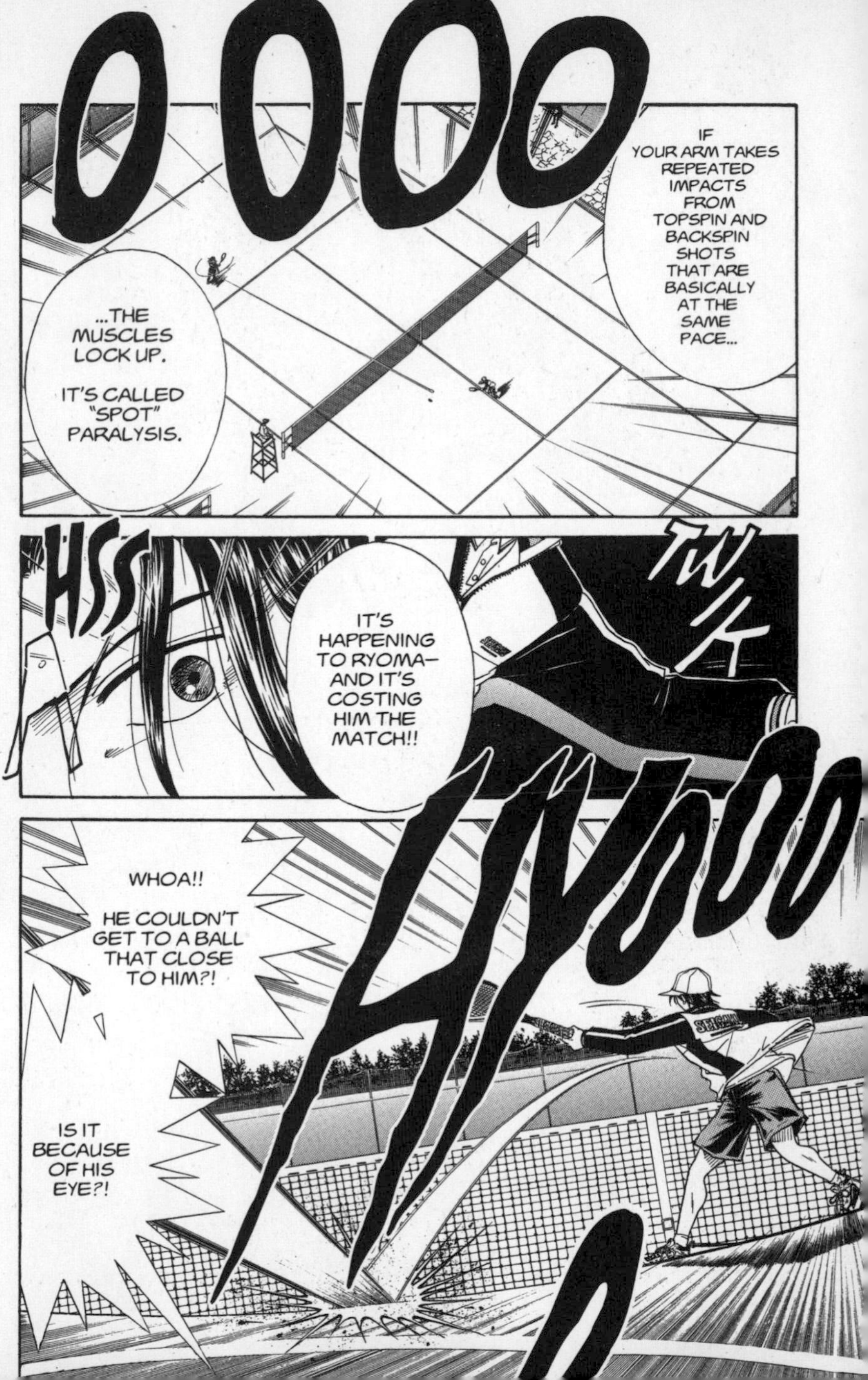
OOOO
IF YOUR ARM TAKES REPEATED IMPACTS FROM TOPSPIN AND BACKSPIN SHOTS THAT ARE BASICALLY AT THE SAME PACE...
...THE MUSCLES LOCK UP.
IT'S CALLED "SPOT" PARALYSIS.
TWIK
IT'S HAPPENING TO RYOMA— AND IT'S COSTING HIM THE MATCH!!
HSS
HYOOO
WHOA!!
HE COULDN'T GET TO A BALL THAT CLOSE TO HIM?!
IS IT BECAUSE OF HIS EYE?!

READ THIS WAY

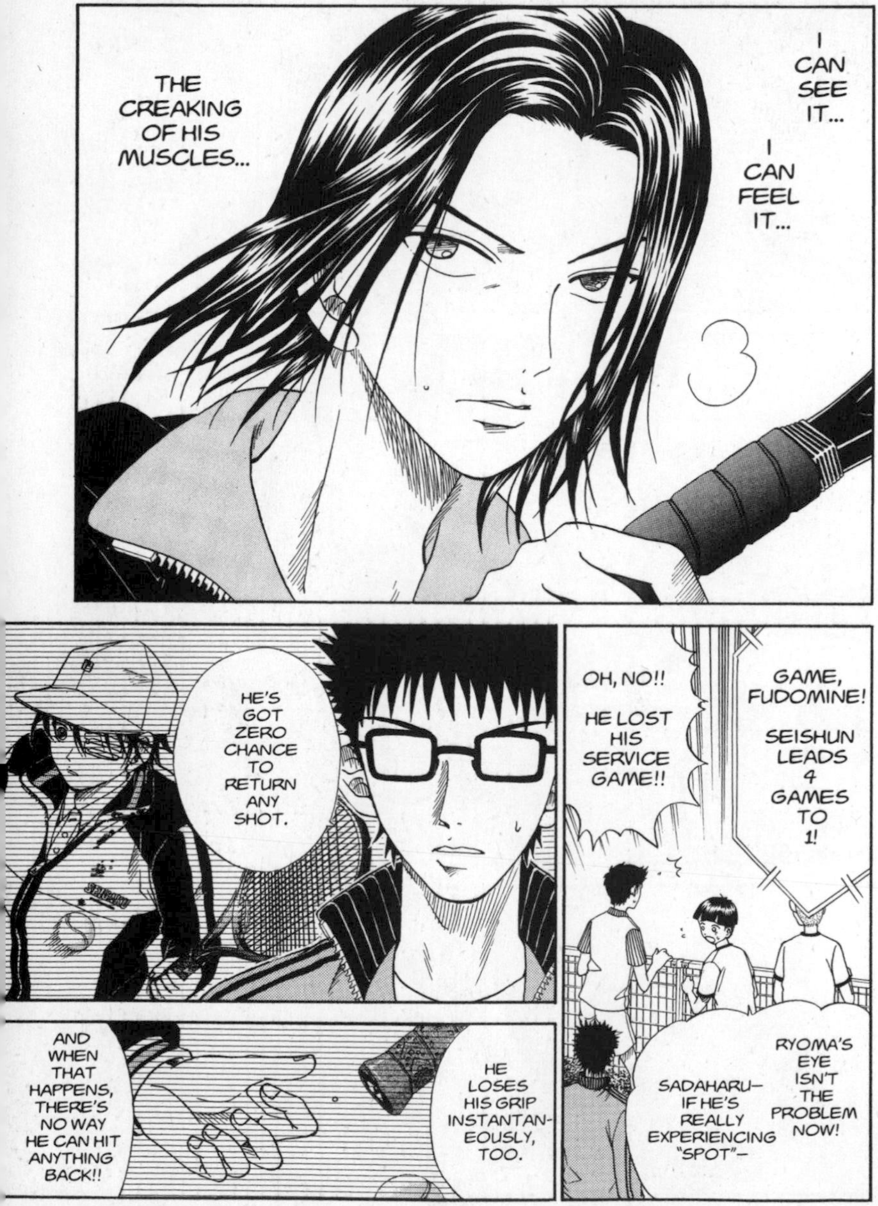

I CAN SEE IT...
I CAN FEEL IT...
THE CREAKING OF HIS MUSCLES...
GAME, FUDOMINE!
SEISHUN LEADS 4 GAMES TO 1!
OH, NO!!
HE LOST HIS SERVICE GAME!!
HE'S GOT ZERO CHANCE TO RETURN ANY SHOT.
RYOMA'S EYE ISN'T THE PROBLEM NOW!
SADAHARU— IF HE'S REALLY EXPERIENCING "SPOT"—
HE LOSES HIS GRIP INSTANTANEOUSLY, TOO.
AND WHEN THAT HAPPENS, THERE'S NO WAY HE CAN HIT ANYTHING BACK!!

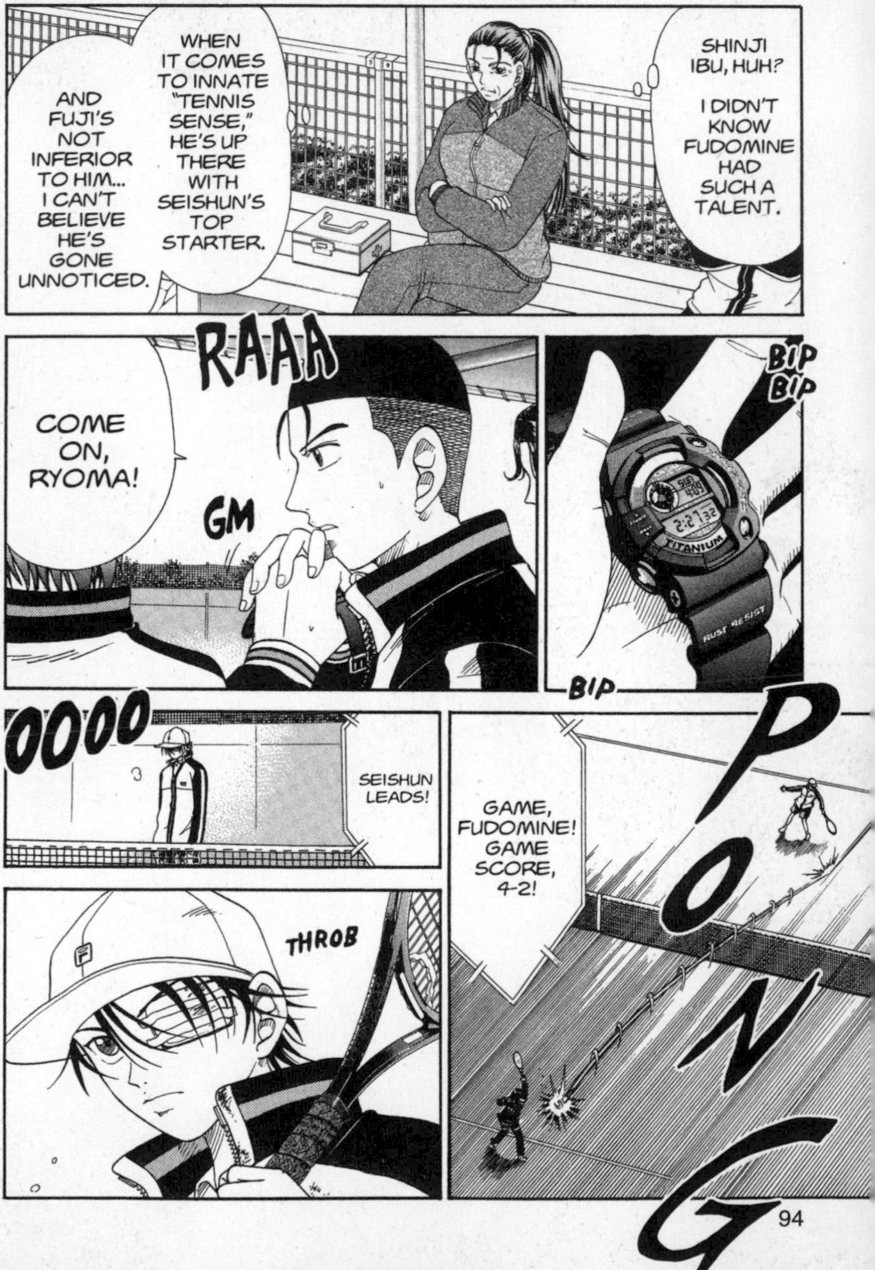
SHINJI IBU, HUH? I DIDN'T KNOW FUDOMINE HAD SUCH A TALENT.
WHEN IT COMES TO INNATE "TENNIS SENSE," HE'S UP THERE WITH SEISHUN'S TOP STARTER.
AND FUJI'S NOT INFERIOR TO HIM... I CAN'T BELIEVE HE'S GONE UNNOTICED.
BIP BIP
TITANIUM
RUST RESIST
BIP
RAAA
COME ON, RYOMA!
GM
PONG
GAME, FUDOMINE! GAME SCORE, 4-2!
OOOO
SEISHUN LEADS!
THROB

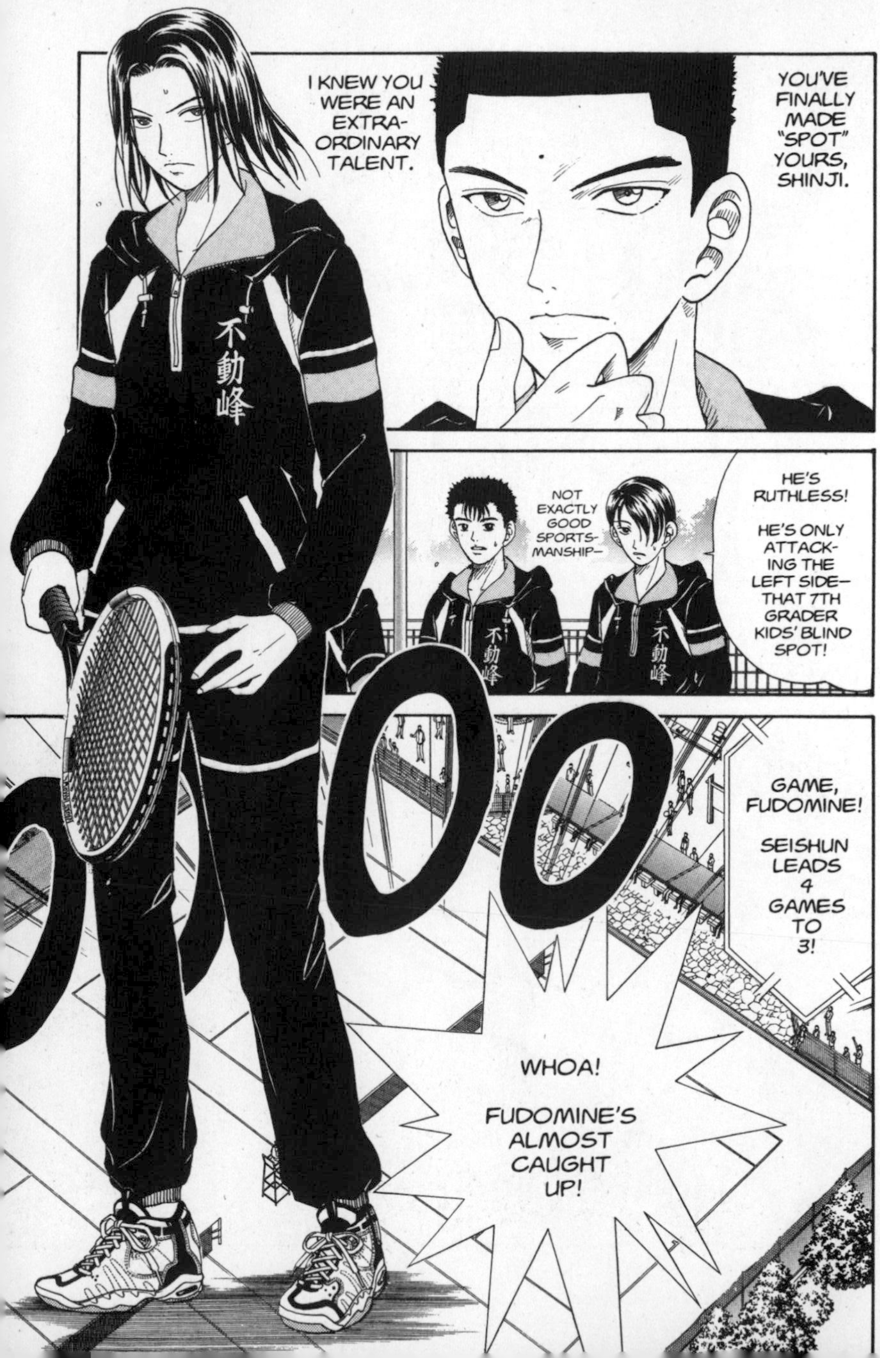
YOU'VE FINALLY MADE "SPOT" YOURS, SHINJI.
I KNEW YOU WERE AN EXTRA-ORDINARY TALENT.
HE'S RUTHLESS!
HE'S ONLY ATTACK-ING THE LEFT SIDE—THAT 7TH GRADER KIDS' BLIND SPOT!
NOT EXACTLY GOOD SPORTS-MANSHIP—
GAME, FUDOMINE!
SEISHUN LEADS 4 GAMES TO 3!
WHOA!
FUDOMINE'S ALMOST CAUGHT UP!

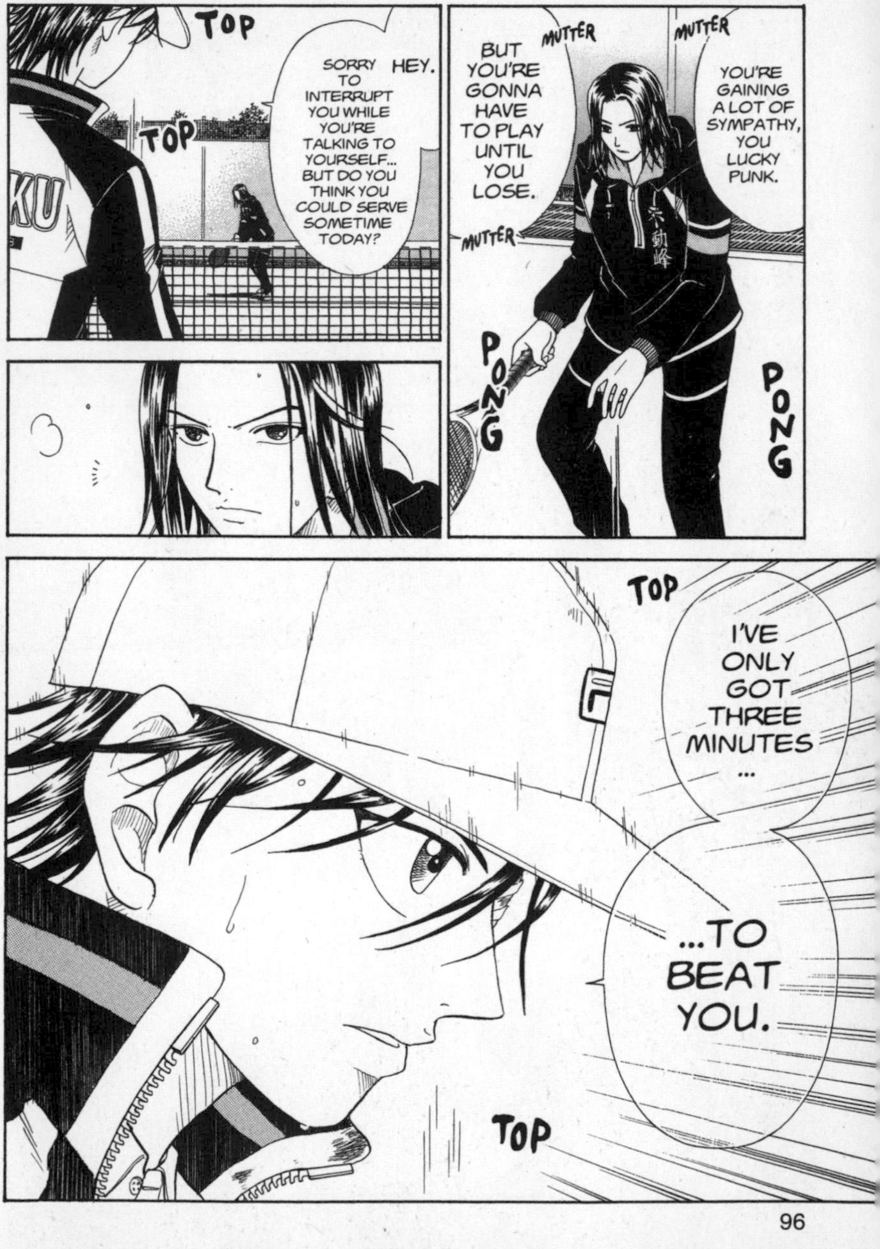
MUTTER
YOU'RE GAINING A LOT OF SYMPATHY, YOU LUCKY PUNK.
MUTTER
BUT YOU'RE GONNA HAVE TO PLAY UNTIL YOU LOSE.
MUTTER
PONG
PONG
TOP
HEY.
SORRY TO INTERRUPT YOU WHILE YOU'RE TALKING TO YOURSELF... BUT DO YOU THINK YOU COULD SERVE SOMETIME TODAY?
TOP
TOP
I'VE ONLY GOT THREE MINUTES ...
...TO BEAT YOU.
TOP

READ THIS WAY

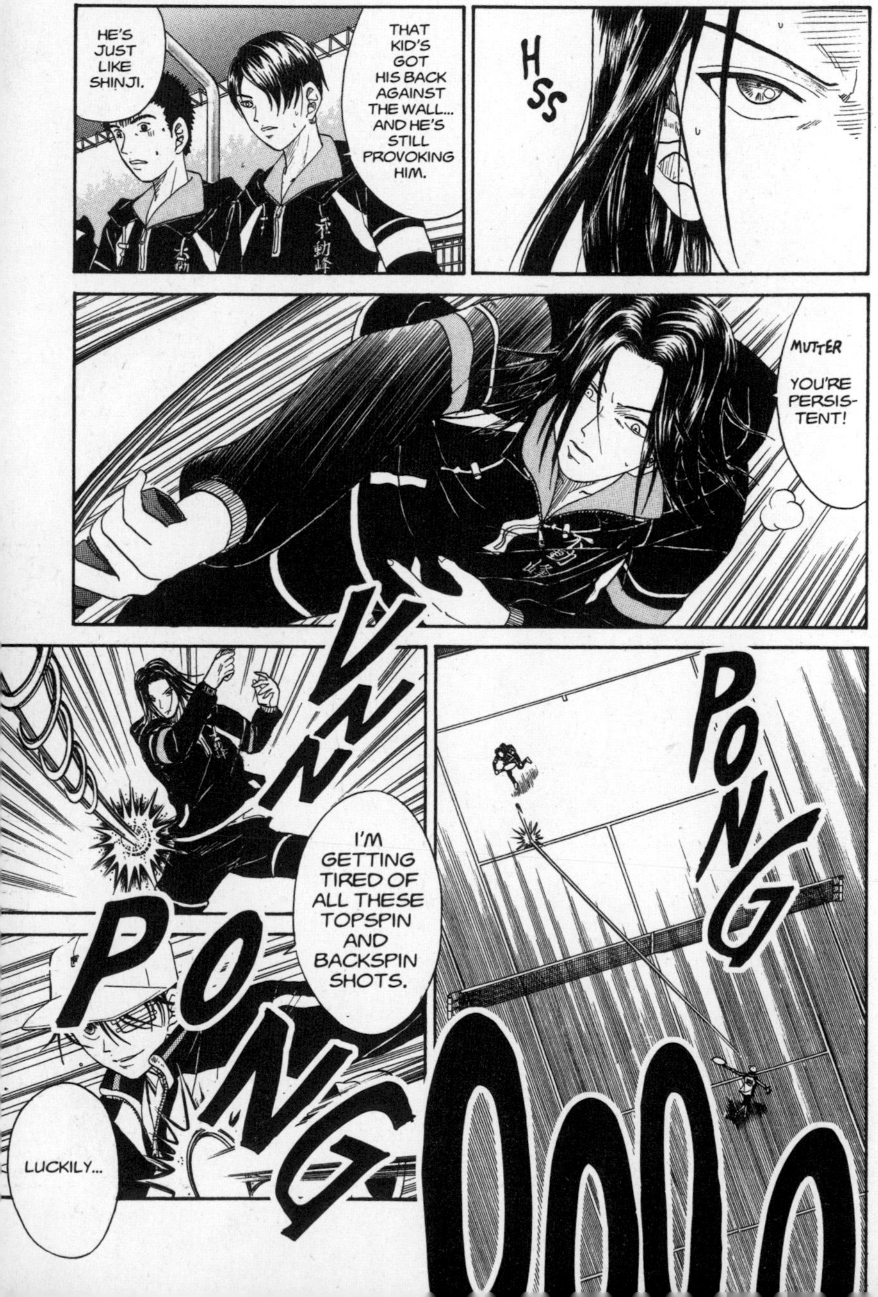
HSS
THAT KID'S GOT HIS BACK AGAINST THE WALL... AND HE'S STILL PROVOKING HIM.
HE'S JUST LIKE SHINJI.
MUTTER
YOU'RE PERSIS-TENT!
PONG
VNN
I'M GETTING TIRED OF ALL THESE TOPSPIN AND BACKSPIN SHOTS.
PONG
OOOO
LUCKILY...

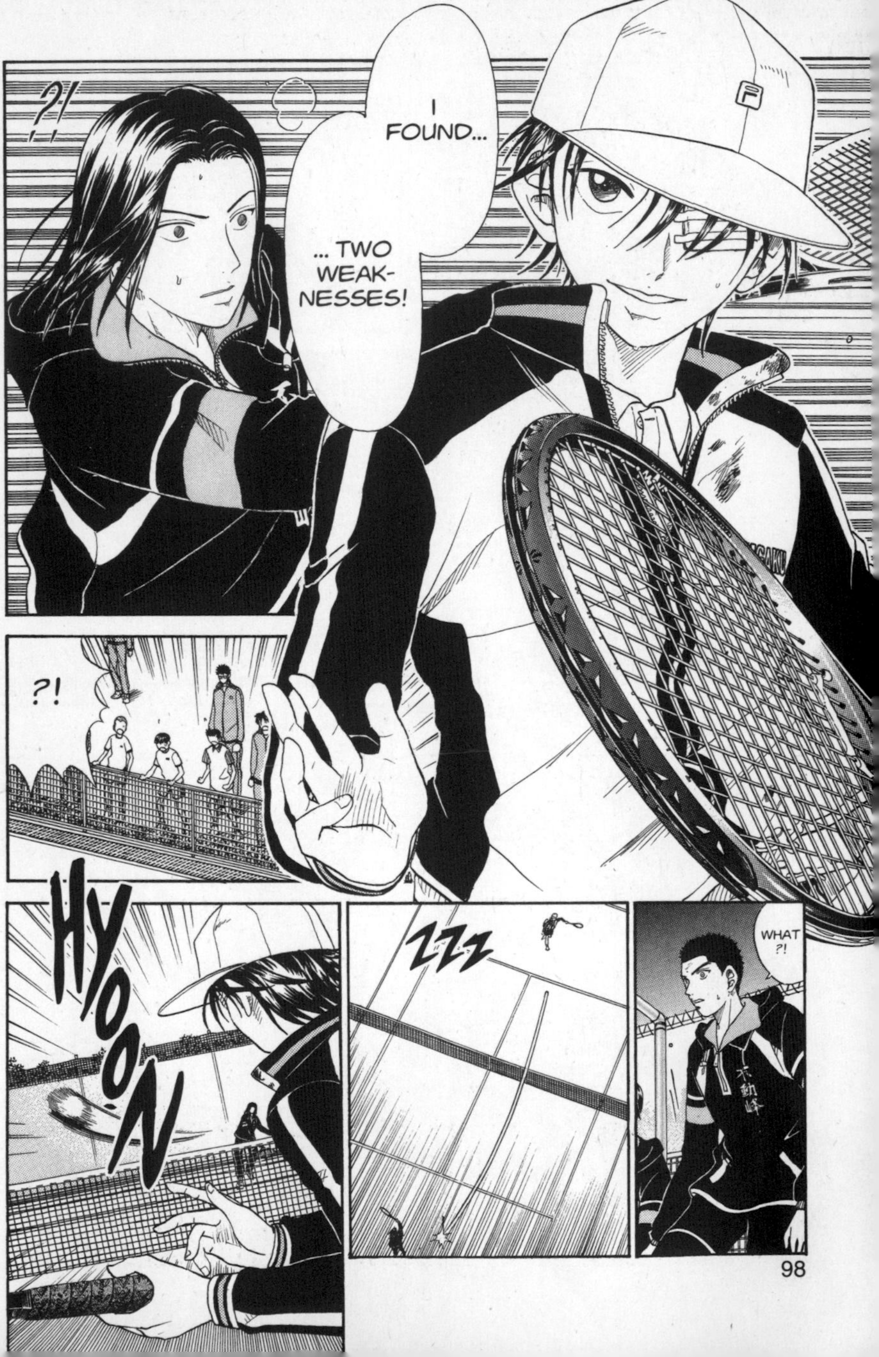
I FOUND...
... TWO WEAK-NESSES!
?!
?!
WHAT ?!
ZZZ
HYOON

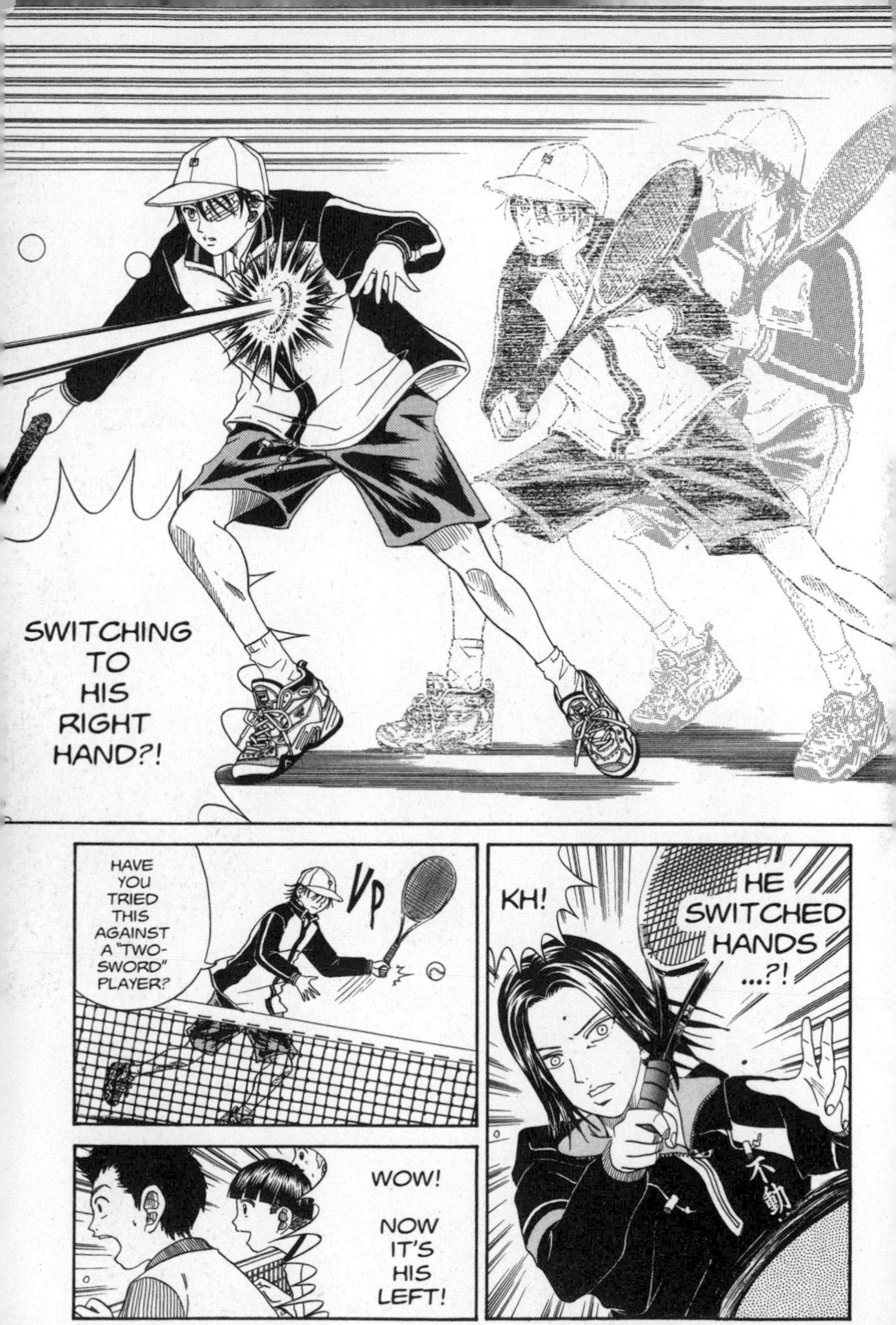
SWITCHING TO HIS RIGHT HAND?!
HE SWITCHED HANDS ...?!
KH!
HAVE YOU TRIED THIS AGAINST A "TWO-SWORD" PLAYER?
VP
WOW!
NOW IT'S HIS LEFT!

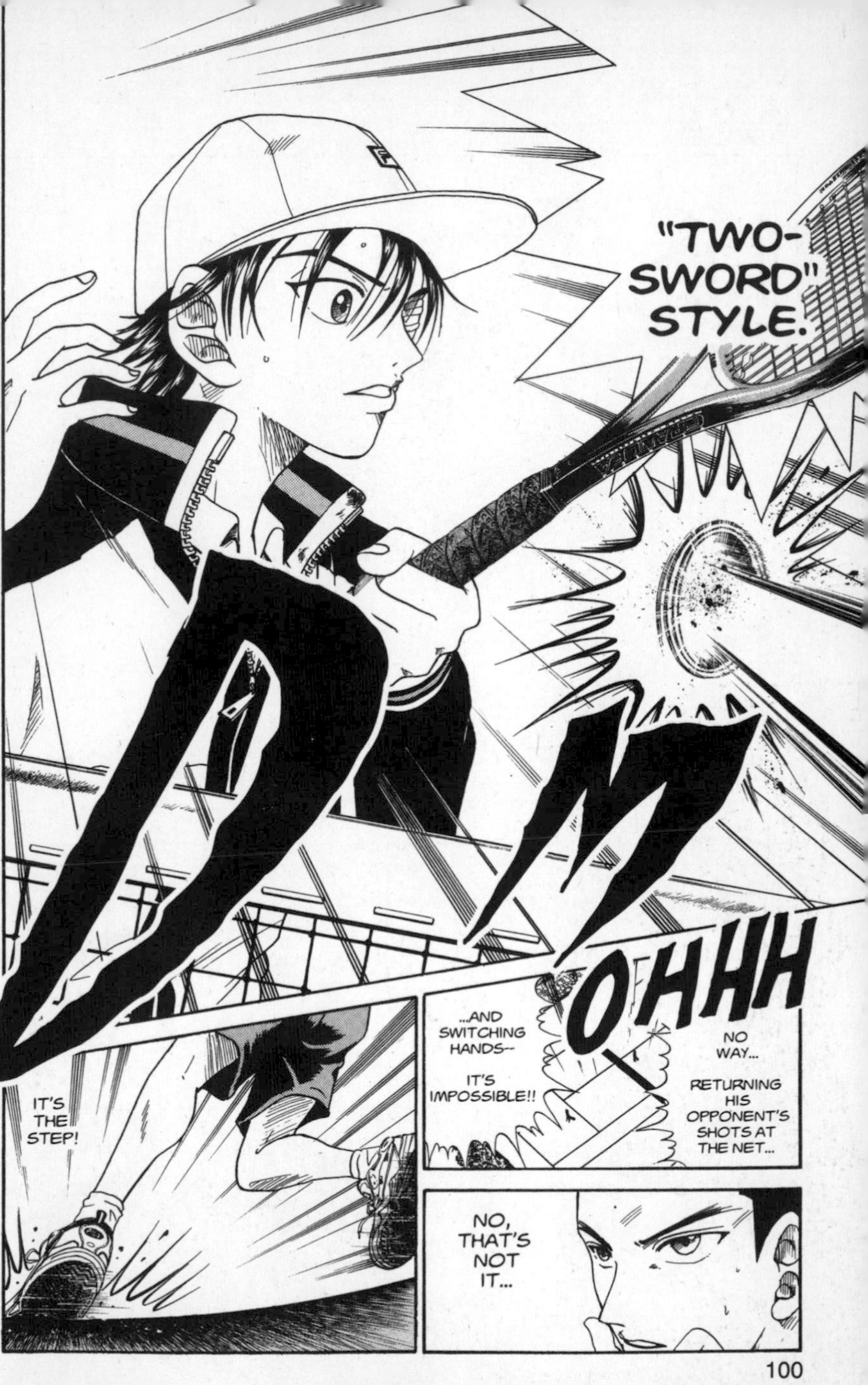
"TWO-SWORD" STYLE.
OHHH
NO WAY... RETURNING HIS OPPONENT'S SHOTS AT THE NET...
...AND SWITCHING HANDS-- IT'S IMPOSSIBLE!!
NO, THAT'S NOT IT...
IT'S THE STEP!

READ THIS WAY

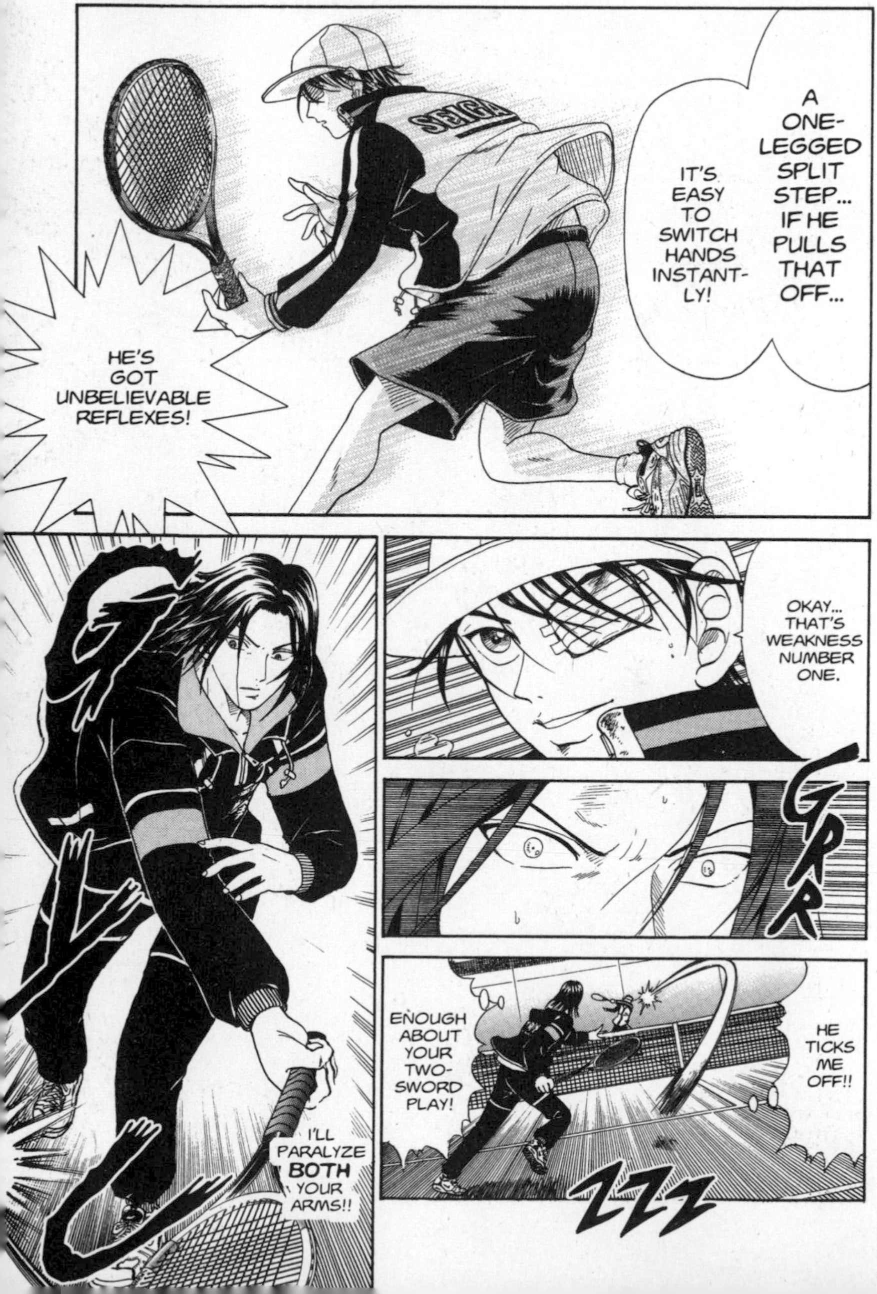
A ONE-LEGGED SPLIT STEP... IF HE PULLS THAT OFF...
IT'S EASY TO SWITCH HANDS INSTANTLY!
HE'S GOT UNBELIEVABLE REFLEXES!
OKAY... THAT'S WEAKNESS NUMBER ONE.
GRR
HE TICKS ME OFF!!
ENOUGH ABOUT YOUR TWO-SWORD PLAY!
ZZZ
I'LL PARALYZE **BOTH** YOUR ARMS!!

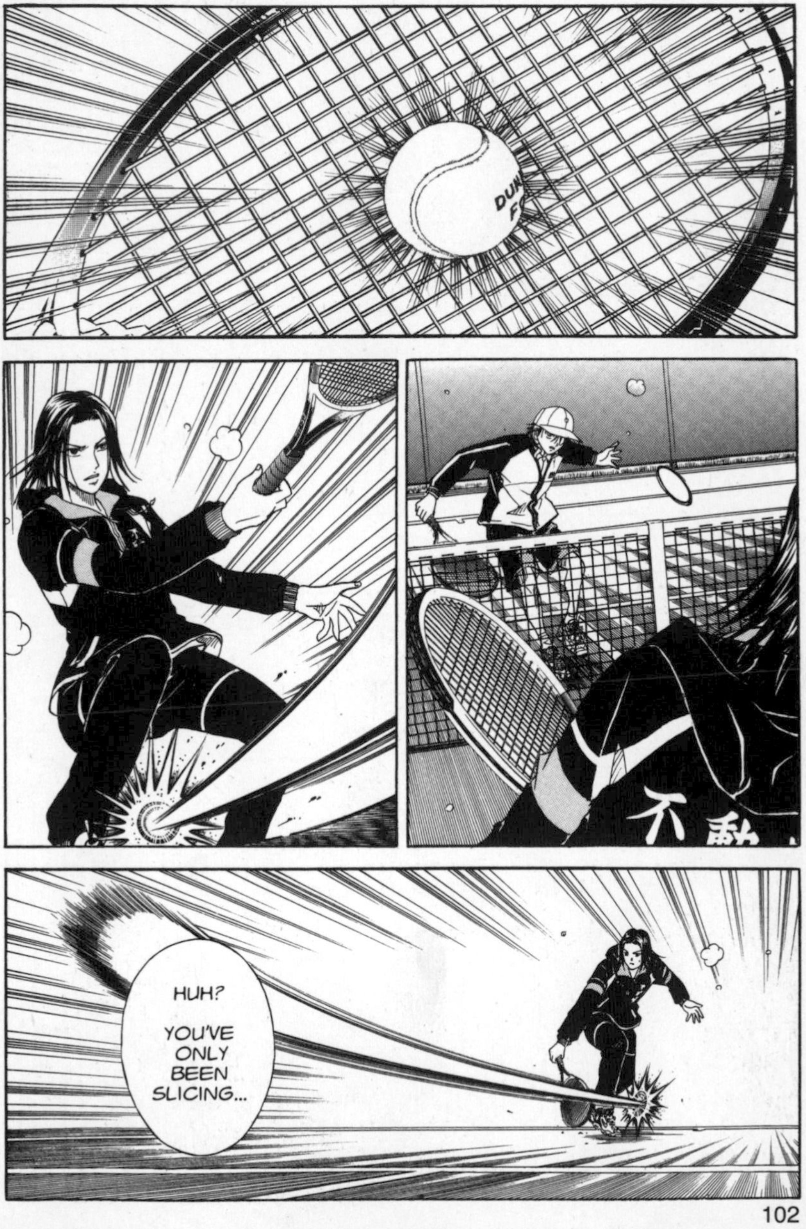
HUH? YOU'VE ONLY BEEN SLICING...

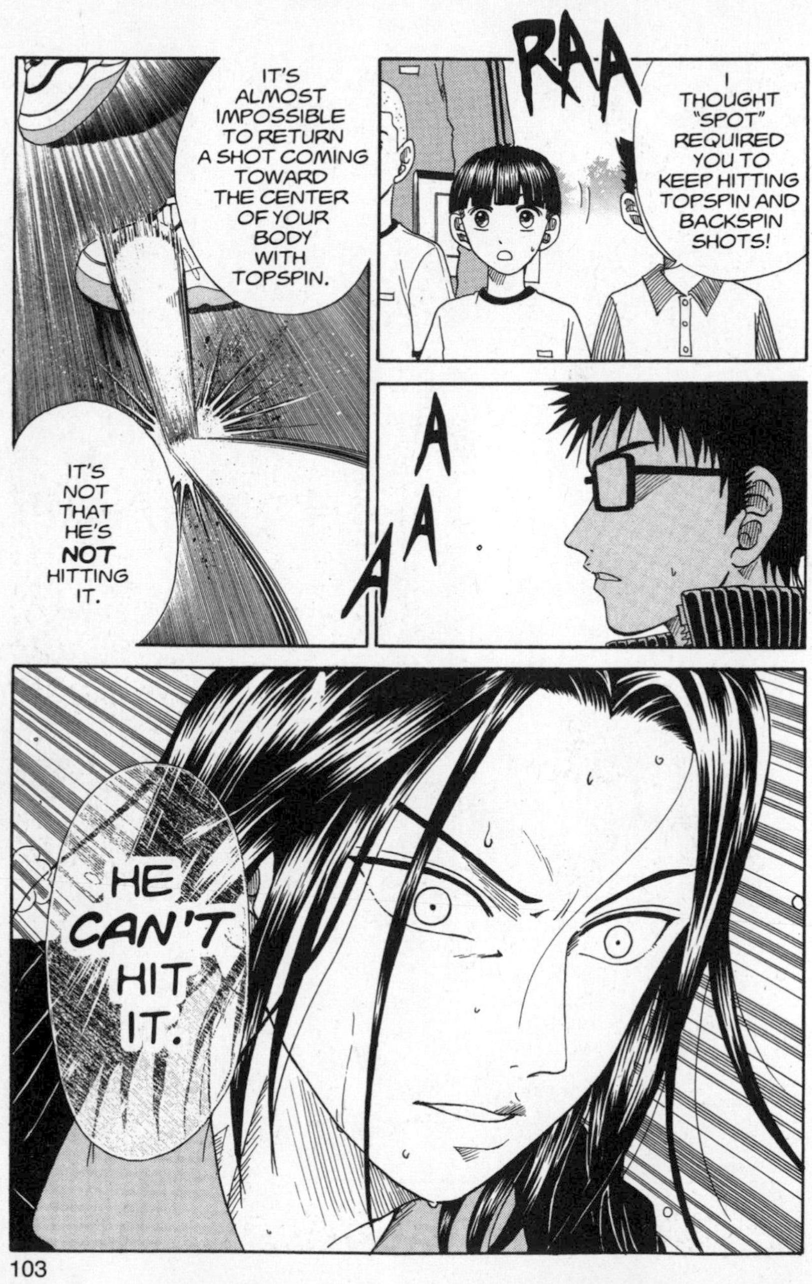
RAA
I THOUGHT "SPOT" REQUIRED YOU TO KEEP HITTING TOPSPIN AND BACKSPIN SHOTS!
AAAA
IT'S ALMOST IMPOSSIBLE TO RETURN A SHOT COMING TOWARD THE CENTER OF YOUR BODY WITH TOPSPIN.
IT'S NOT THAT HE'S **NOT** HITTING IT.
HE **CAN'T** HIT IT.

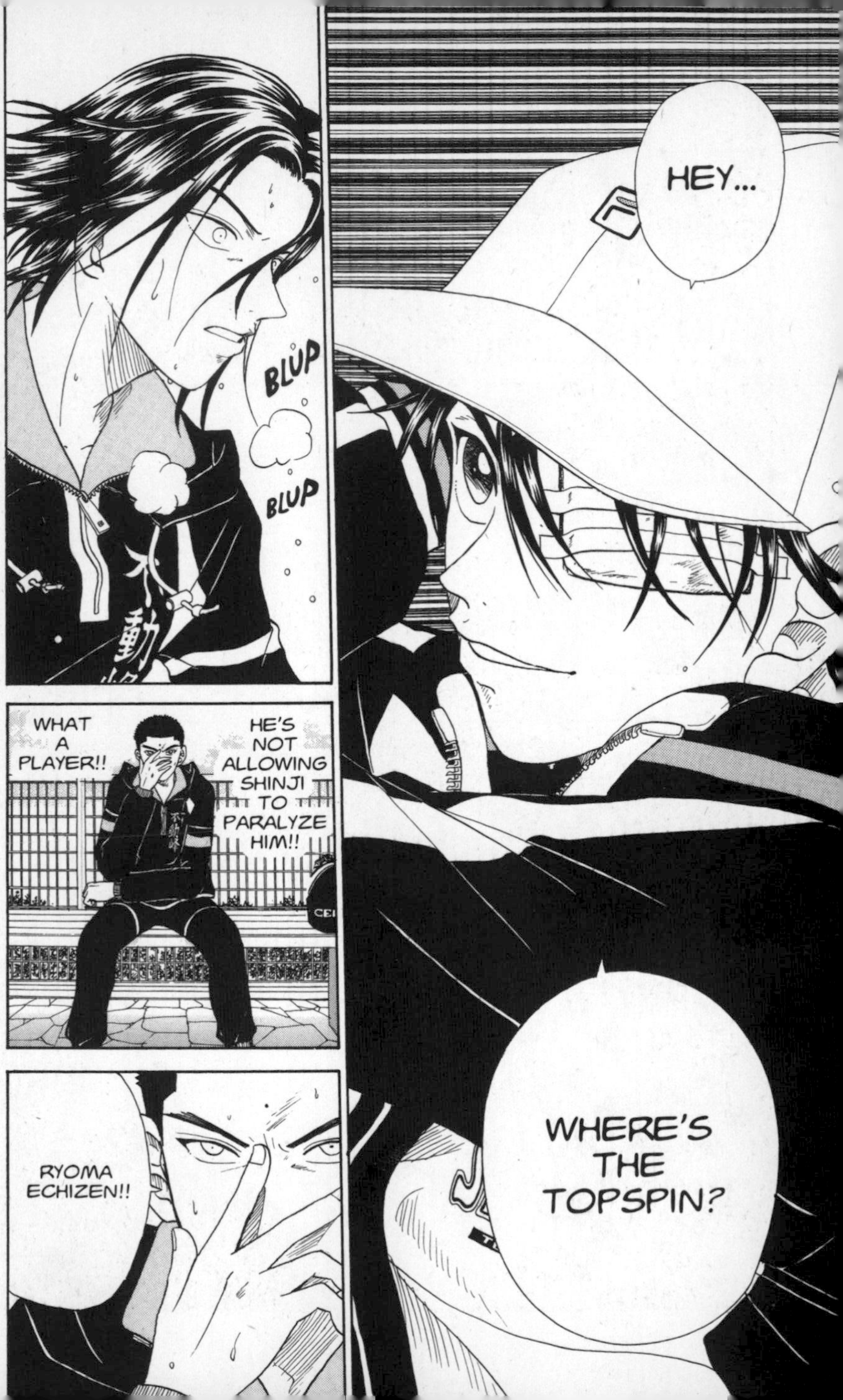
HEY...
WHERE'S THE TOPSPIN?
BLUP
BLUP
HE'S NOT ALLOWING SHINJI TO PARALYZE HIM!!
WHAT A PLAYER!!
RYOMA ECHIZEN!!

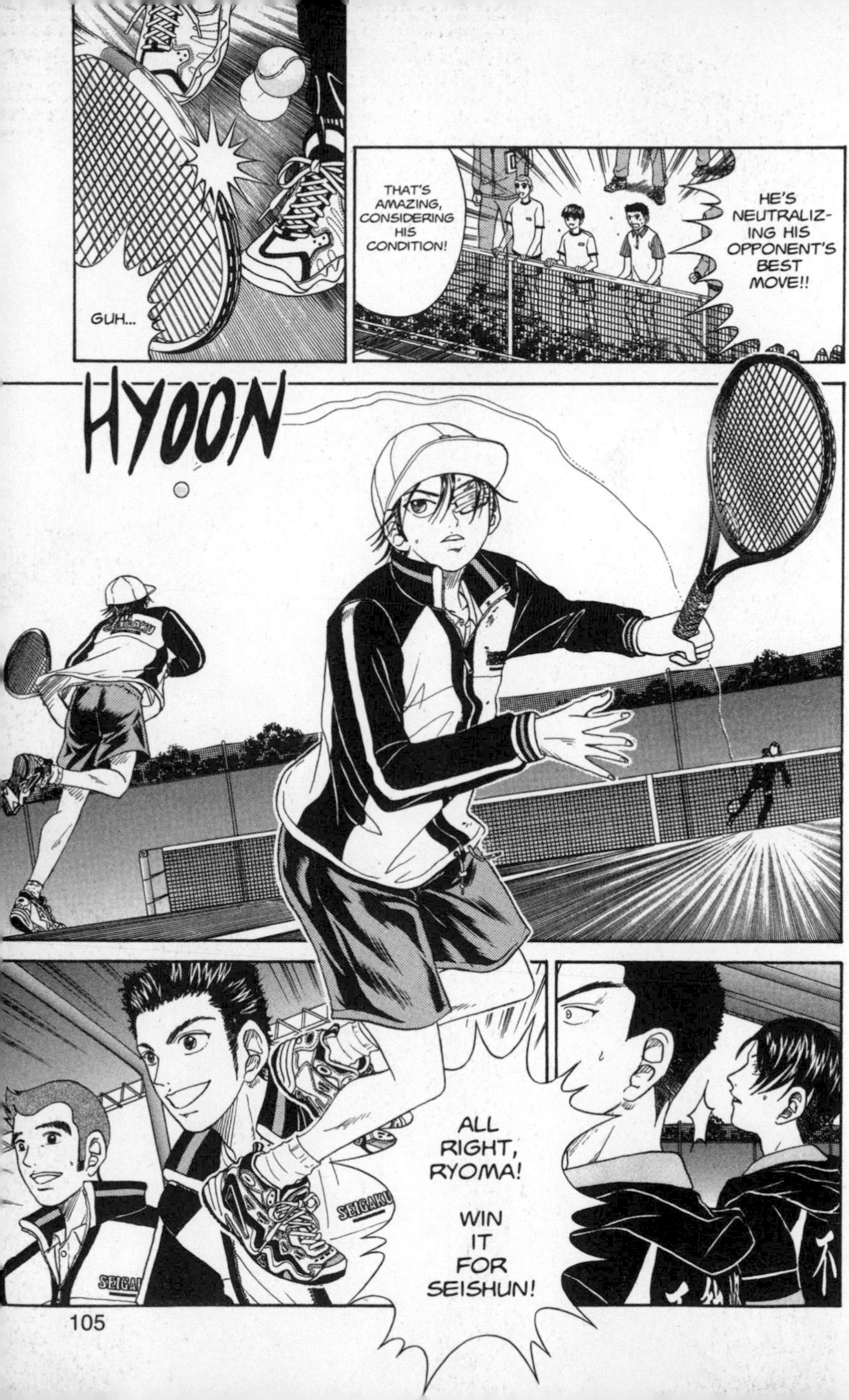
HE'S NEUTRALIZING HIS OPPONENT'S BEST MOVE!!
THAT'S AMAZING, CONSIDERING HIS CONDITION!
GUH...
HYOON
ALL RIGHT, RYOMA!
WIN IT FOR SEISHUN!

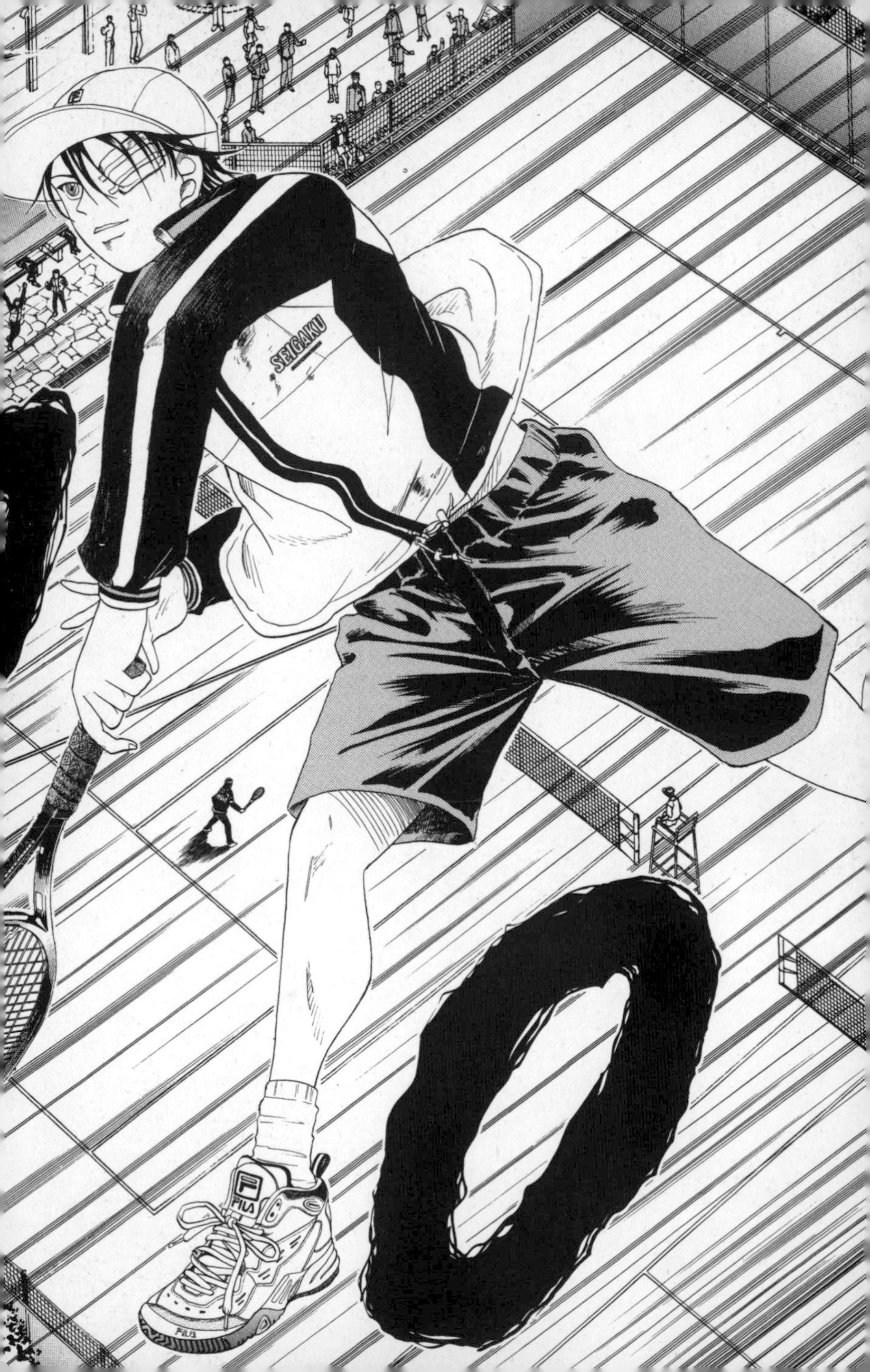
SEIGAKU
FILA

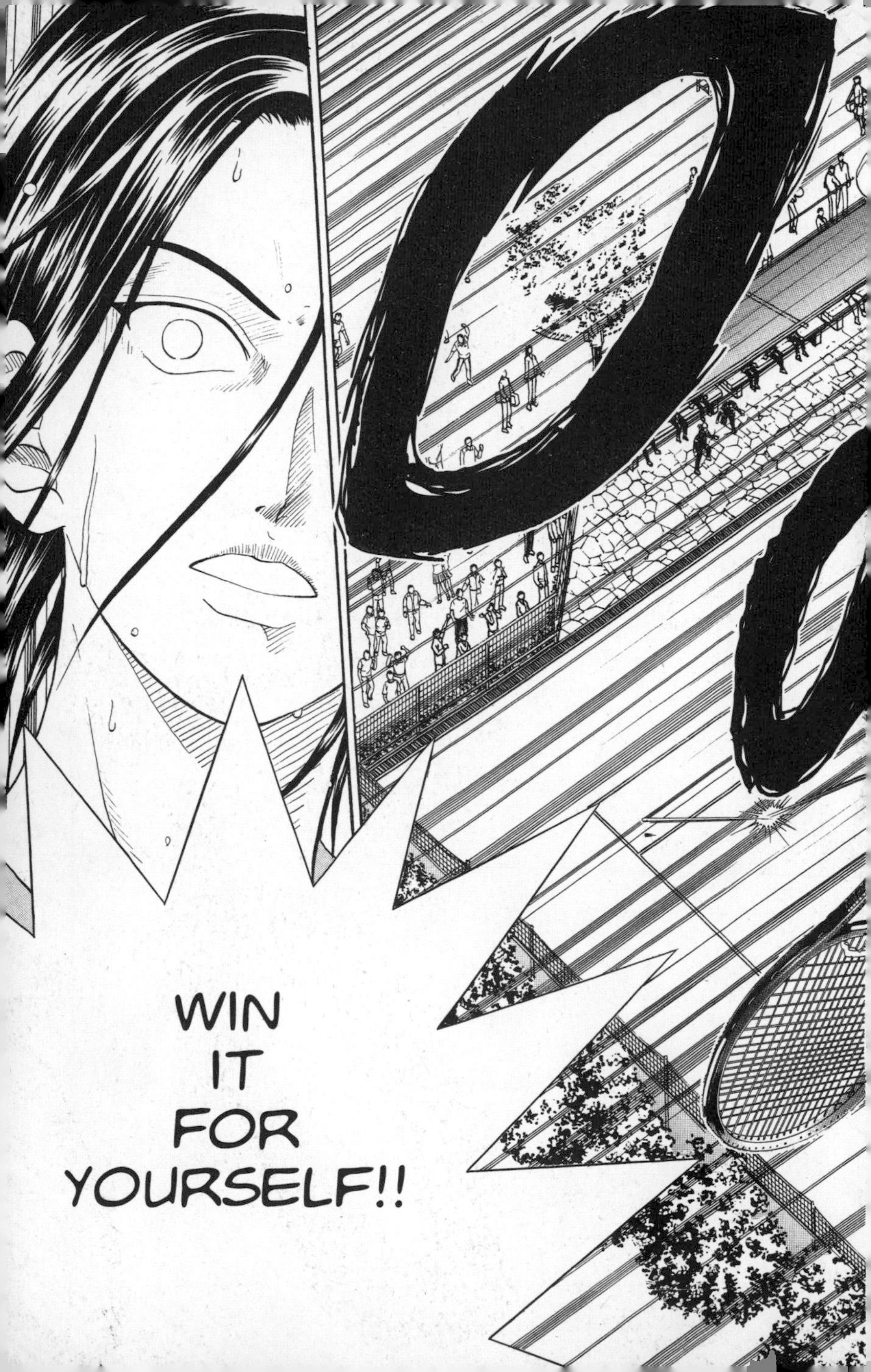
WIN IT FOR YOURSELF!!

THANKS FOR READING PRINCE OF TENNIS VOLUME 5.
(IN VOLUME 4, I WROTE "THANK YOU FOR READING VOLUME 3—."
THOSE WITH THE FIRST PRINTING, CHECK IT OUT.) I'VE BEEN
RECEIVING GIFTS AND HANDMADE ITEMS FROM READERS.
THANK YOU VERY MUCH!! AS I WRITE THIS IN AUGUST 2000, IT'S THE 1ST
ANNIVERSARY OF THE SERIES. THANKS!

THE WINNER OF LAST VOLUME'S "CHOOSE THE COLOR KEY OF VOLUME 5"
IS GENIUS 35. IT WAS VERY CLOSE. I THOUGHT 35 HAD THE EDGE BECAUSE THERE
WERE MORE CHARACTERS IN IT, BUT AVID FANS OF 43 MADE A BIG PUSH.
DURING THE SHORT SUBMISSION PERIOD, THE VOTES WERE 465 TO 391!!
OF COURSE, EACH VOTE CAME WITH A WARM LETTER. I'M SURE YOU'VE
NOTICED, BUT I LOVE FAN LETTERS. UNFORTUNATELY, I HAVEN'T BEEN ABLE
TO RESPOND TO MANY OF THEM... I'M VERY SORRY. I'M TRYING TO COME UP
WITH FUN PROJECTS IN RESPONSE TO EVERYBODY'S SUPPORT. THERE ARE
PROBABLY A FEW OF YOU WHO THOUGHT, "HEY! I THINK I WROTE THAT IN MY
LETTER...!" WELL, YOU'RE RIGHT. BESIDES THE MAIN STORY, THIS VOLUME
INCLUDES A YOMIKIRI (A STAND-ALONE STORY). HOPE YOU ENJOY IT!

KEEP SUPPORTING PRINCE OF TENNIS AND RYOMA!

SEE YOU IN THE NEXT VOLUME!

TAKESHI KONOMI

T. KONOMI
2000. 8. 25

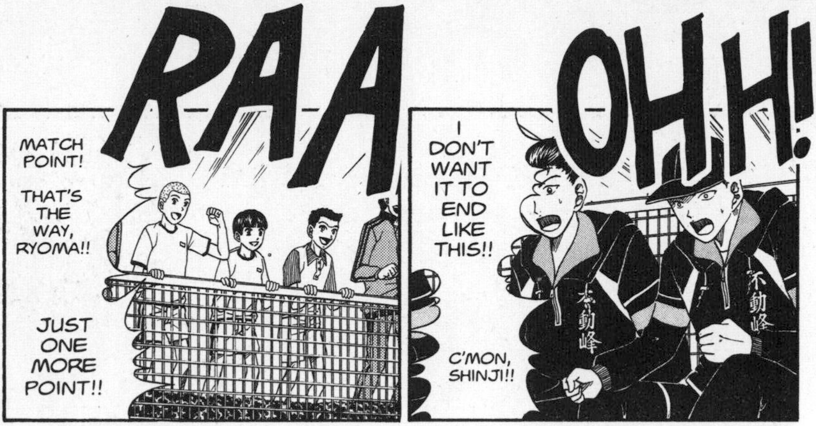
RAAOHH!
I DON'T WANT IT TO END LIKE THIS!!
C'MON, SHINJI!!
不動峰
不動峰
MATCH POINT!
THAT'S THE WAY, RYOMA!!
JUST ONE MORE POINT!!

Genius 40: Champion

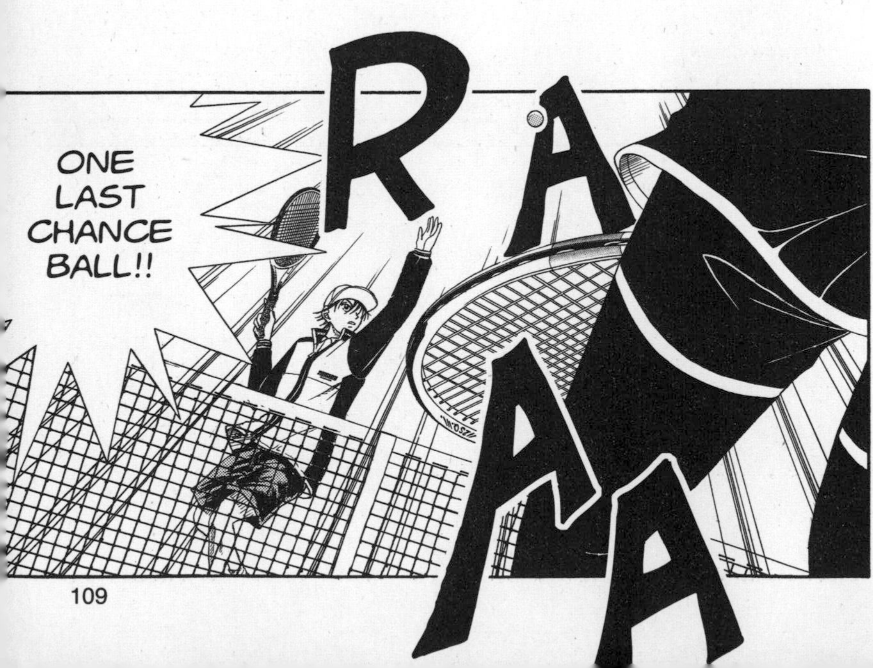
RAAAA
ONE LAST CHANCE BALL!!

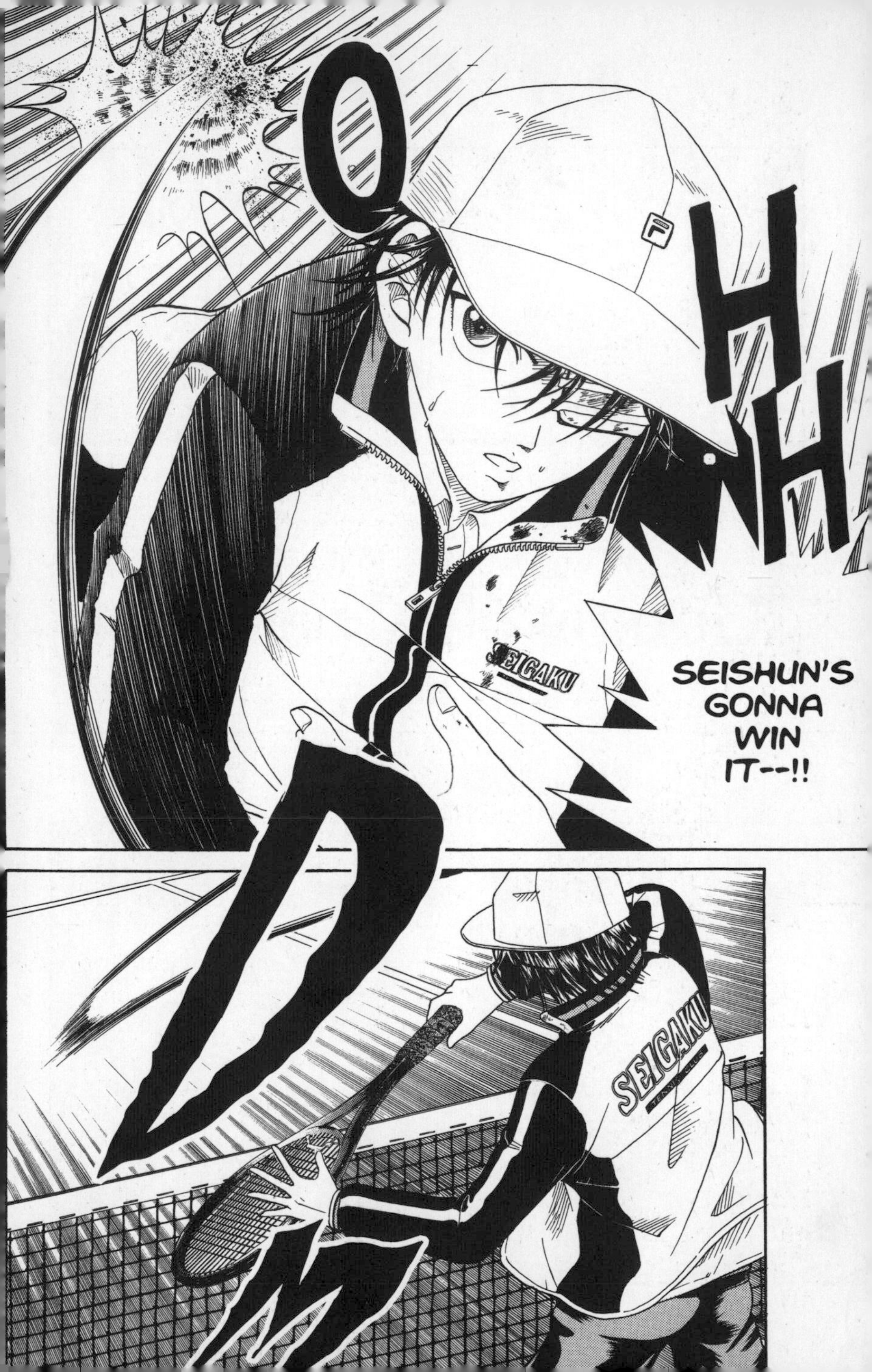
OHHH
SEISHUN'S GONNA WIN IT--!!

« READ THIS WAY «

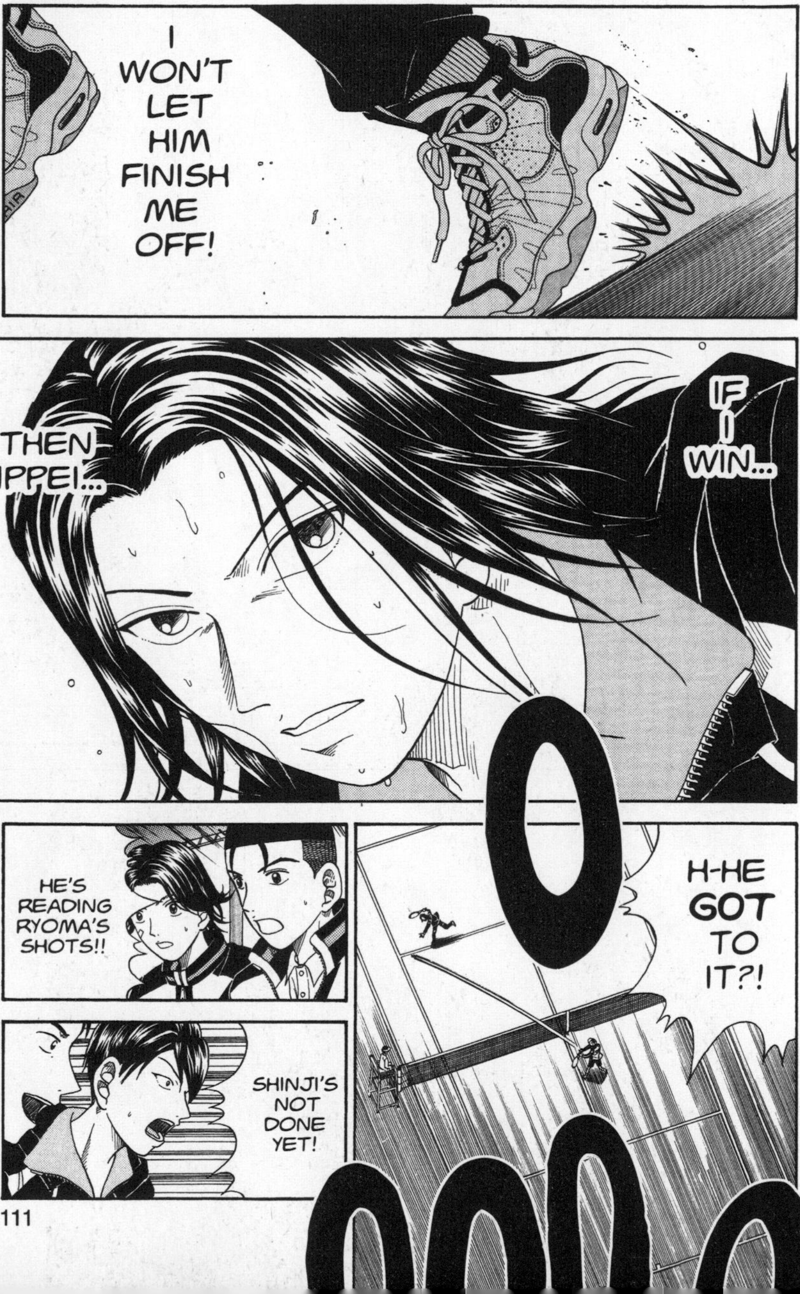
I WON'T LET HIM FINISH ME OFF!
IF I WIN...
...THEN KIPPEI...
H-HE GOT TO IT?!
OOOOO
HE'S READING RYOMA'S SHOTS!!
SHINJI'S NOT DONE YET!

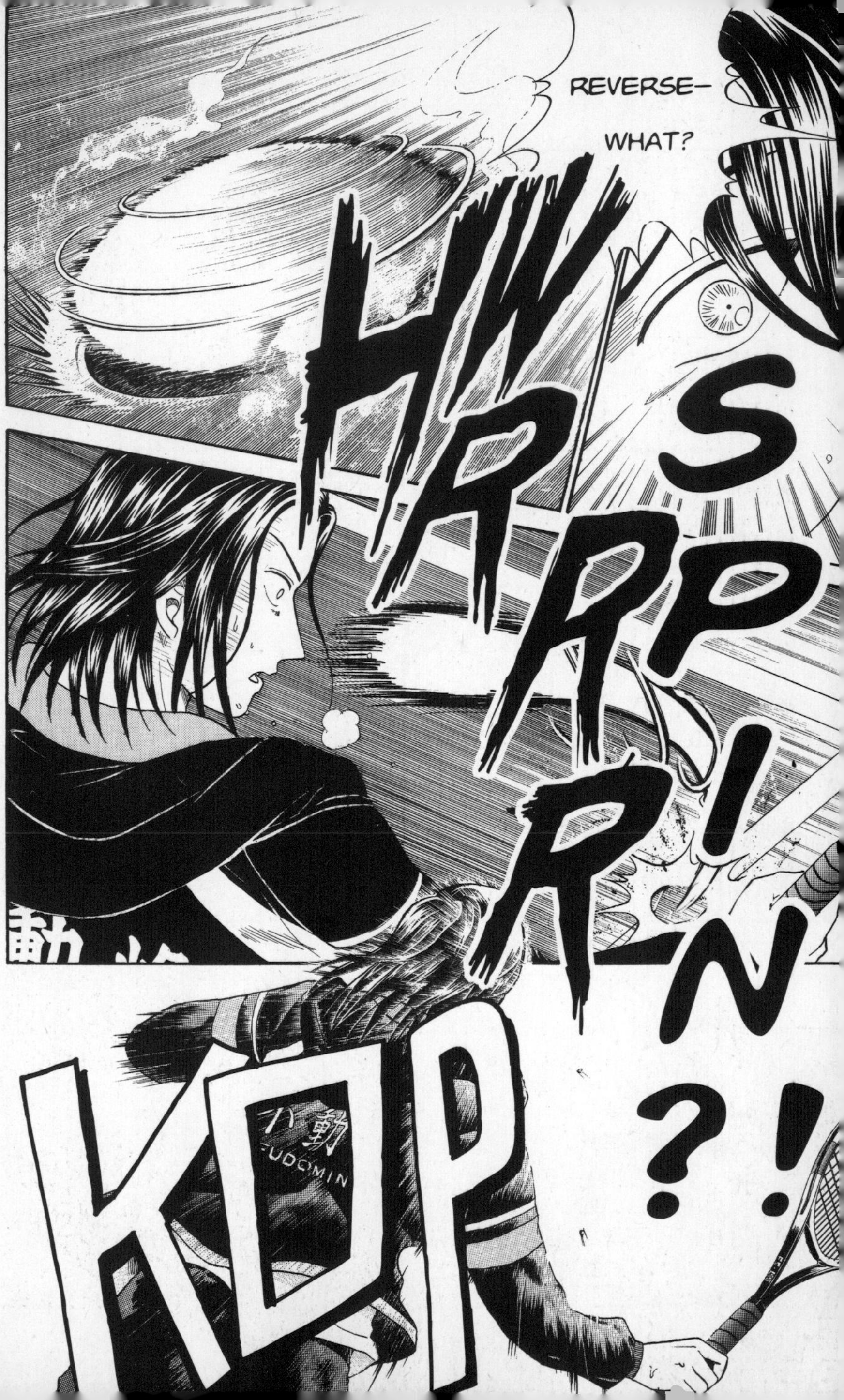
REVERSE-
WHAT?
HWRRRR
SPIN?!
FUDOMIN
KDP

READ THIS WAY

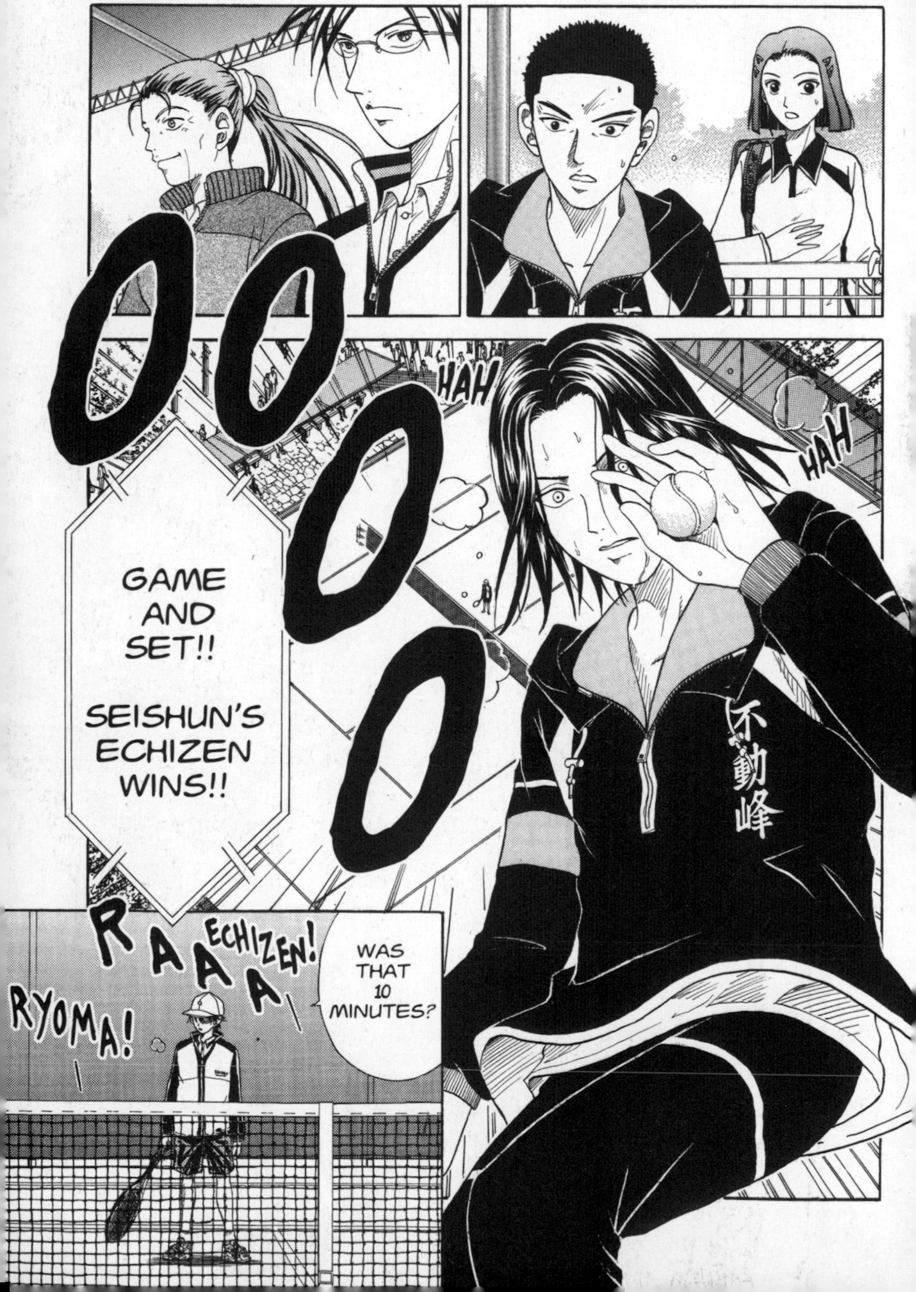
HAH
HAH
OOOOO
GAME AND SET!! SEISHUN'S ECHIZEN WINS!!
不動峰
WAS THAT 10 MINUTES?
ECHIZEN!
RAAA
RYOMA!

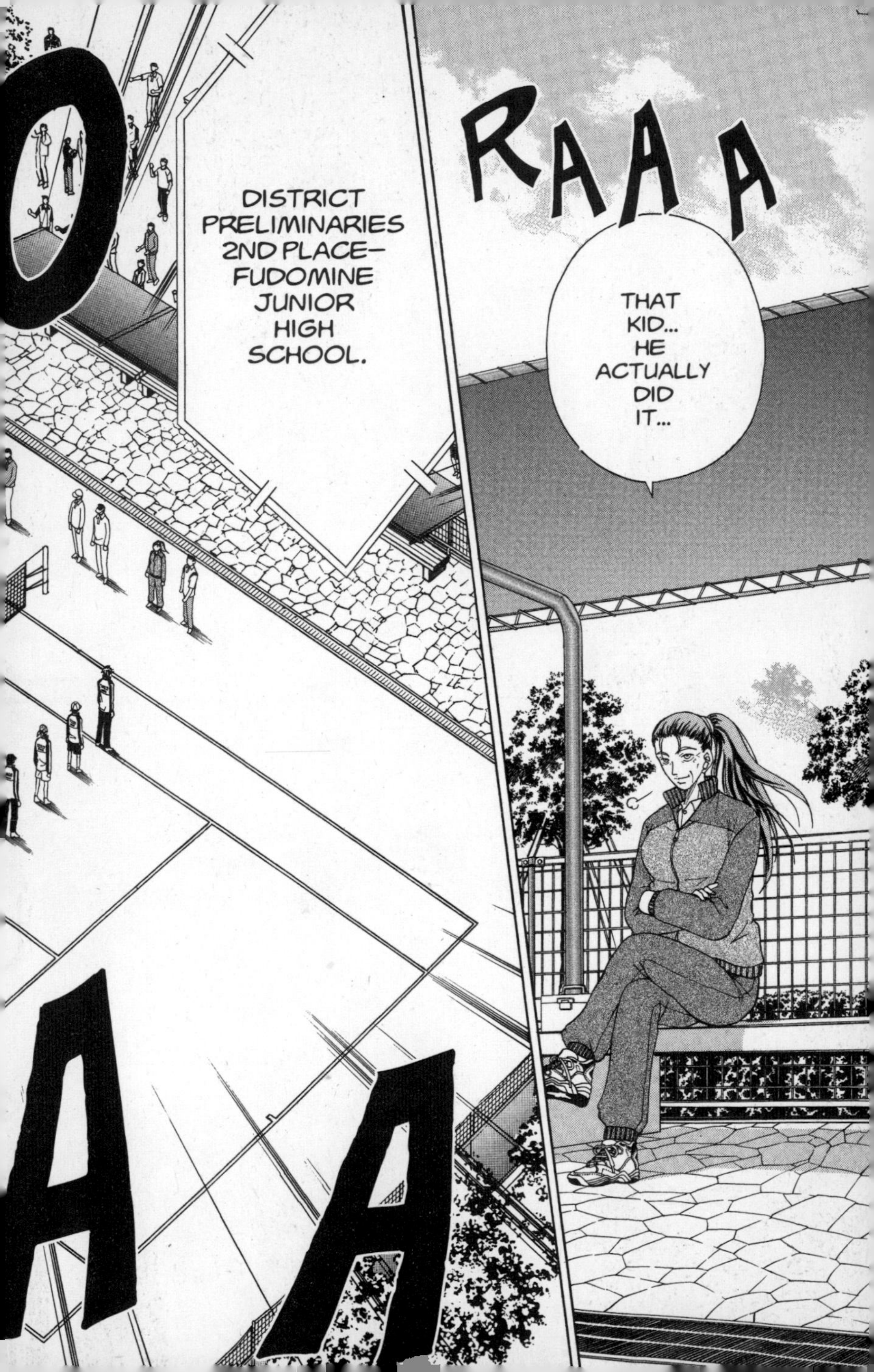
RAAA
THAT KID... HE ACTUALLY DID IT...
DISTRICT PRELIMINARIES 2ND PLACE—FUDOMINE JUNIOR HIGH SCHOOL.
O
A
A

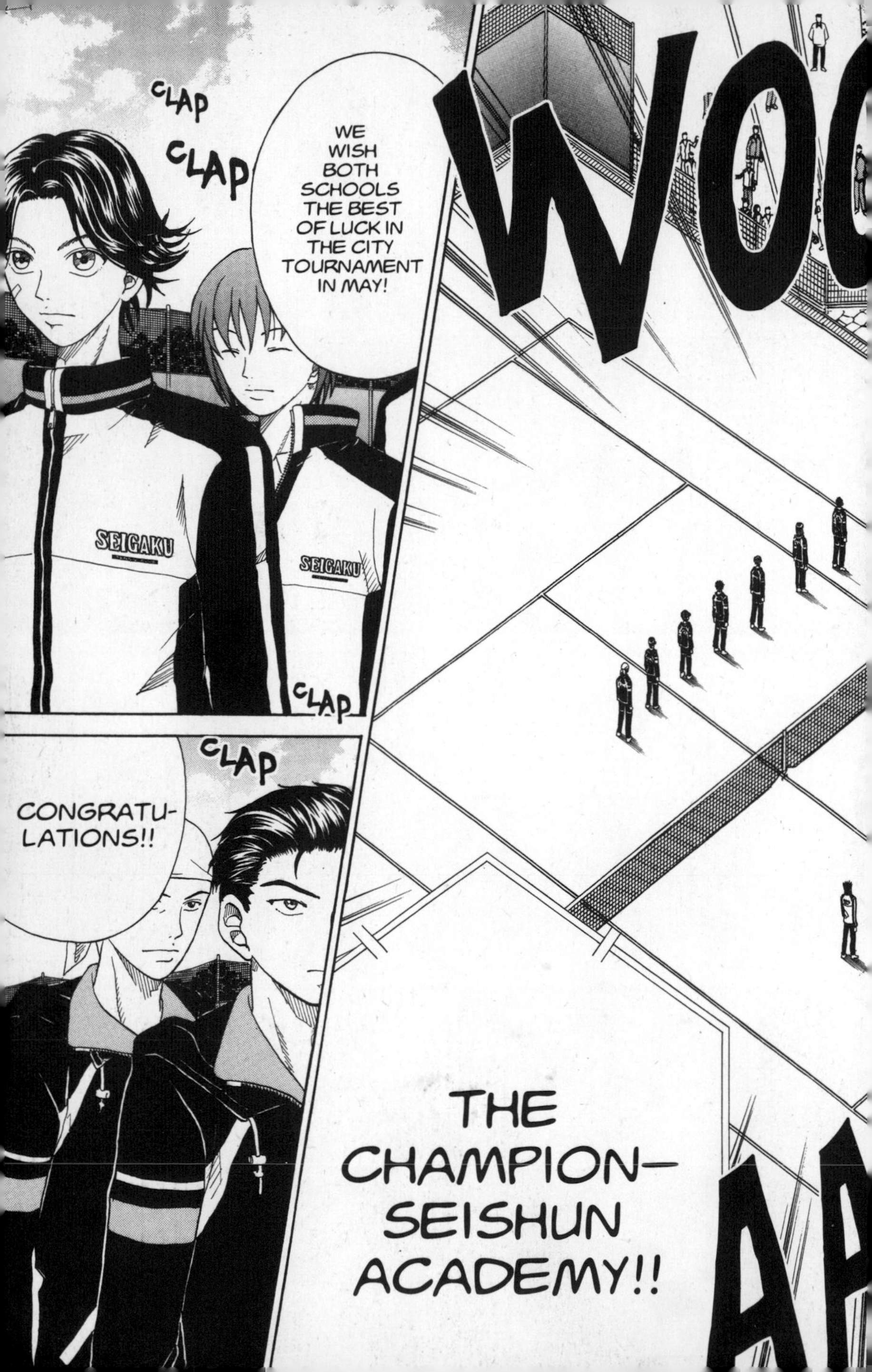
WOO
THE CHAMPION— SEISHUN ACADEMY!!
A
CLAP
CLAP
WE WISH BOTH SCHOOLS THE BEST OF LUCK IN THE CITY TOURNAMENT IN MAY!
SEIGAKU
SEIGAKU
CLAP
CLAP
CONGRATU-LATIONS!!

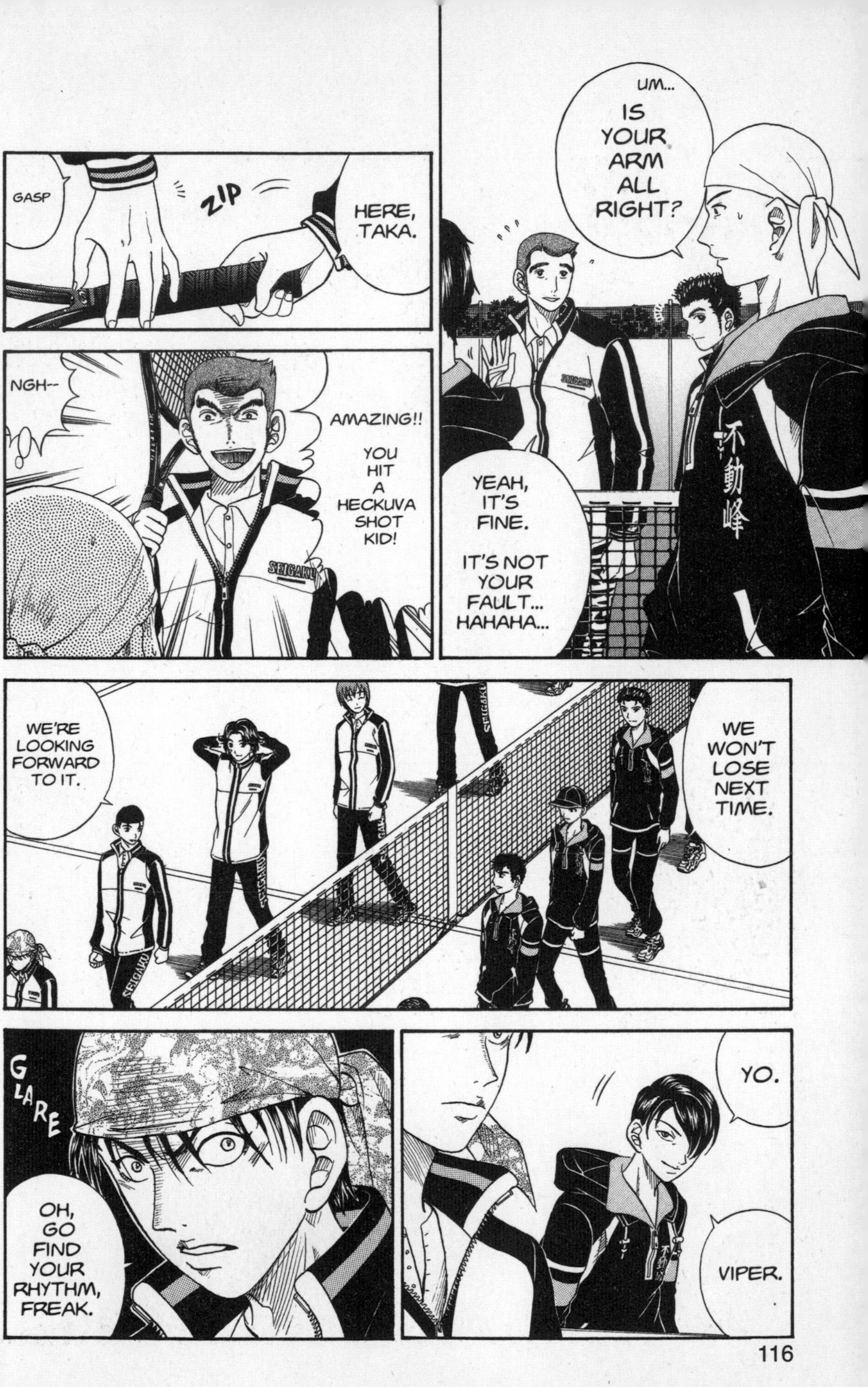
UM...
IS YOUR ARM ALL RIGHT?
YEAH, IT'S FINE.
IT'S NOT YOUR FAULT... HAHAHA...
HERE, TAKA.
ZIP
GASP
AMAZING!!
YOU HIT A HECKUVA SHOT KID!
NGH--
WE WON'T LOSE NEXT TIME.
WE'RE LOOKING FORWARD TO IT.
YO.
VIPER.
GLARE
OH, GO FIND YOUR RHYTHM, FREAK.

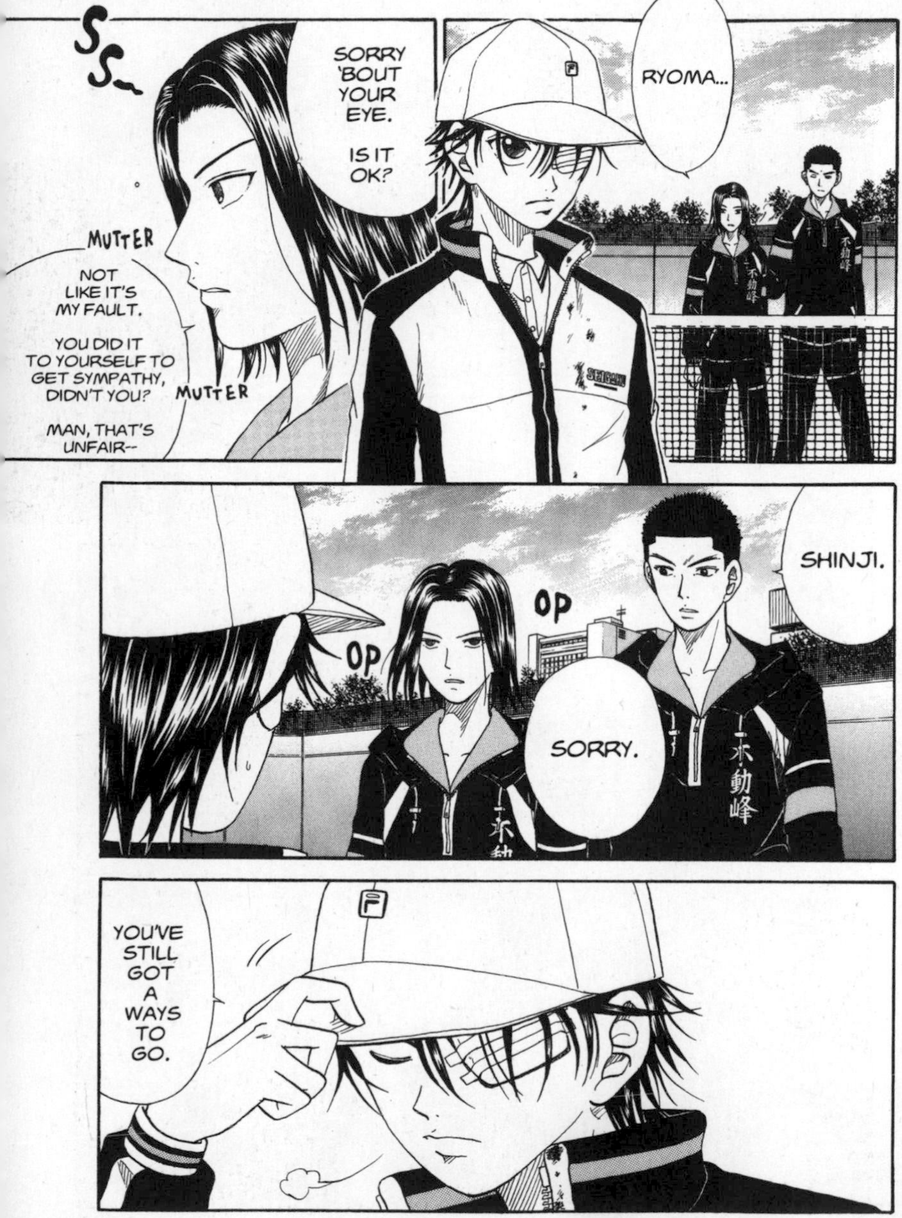
RYOMA...
SORRY 'BOUT YOUR EYE.
IS IT OK?
SS
MUTTER
NOT LIKE IT'S MY FAULT.
YOU DID IT TO YOURSELF TO GET SYMPATHY, DIDN'T YOU?
MUTTER
MAN, THAT'S UNFAIR--
SHINJI.
OP
OP
SORRY.
YOU'VE STILL GOT A WAYS TO GO.

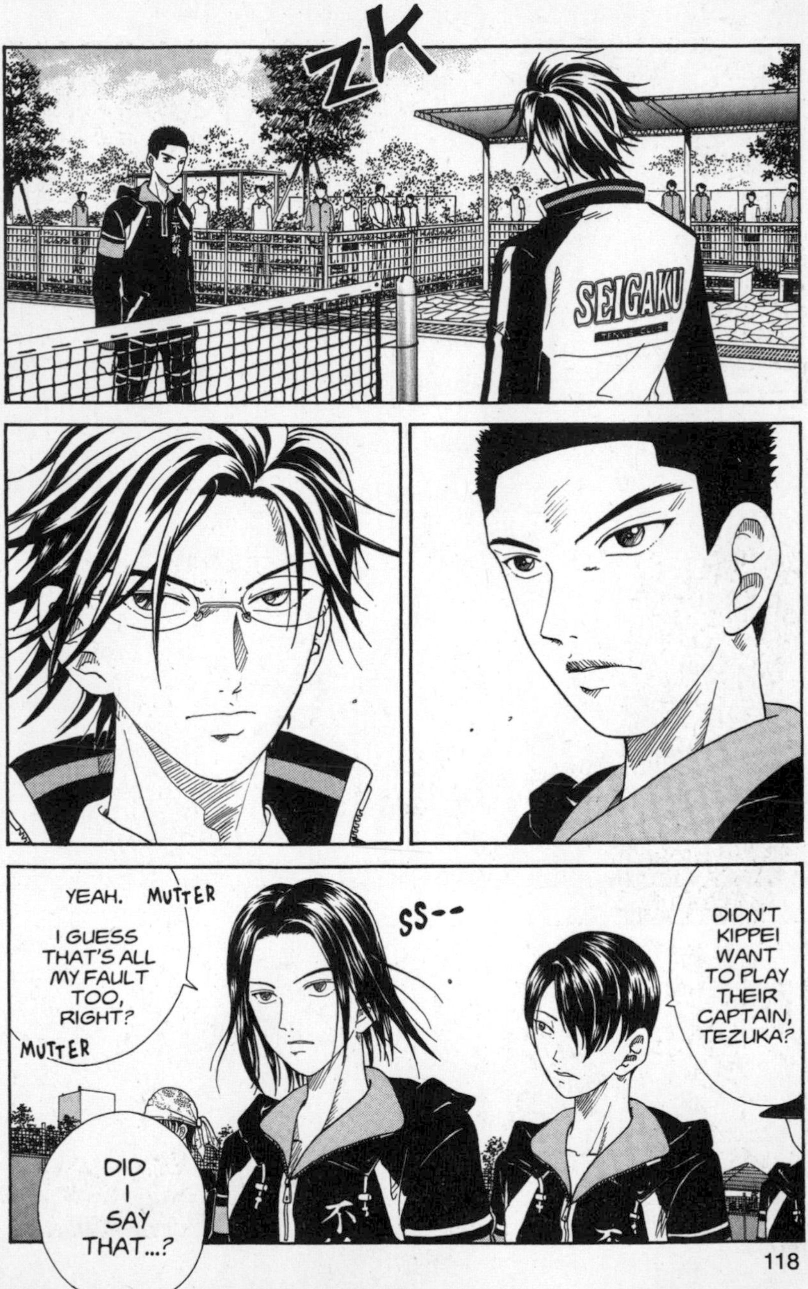
ZK
DIDN'T KIPPEI WANT TO PLAY THEIR CAPTAIN, TEZUKA?
SS--
YEAH.
MUTTER
I GUESS THAT'S ALL MY FAULT TOO, RIGHT?
MUTTER
DID I SAY THAT...?

READ THIS WAY

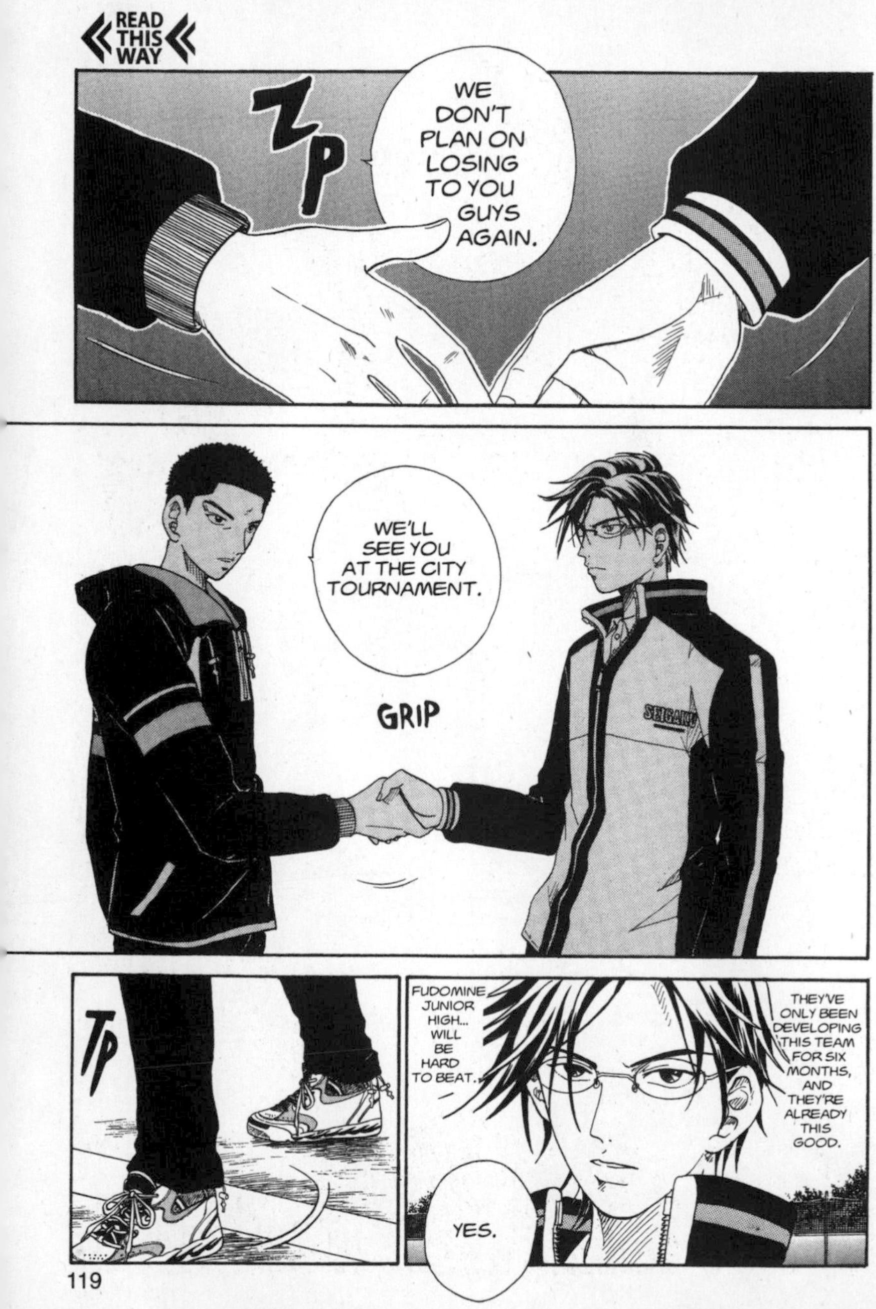

ZP
WE DON'T PLAN ON LOSING TO YOU GUYS AGAIN.
WE'LL SEE YOU AT THE CITY TOURNAMENT.
GRIP
THEY'VE ONLY BEEN DEVELOPING THIS TEAM FOR SIX MONTHS, AND THEY'RE ALREADY THIS GOOD.
FUDOMINE JUNIOR HIGH... WILL BE HARD TO BEAT.
YES.
TP

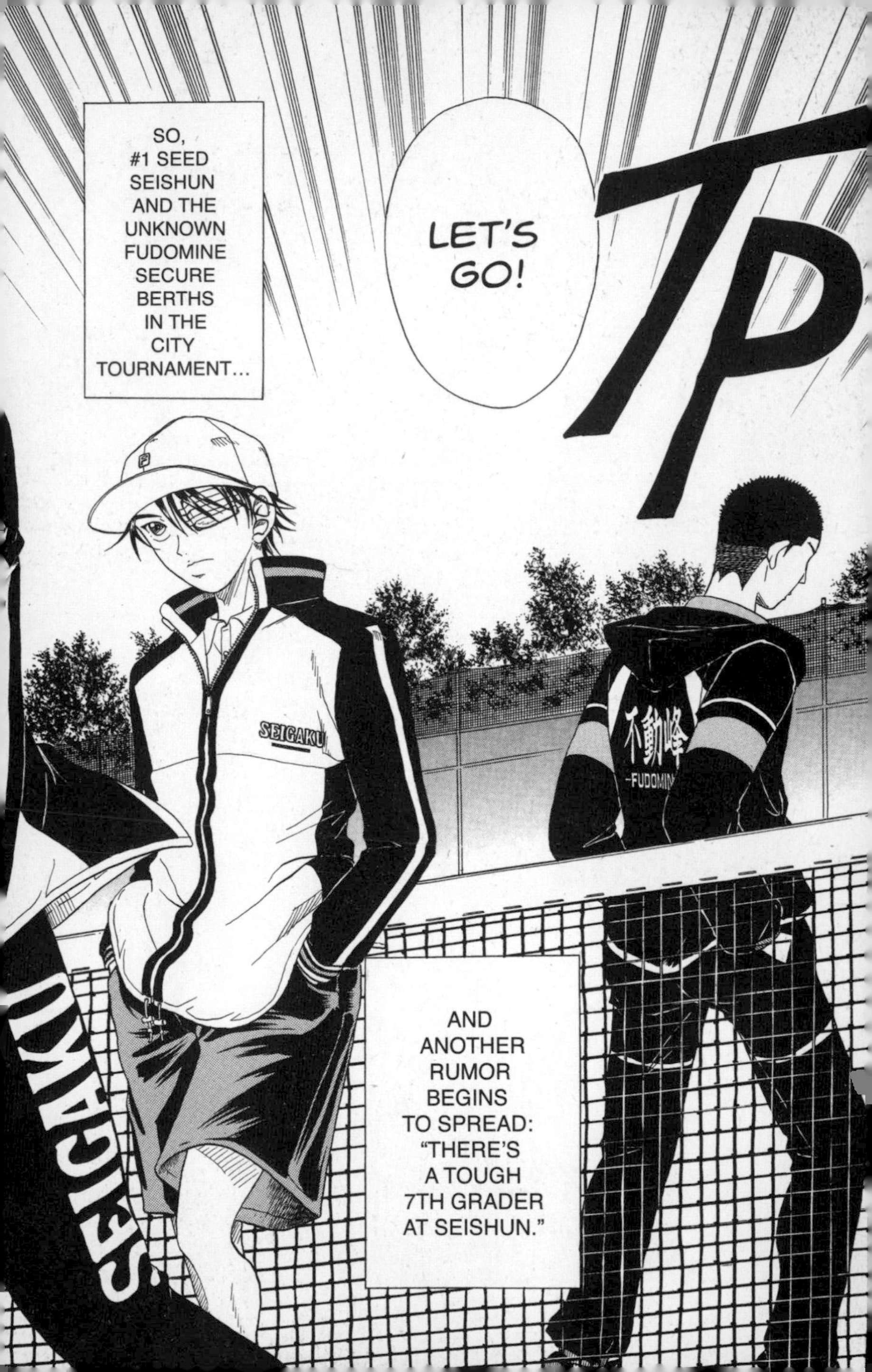
TP
LET'S GO!
SO, #1 SEED SEISHUN AND THE UNKNOWN FUDOMINE SECURE BERTHS IN THE CITY TOURNAMENT...
AND ANOTHER RUMOR BEGINS TO SPREAD: "THERE'S A TOUGH 7TH GRADER AT SEISHUN."

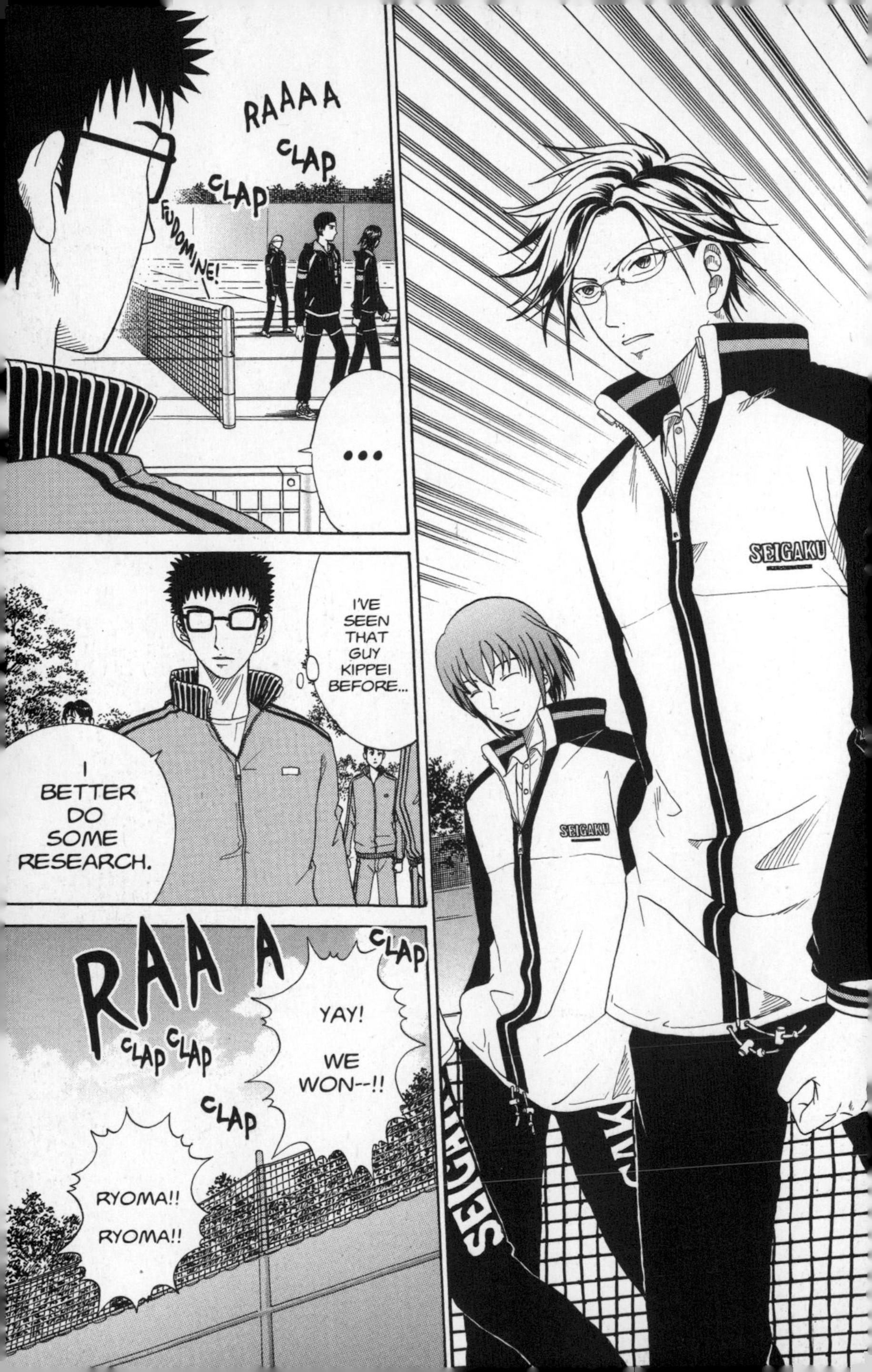
SEIGAKU
SEIGAKU
SEIGAKU
RAAAA
CLAP
CLAP
FUDOMINE!
...
I'VE SEEN THAT GUY KIPPEI BEFORE...
I BETTER DO SOME RESEARCH.
CLAP
YAY! WE WON--!!
RAA A
CLAP CLAP
CLAP
RYOMA!! RYOMA!!

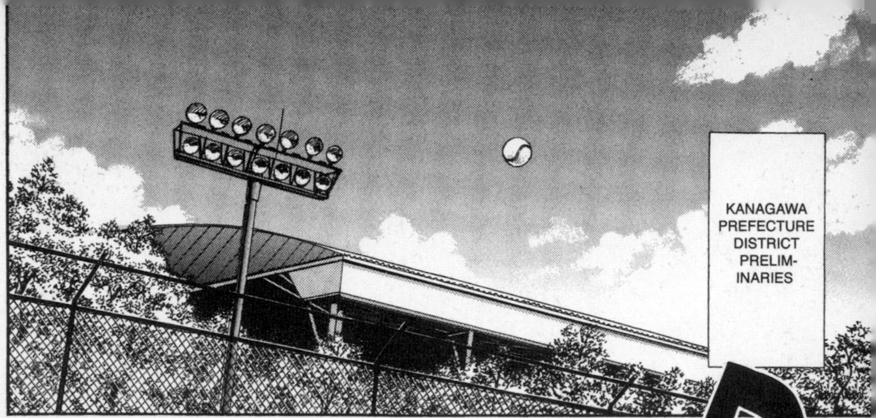
KANAGAWA PREFECTURE DISTRICT PRELIM-INARIES

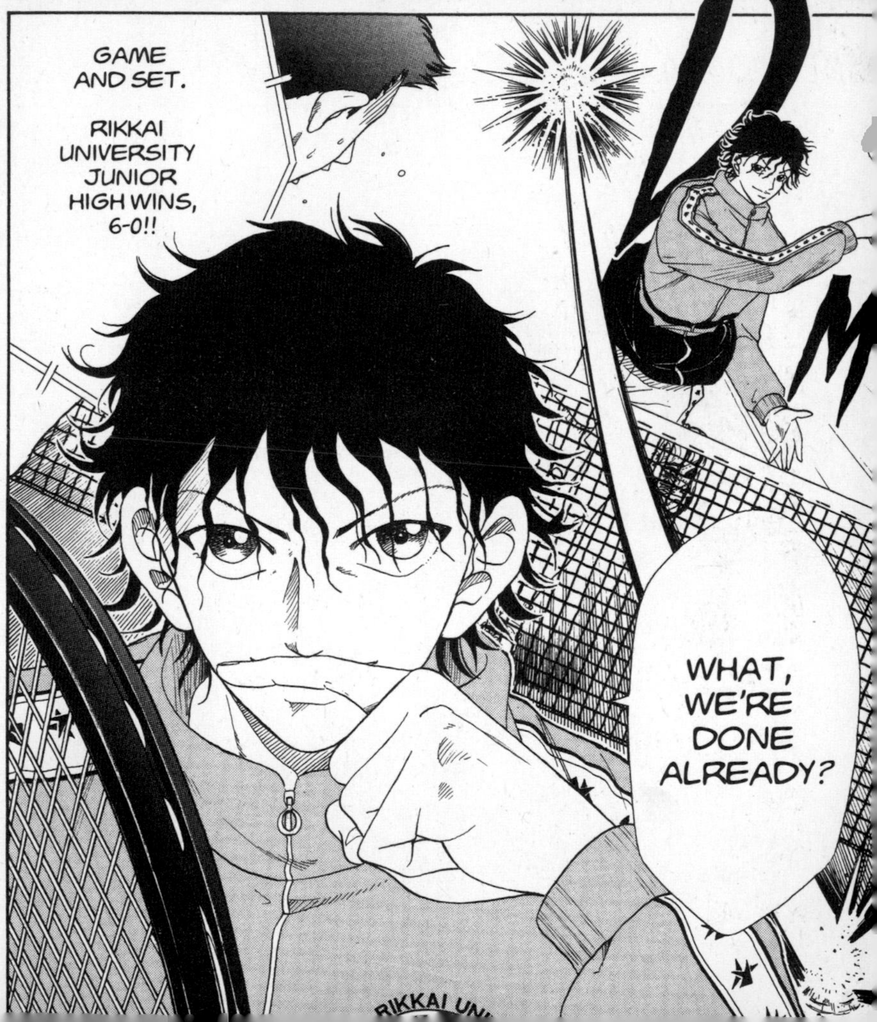
GAME AND SET.
RIKKAI UNIVERSITY JUNIOR HIGH WINS, 6-0!!
WHAT, WE'RE DONE ALREADY?

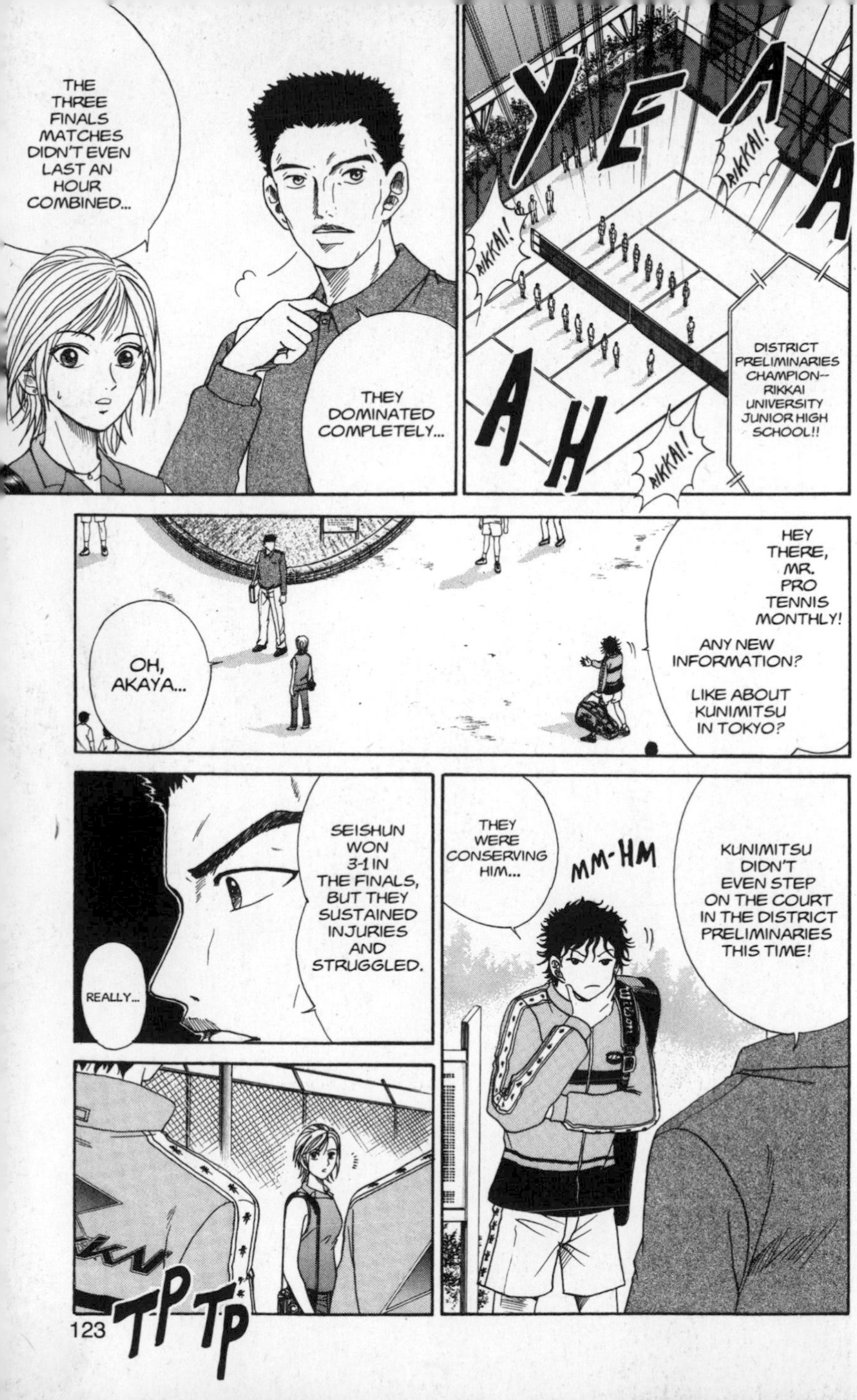
YEAAAAH
RIKKAI!
RIKKAI!
RIKKAI!
DISTRICT PRELIMINARIES CHAMPION-- RIKKAI UNIVERSITY JUNIOR HIGH SCHOOL!!
THE THREE FINALS MATCHES DIDN'T EVEN LAST AN HOUR COMBINED...
THEY DOMINATED COMPLETELY...
HEY THERE, MR. PRO TENNIS MONTHLY!
ANY NEW INFORMATION?
LIKE ABOUT KUNIMITSU IN TOKYO?
OH, AKAYA...
KUNIMITSU DIDN'T EVEN STEP ON THE COURT IN THE DISTRICT PRELIMINARIES THIS TIME!
MM-HM
THEY WERE CONSERVING HIM...
SEISHUN WON 3-1 IN THE FINALS, BUT THEY SUSTAINED INJURIES AND STRUGGLED.
REALLY...
TP TP

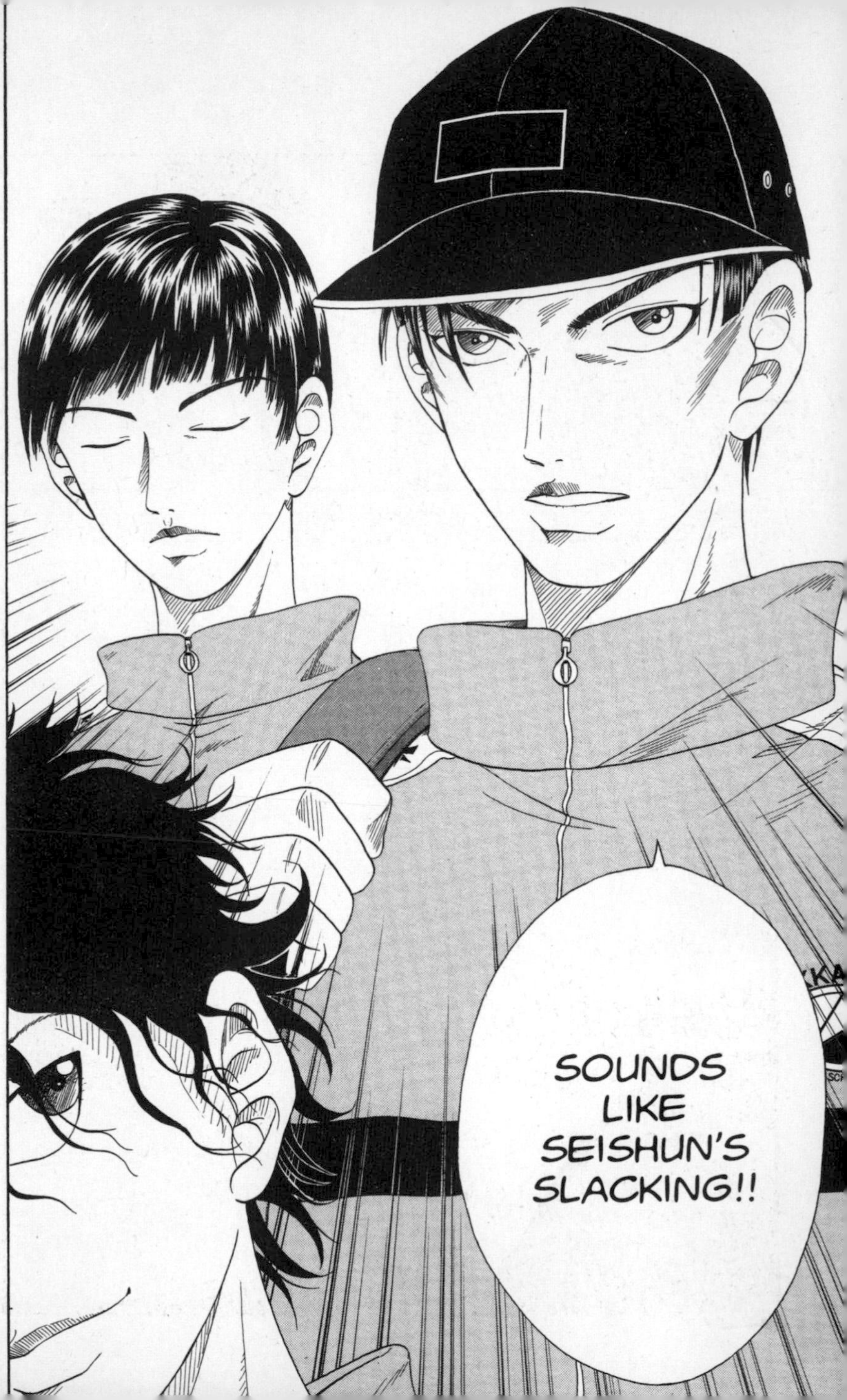
SOUNDS LIKE SEISHUN'S SLACKING!!

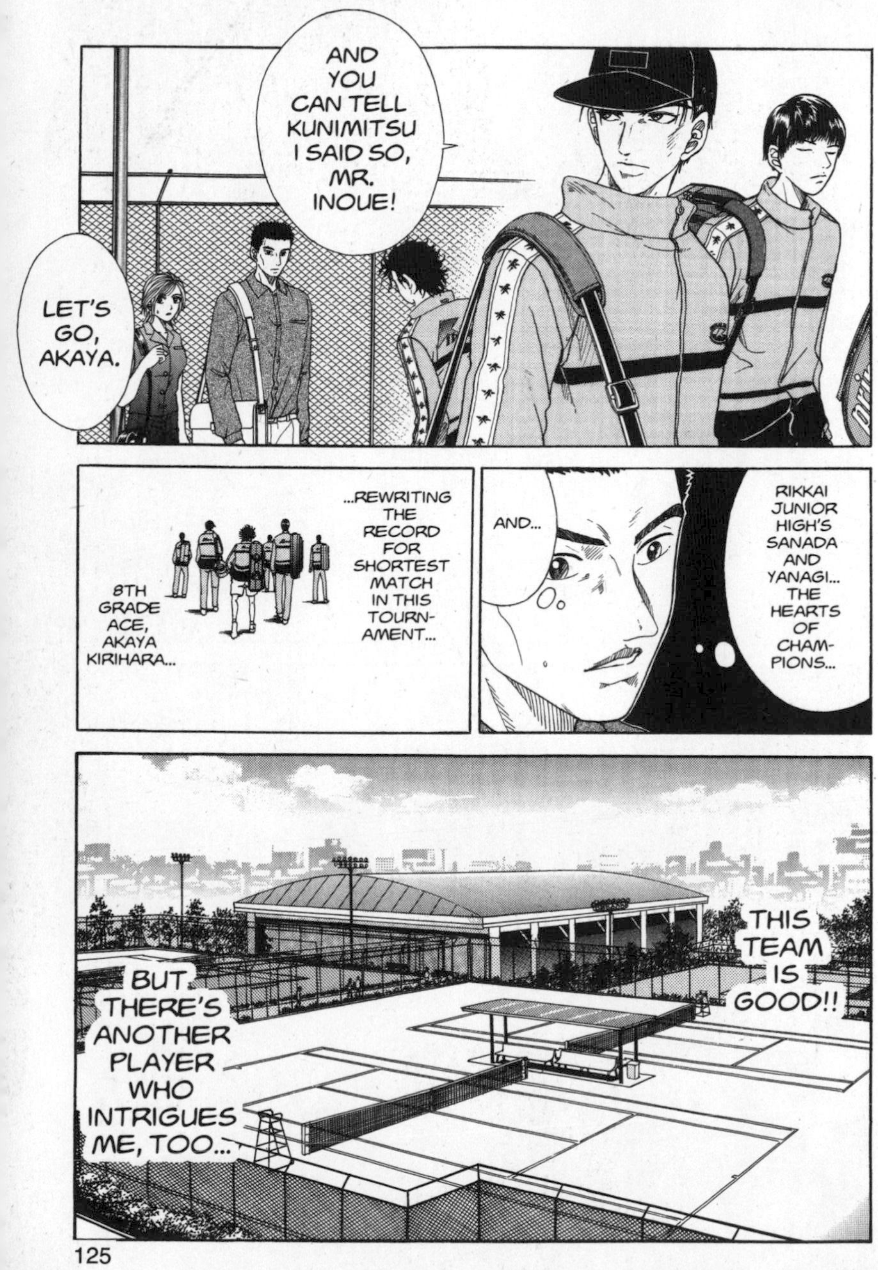
AND YOU CAN TELL KUNIMITSU I SAID SO, MR. INOUE!
LET'S GO, AKAYA.
RIKKAI JUNIOR HIGH'S SANADA AND YANAGI... THE HEARTS OF CHAMPIONS...
AND...
8TH GRADE ACE, AKAYA KIRIHARA...
...REWRITING THE RECORD FOR SHORTEST MATCH IN THIS TOURNAMENT...
THIS TEAM IS GOOD!!
BUT THERE'S ANOTHER PLAYER WHO INTRIGUES ME, TOO...

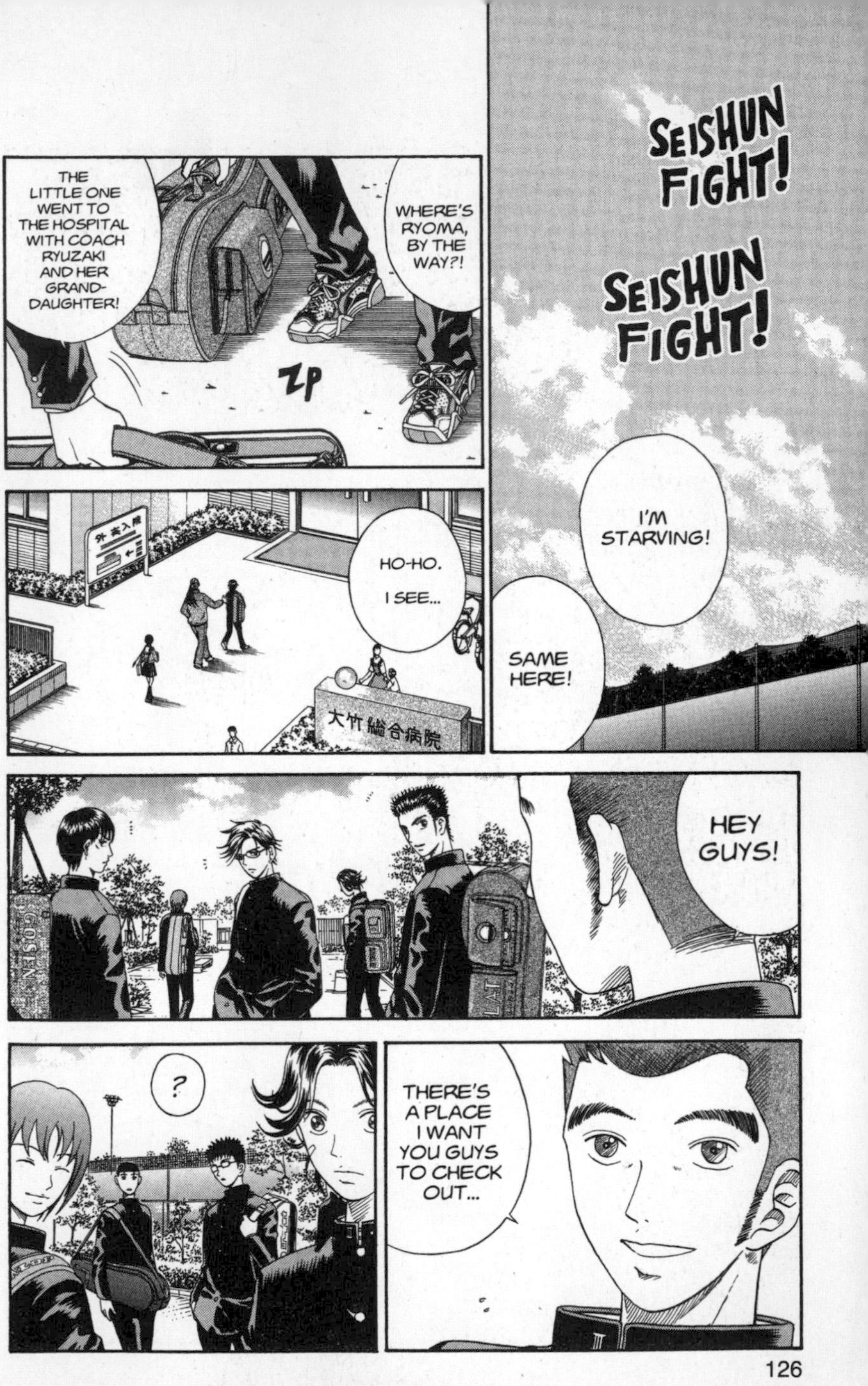
SEISHUN FIGHT!
SEISHUN FIGHT!
I'M STARVING!
SAME HERE!
WHERE'S RYOMA, BY THE WAY?!
THE LITTLE ONE WENT TO THE HOSPITAL WITH COACH RYUZAKI AND HER GRAND-DAUGHTER!
ZP
HO-HO. I SEE...
大竹総合病院
HEY GUYS!
GOSEN
THERE'S A PLACE I WANT YOU GUYS TO CHECK OUT...
?

READ THIS WAY

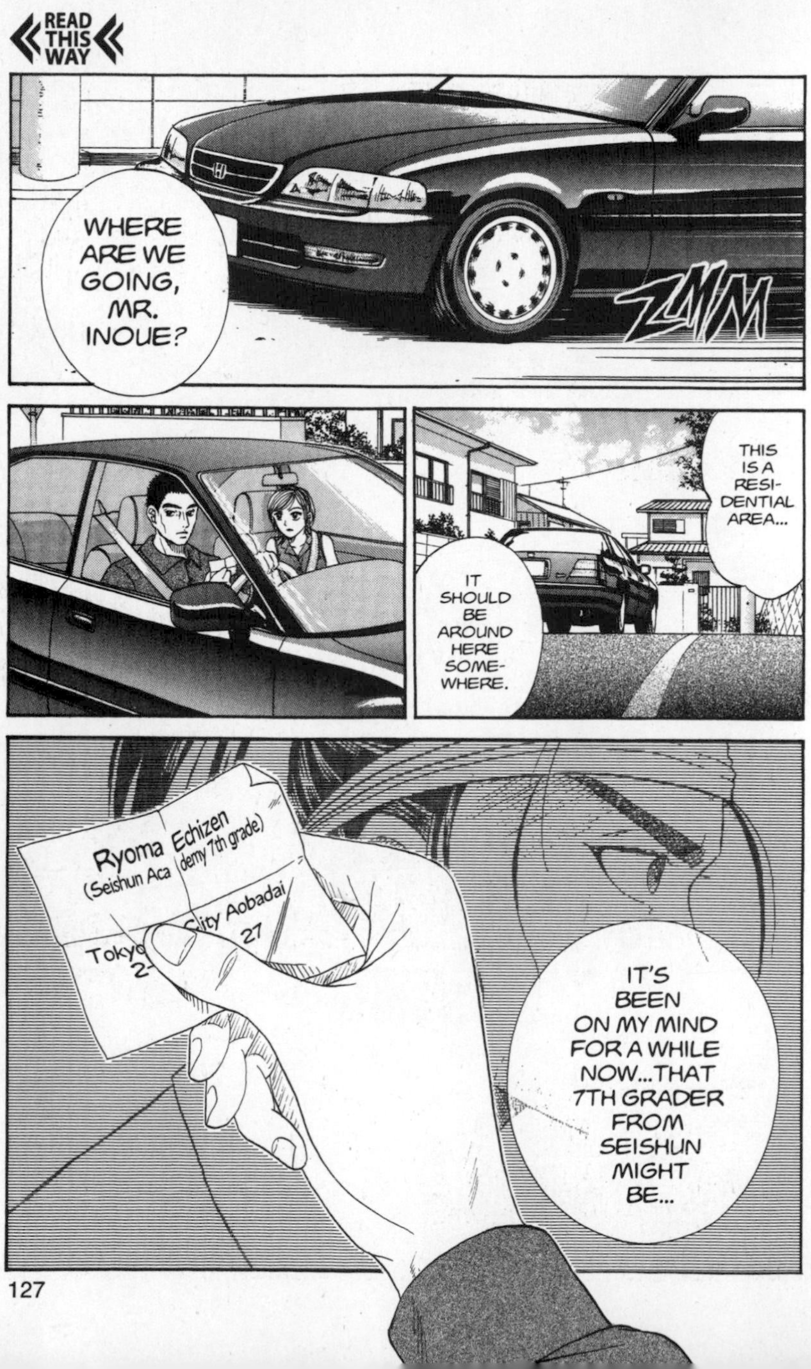
WHERE ARE WE GOING, MR. INOUE?
ZMM
THIS IS A RESIDENTIAL AREA...
IT SHOULD BE AROUND HERE SOMEWHERE.
Ryoma Echizen
(Seishun Aca demy 7th grade)
Tokyo City Aobadai
2- 27
IT'S BEEN ON MY MIND FOR A WHILE NOW...THAT 7TH GRADER FROM SEISHUN MIGHT BE...

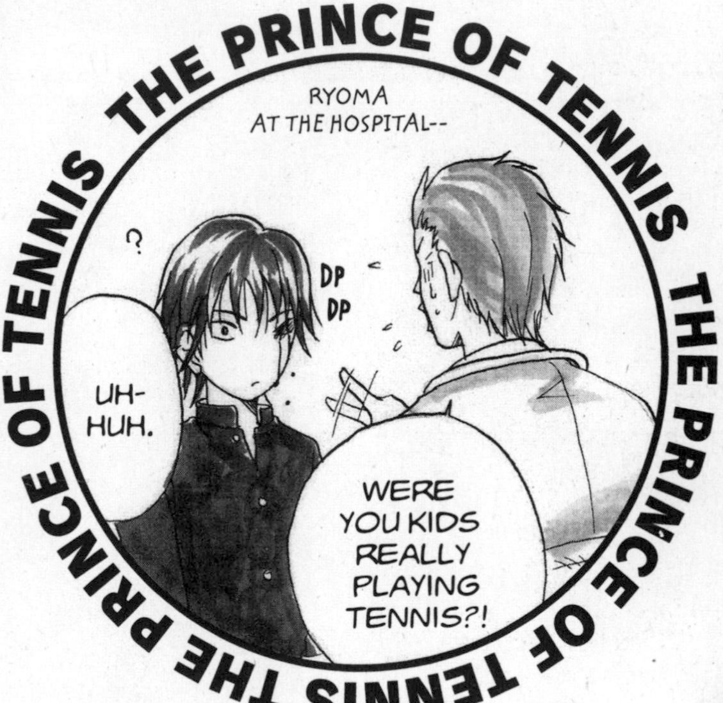
THE PRINCE OF TENNIS THE PRINCE OF TENNIS THE PRINCE OF TENNIS
RYOMA AT THE HOSPITAL--
WERE YOU KIDS REALLY PLAYING TENNIS?!
DP DP
UH-HUH.
?

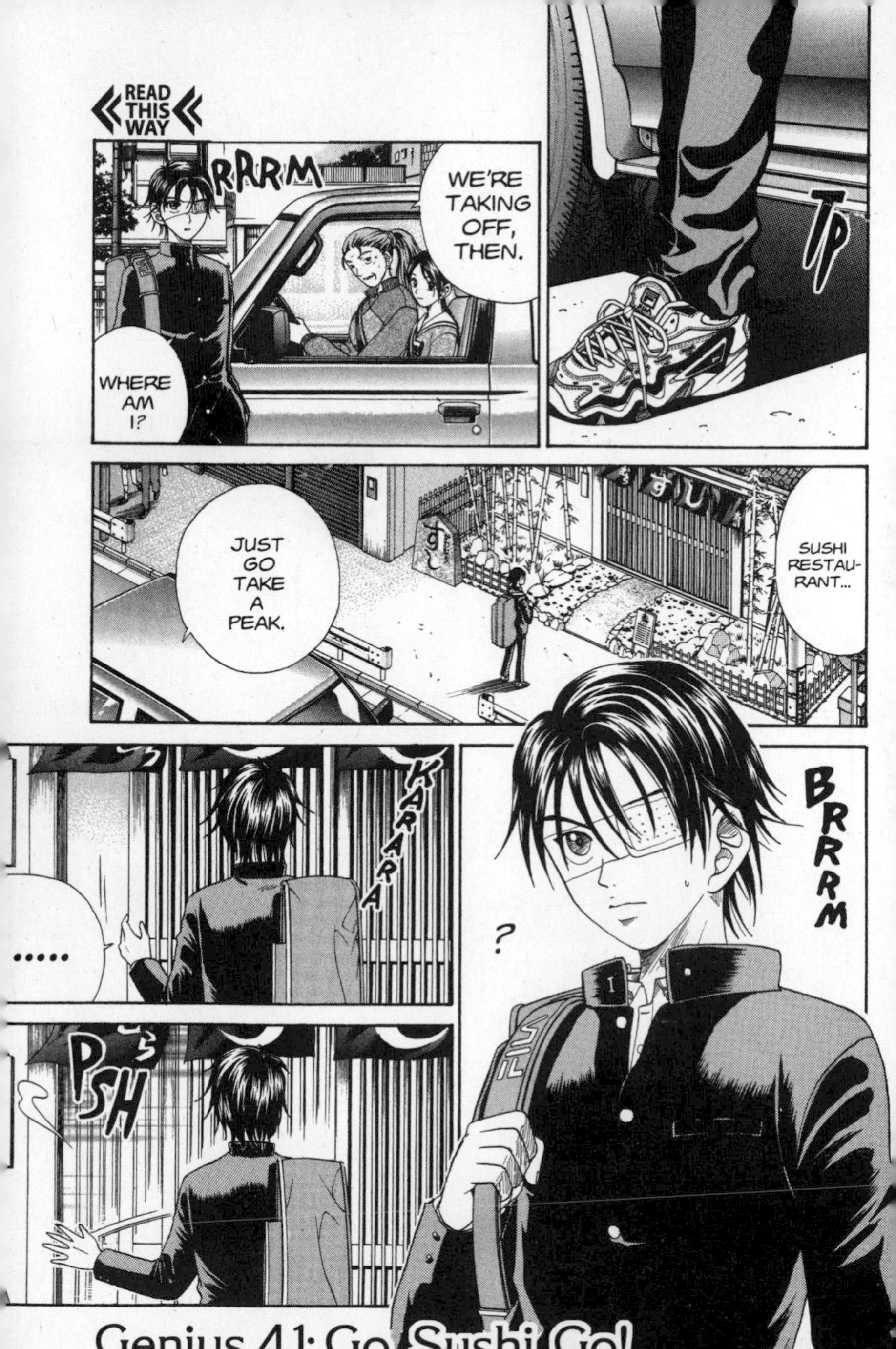
READ THIS WAY
TP
RRRM
WE'RE TAKING OFF, THEN.
WHERE AM I?
SUSHI RESTAURANT...
JUST GO TAKE A PEAK.
BRRRM
?
KARARA
.....
PSH

Genius 41: Go, Sushi, Go!

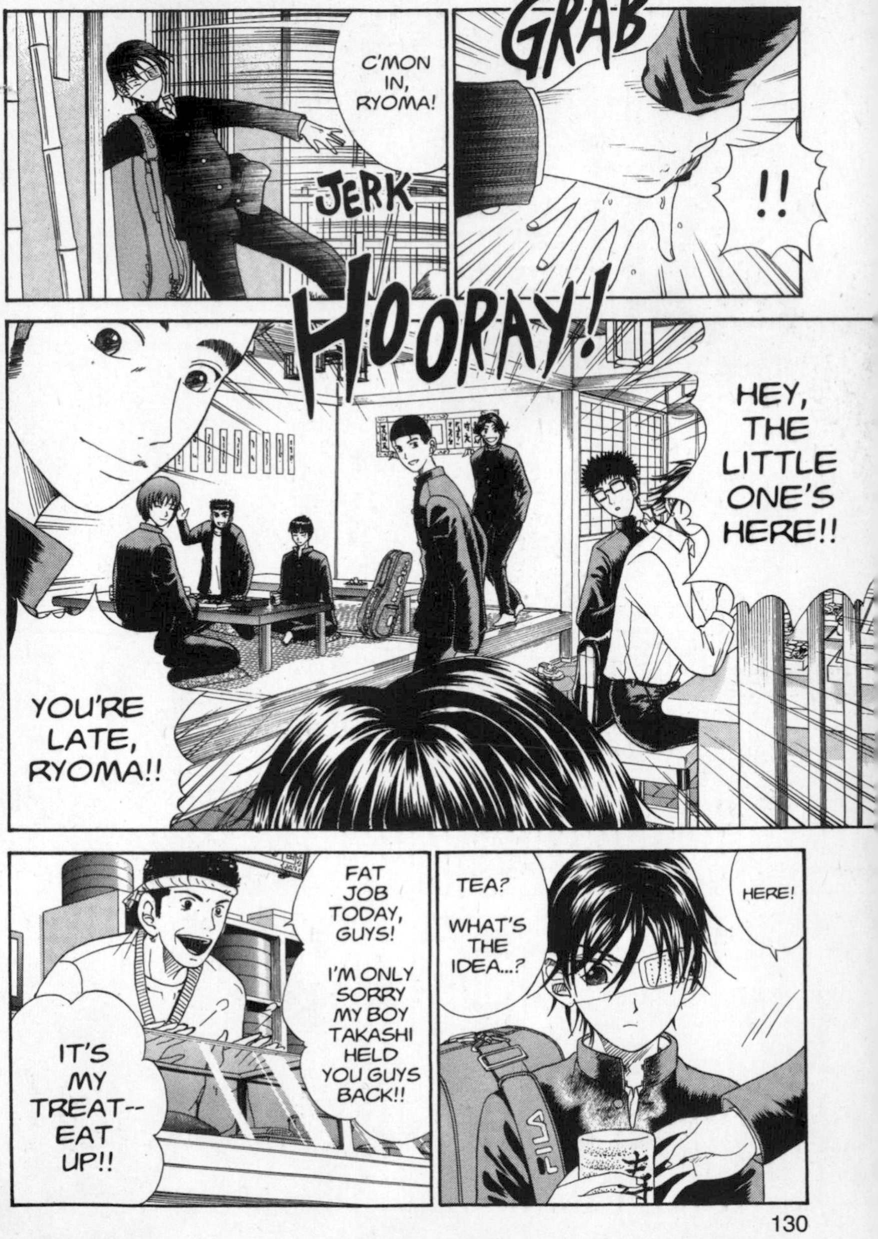
GRAB
!!
C'MON IN, RYOMA!
JERK
HOORAY!
HEY, THE LITTLE ONE'S HERE!!
YOU'RE LATE, RYOMA!!
HERE!
TEA? WHAT'S THE IDEA...?
FAT JOB TODAY, GUYS! I'M ONLY SORRY MY BOY TAKASHI HELD YOU GUYS BACK!!
IT'S MY TREAT--EAT UP!!

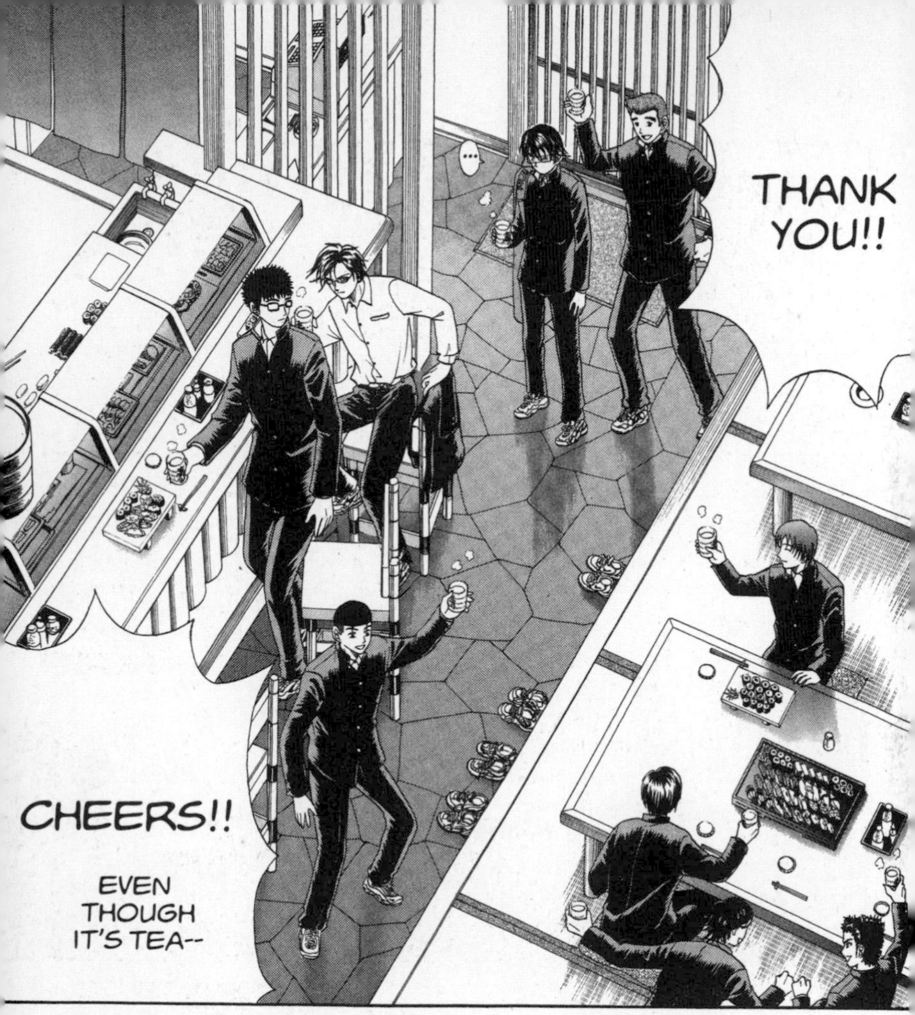
THANK YOU!!
...
CHEERS!!
EVEN THOUGH IT'S TEA--

Genius 41:

Go, Sushi, Go!

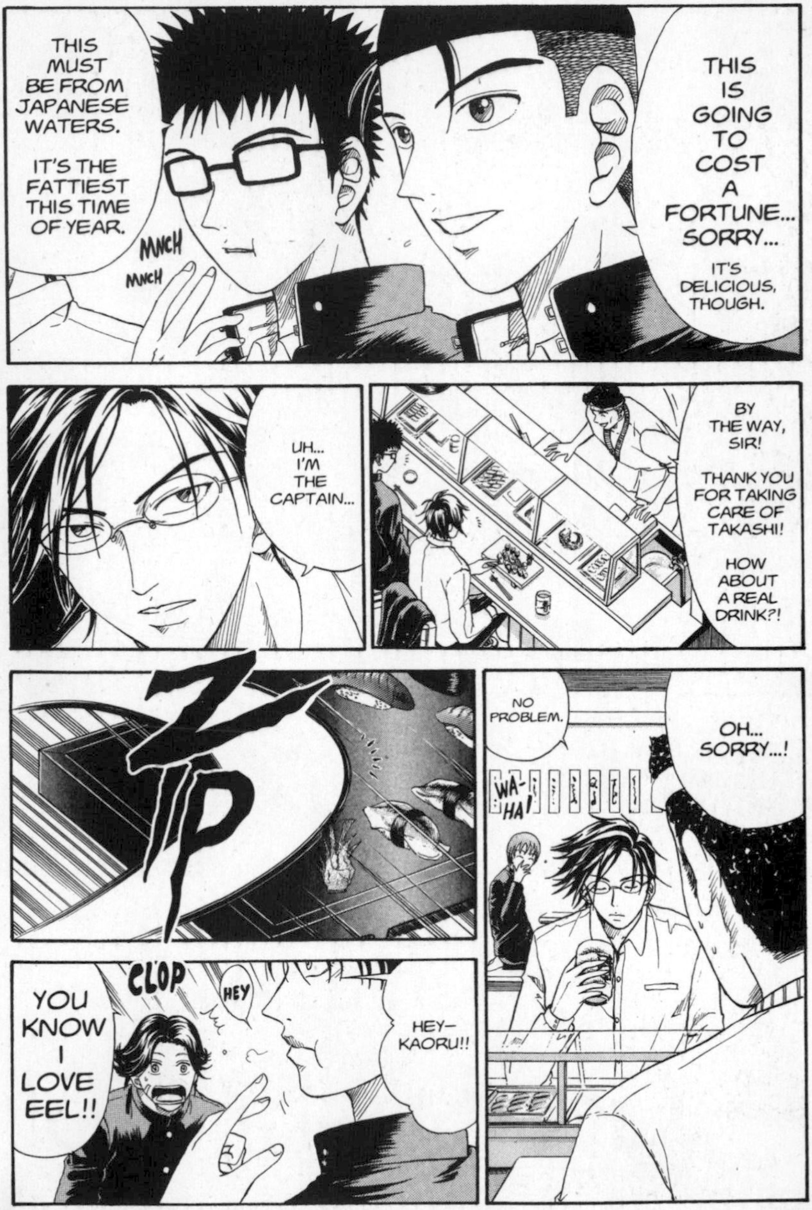
THIS IS GOING TO COST A FORTUNE... SORRY...
IT'S DELICIOUS, THOUGH.
THIS MUST BE FROM JAPANESE WATERS.
IT'S THE FATTIEST THIS TIME OF YEAR.
MNCH
MNCH
BY THE WAY, SIR!
THANK YOU FOR TAKING CARE OF TAKASHI!
HOW ABOUT A REAL DRINK?!
UH... I'M THE CAPTAIN...
OH... SORRY...!
NO PROBLEM.
WA-HA
ZIP
HEY-KAORU!!
HEY
CLOP
YOU KNOW I LOVE EEL!!

READ THIS WAY

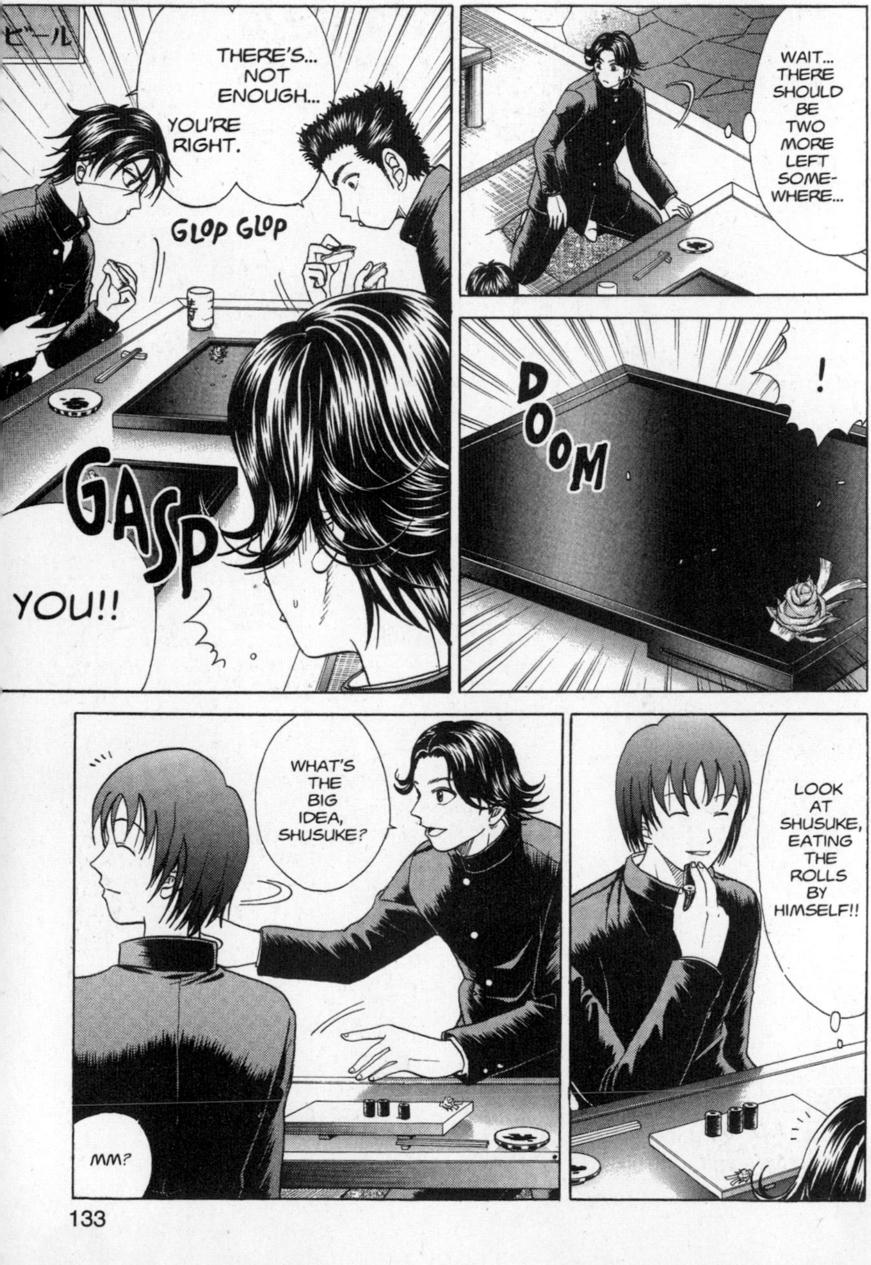

WAIT... THERE SHOULD BE TWO MORE LEFT SOME-WHERE...
!
DOOM
ビール
THERE'S... NOT ENOUGH...
YOU'RE RIGHT.
GLOP GLOP
GASP
YOU!!
LOOK AT SHUSUKE, EATING THE ROLLS BY HIMSELF!!
WHAT'S THE BIG IDEA, SHUSUKE?
MM?

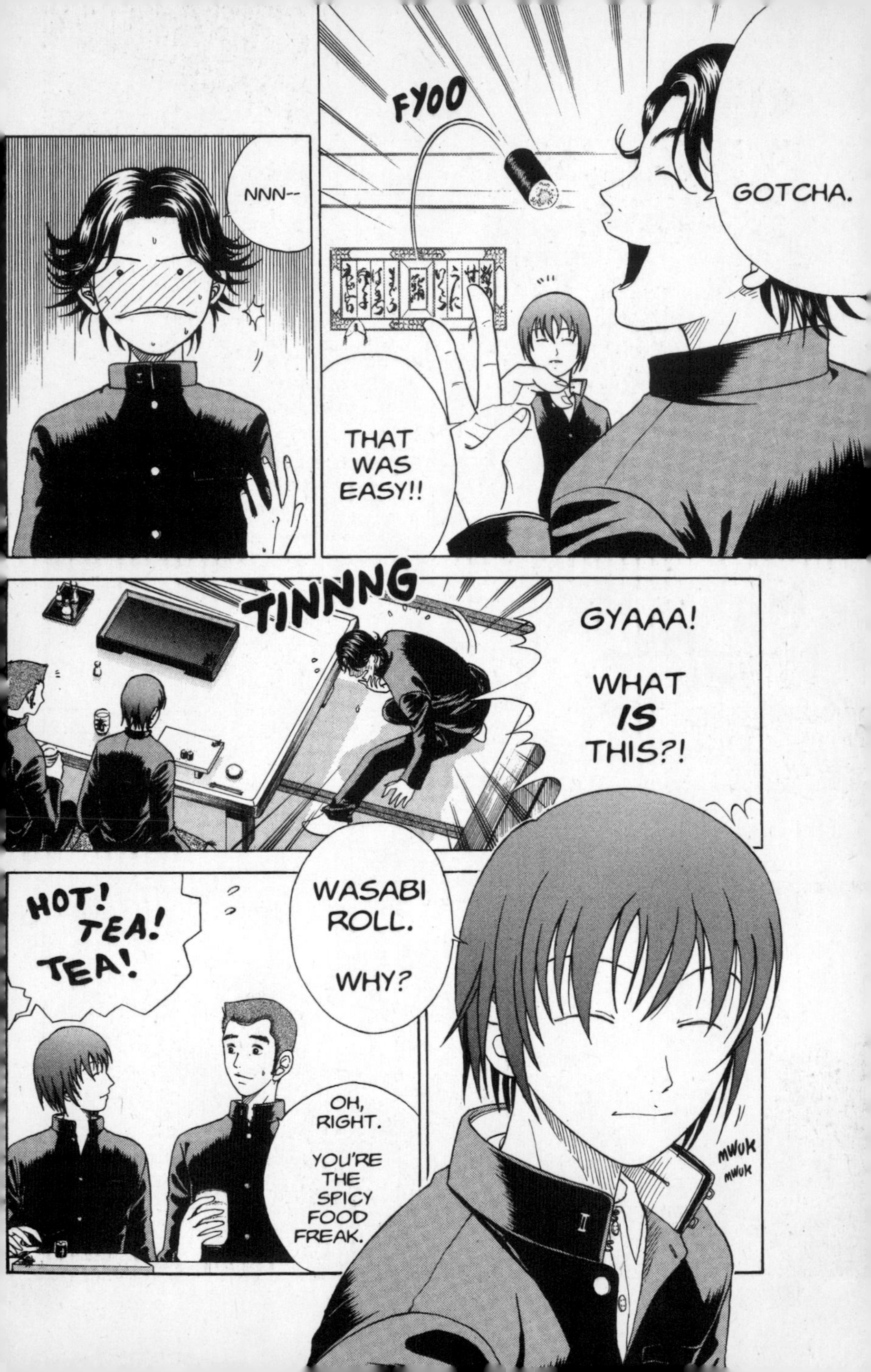
GOTCHA.
FYOO
THAT WAS EASY!!
NNN--
TINNNG
GYAAA!
WHAT *IS* THIS?!
WASABI ROLL.
WHY?
MWUK MWUK
HOT! TEA! TEA!
OH, RIGHT.
YOU'RE THE SPICY FOOD FREAK.

READ THIS WAY

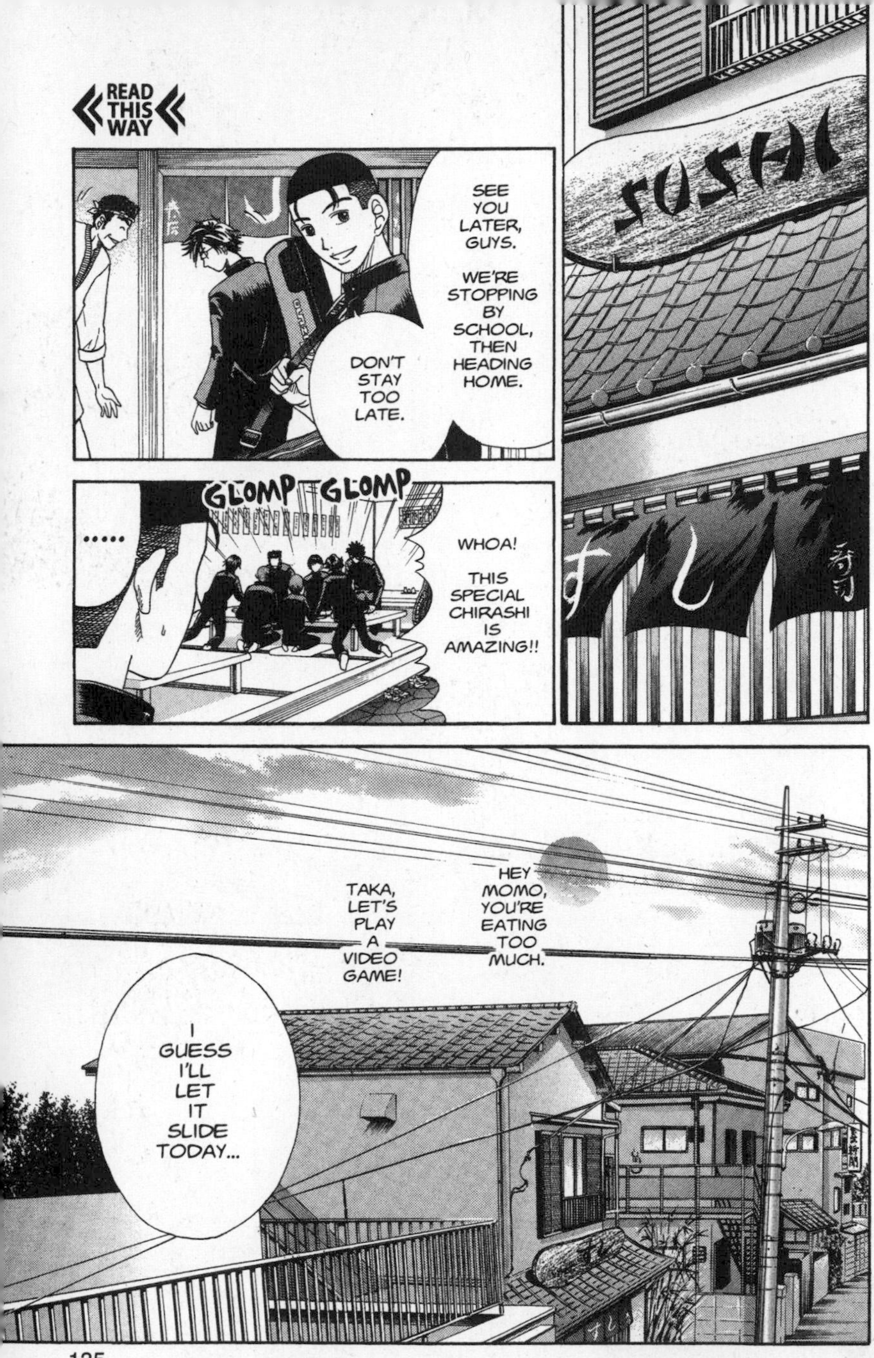
SUSHI
すし
SEE YOU LATER, GUYS. WE'RE STOPPING BY SCHOOL, THEN HEADING HOME.
DON'T STAY TOO LATE.
WHOA! THIS SPECIAL CHIRASHI IS AMAZING!!
GLOMP GLOMP
.....
HEY MOMO, YOU'RE EATING TOO MUCH.
TAKA, LET'S PLAY A VIDEO GAME!
I GUESS I'LL LET IT SLIDE TODAY...

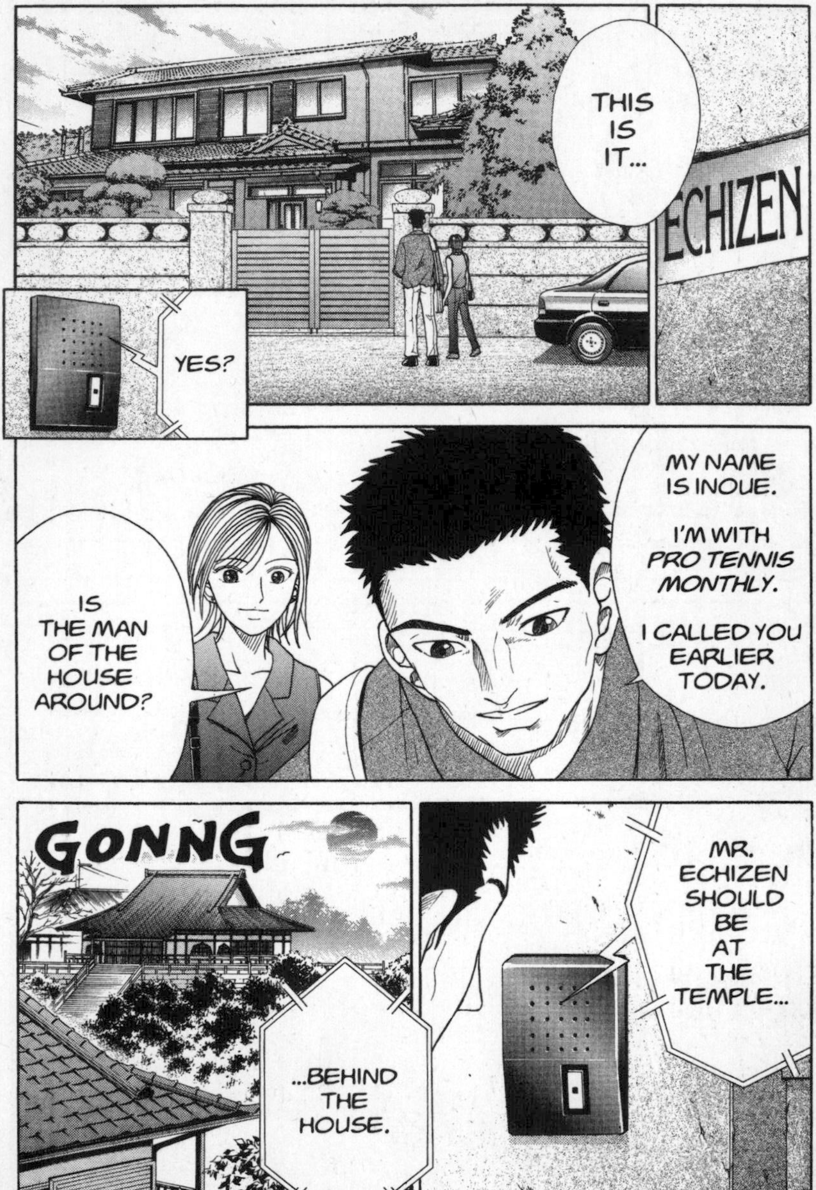
THIS IS IT...
ECHIZEN
YES?
MY NAME IS INOUE.
I'M WITH *PRO TENNIS MONTHLY.*
I CALLED YOU EARLIER TODAY.
IS THE MAN OF THE HOUSE AROUND?
MR. ECHIZEN SHOULD BE AT THE TEMPLE...
GONNG
...BEHIND THE HOUSE.

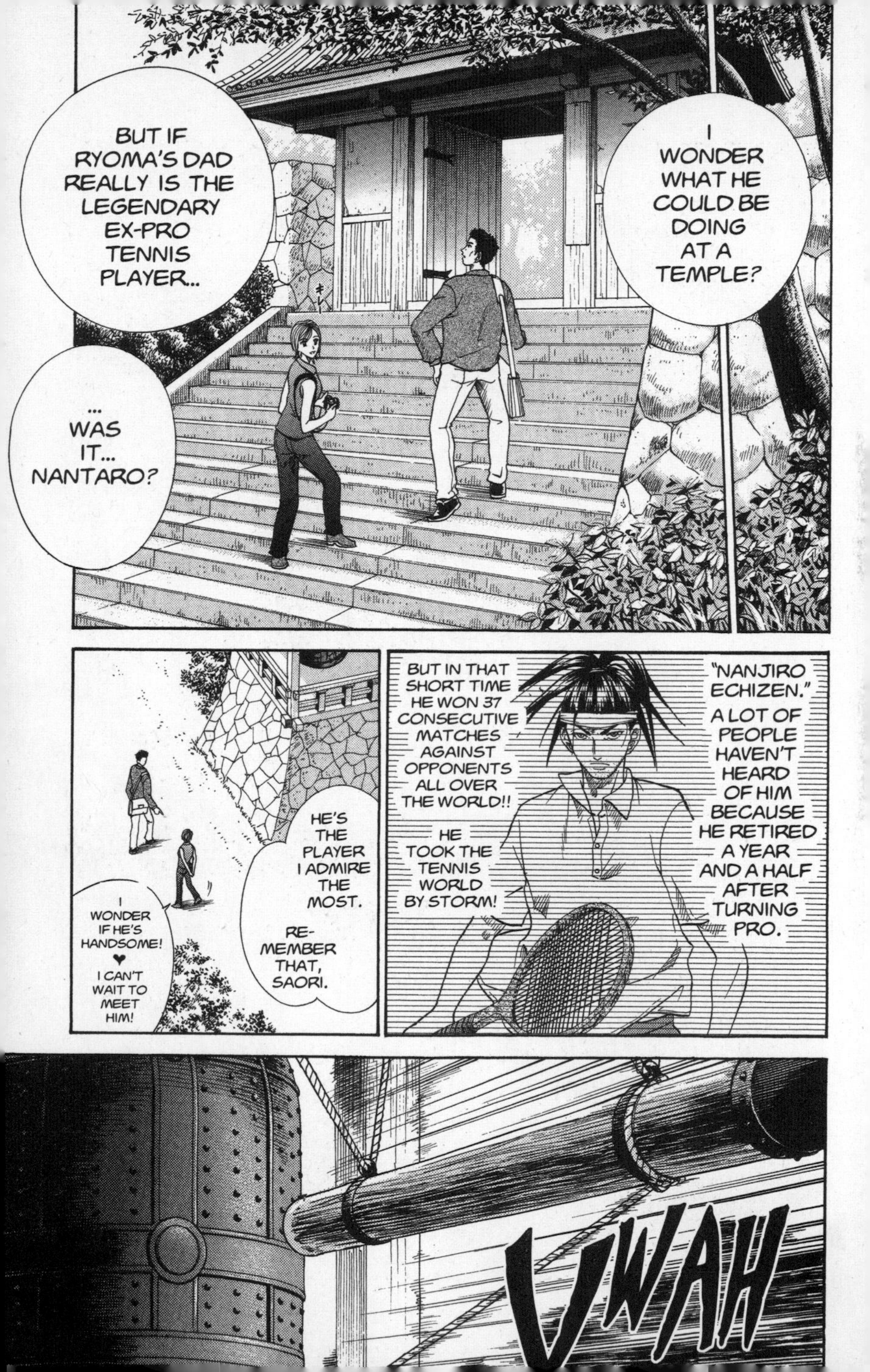
I WONDER WHAT HE COULD BE DOING AT A TEMPLE?
BUT IF RYOMA'S DAD REALLY IS THE LEGENDARY EX-PRO TENNIS PLAYER...
... WAS IT... NANTARO?
"NANJIRO ECHIZEN." A LOT OF PEOPLE HAVEN'T HEARD OF HIM BECAUSE HE RETIRED A YEAR AND A HALF AFTER TURNING PRO.
BUT IN THAT SHORT TIME HE WON 37 CONSECUTIVE MATCHES AGAINST OPPONENTS ALL OVER THE WORLD!!
HE TOOK THE TENNIS WORLD BY STORM!
HE'S THE PLAYER I ADMIRE THE MOST.
RE-MEMBER THAT, SAORI.
I WONDER IF HE'S HANDSOME! ❤ I CAN'T WAIT TO MEET HIM!
VWAH

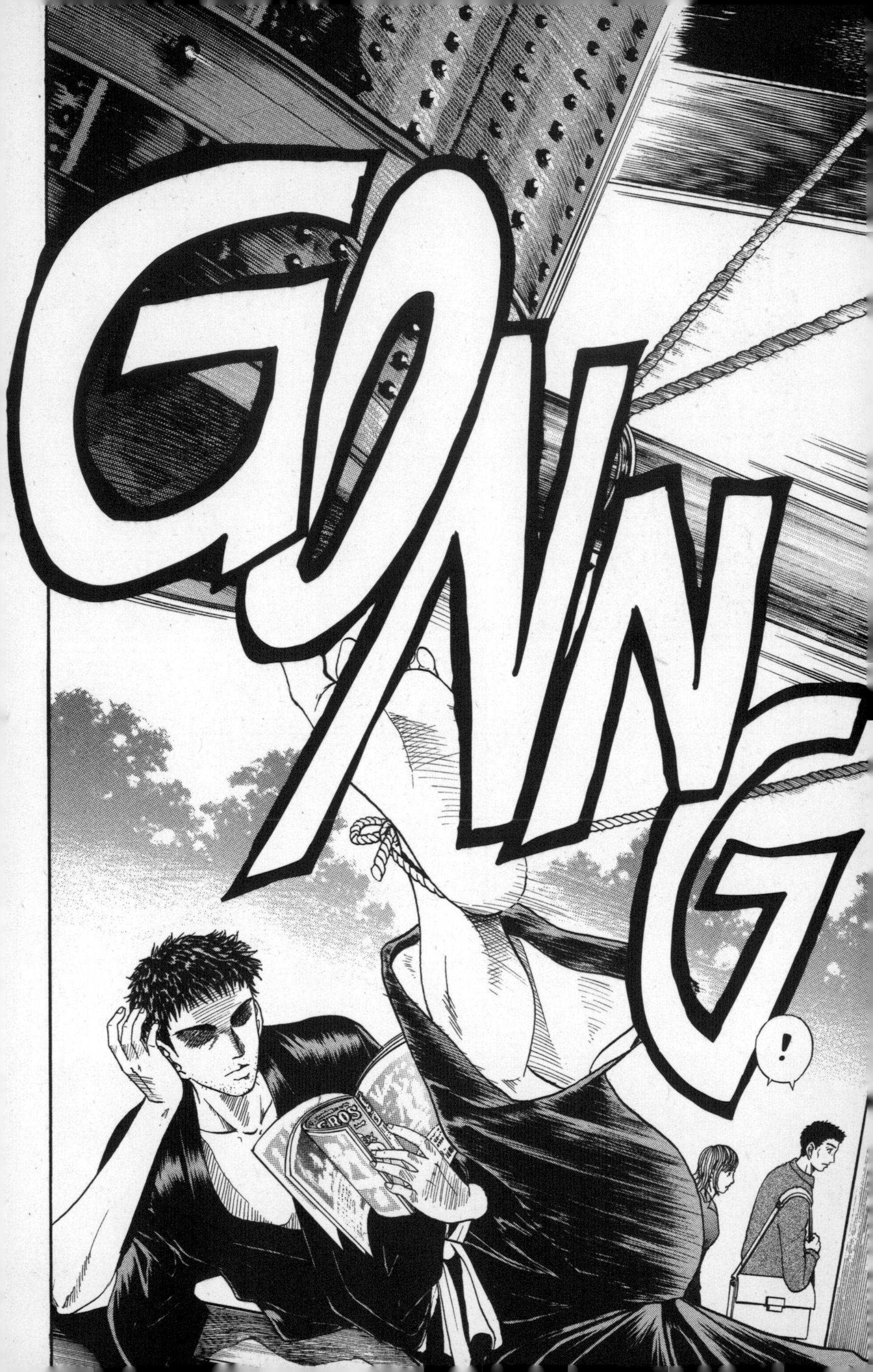
GONNG
!

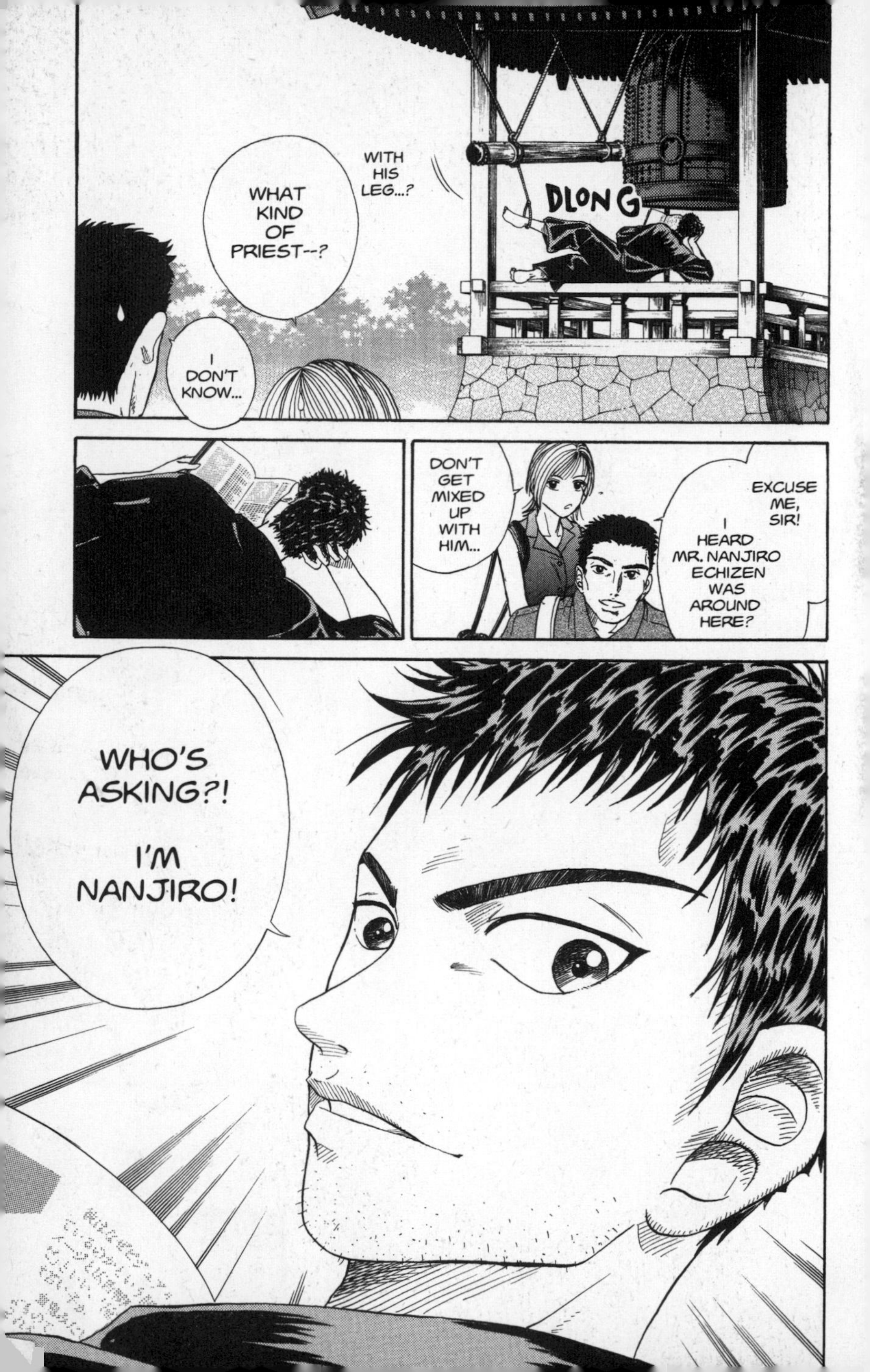
WITH HIS LEG...?
DLONG
WHAT KIND OF PRIEST--?
I DON'T KNOW...
EXCUSE ME, SIR!
I HEARD MR. NANJIRO ECHIZEN WAS AROUND HERE?
DON'T GET MIXED UP WITH HIM...
WHO'S ASKING?!
I'M NANJIRO!

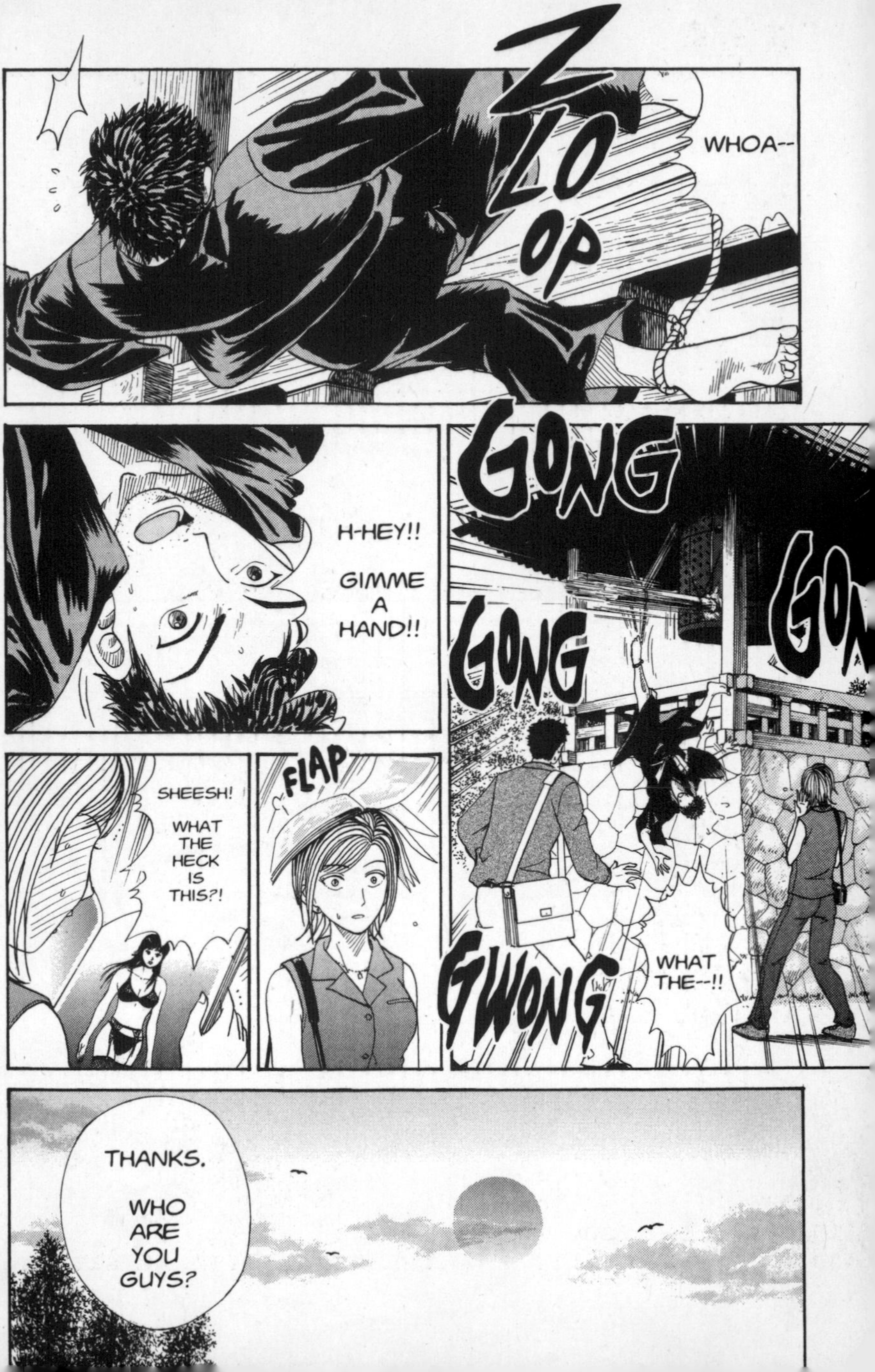
ZLOOP
WHOA--
GONG
GONG
GON
GWONG
WHAT THE--!!
H-HEY!! GIMME A HAND!!
FLAP
SHEESH! WHAT THE HECK IS THIS?!
THANKS. WHO ARE YOU GUYS?

READ THIS WAY

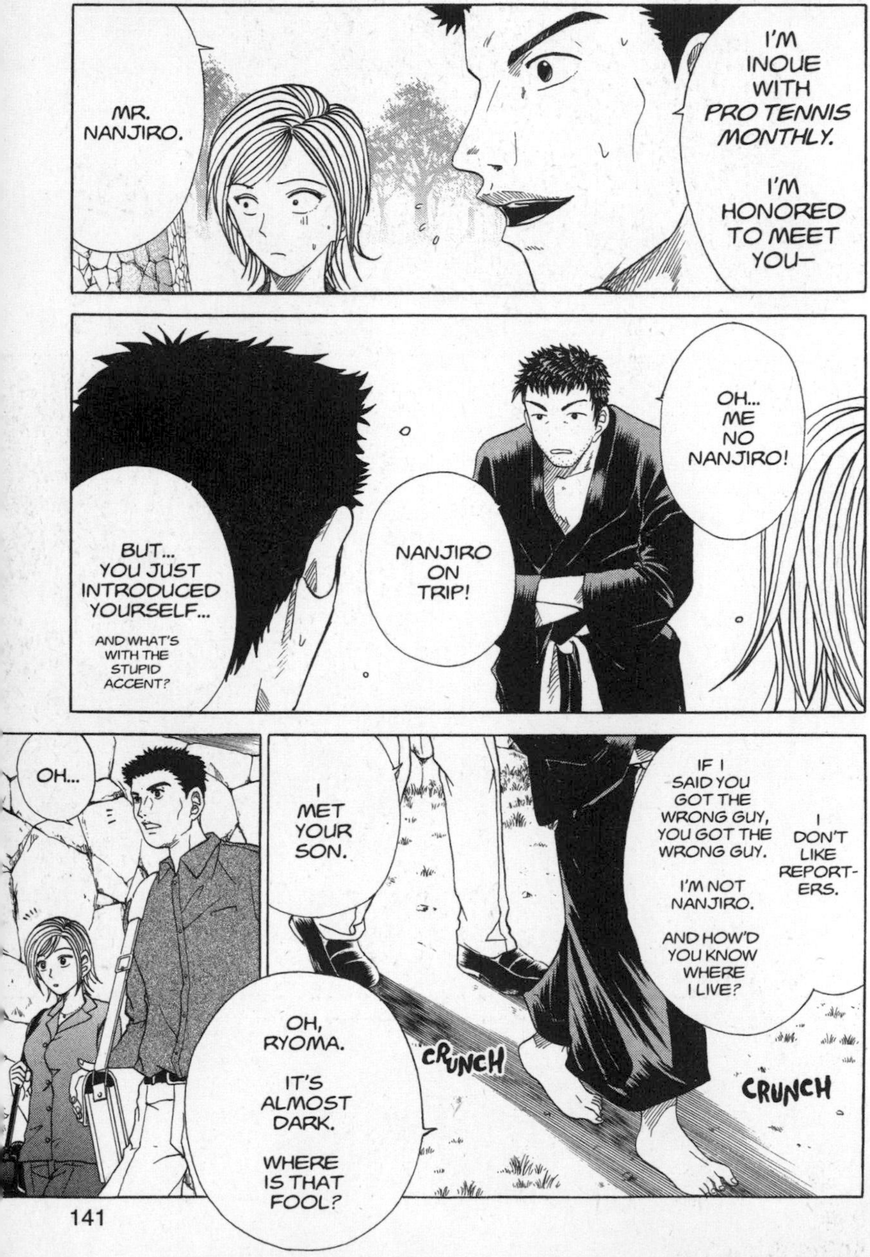
I'M INOUE WITH PRO TENNIS MONTHLY.
I'M HONORED TO MEET YOU—
MR. NANJIRO.
OH... ME NO NANJIRO!
NANJIRO ON TRIP!
BUT... YOU JUST INTRODUCED YOURSELF...
AND WHAT'S WITH THE STUPID ACCENT?
I DON'T LIKE REPORTERS.
IF I SAID YOU GOT THE WRONG GUY, YOU GOT THE WRONG GUY.
I'M NOT NANJIRO.
AND HOW'D YOU KNOW WHERE I LIVE?
CRUNCH
CRUNCH
I MET YOUR SON.
OH...
OH, RYOMA.
IT'S ALMOST DARK.
WHERE IS THAT FOOL?

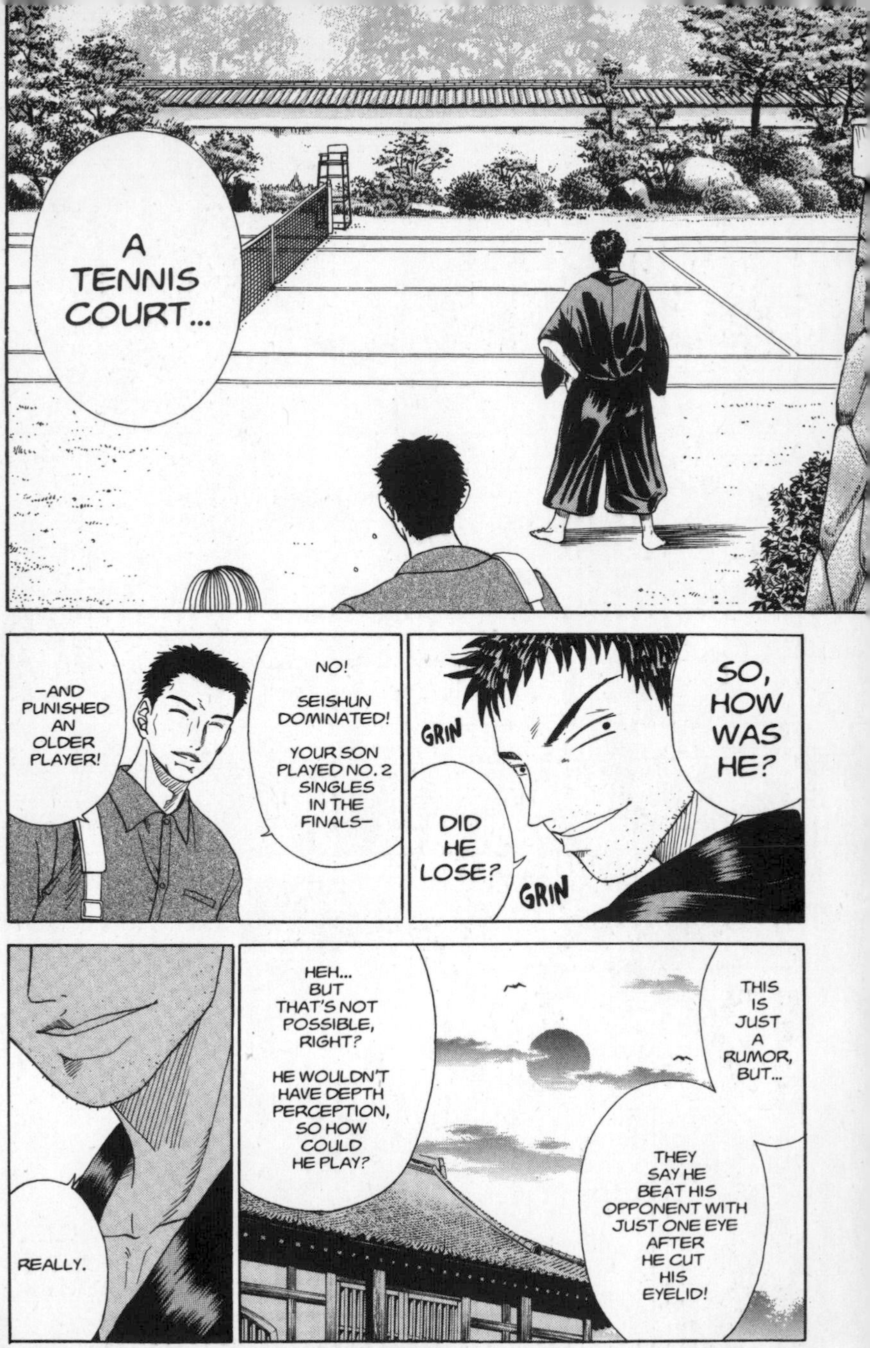
A TENNIS COURT...
SO, HOW WAS HE?
GRIN
DID HE LOSE?
GRIN
NO! SEISHUN DOMINATED! YOUR SON PLAYED NO. 2 SINGLES IN THE FINALS–
–AND PUNISHED AN OLDER PLAYER!
THIS IS JUST A RUMOR, BUT...
THEY SAY HE BEAT HIS OPPONENT WITH JUST ONE EYE AFTER HE CUT HIS EYELID!
HEH... BUT THAT'S NOT POSSIBLE, RIGHT? HE WOULDN'T HAVE DEPTH PERCEPTION, SO HOW COULD HE PLAY?
REALLY.

READ THIS WAY

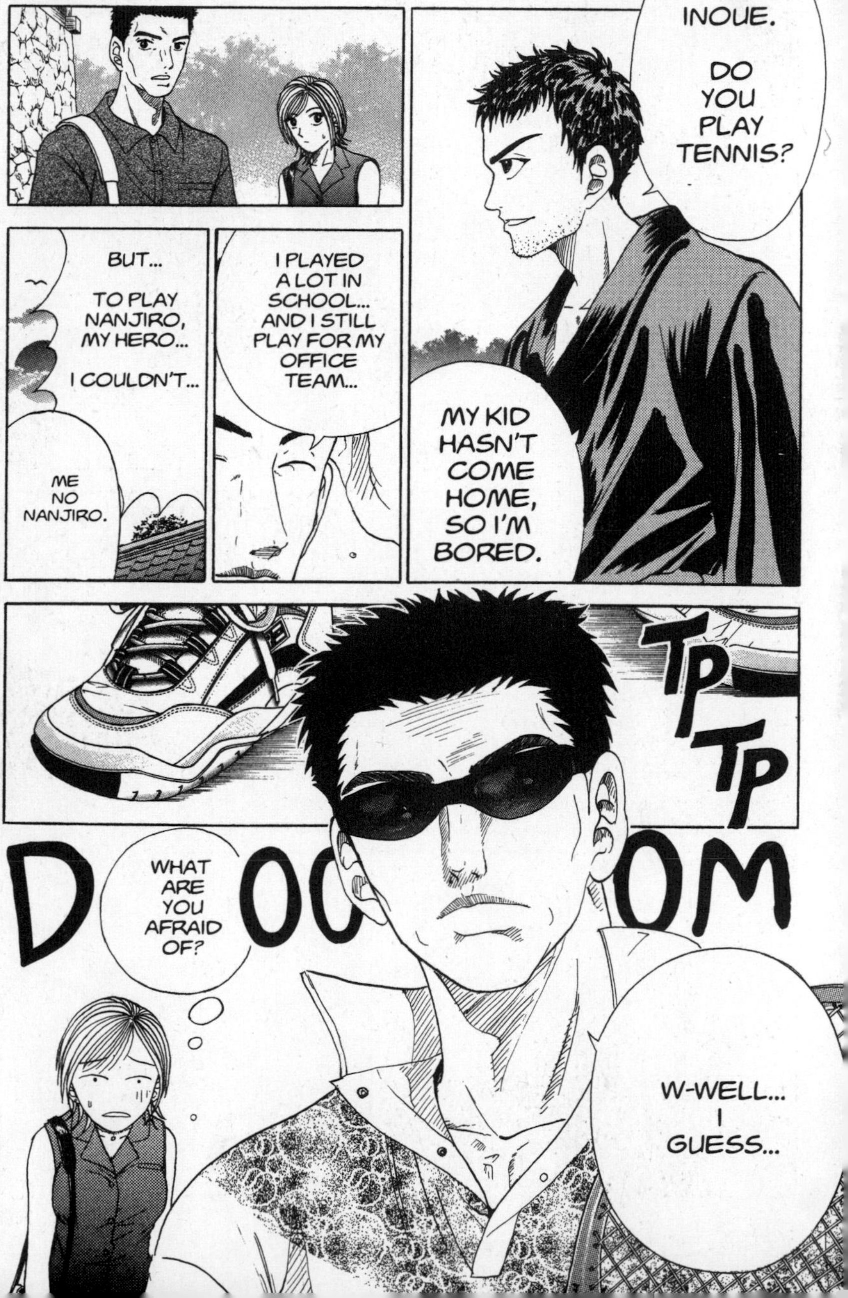
INOUE.
DO YOU PLAY TENNIS?
MY KID HASN'T COME HOME, SO I'M BORED.
I PLAYED A LOT IN SCHOOL... AND I STILL PLAY FOR MY OFFICE TEAM...
BUT...
TO PLAY NANJIRO, MY HERO...
I COULDN'T...
ME NO NANJIRO.
TP TP
DOOOOM
WHAT ARE YOU AFRAID OF?
W-WELL... I GUESS...

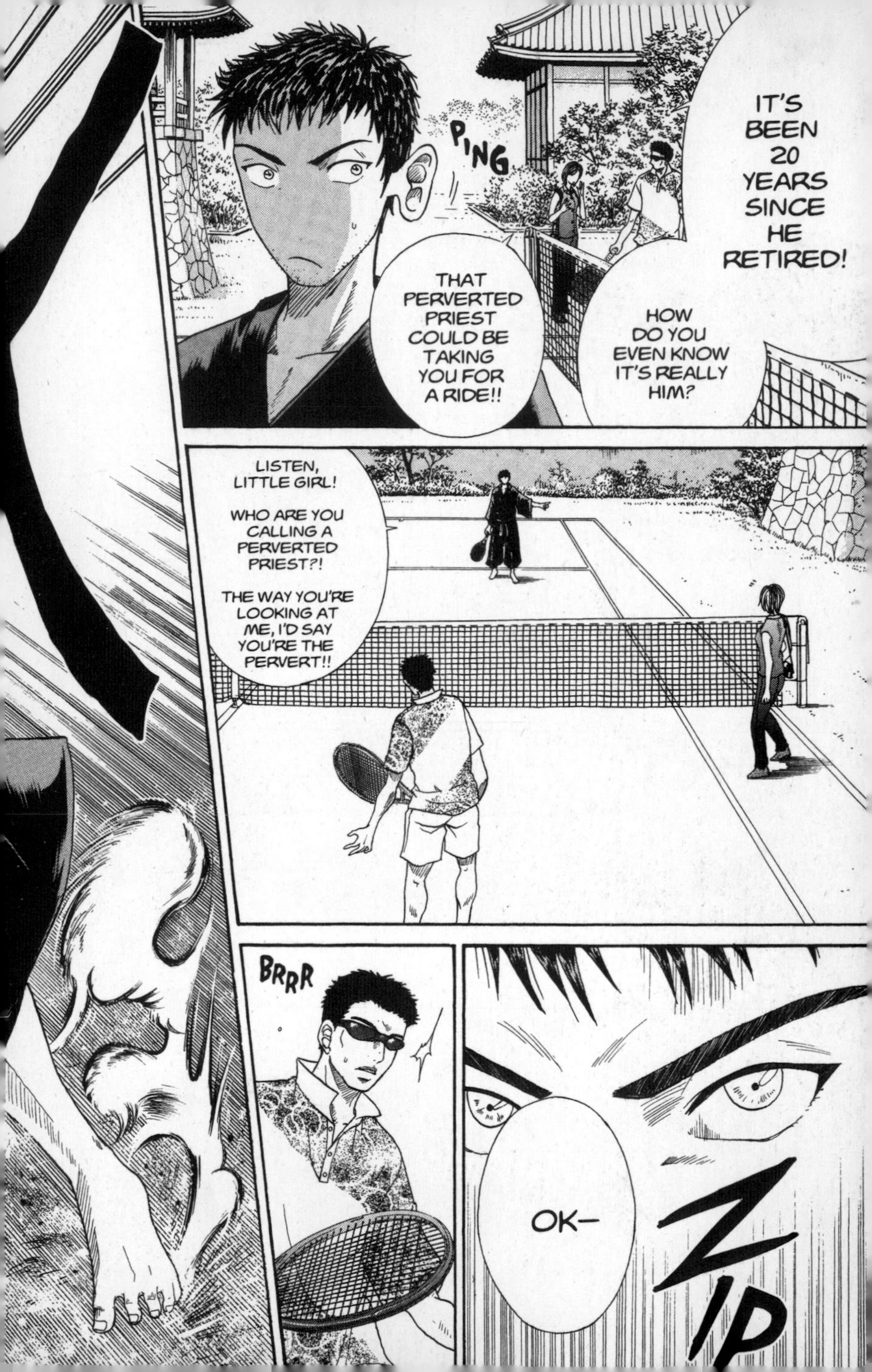
IT'S BEEN 20 YEARS SINCE HE RETIRED!
HOW DO YOU EVEN KNOW IT'S REALLY HIM?
PING
THAT PERVERTED PRIEST COULD BE TAKING YOU FOR A RIDE!!
LISTEN, LITTLE GIRL!
WHO ARE YOU CALLING A PERVERTED PRIEST?!
THE WAY YOU'RE LOOKING AT ME, I'D SAY YOU'RE THE PERVERT!!
OK-
ZIP
BRRR

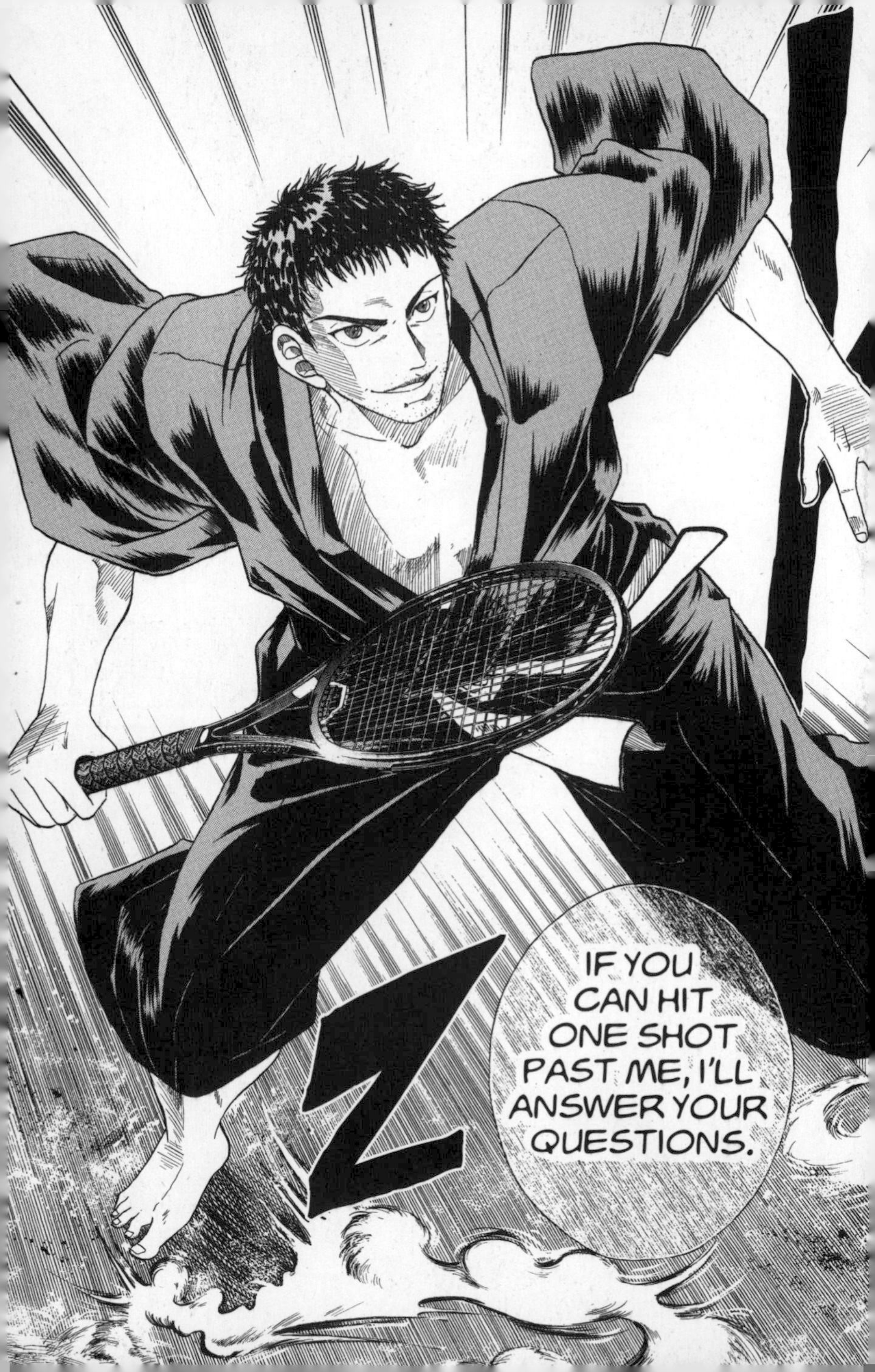
IF YOU CAN HIT ONE SHOT PAST ME, I'LL ANSWER YOUR QUESTIONS.

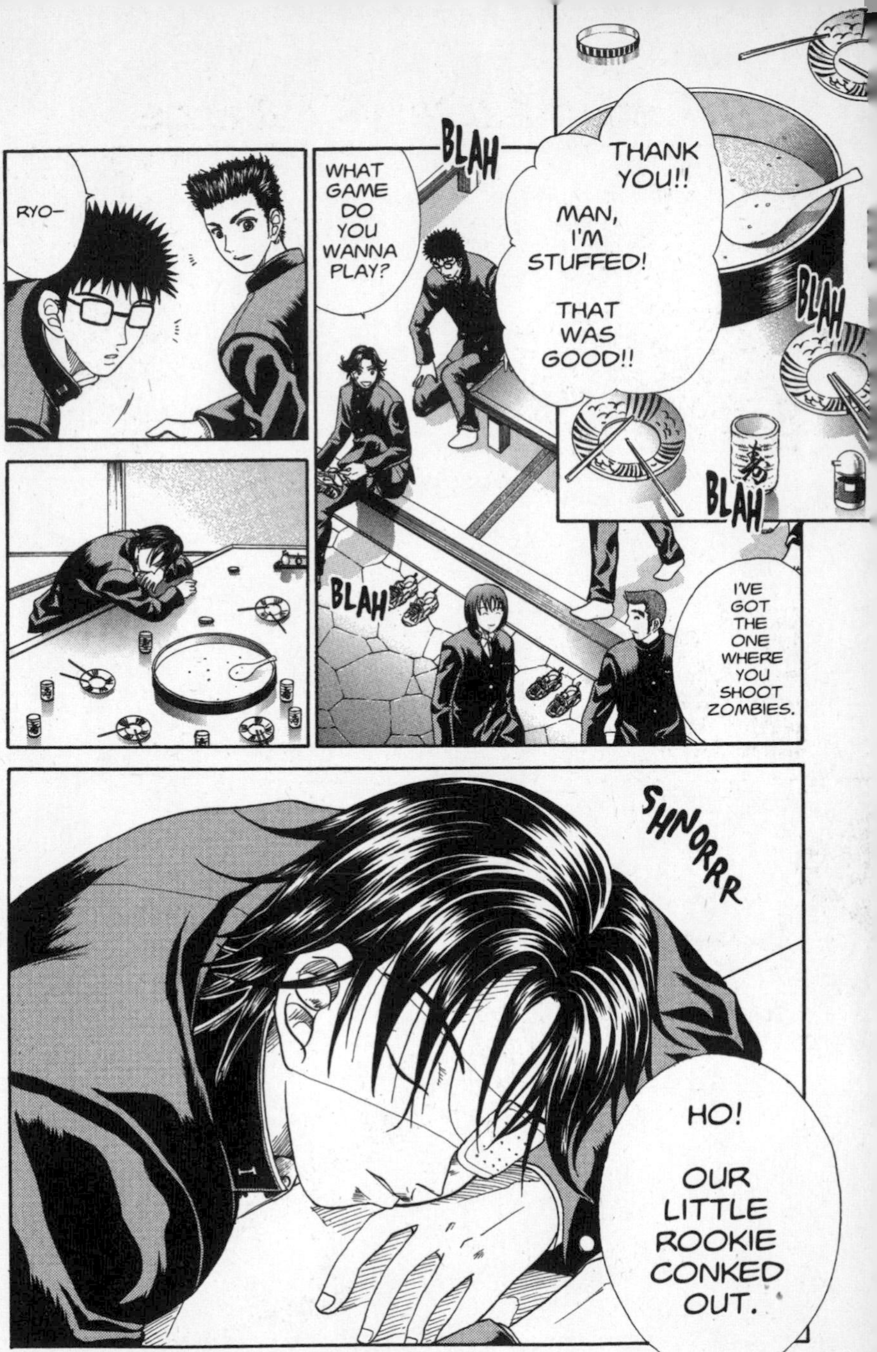
BLAH
THANK YOU!!
MAN, I'M STUFFED!
THAT WAS GOOD!!
BLAH
BLAH
WHAT GAME DO YOU WANNA PLAY?
BLAH
I'VE GOT THE ONE WHERE YOU SHOOT ZOMBIES.
RYO-
SHNORRR
HO!
OUR LITTLE ROOKIE CONKED OUT.

Genius 42: New Challenge

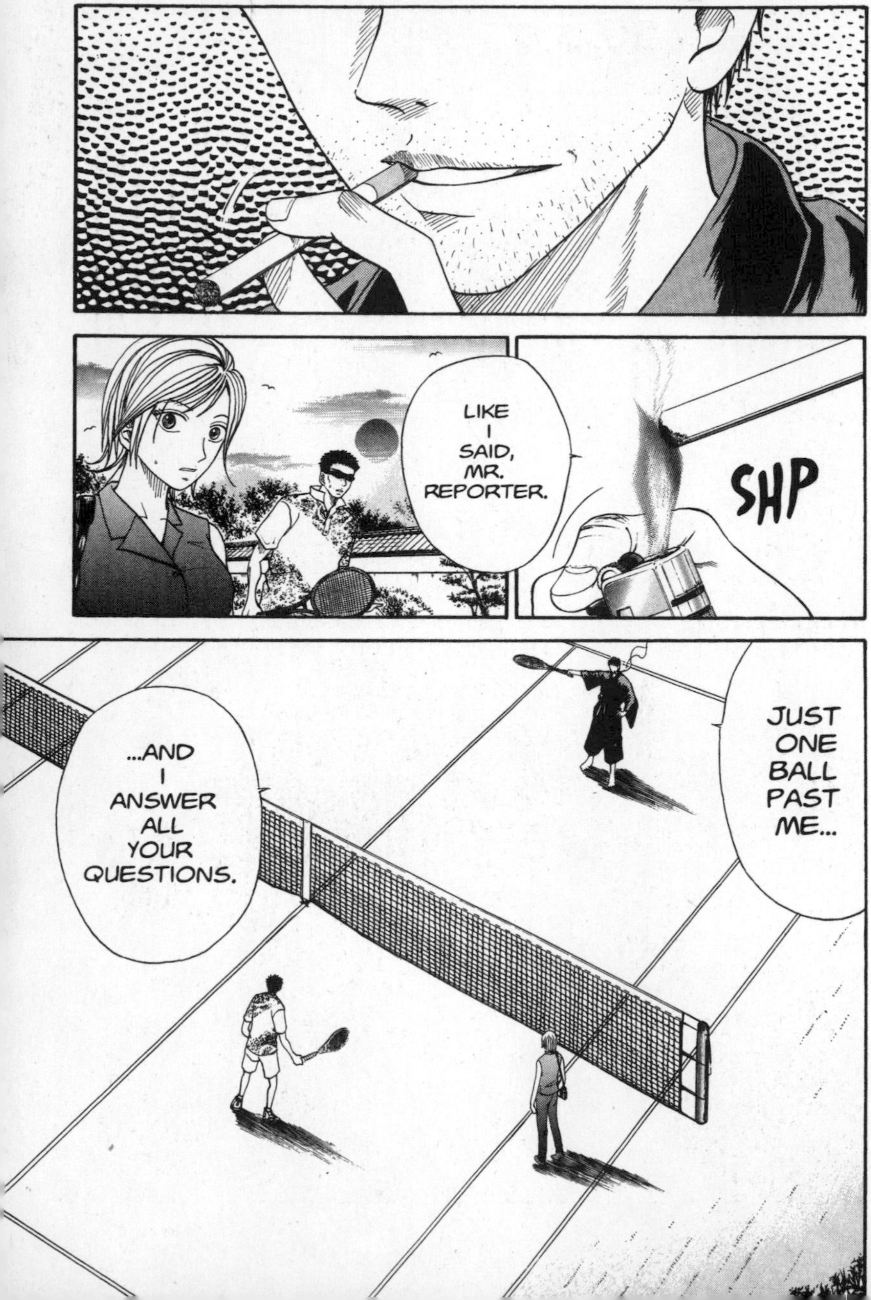
SHP
LIKE I SAID, MR. REPORTER.
JUST ONE BALL PAST ME...
...AND I ANSWER ALL YOUR QUESTIONS.

Genius 42: New Challenge

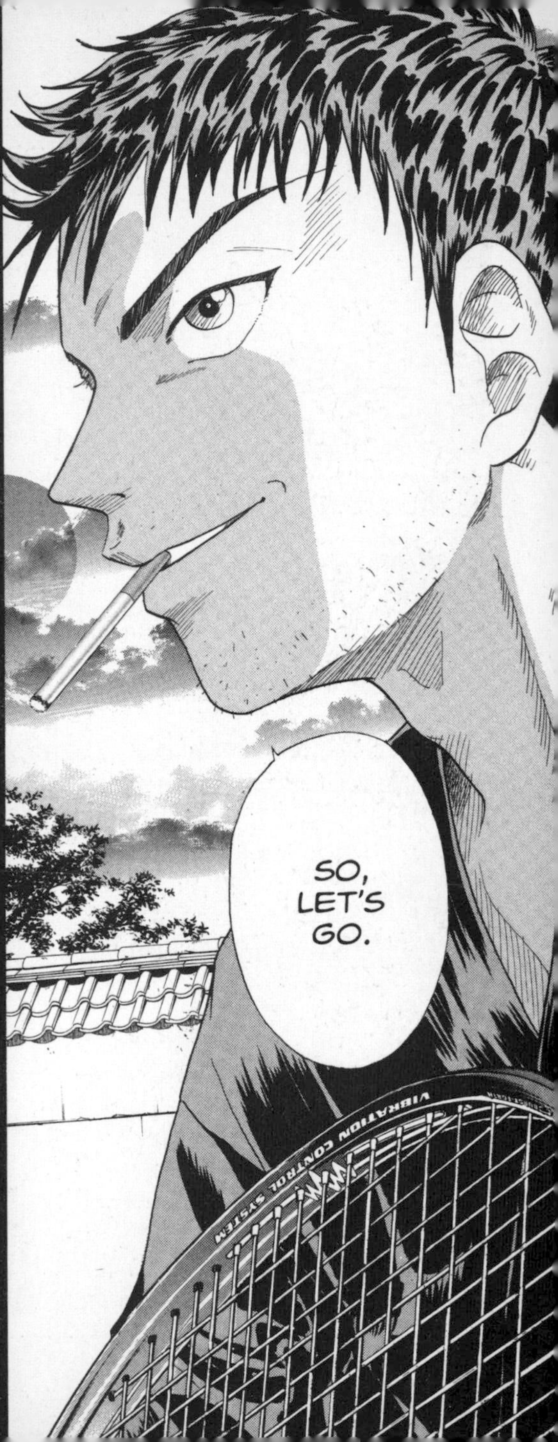
SO, LET'S GO.
VIBRATION CONTROL SYSTEM

READ THIS WAY

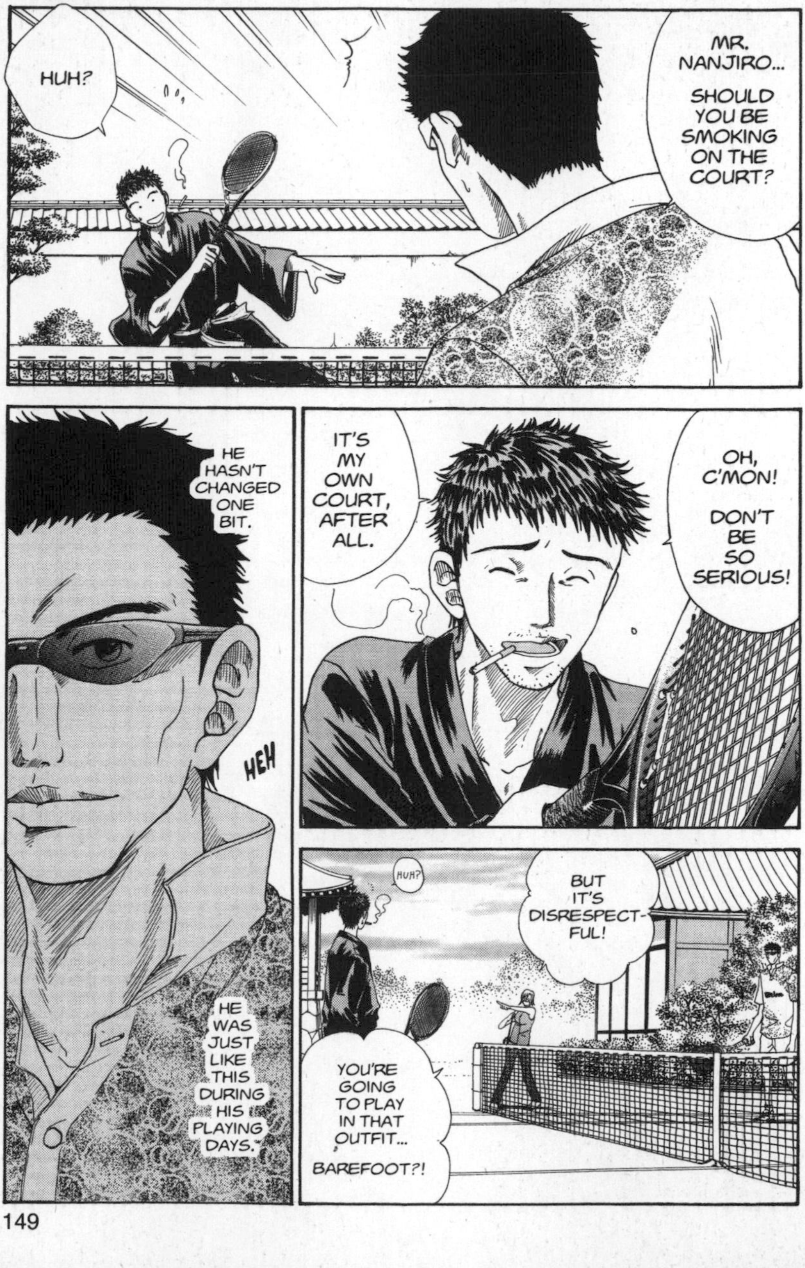

MR. NANJIRO... SHOULD YOU BE SMOKING ON THE COURT?
HUH?
OH, C'MON! DON'T BE SO SERIOUS!
IT'S MY OWN COURT, AFTER ALL.
BUT IT'S DISRESPECT-FUL!
HUH?
YOU'RE GOING TO PLAY IN THAT OUTFIT... BAREFOOT?!
HE HASN'T CHANGED ONE BIT.
HEH
HE WAS JUST LIKE THIS DURING HIS PLAYING DAYS.

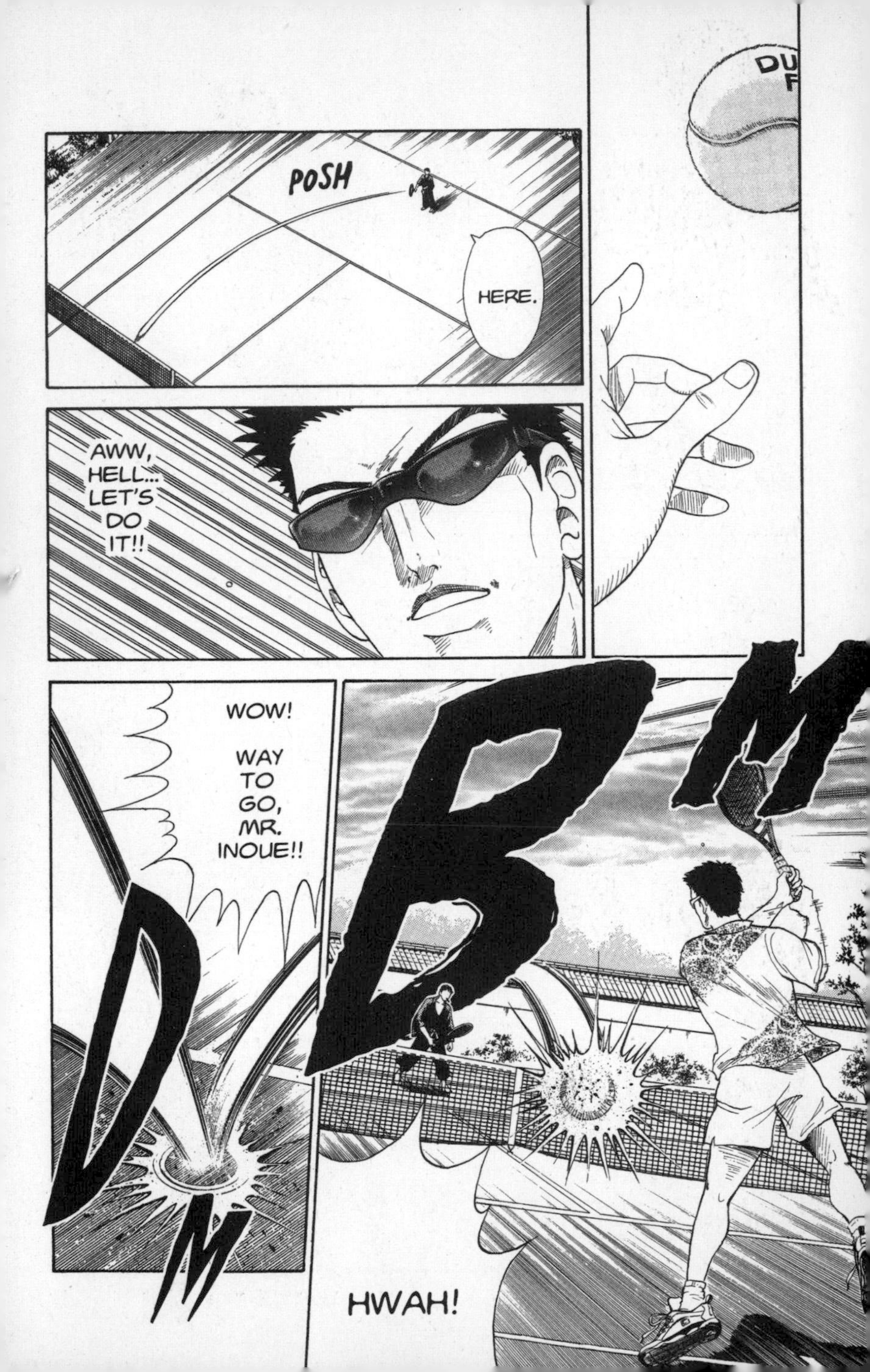
POSH
HERE.
AWW, HELL... LET'S DO IT!!
HWAH!
WOW!
WAY TO GO, MR. INOUE!!

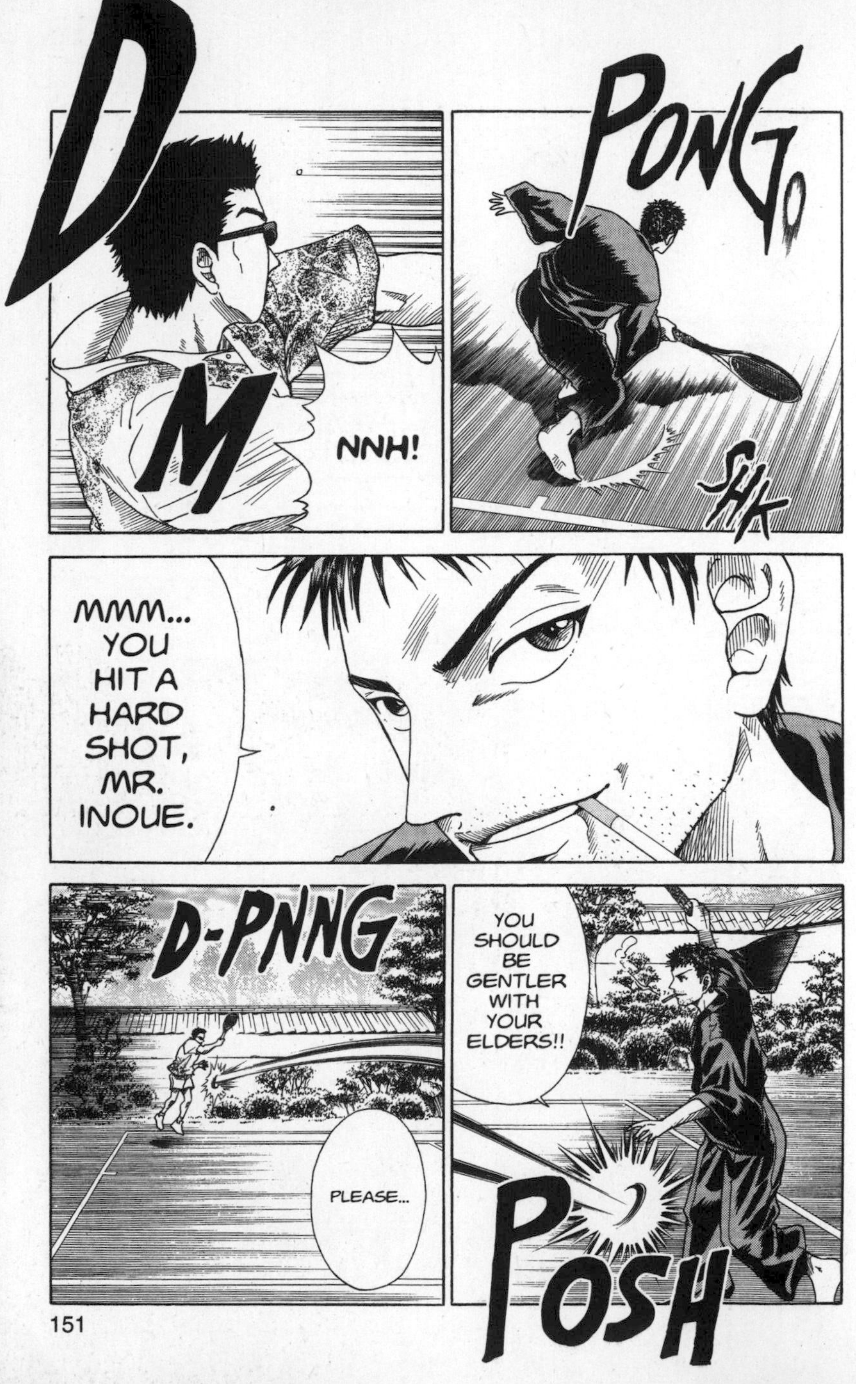
PONG
SHK
DM
NNH!
MMM... YOU HIT A HARD SHOT, MR. INOUE.
YOU SHOULD BE GENTLER WITH YOUR ELDERS!!
POSH
D-PNNG
PLEASE...

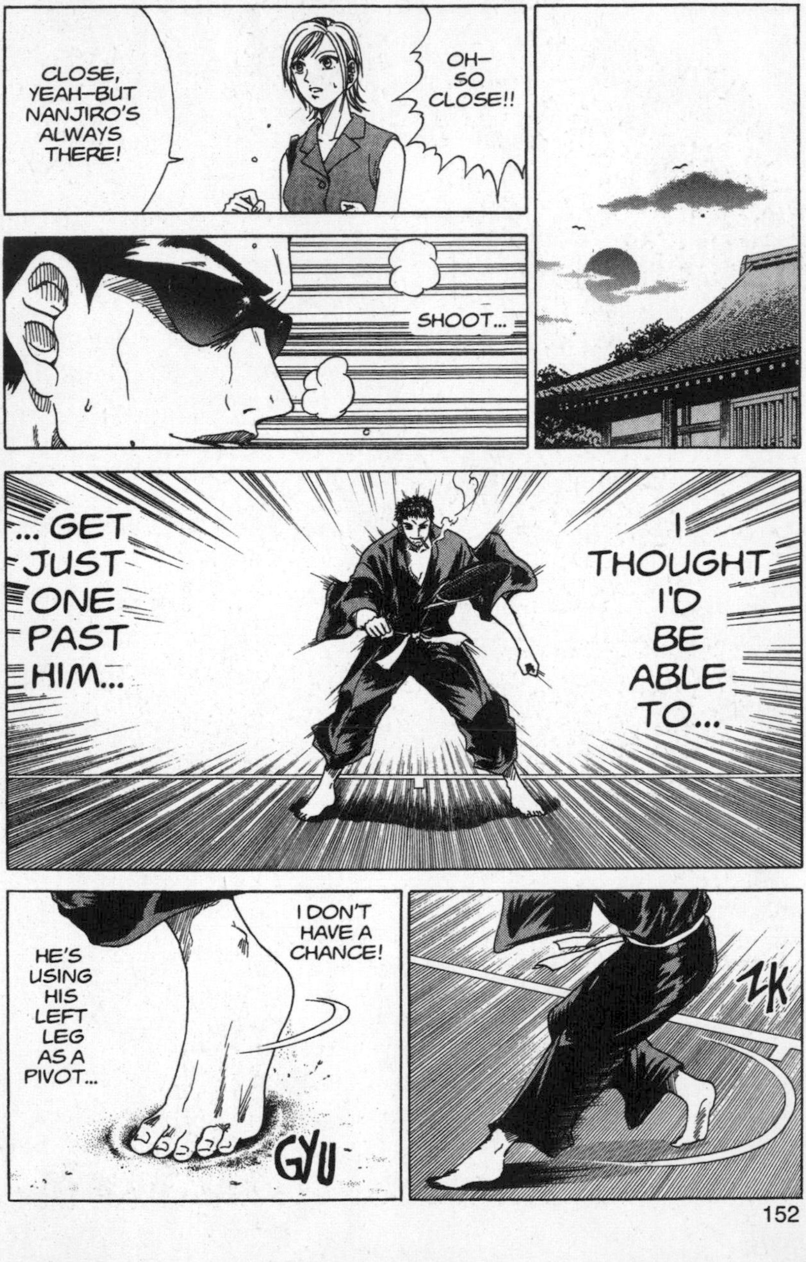
OH— SO CLOSE!!
CLOSE, YEAH—BUT NANJIRO'S ALWAYS THERE!
SHOOT...
I THOUGHT I'D BE ABLE TO...
... GET JUST ONE PAST HIM...
ZK
I DON'T HAVE A CHANCE!
HE'S USING HIS LEFT LEG AS A PIVOT...
GYU

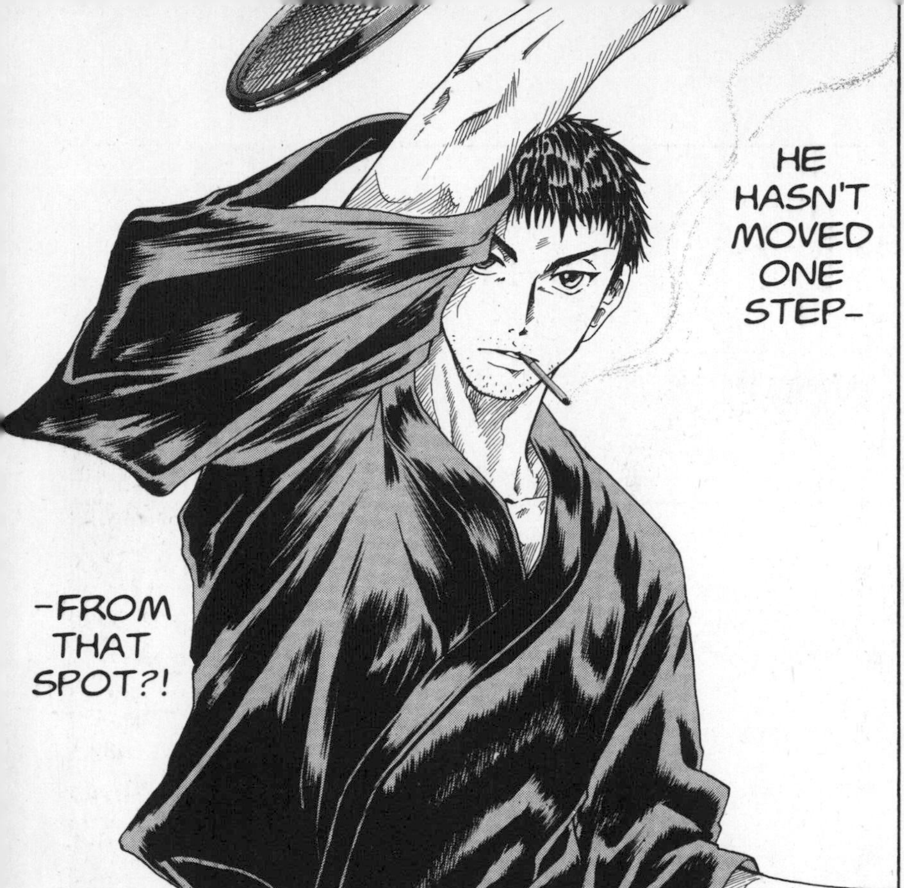
HE HASN'T MOVED ONE STEP-
-FROM THAT SPOT?!

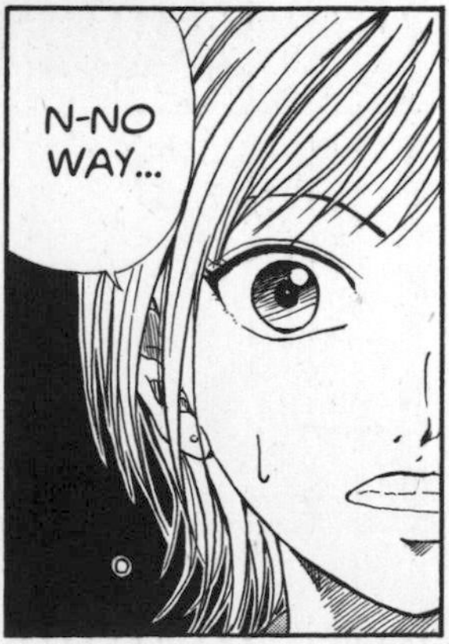
N-NO WAY...

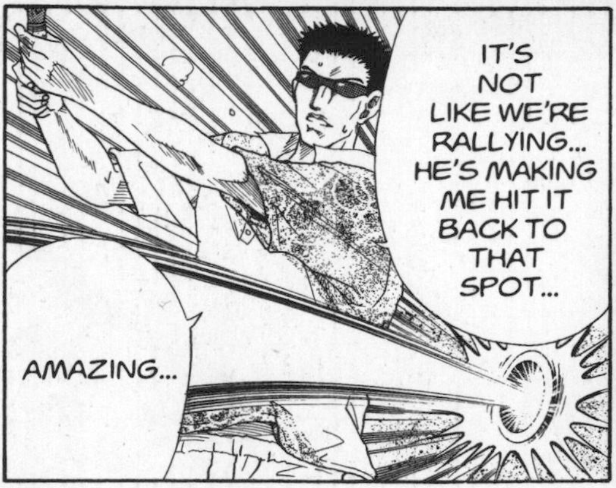
IT'S NOT LIKE WE'RE RALLYING... HE'S MAKING ME HIT IT BACK TO THAT SPOT...
AMAZING...

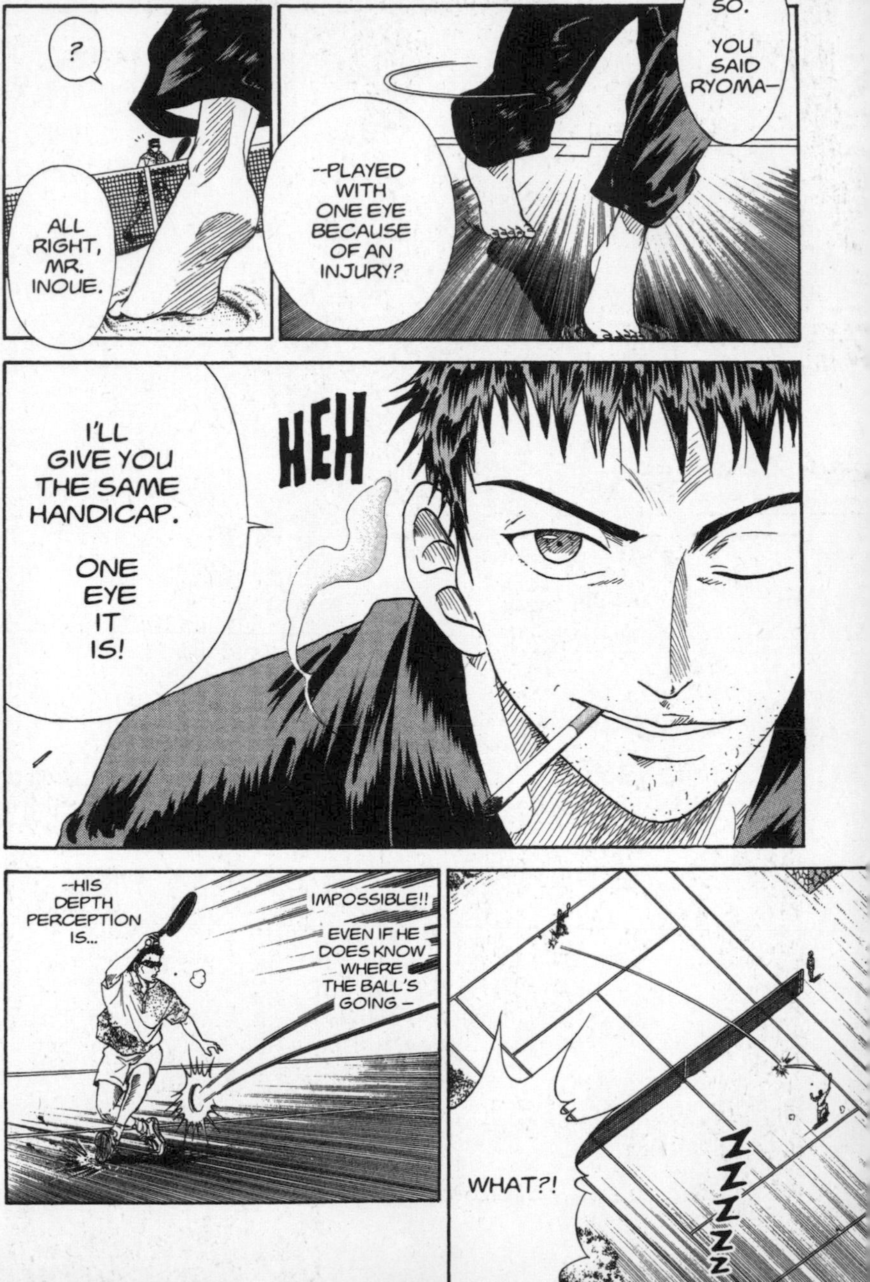
SO. YOU SAID RYOMA—
--PLAYED WITH ONE EYE BECAUSE OF AN INJURY?
?
ALL RIGHT, MR. INOUE.
HEH
I'LL GIVE YOU THE SAME HANDICAP. ONE EYE IT IS!
WHAT?!
ZZZZZZ
IMPOSSIBLE!!
EVEN IF HE DOES KNOW WHERE THE BALL'S GOING –
--HIS DEPTH PERCEPTION IS...

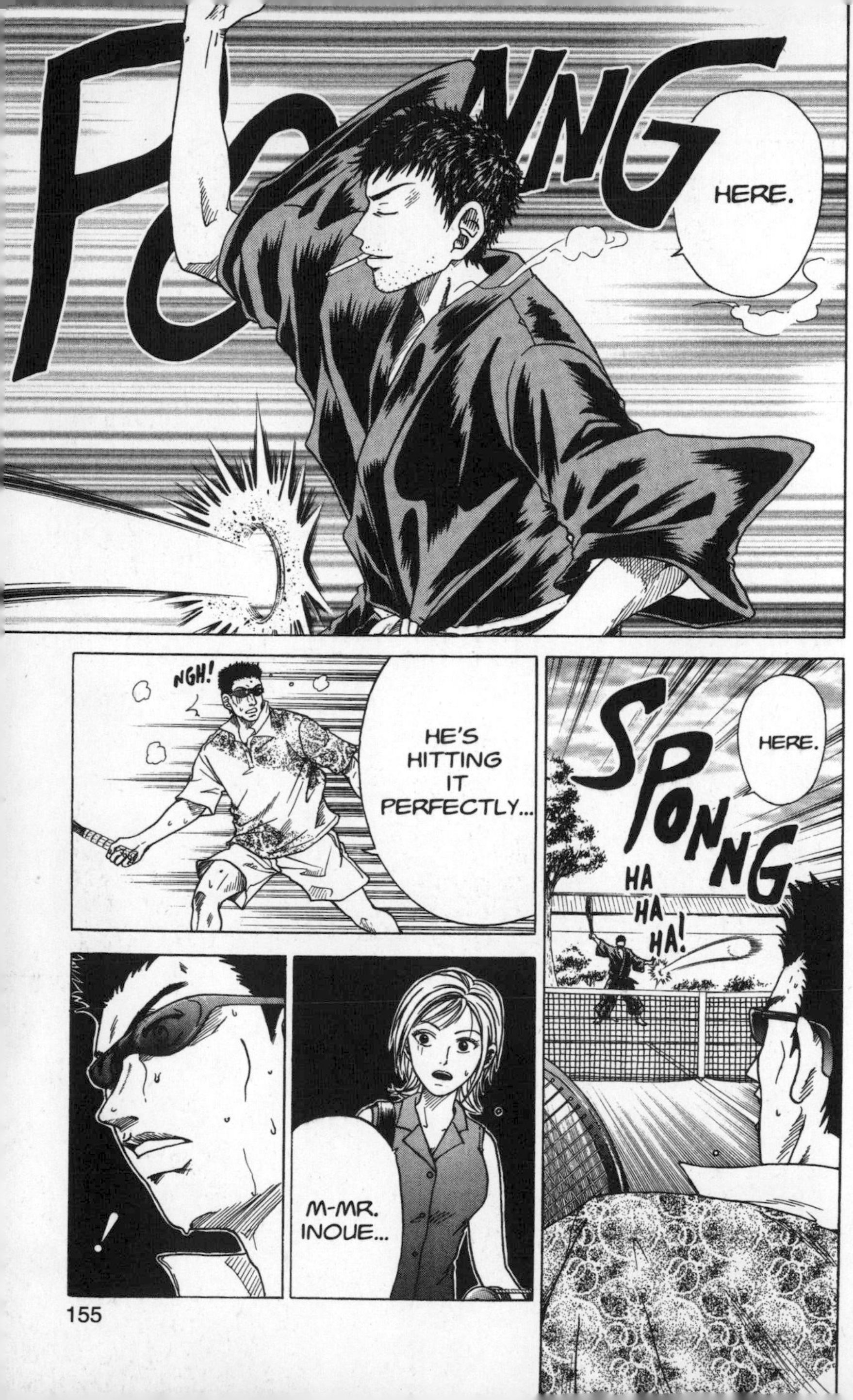
HERE.
HERE.
SPONNG
HA HA HA!
HE'S HITTING IT PERFECTLY...
NGH!
M-MR. INOUE...
!

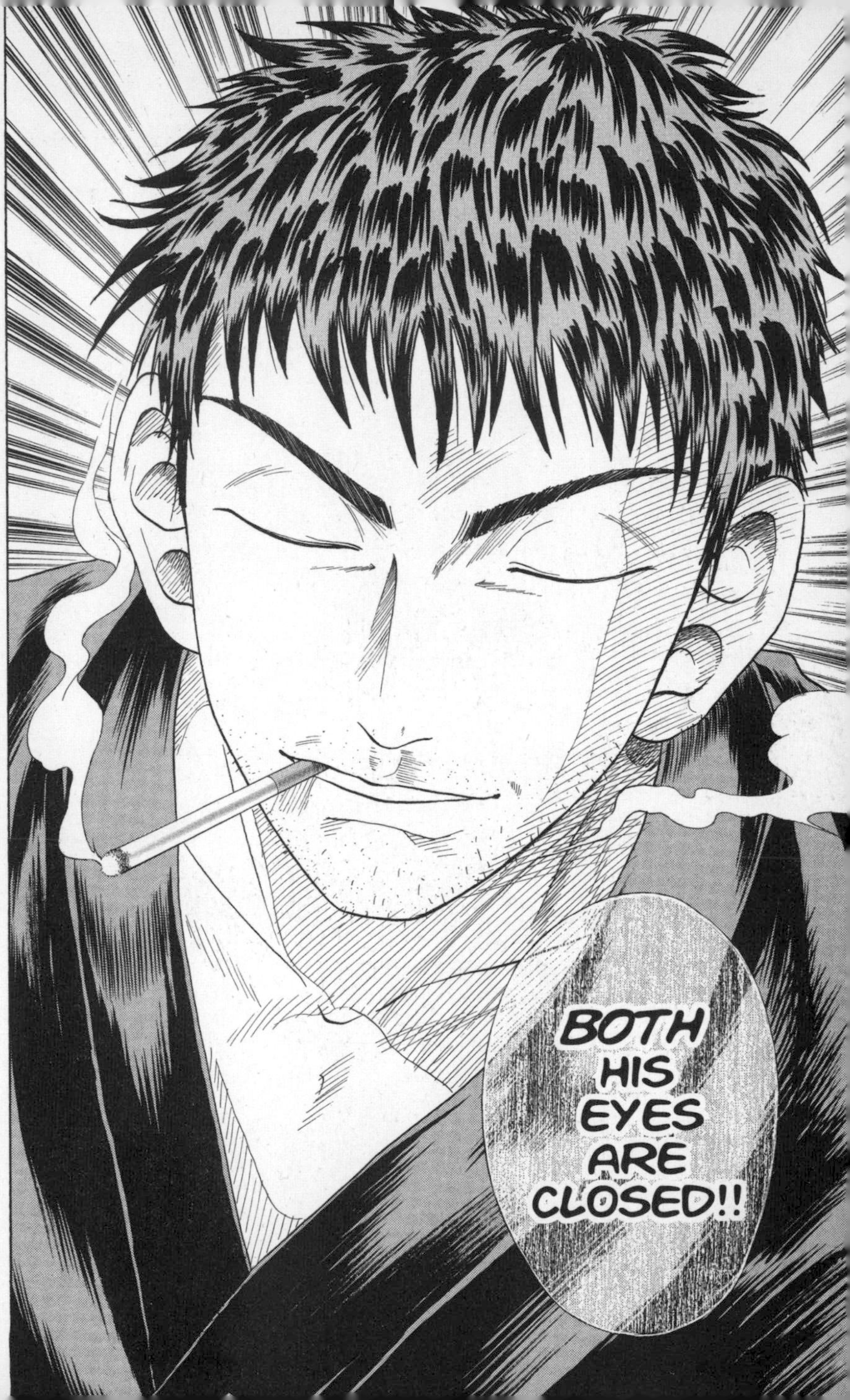
BOTH HIS EYES ARE CLOSED!!

READ THIS WAY

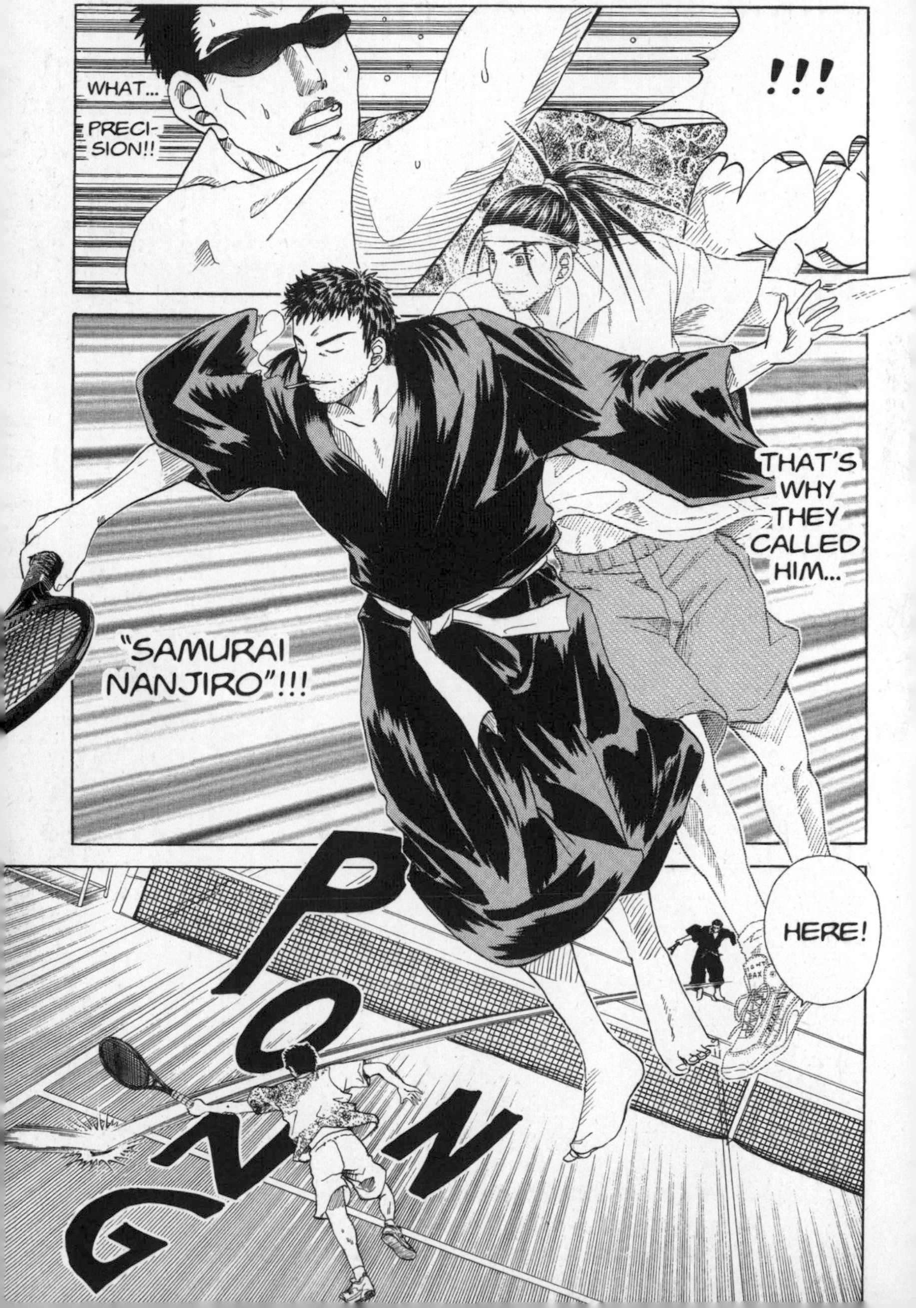
!!!
WHAT...
PRECISION!!
THAT'S WHY THEY CALLED HIM...
"SAMURAI NANJIRO"!!!
HERE!
PONG

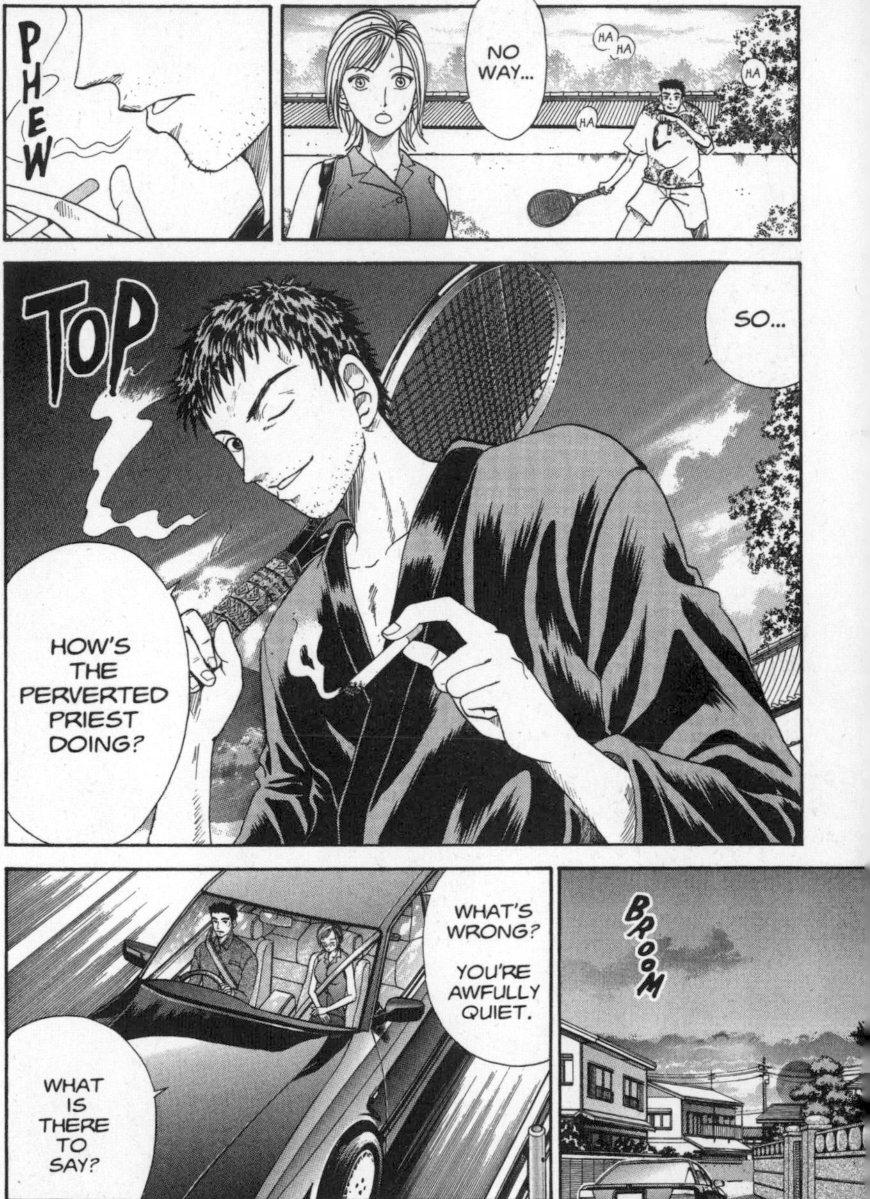
NO WAY...
HA
HA
HA
HA
PHEW
SO...
TOP
HOW'S THE PERVERTED PRIEST DOING?
BROOM
WHAT'S WRONG?
YOU'RE AWFULLY QUIET.
WHAT IS THERE TO SAY?

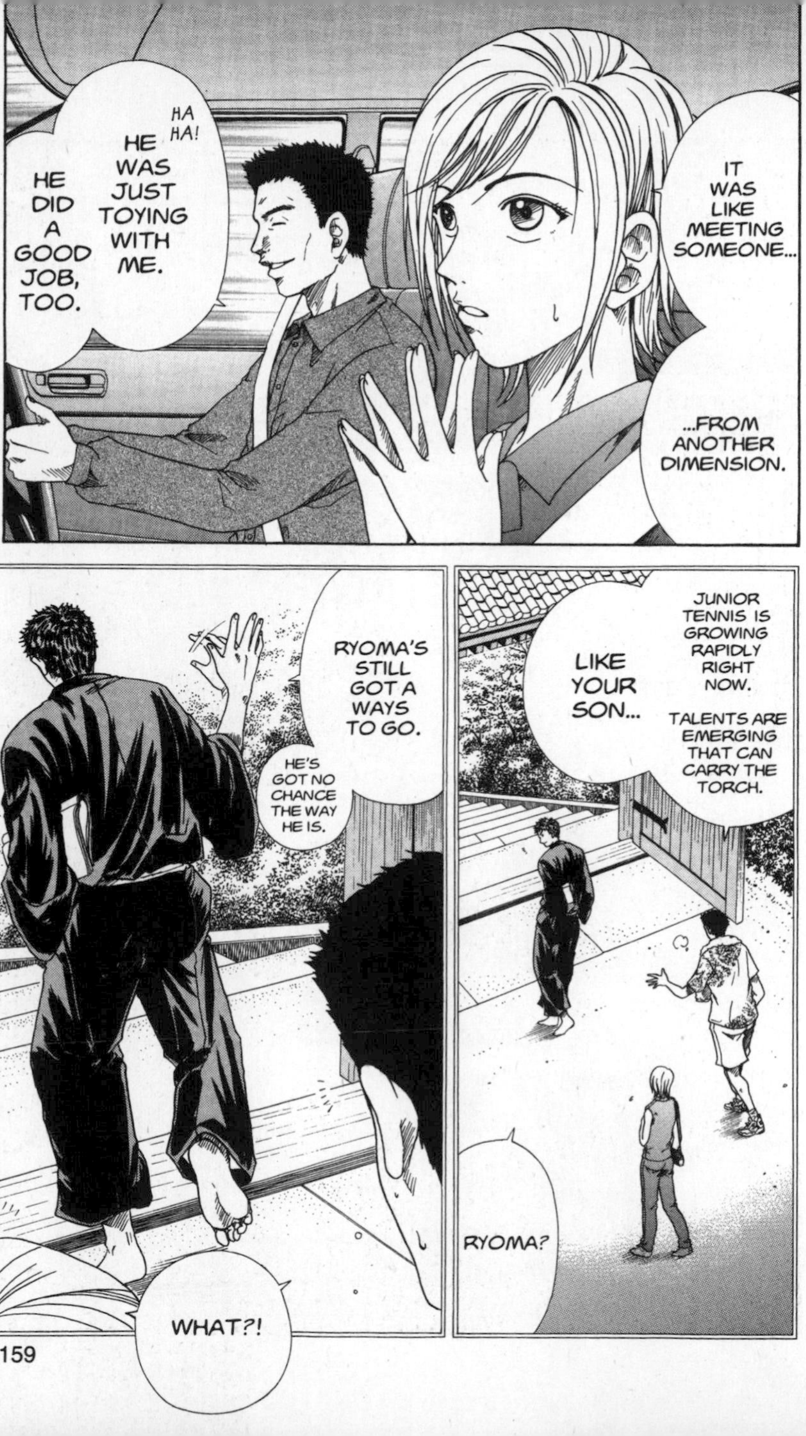
IT WAS LIKE MEETING SOMEONE...
...FROM ANOTHER DIMENSION.
HA HA!
HE WAS JUST TOYING WITH ME.
HE DID A GOOD JOB, TOO.
JUNIOR TENNIS IS GROWING RAPIDLY RIGHT NOW.
TALENTS ARE EMERGING THAT CAN CARRY THE TORCH.
LIKE YOUR SON...
RYOMA?
RYOMA'S STILL GOT A WAYS TO GO.
HE'S GOT NO CHANCE THE WAY HE IS.
WHAT?!

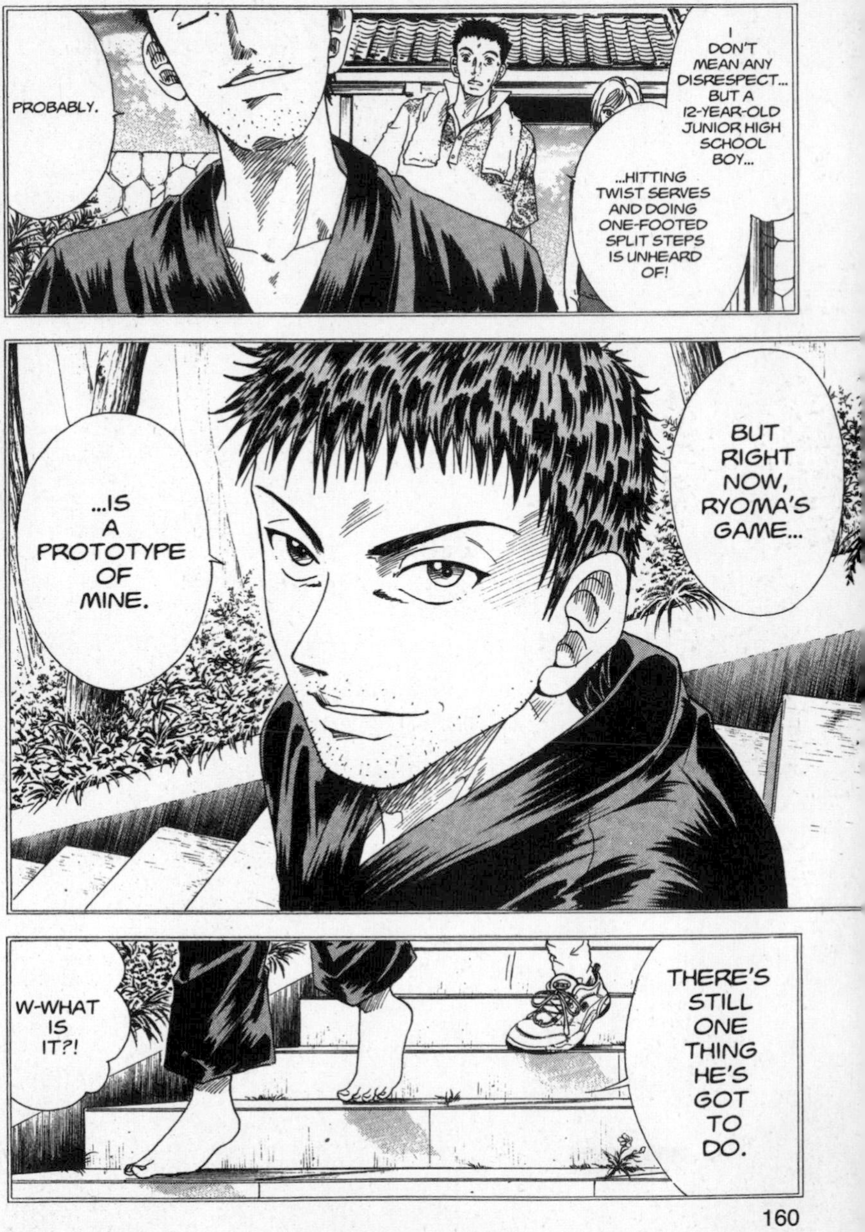
I DON'T MEAN ANY DISRESPECT... BUT A 12-YEAR-OLD JUNIOR HIGH SCHOOL BOY...
...HITTING TWIST SERVES AND DOING ONE-FOOTED SPLIT STEPS IS UNHEARD OF!
PROBABLY.
BUT RIGHT NOW, RYOMA'S GAME...
...IS A PROTOTYPE OF MINE.
THERE'S STILL ONE THING HE'S GOT TO DO.
W-WHAT IS IT?!

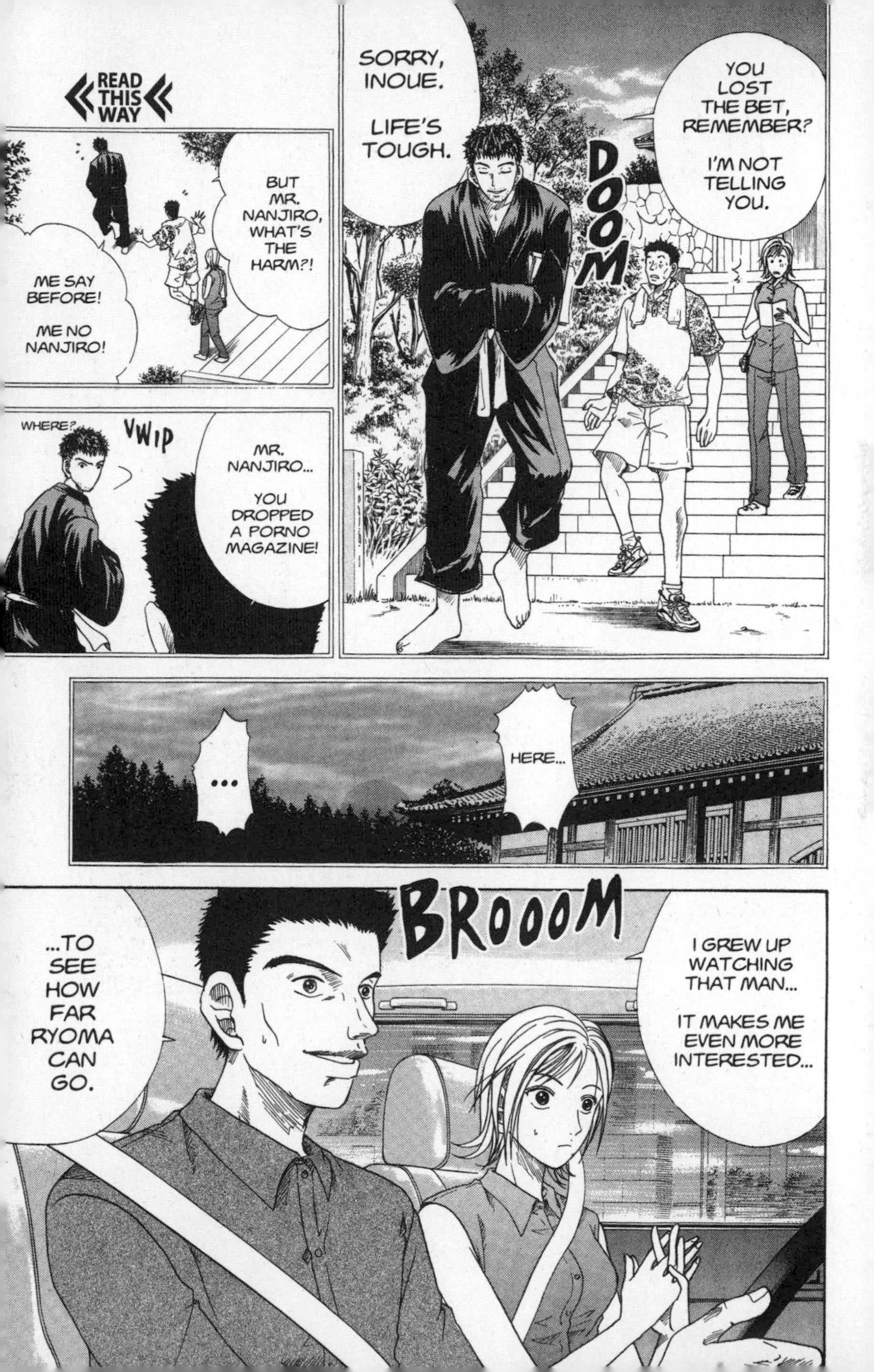
READ THIS WAY
YOU LOST THE BET, REMEMBER? I'M NOT TELLING YOU.
SORRY, INOUE. LIFE'S TOUGH.
DOOM
BUT MR. NANJIRO, WHAT'S THE HARM?!
ME SAY BEFORE! ME NO NANJIRO!
MR. NANJIRO... YOU DROPPED A PORNO MAGAZINE!
VWIP
WHERE?
HERE...
...
I GREW UP WATCHING THAT MAN... IT MAKES ME EVEN MORE INTERESTED...
BROOOM
...TO SEE HOW FAR RYOMA CAN GO.

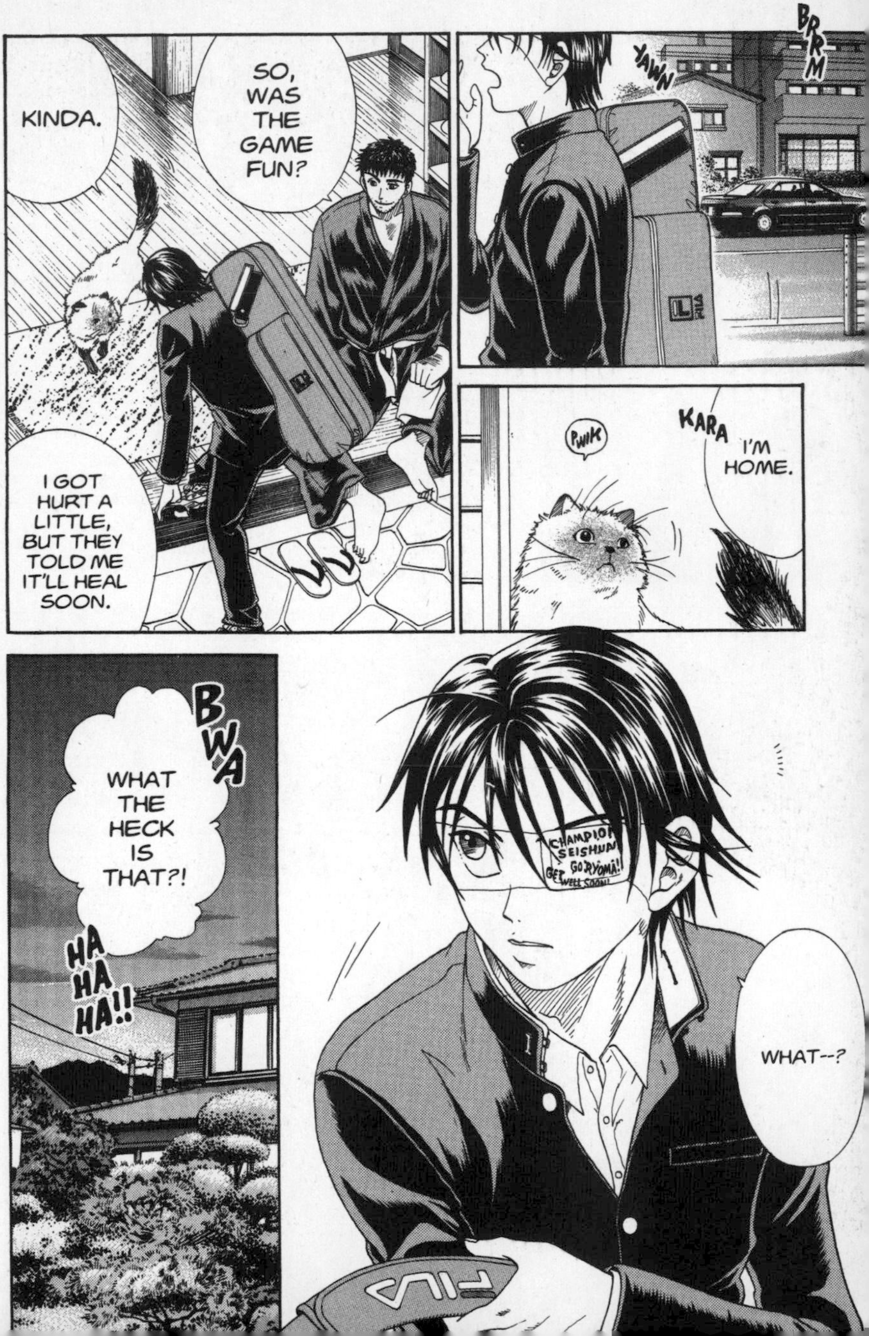
BRRRM
YAWN
KARA
I'M HOME.
PWIK?
SO, WAS THE GAME FUN?
KINDA.
I GOT HURT A LITTLE, BUT THEY TOLD ME IT'LL HEAL SOON.
WHAT--?
BWA
WHAT THE HECK IS THAT?!
HA HA HA!!

READ THIS WAY

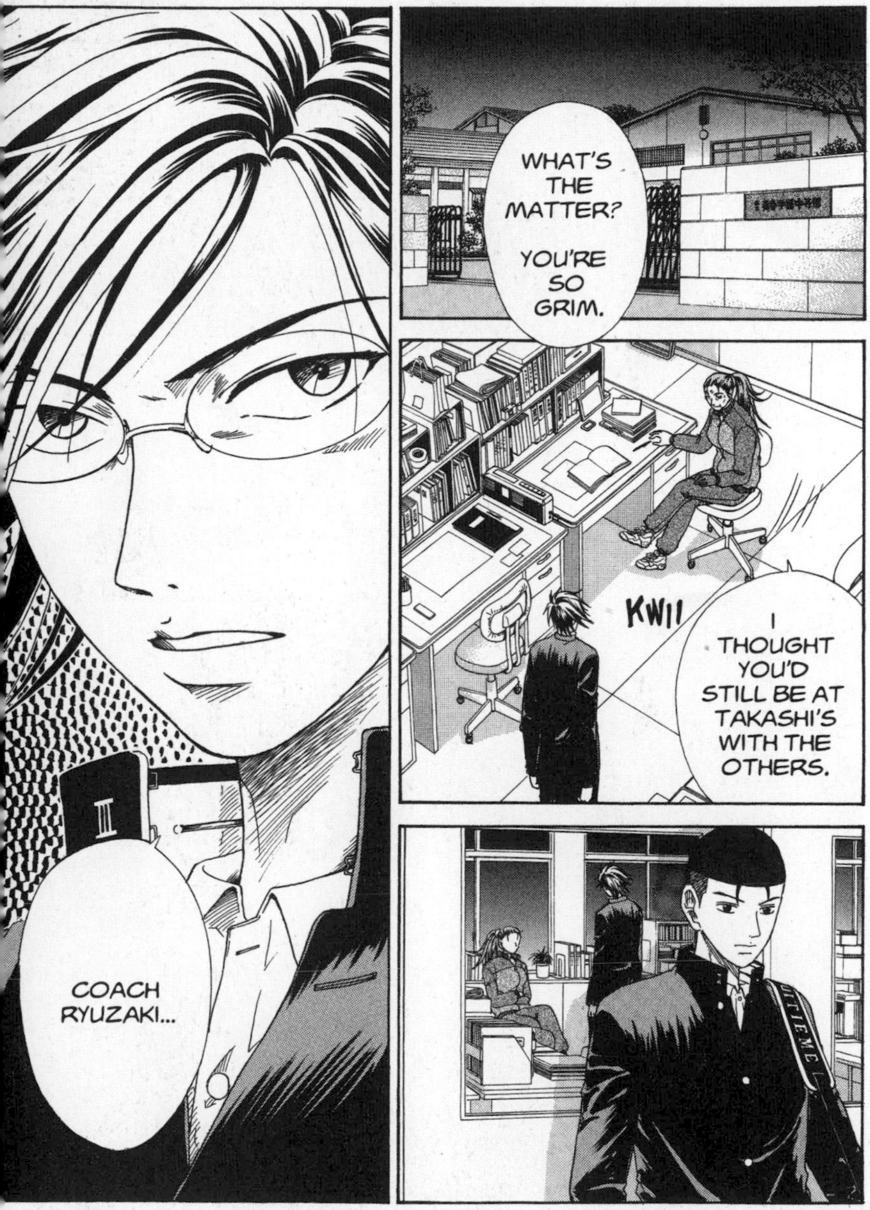
WHAT'S THE MATTER? YOU'RE SO GRIM.
KWII
I THOUGHT YOU'D STILL BE AT TAKASHI'S WITH THE OTHERS.
COACH RYUZAKI...

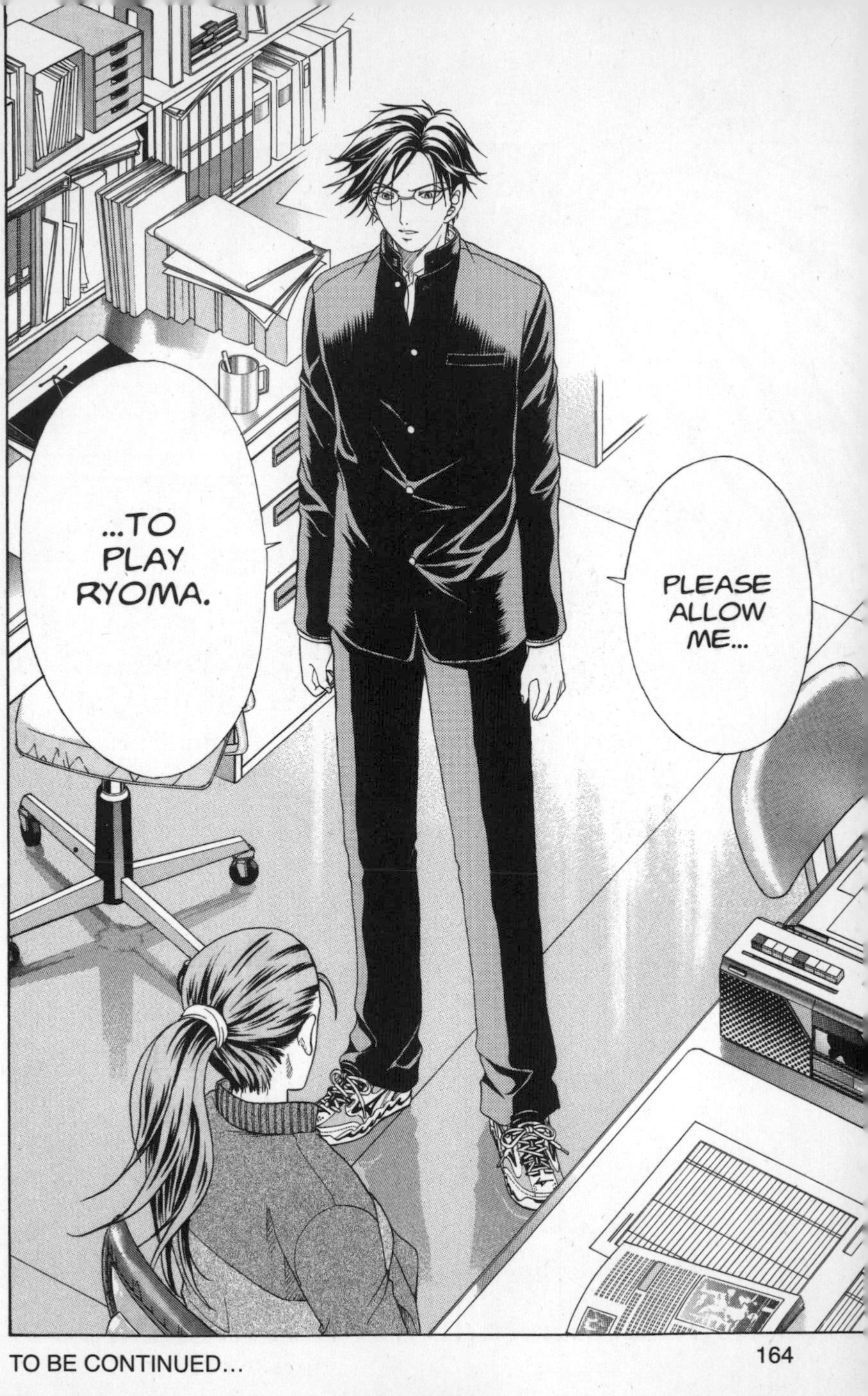
PLEASE ALLOW ME...
...TO PLAY RYOMA.

TO BE CONTINUED…

テニスの王子様

THE PRINCE OF TENNIS™

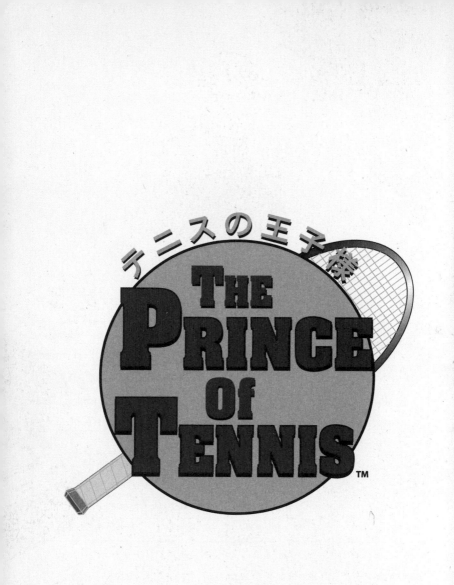

A WORD BEFORE READING THE SHORT STORY

THE FOLLOWING STORY IS THE PREQUEL TO "THE PRINCE OF TENNIS," THE SHORT STORY
VERSION. IT APPEARED IN SHONEN JUMP A YEAR BEFORE THE PRINCE OF TENNIS WAS PUBLISHED.
THE ART IS THE SAME AS WHEN IT WAS DRAWN, BUT I'VE TRIED TO UPDATE THE DIALOGUE,
SO THERE MAY BE SOME INCONSISTENCIES. WHEN I WROTE THIS SHORT STORY, I WAS THINKING
OF A COMPLETELY DIFFERENT KIND OF CHARACTER, AND IT TOOK PLACE IN HIGH SCHOOL.

ORIGINALLY, "RYOMA" WAS THE NAME OF THE ANTAGONIST IN THIS STORY.

THE MAIN CHARACTER'S NAME WAS "KINTARO TOYAMA". BUT THEN I CHANGED IT TO
"ECHIZEN"(THE MAIN CHARACTER'S DAD WAS ORIGINALLY NAMED "NANJIRO ECHIZEN" TOO,
FROM OLD JAPANESE HISTORICAL DRAMAS). IN THE END, THIS STORY WAS POPULAR ENOUGH
FOR RYOMA TO RETAIN HIS STATUS AS THE MAIN CHARACTER.   -- TAKESHI KONOMI

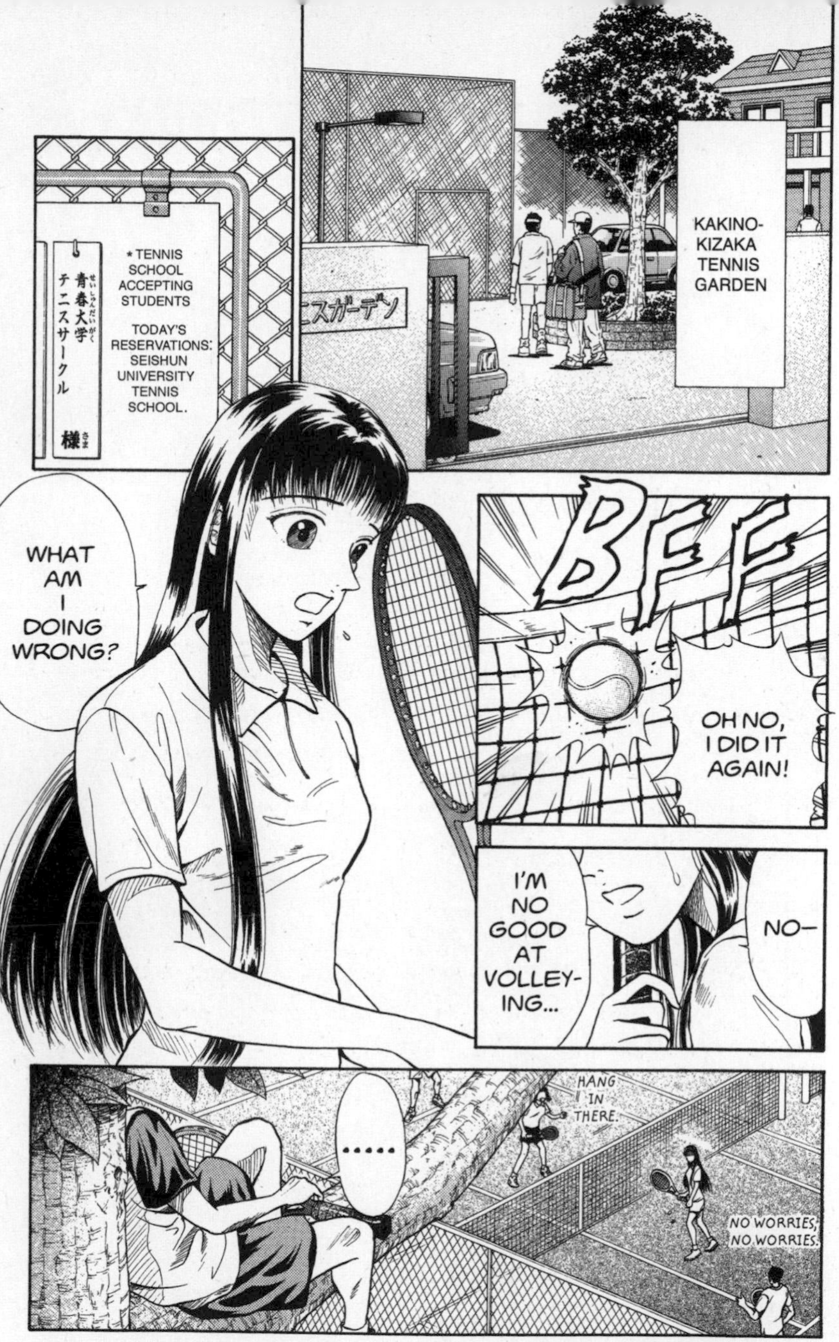
KAKINO-KIZAKA TENNIS GARDEN
ニスガーデン
青春大学テニスサークル様
*TENNIS SCHOOL ACCEPTING STUDENTS
TODAY'S RESERVATIONS: SEISHUN UNIVERSITY TENNIS SCHOOL.
BFF
OH NO, I DID IT AGAIN!
NO—
I'M NO GOOD AT VOLLEYING...
WHAT AM I DOING WRONG?
NO WORRIES, NO WORRIES.
HANG IN THERE.
.....

 Special Short Story: The Prince Of Tennis

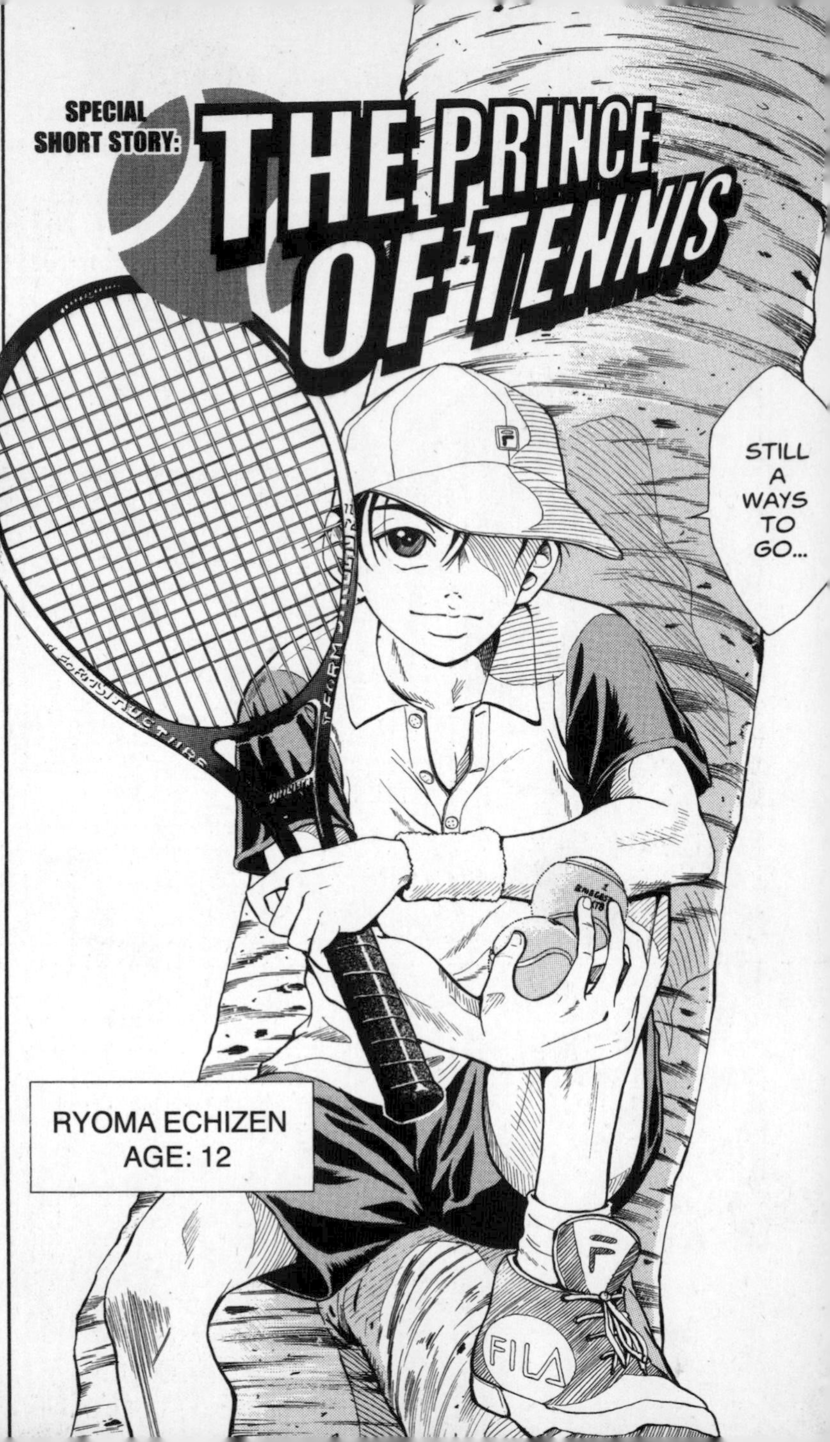
SPECIAL SHORT STORY: THE PRINCE OF TENNIS
STILL A WAYS TO GO...
RYOMA ECHIZEN AGE: 12
FILA

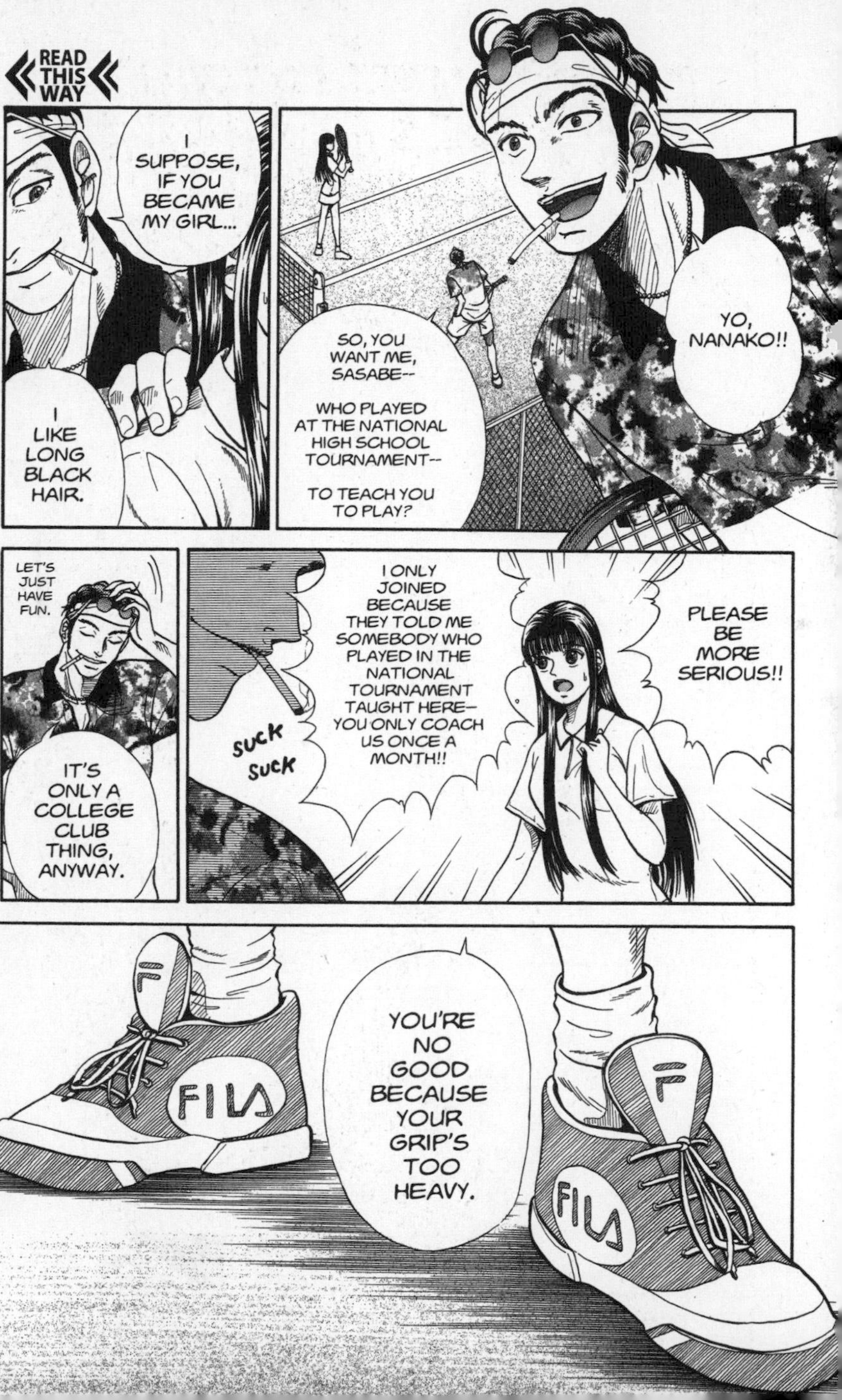
READ THIS WAY
YO, NANAKO!!
SO, YOU WANT ME, SASABE-- WHO PLAYED AT THE NATIONAL HIGH SCHOOL TOURNAMENT-- TO TEACH YOU TO PLAY?
I SUPPOSE, IF YOU BECAME MY GIRL...
I LIKE LONG BLACK HAIR.
PLEASE BE MORE SERIOUS!!
I ONLY JOINED BECAUSE THEY TOLD ME SOMEBODY WHO PLAYED IN THE NATIONAL TOURNAMENT TAUGHT HERE— YOU ONLY COACH US ONCE A MONTH!!
SUCK SUCK
LET'S JUST HAVE FUN.
IT'S ONLY A COLLEGE CLUB THING, ANYWAY.
YOU'RE NO GOOD BECAUSE YOUR GRIP'S TOO HEAVY.

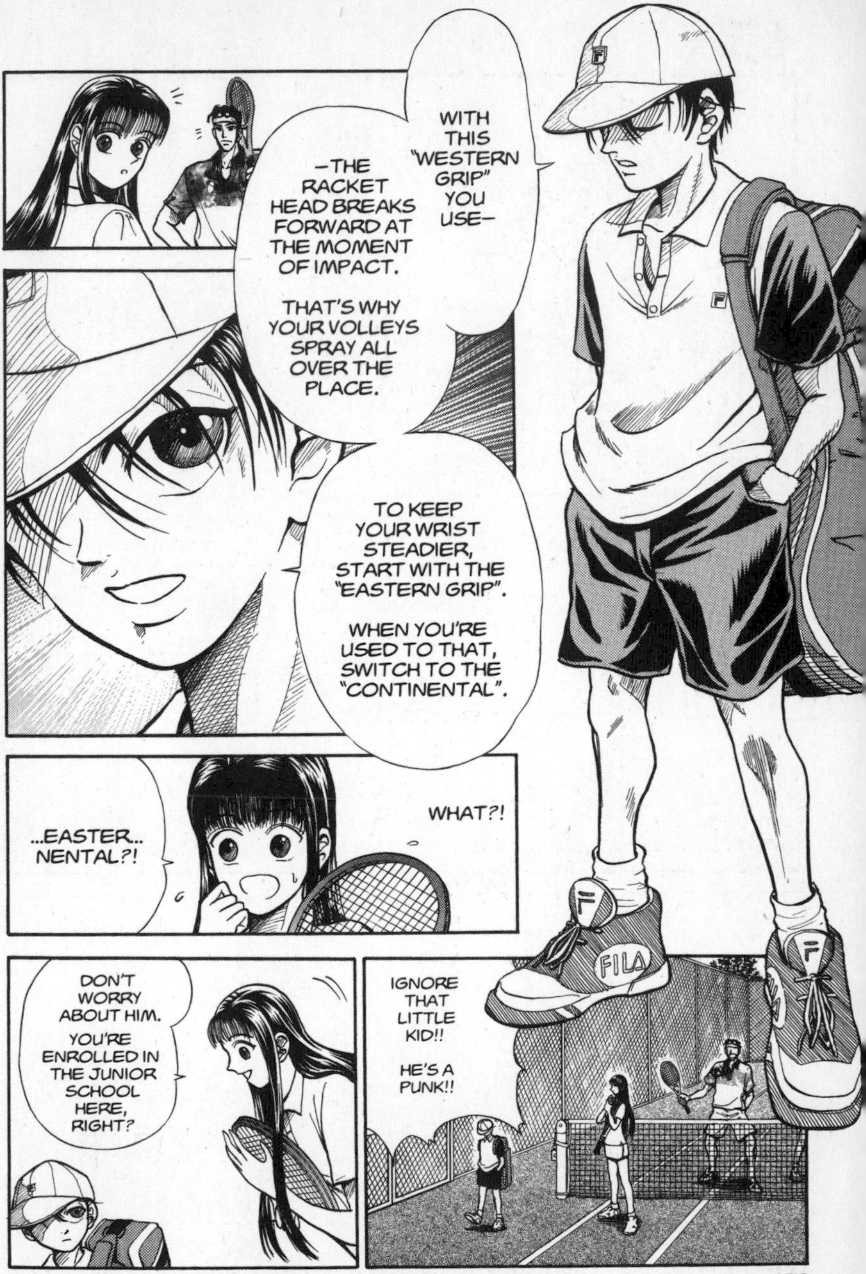
WITH THIS "WESTERN GRIP" YOU USE—
—THE RACKET HEAD BREAKS FORWARD AT THE MOMENT OF IMPACT.
THAT'S WHY YOUR VOLLEYS SPRAY ALL OVER THE PLACE.
TO KEEP YOUR WRIST STEADIER, START WITH THE "EASTERN GRIP".
WHEN YOU'RE USED TO THAT, SWITCH TO THE "CONTINENTAL".
WHAT?!
...EASTER... NENTAL?!
FILA
IGNORE THAT LITTLE KID!!
HE'S A PUNK!!
DON'T WORRY ABOUT HIM.
YOU'RE ENROLLED IN THE JUNIOR SCHOOL HERE, RIGHT?

READ THIS WAY

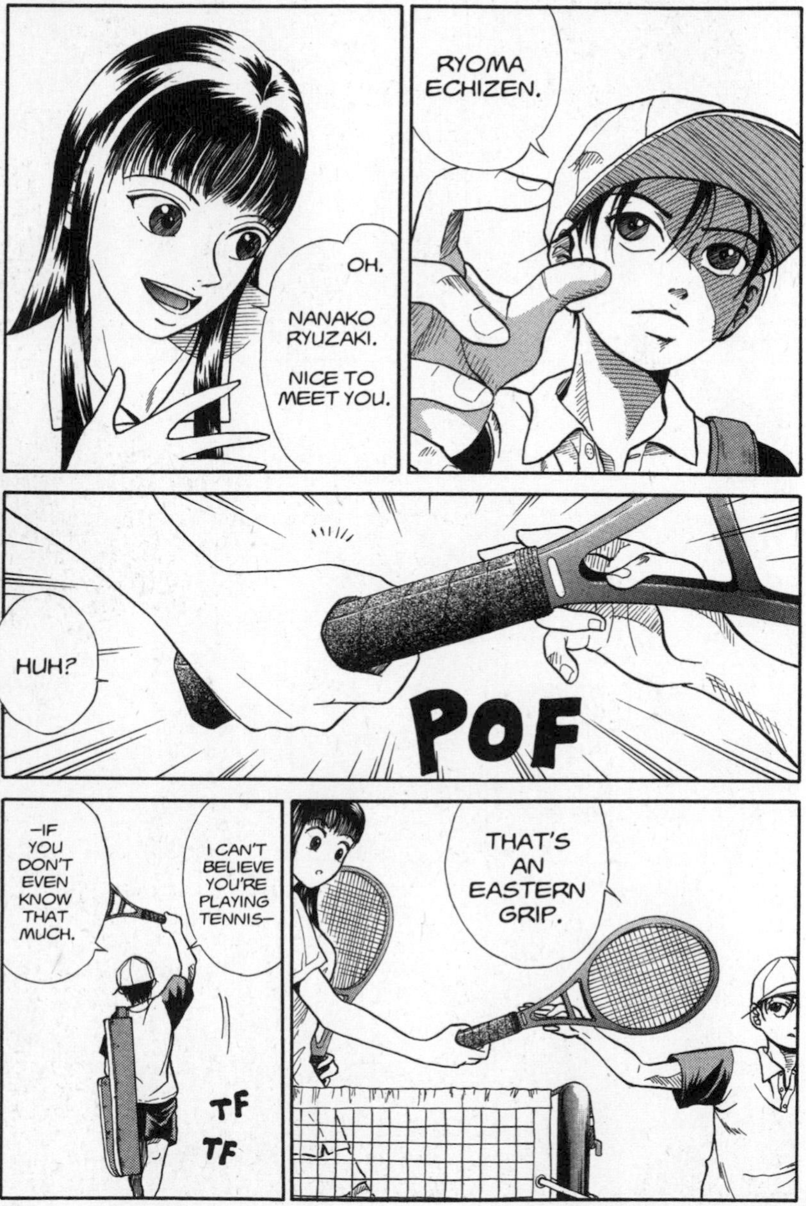

RYOMA ECHIZEN.
OH.
NANAKO RYUZAKI.
NICE TO MEET YOU.
HUH?
POF
THAT'S AN EASTERN GRIP.
I CAN'T BELIEVE YOU'RE PLAYING TENNIS—
—IF YOU DON'T EVEN KNOW THAT MUCH.
TF
TF

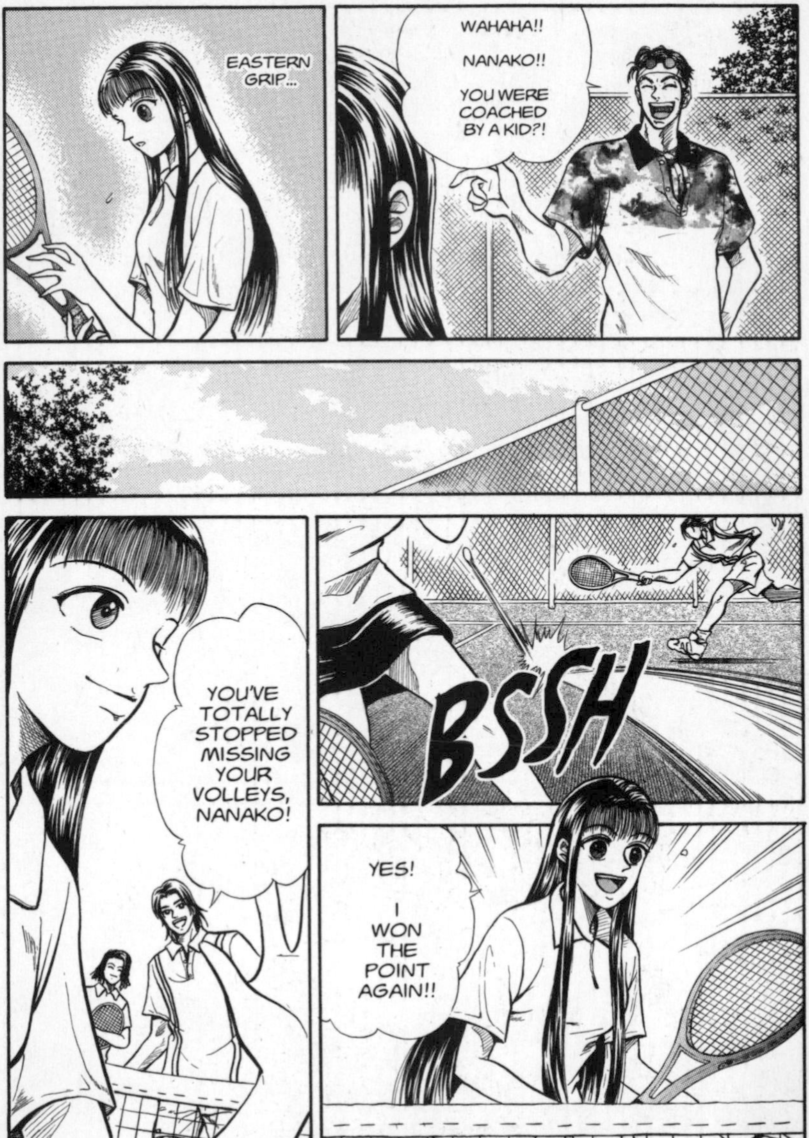
WAHAHA!! NANAKO!! YOU WERE COACHED BY A KID?!
EASTERN GRIP...
BSSH
YES! I WON THE POINT AGAIN!!
YOU'VE TOTALLY STOPPED MISSING YOUR VOLLEYS, NANAKO!

READ THIS WAY

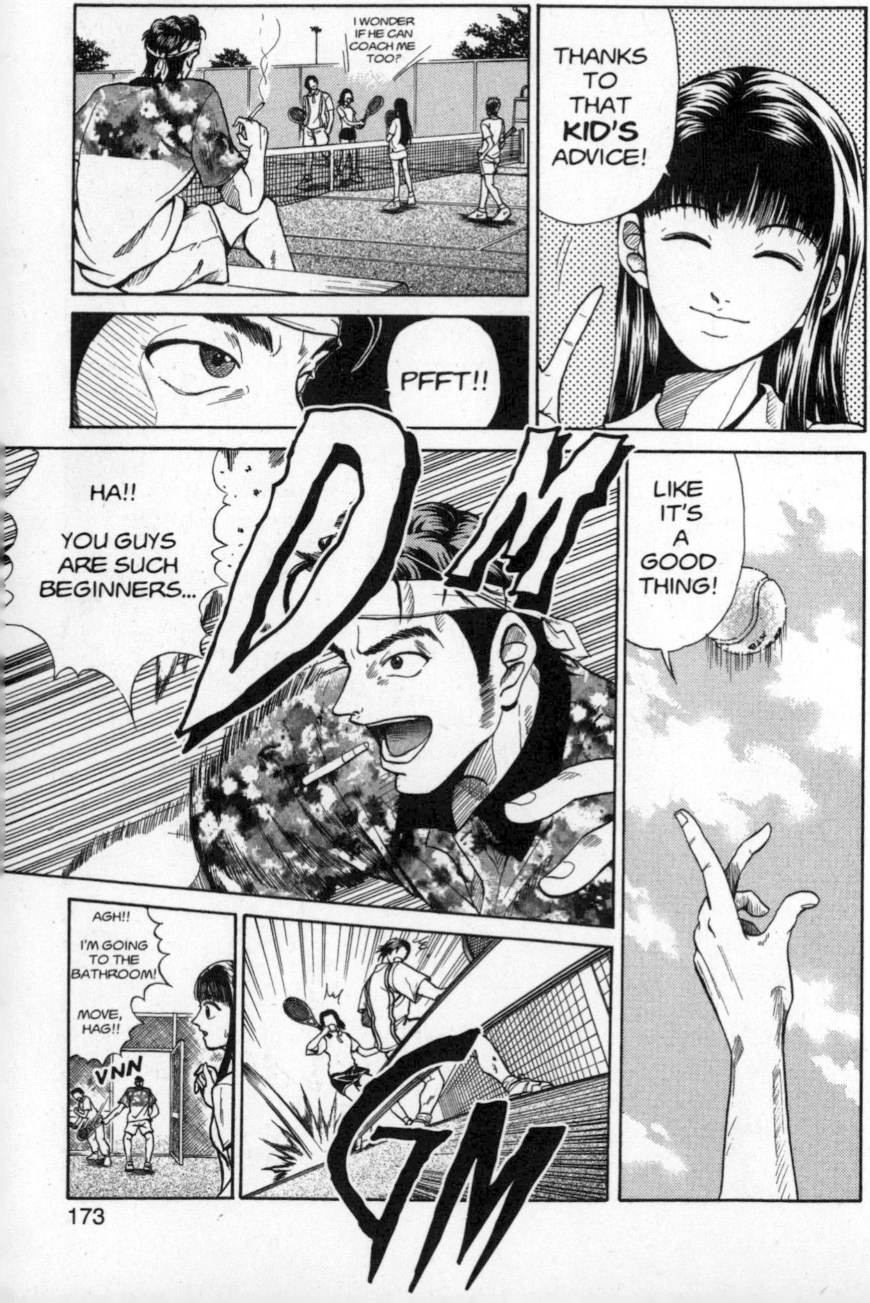

THANKS TO THAT KID'S ADVICE!
I WONDER IF HE CAN COACH ME TOO?
PFFT!!
LIKE IT'S A GOOD THING!
HA!!
YOU GUYS ARE SUCH BEGINNERS...
DM
GM
AGH!!
I'M GOING TO THE BATHROOM!
MOVE, HAG!!
VNN

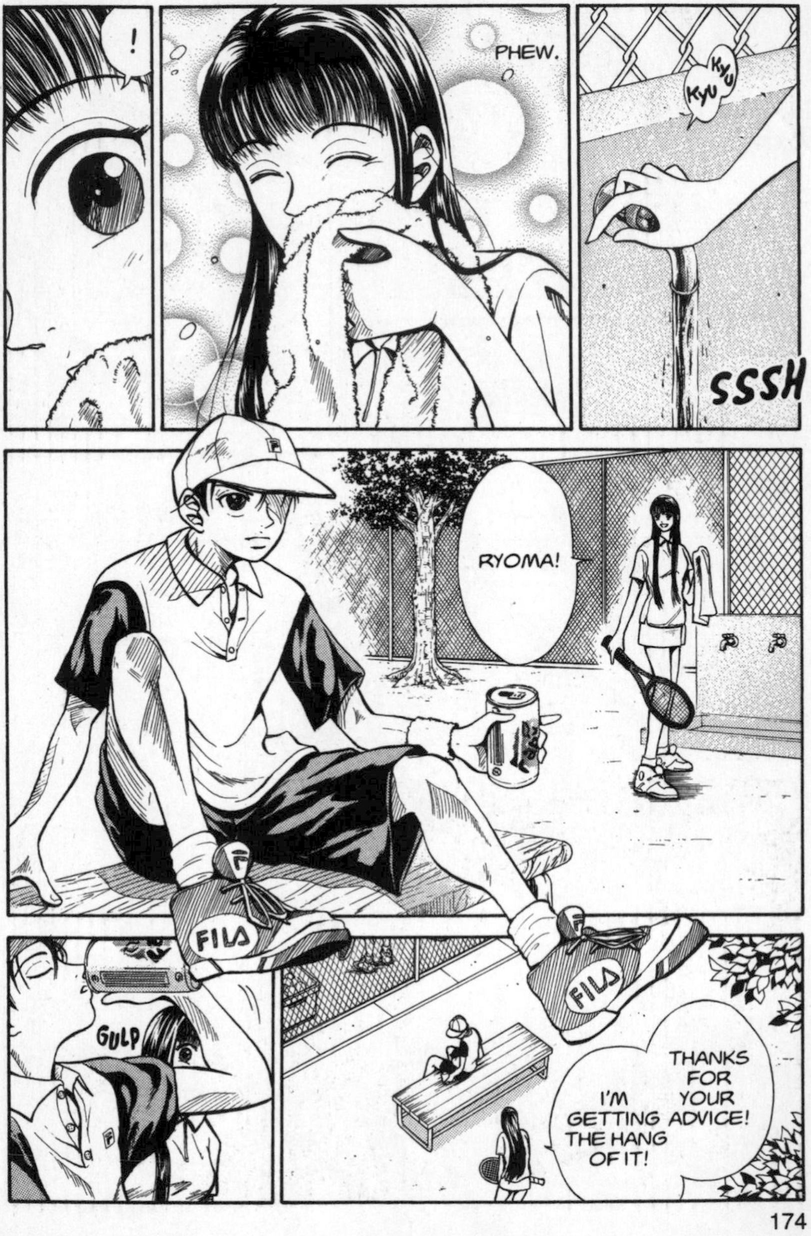
KYU KYU
SSSH
PHEW.
!
RYOMA!
THANKS FOR YOUR ADVICE!
I'M GETTING THE HANG OF IT!
GULP

READ THIS WAY

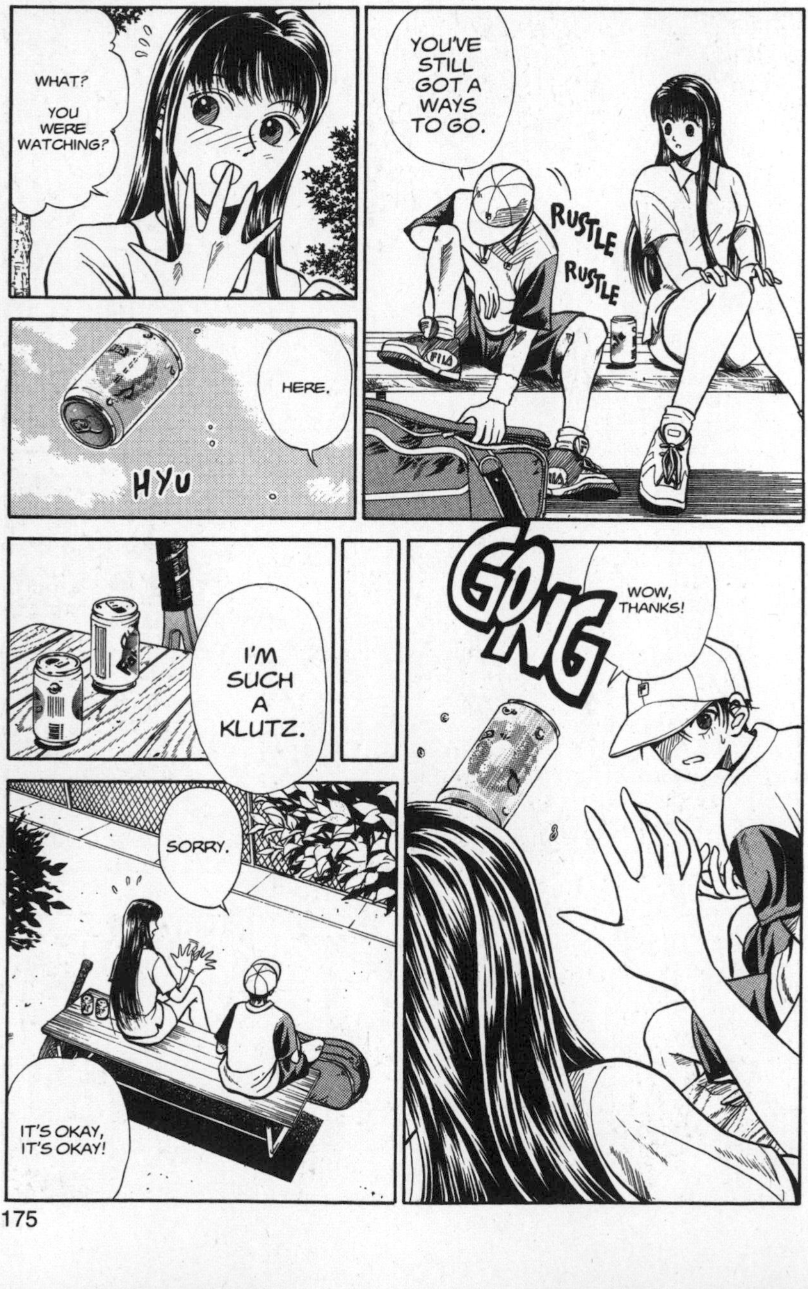

YOU'VE STILL GOT A WAYS TO GO.
RUSTLE
RUSTLE
WHAT? YOU WERE WATCHING?
HERE.
HYU
WOW, THANKS!
GONG
I'M SUCH A KLUTZ.
SORRY.
IT'S OKAY, IT'S OKAY!

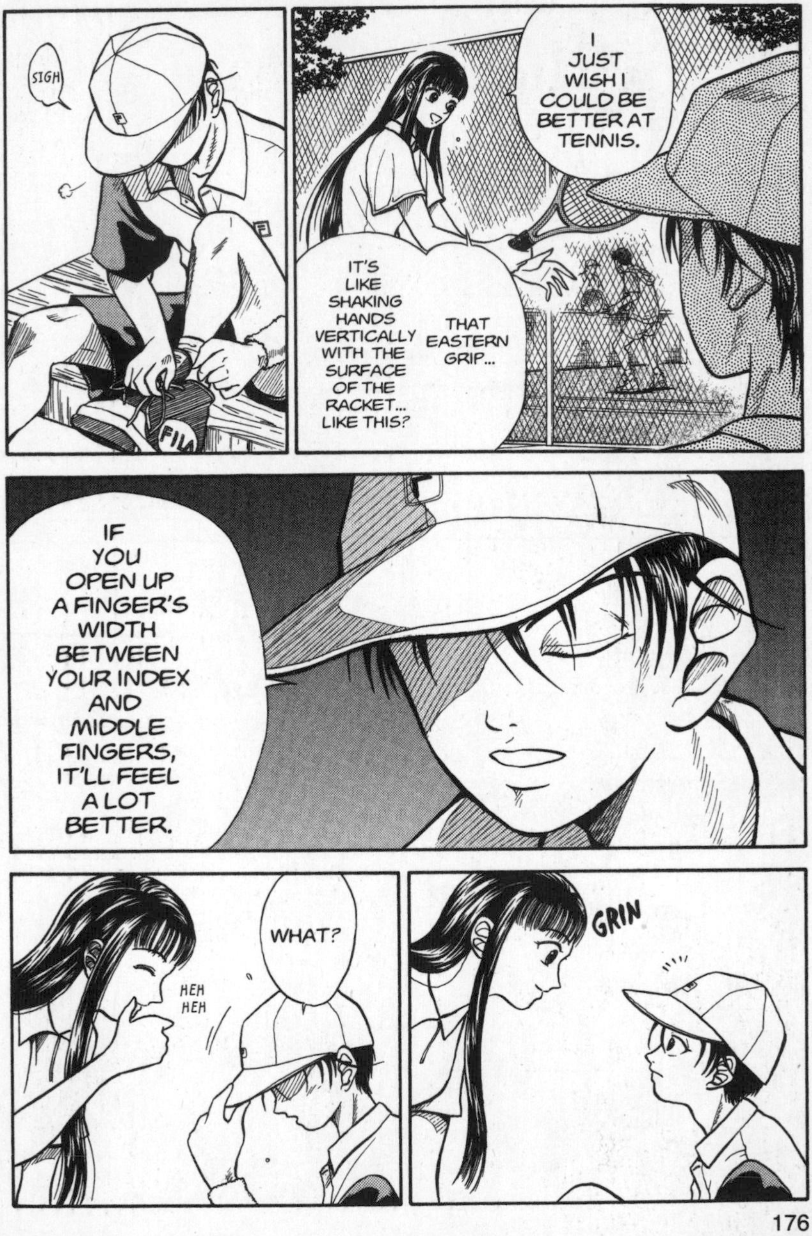
I JUST WISH I COULD BE BETTER AT TENNIS.
THAT EASTERN GRIP...
IT'S LIKE SHAKING HANDS VERTICALLY WITH THE SURFACE OF THE RACKET... LIKE THIS?
SIGH
FILA
IF YOU OPEN UP A FINGER'S WIDTH BETWEEN YOUR INDEX AND MIDDLE FINGERS, IT'LL FEEL A LOT BETTER.
GRIN
WHAT?
HEH HEH

READ THIS WAY

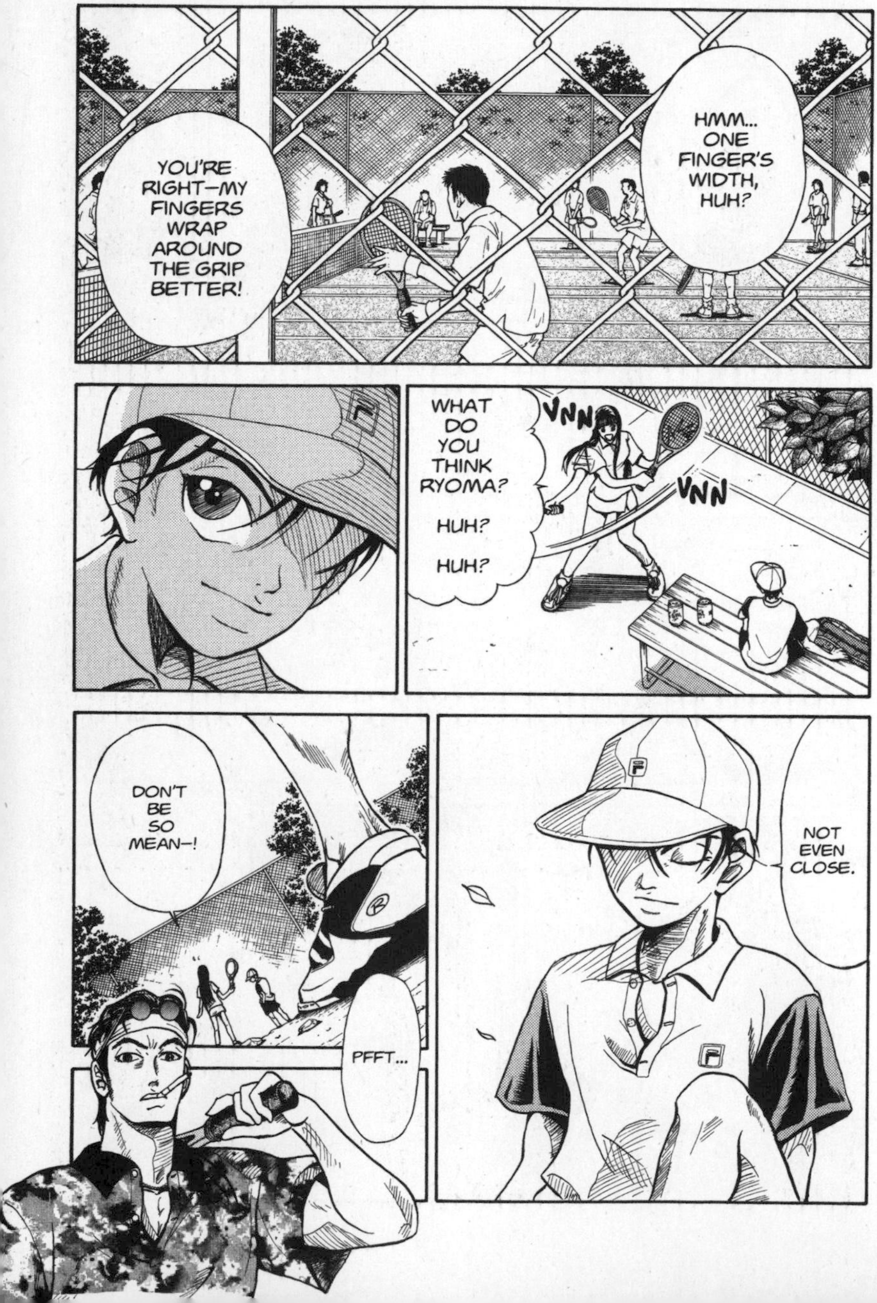
HMM... ONE FINGER'S WIDTH, HUH?
YOU'RE RIGHT—MY FINGERS WRAP AROUND THE GRIP BETTER!
VNN
WHAT DO YOU THINK RYOMA?
HUH?
HUH?
VNN
NOT EVEN CLOSE.
DON'T BE SO MEAN—!
PFFT...

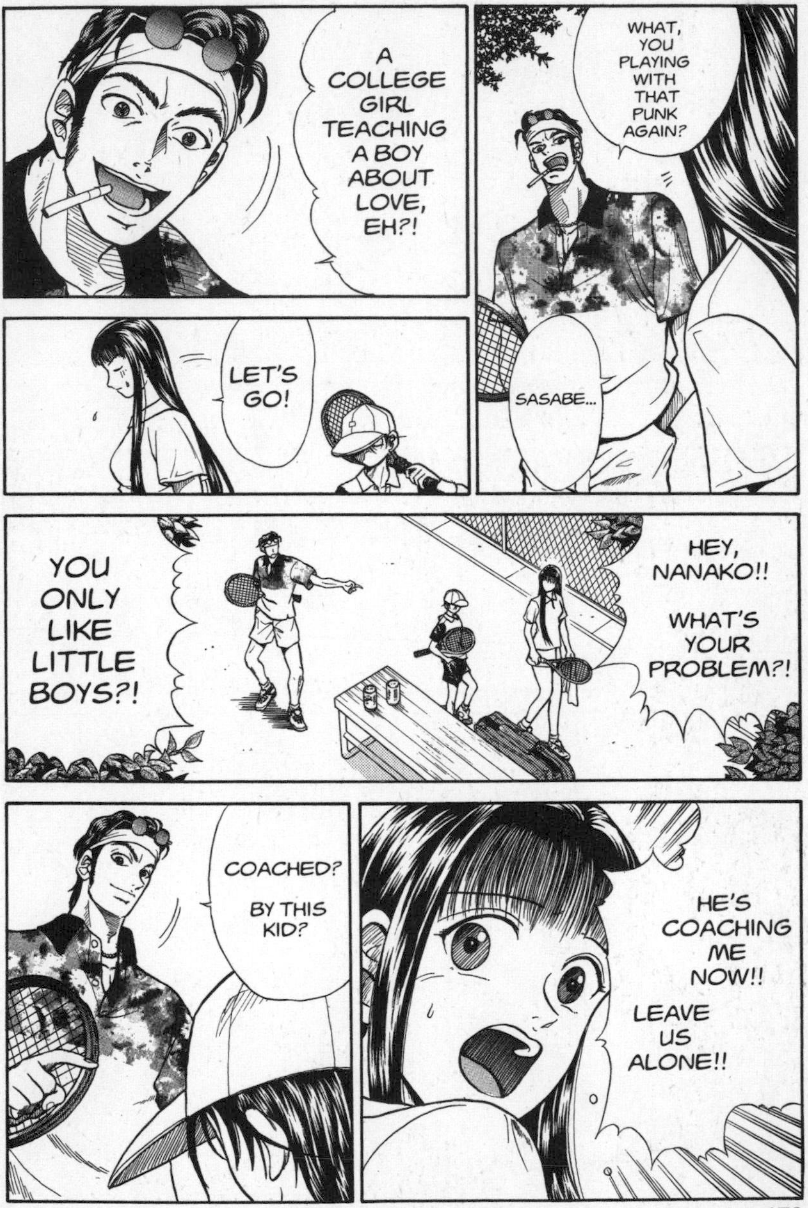
WHAT, YOU PLAYING WITH THAT PUNK AGAIN?
SASABE...
A COLLEGE GIRL TEACHING A BOY ABOUT LOVE, EH?!
LET'S GO!
HEY, NANAKO!!
WHAT'S YOUR PROBLEM?!
YOU ONLY LIKE LITTLE BOYS?!
HE'S COACHING ME NOW!!
LEAVE US ALONE!!
COACHED?
BY THIS KID?

READ THIS WAY

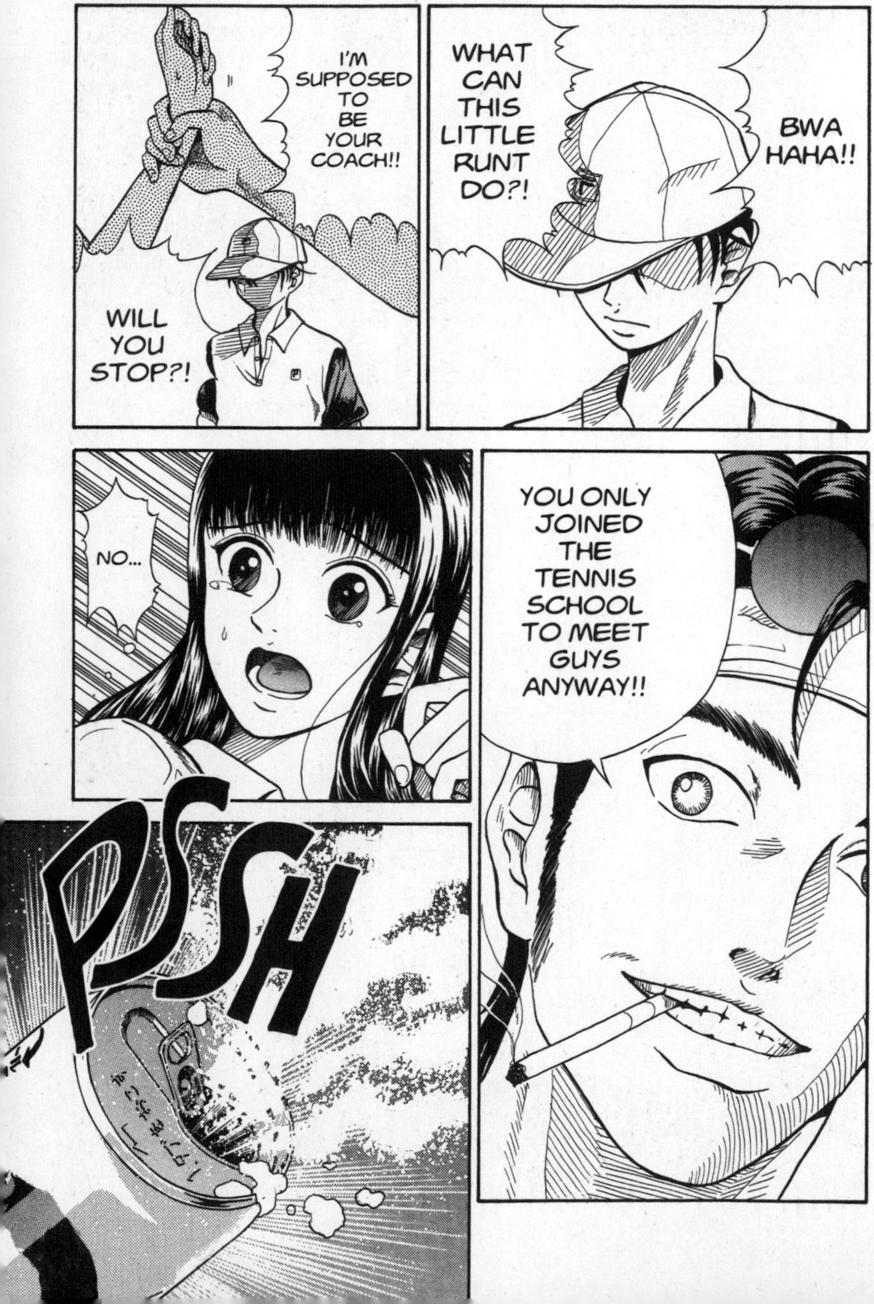
BWA HAHA!!
WHAT CAN THIS LITTLE RUNT DO?!
I'M SUPPOSED TO BE YOUR COACH!!
WILL YOU STOP?!
YOU ONLY JOINED THE TENNIS SCHOOL TO MEET GUYS ANYWAY!!
NO...
PSSH

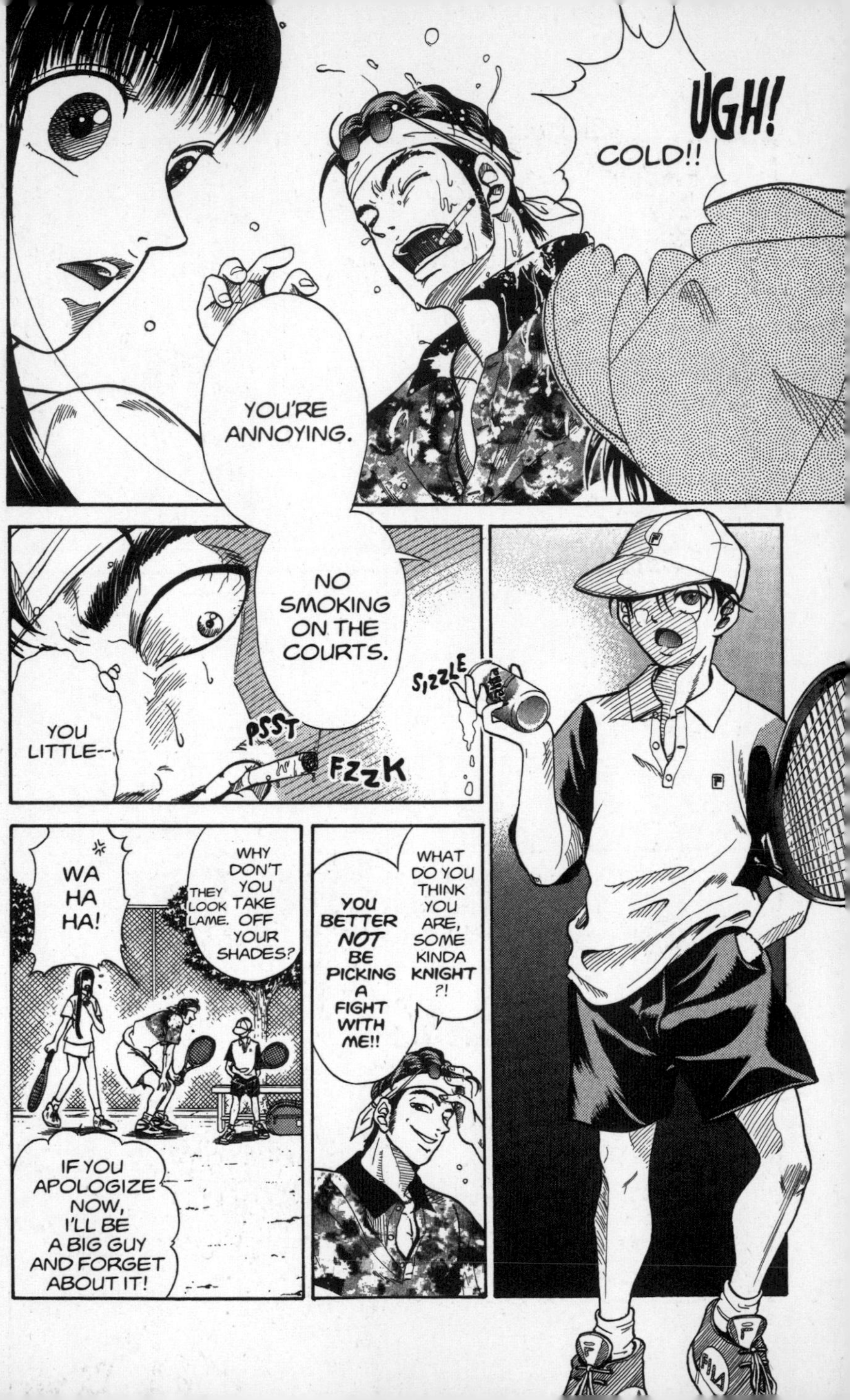
UGH!
COLD!!
YOU'RE ANNOYING.
SIZZLE
NO SMOKING ON THE COURTS.
PSST
FZZK
YOU LITTLE--
WHAT DO YOU THINK YOU ARE, SOME KINDA KNIGHT?!
YOU BETTER NOT BE PICKING A FIGHT WITH ME!!
WA HA HA!
WHY DON'T YOU TAKE OFF YOUR SHADES?
THEY LOOK LAME.
IF YOU APOLOGIZE NOW, I'LL BE A BIG GUY AND FORGET ABOUT IT!

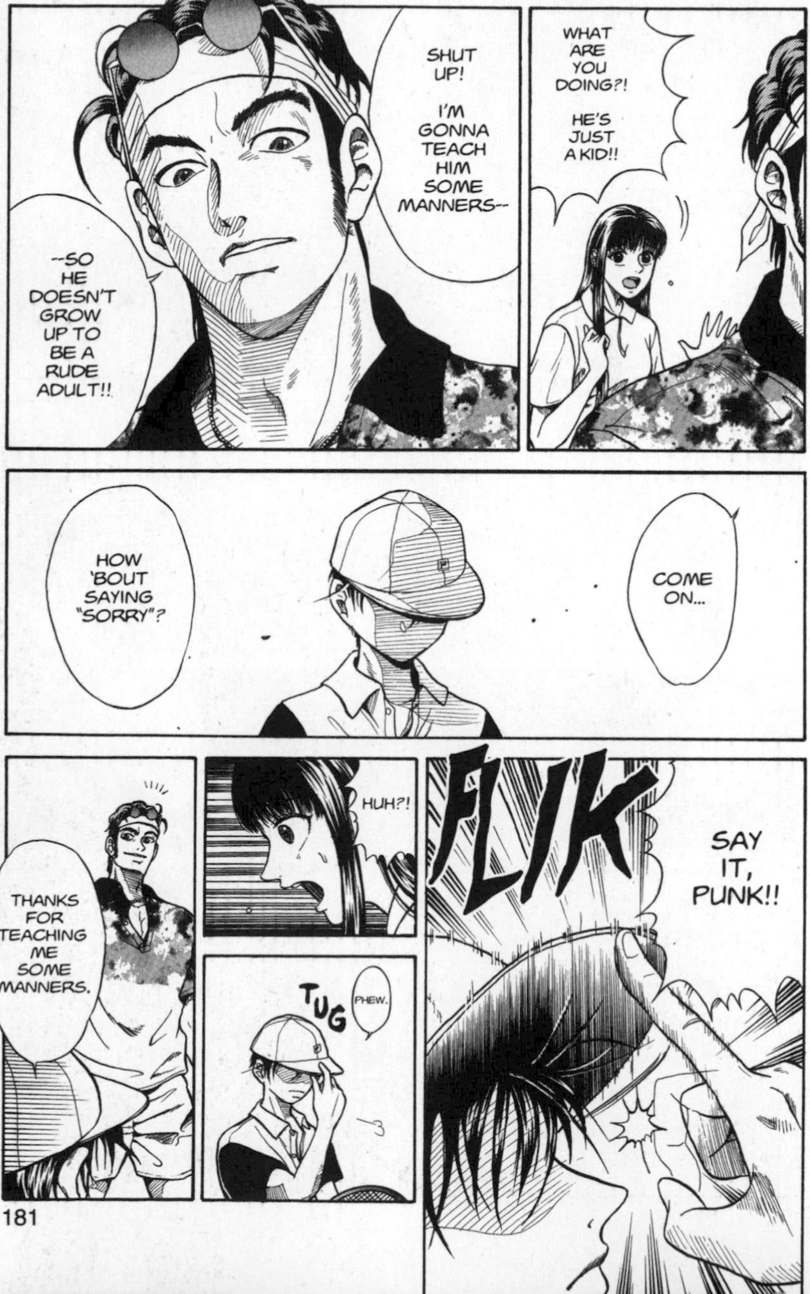
WHAT ARE YOU DOING?! HE'S JUST A KID!!
SHUT UP! I'M GONNA TEACH HIM SOME MANNERS--
--SO HE DOESN'T GROW UP TO BE A RUDE ADULT!!
COME ON...
HOW 'BOUT SAYING "SORRY"?
FLIK
SAY IT, PUNK!!
HUH?!
TUG
PHEW.
THANKS FOR TEACHING ME SOME MANNERS.

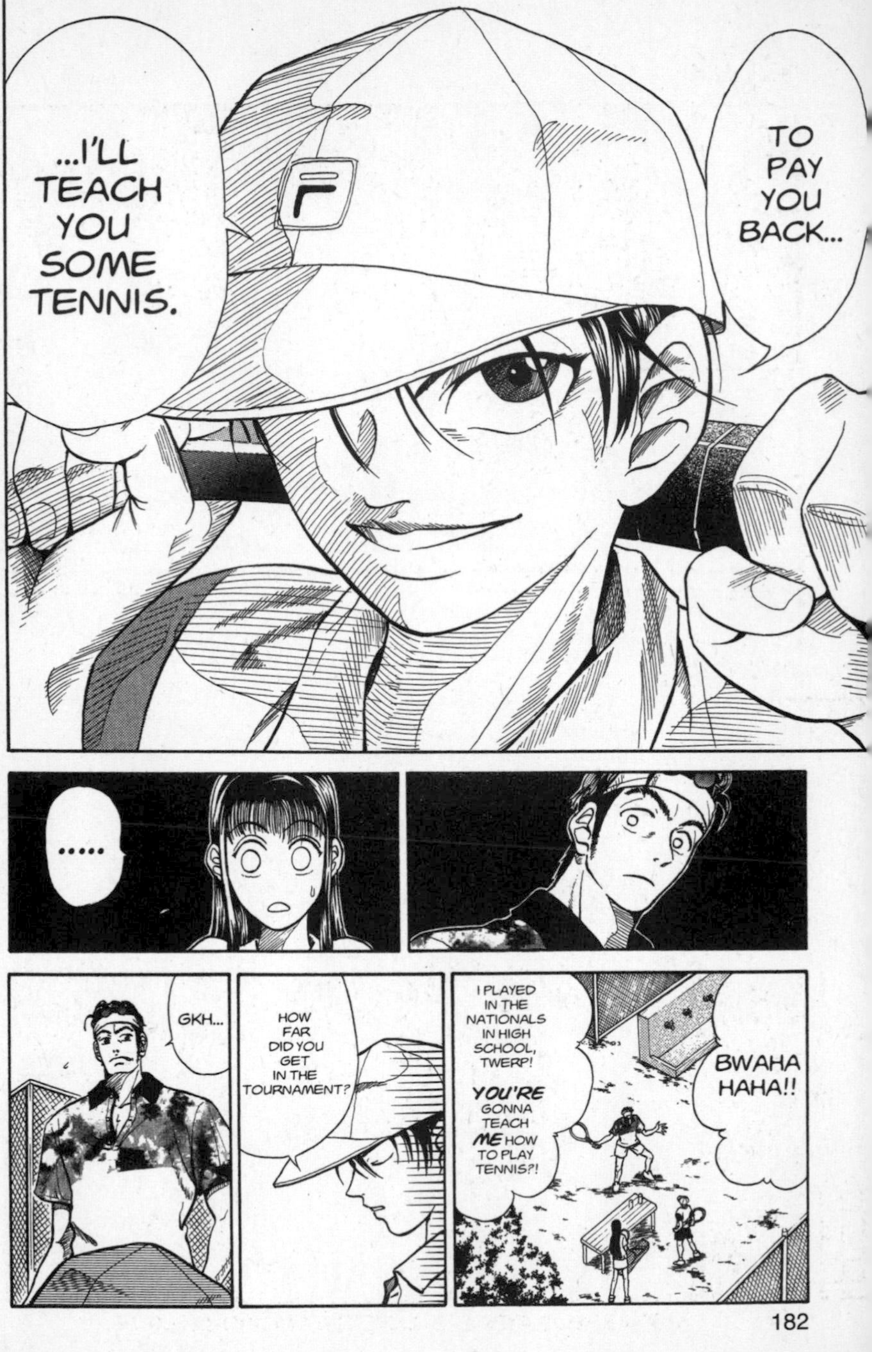
TO PAY YOU BACK...
...I'LL TEACH YOU SOME TENNIS.
......
BWAHA HAHA!!
I PLAYED IN THE NATIONALS IN HIGH SCHOOL, TWERP! YOU'RE GONNA TEACH ME HOW TO PLAY TENNIS?!
HOW FAR DID YOU GET IN THE TOURNAMENT?
GKH...

READ THIS WAY

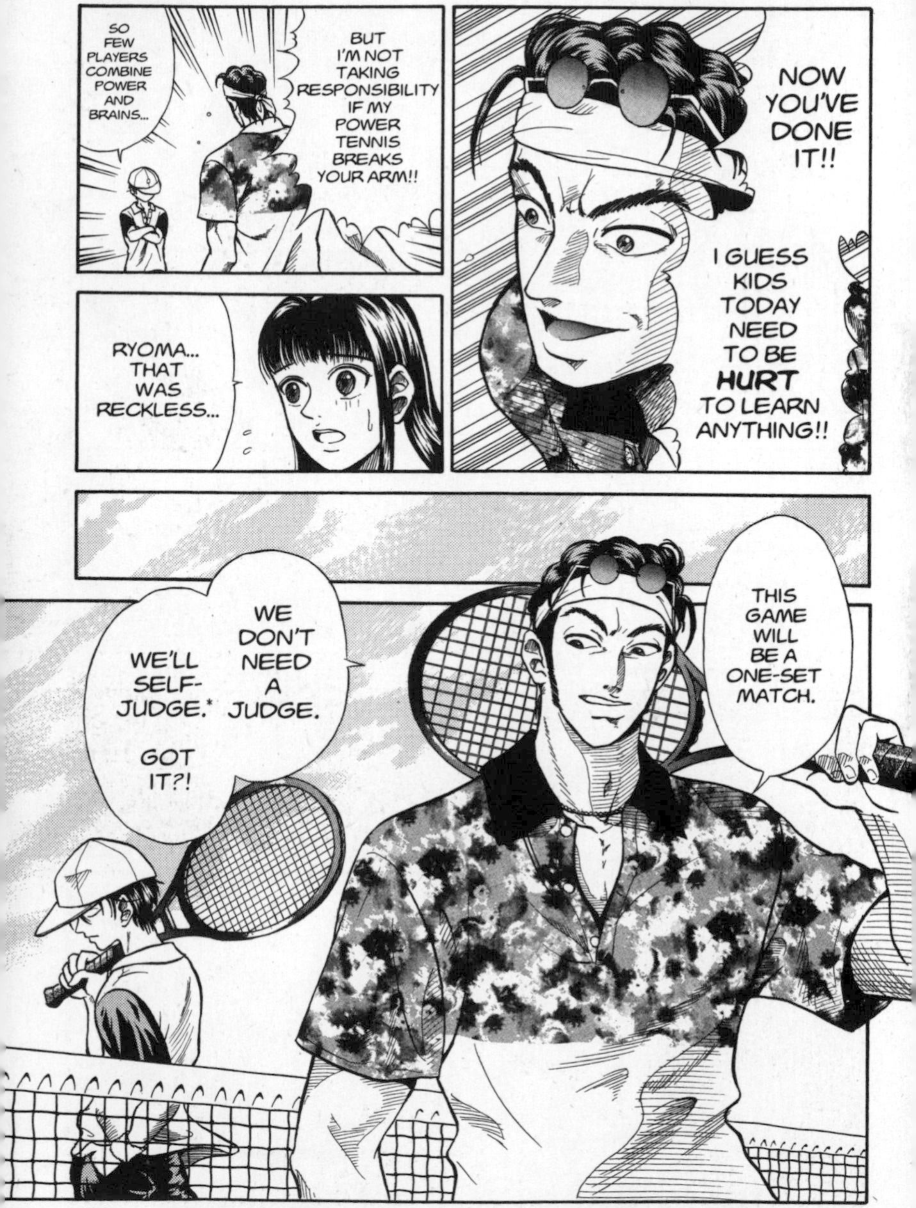
NOW YOU'VE DONE IT!!
I GUESS KIDS TODAY NEED TO BE **HURT** TO LEARN ANYTHING!!
SO FEW PLAYERS COMBINE POWER AND BRAINS...
BUT I'M NOT TAKING RESPONSIBILITY IF MY POWER TENNIS BREAKS YOUR ARM!!
RYOMA... THAT WAS RECKLESS...
THIS GAME WILL BE A ONE-SET MATCH.
WE DON'T NEED A JUDGE.
WE'LL SELF-JUDGE.* GOT IT?!

* WHEN THE PLAYERS JUDGE THEIR OWN COURTS.

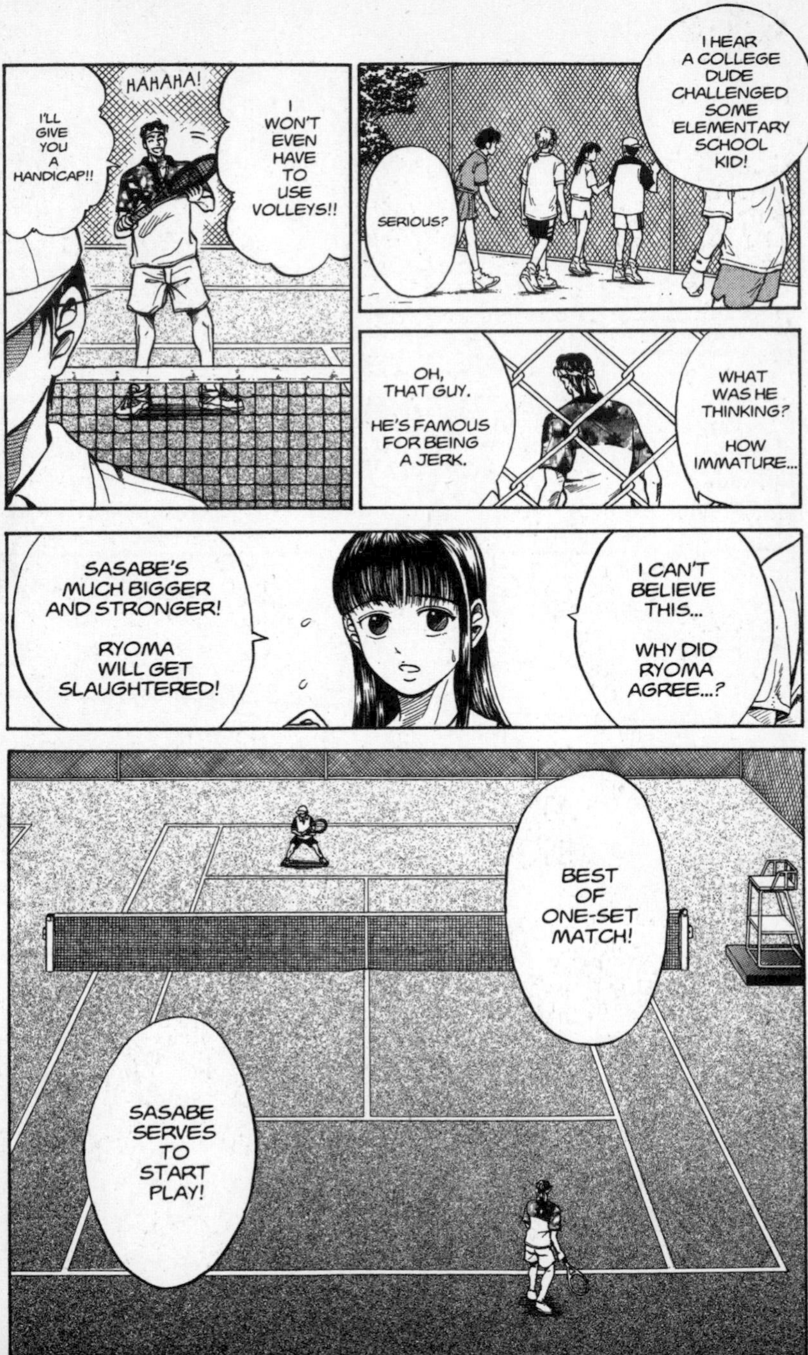
I HEAR A COLLEGE DUDE CHALLENGED SOME ELEMENTARY SCHOOL KID!
SERIOUS?
WHAT WAS HE THINKING? HOW IMMATURE...
OH, THAT GUY. HE'S FAMOUS FOR BEING A JERK.
I WON'T EVEN HAVE TO USE VOLLEYS!!
HAHAHA!
I'LL GIVE YOU A HANDICAP!!
I CAN'T BELIEVE THIS... WHY DID RYOMA AGREE...?
SASABE'S MUCH BIGGER AND STRONGER! RYOMA WILL GET SLAUGHTERED!
BEST OF ONE-SET MATCH!
SASABE SERVES TO START PLAY!

READ THIS WAY

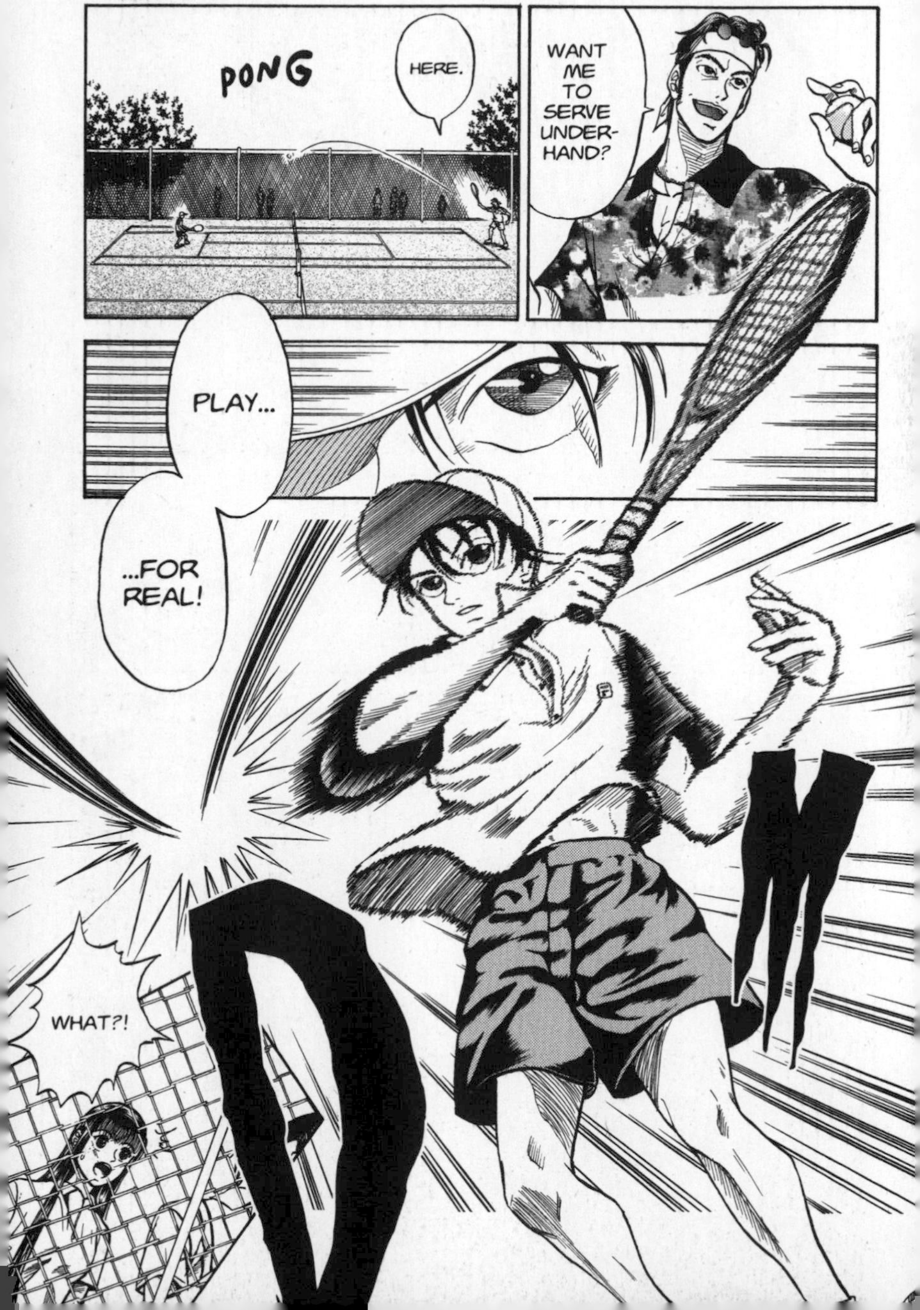
WANT ME TO SERVE UNDER-HAND?
HERE.
PONG
PLAY...
...FOR REAL!
WHAT?!

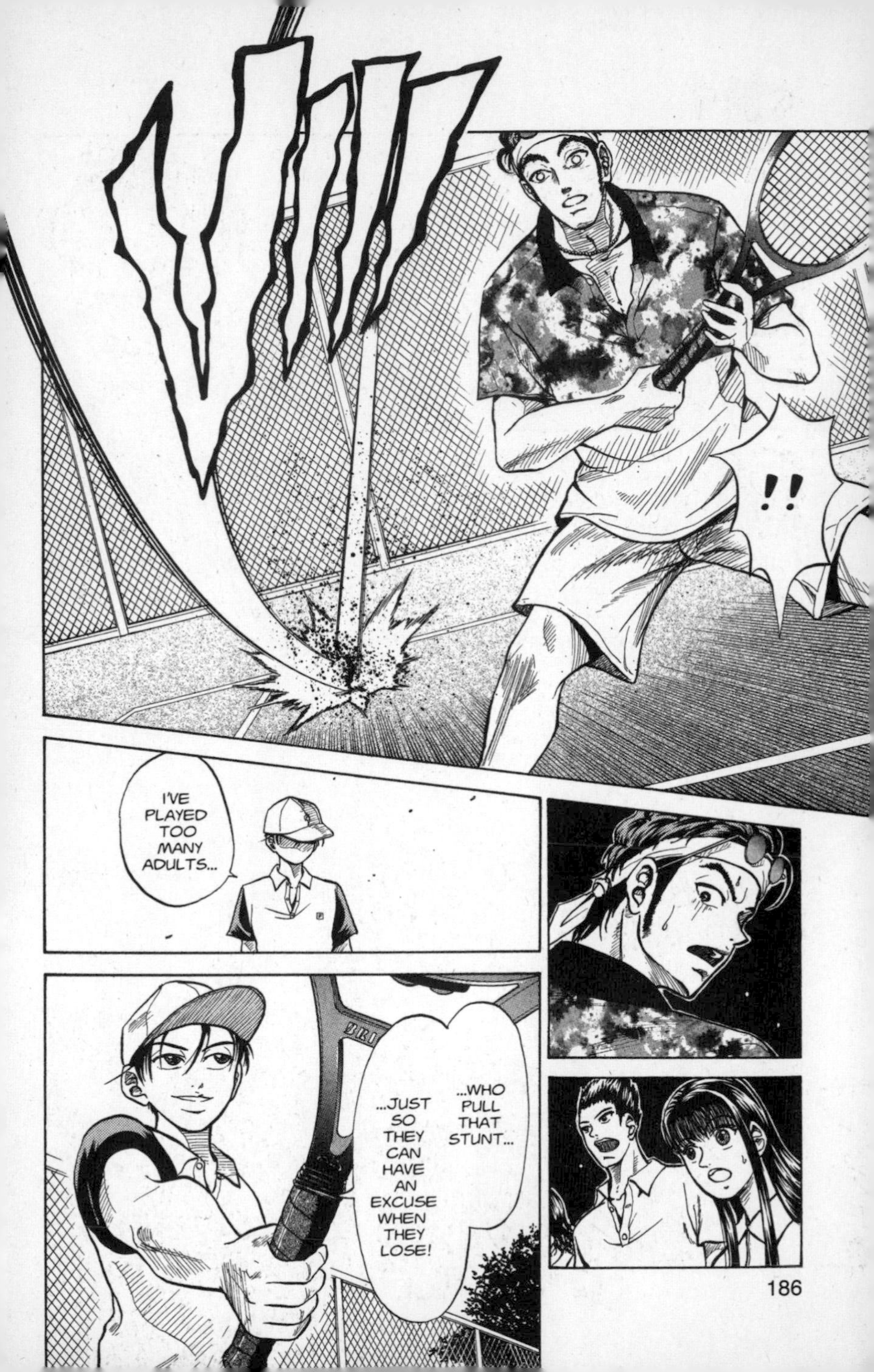
!!
I'VE PLAYED TOO MANY ADULTS...
...WHO PULL THAT STUNT...
...JUST SO THEY CAN HAVE AN EXCUSE WHEN THEY LOSE!

READ THIS WAY

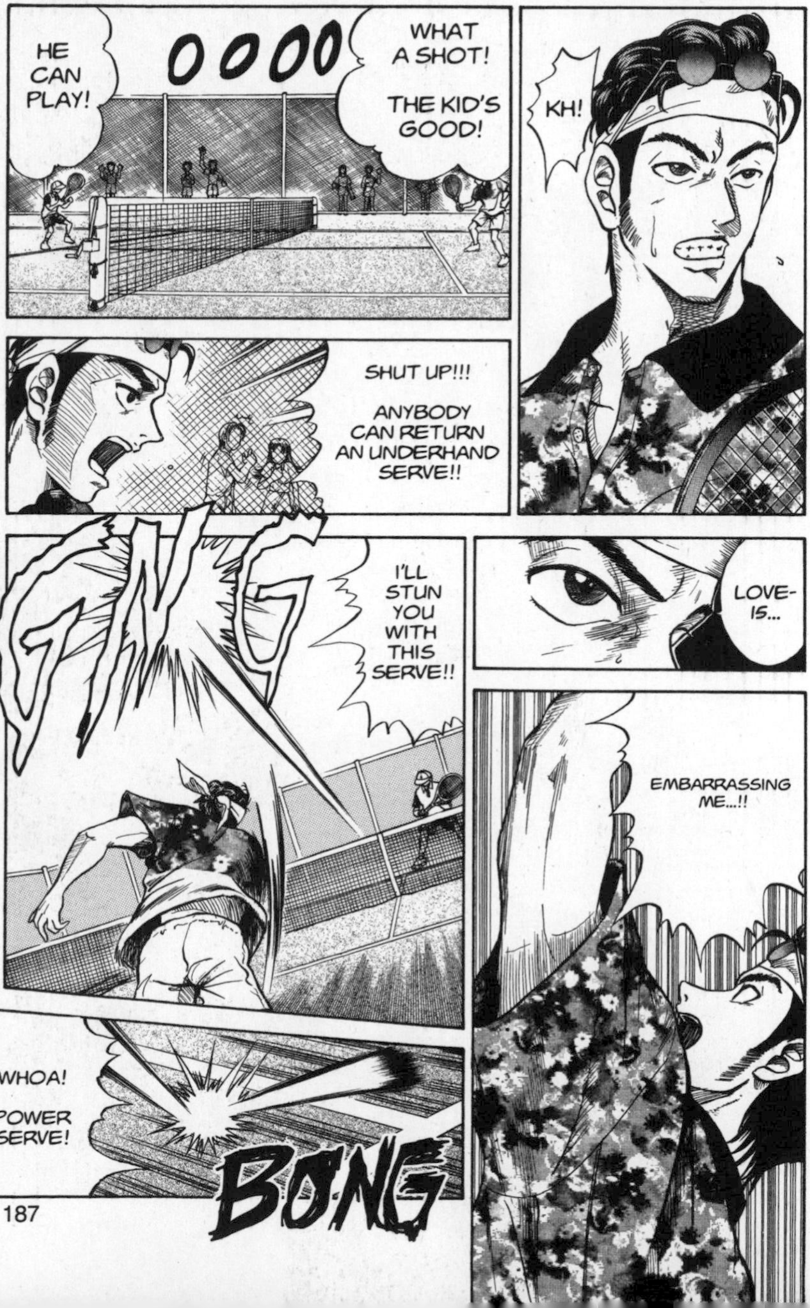
KH!
WHAT A SHOT!
THE KID'S GOOD!
OOOO
HE CAN PLAY!
SHUT UP!!!
ANYBODY CAN RETURN AN UNDERHAND SERVE!!
LOVE-IS...
EMBARRASSING ME...!!
I'LL STUN YOU WITH THIS SERVE!!
GING
BONG
WHOA!
POWER SERVE!

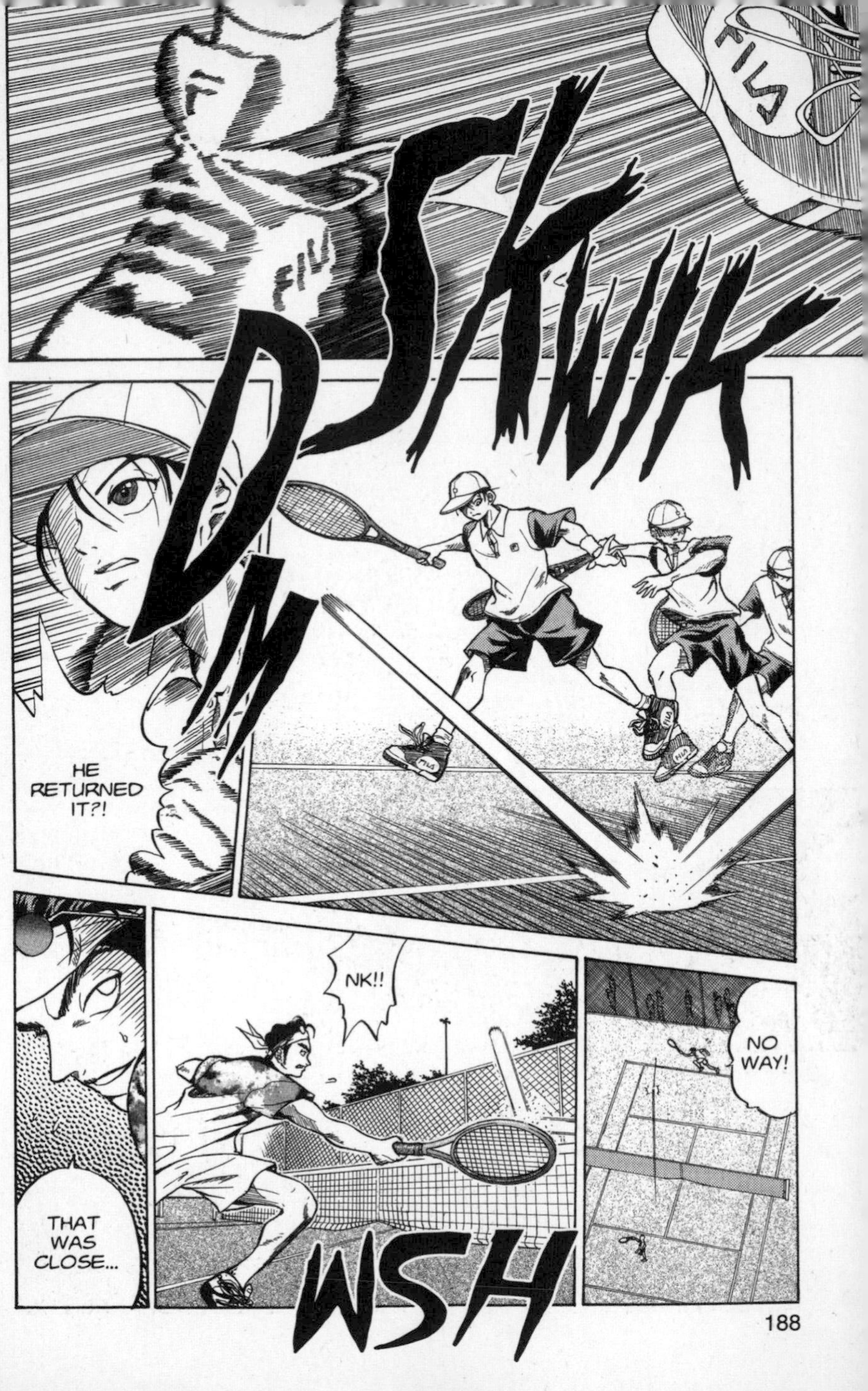
HE RETURNED IT?!
NO WAY!
NK!!
WSH
THAT WAS CLOSE...

READ THIS WAY

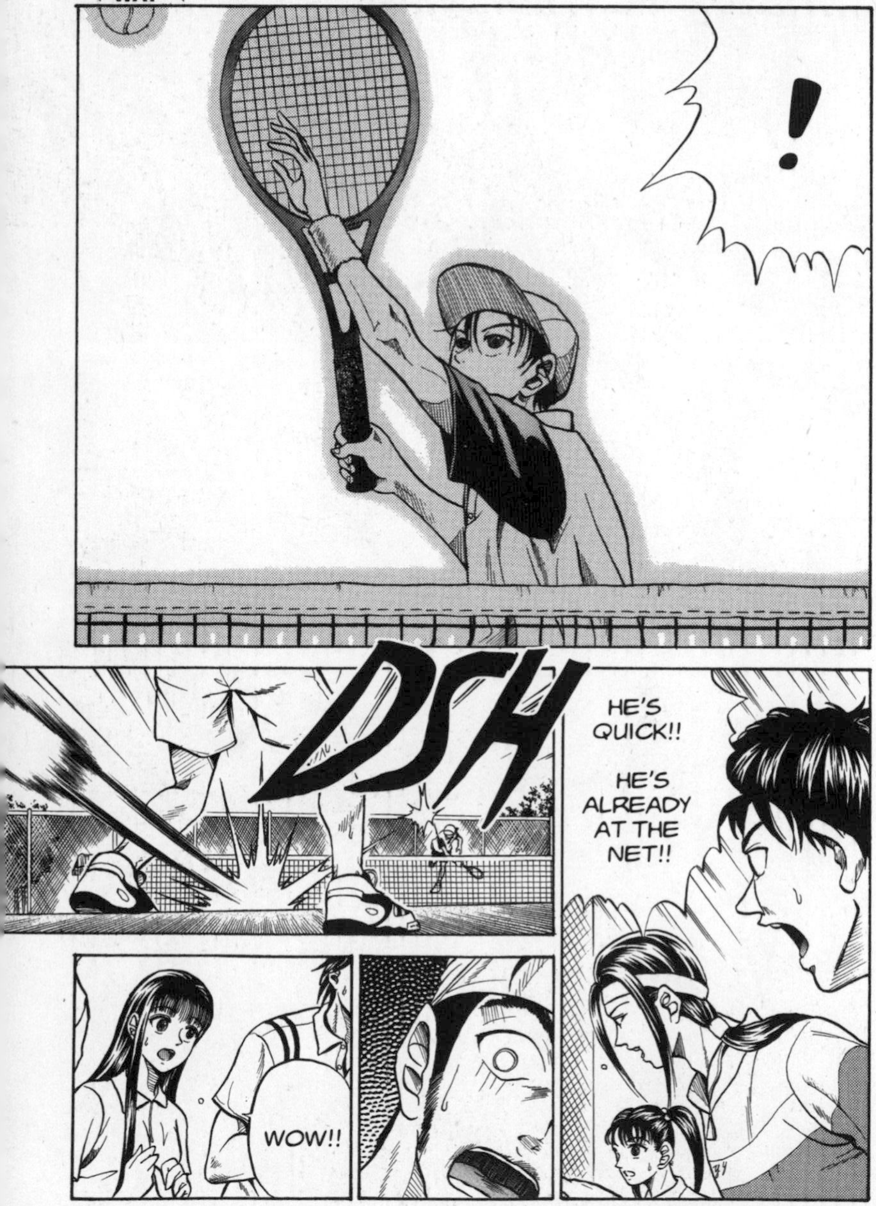
!
HE'S QUICK!!
HE'S ALREADY AT THE NET!!
DSH
WOW!!

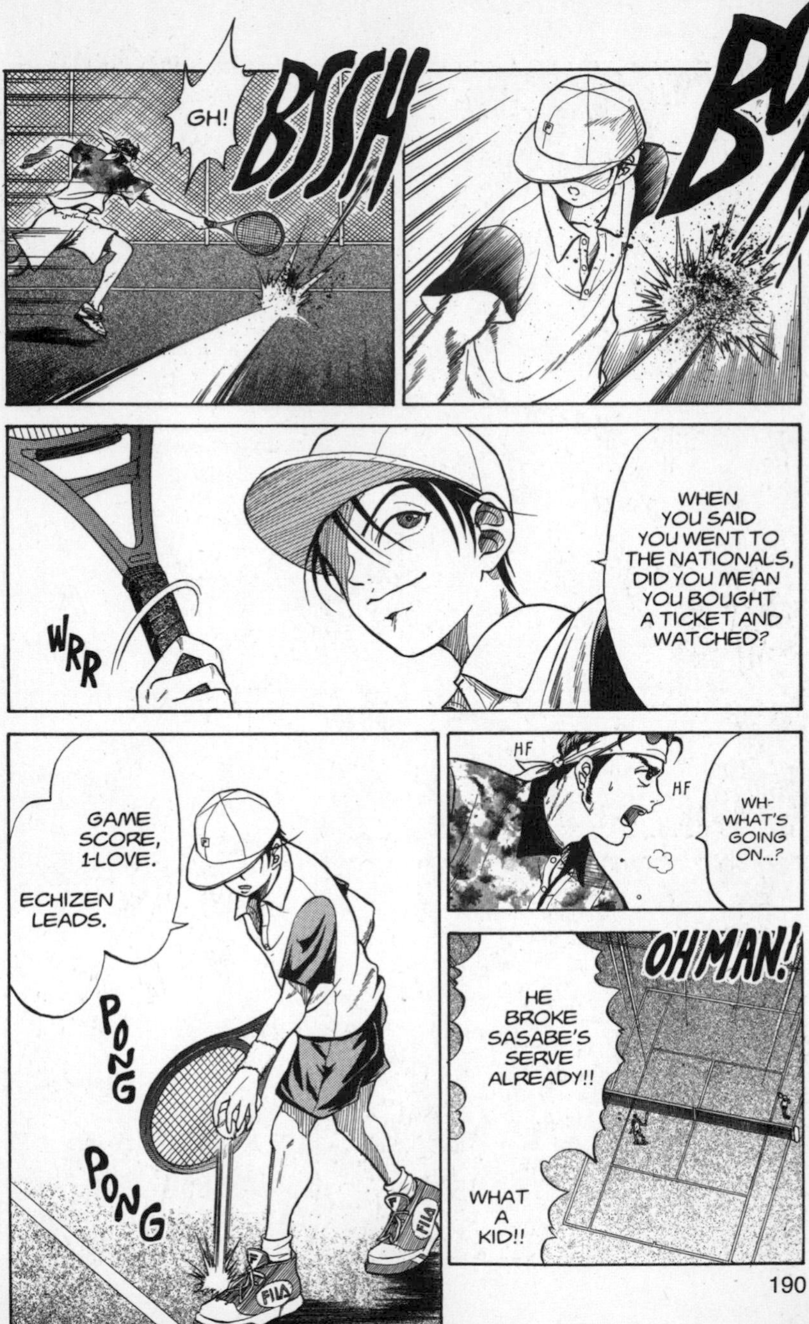
BOOM
GH!
BISH
WHEN YOU SAID YOU WENT TO THE NATIONALS, DID YOU MEAN YOU BOUGHT A TICKET AND WATCHED?
WRR
HF
HF
WH- WHAT'S GOING ON...?
OH MAN!
HE BROKE SASABE'S SERVE ALREADY!!
WHAT A KID!!
GAME SCORE, 1-LOVE.
ECHIZEN LEADS.
PONG
PONG

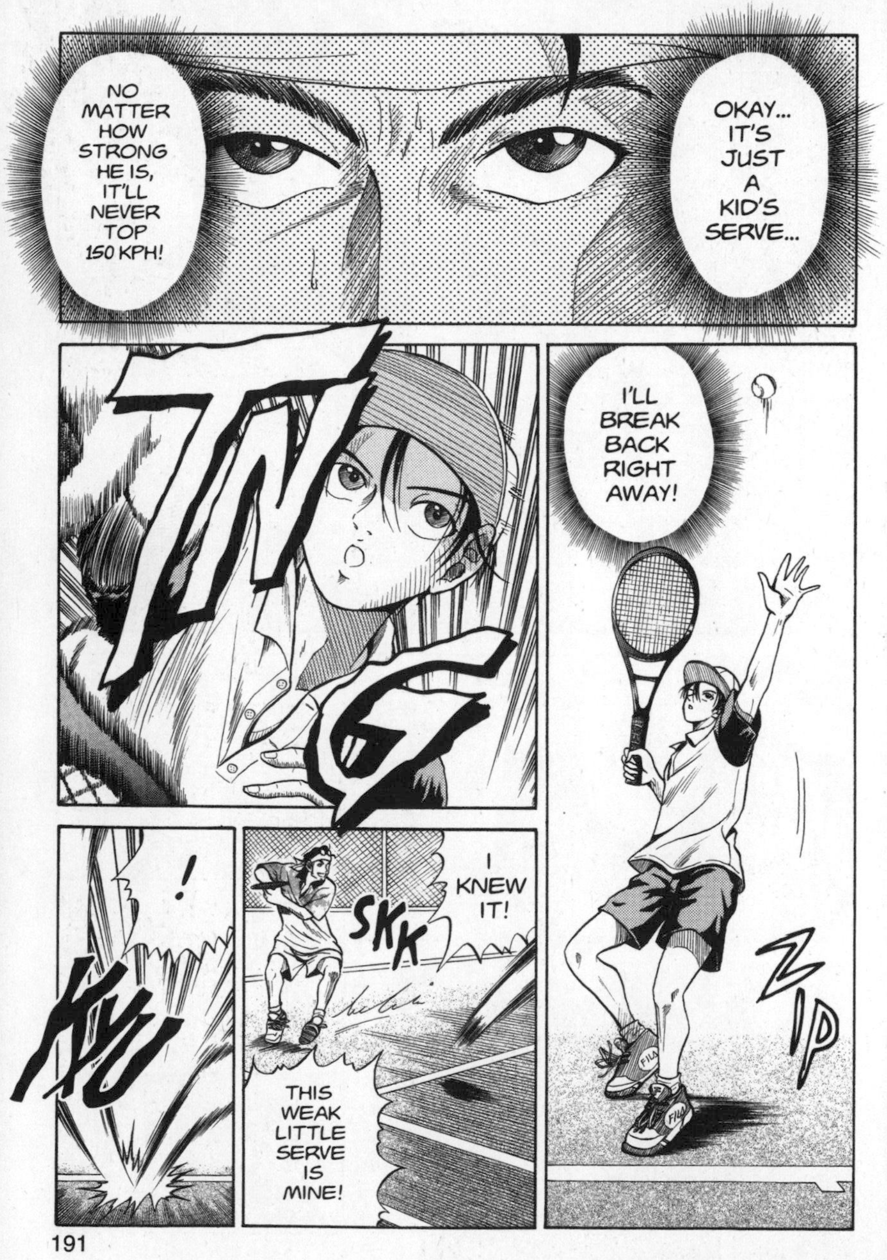
OKAY... IT'S JUST A KID'S SERVE...
NO MATTER HOW STRONG HE IS, IT'LL NEVER TOP 150 KPH!
I'LL BREAK BACK RIGHT AWAY!
ZIP
TNG
I KNEW IT!
SKK
THIS WEAK LITTLE SERVE IS MINE!
!
KYU

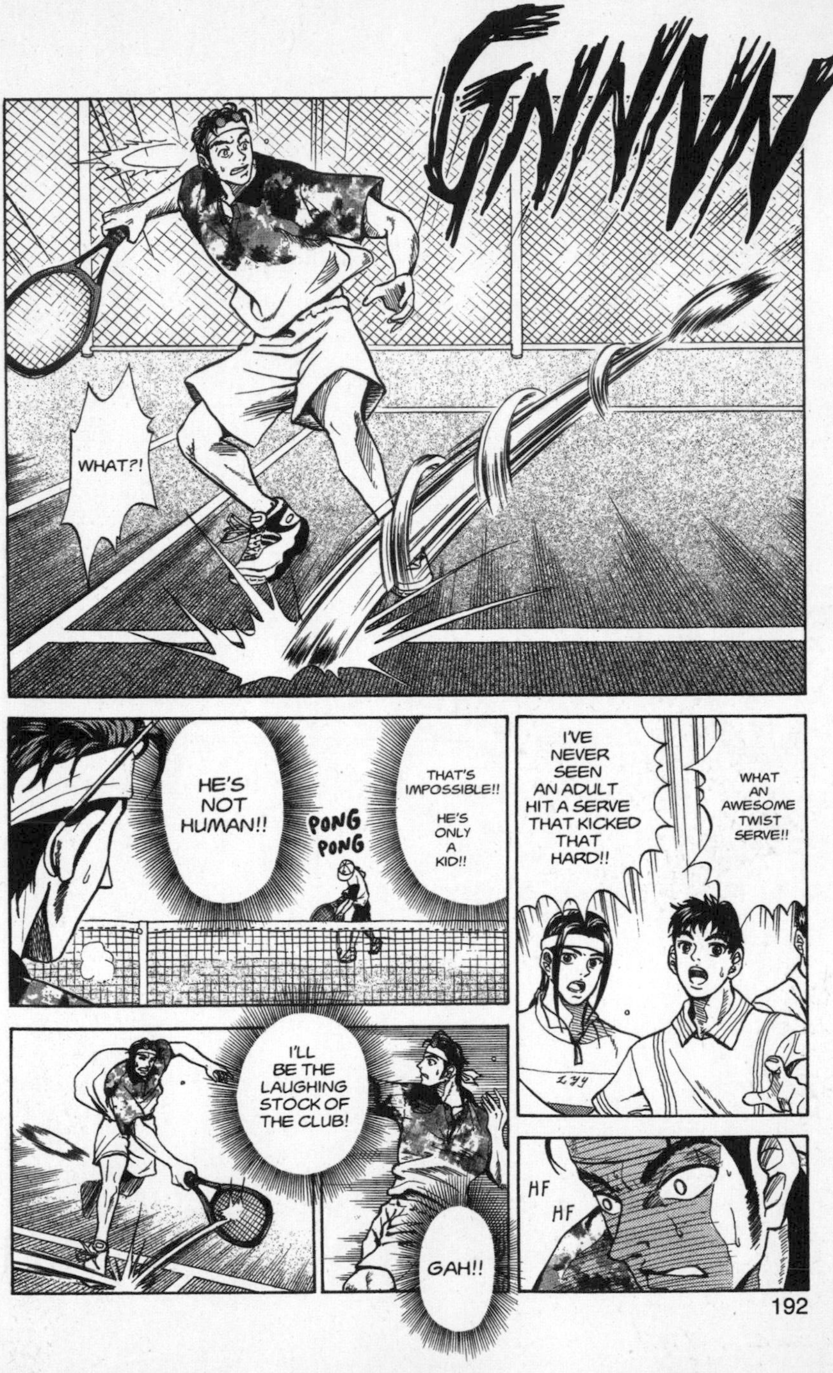
GNNNN
WHAT?!
WHAT AN AWESOME TWIST SERVE!!
I'VE NEVER SEEN AN ADULT HIT A SERVE THAT KICKED THAT HARD!!
THAT'S IMPOSSIBLE!! HE'S ONLY A KID!!
PONG PONG
HE'S NOT HUMAN!!
HF HF
I'LL BE THE LAUGHING STOCK OF THE CLUB!
GAH!!

READ THIS WAY

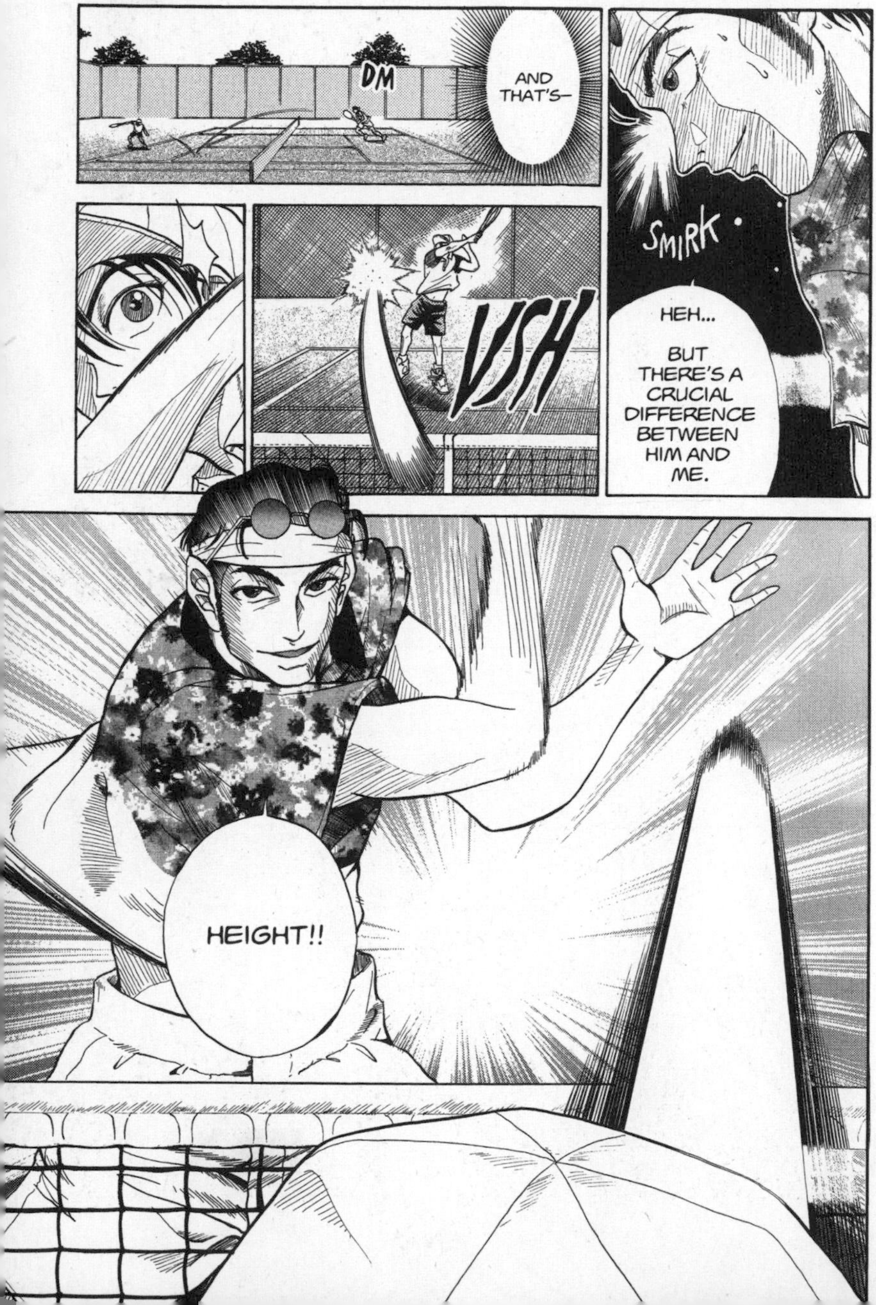
SMIRK
HEH... BUT THERE'S A CRUCIAL DIFFERENCE BETWEEN HIM AND ME.
DM
AND THAT'S—
VSH
HEIGHT!!

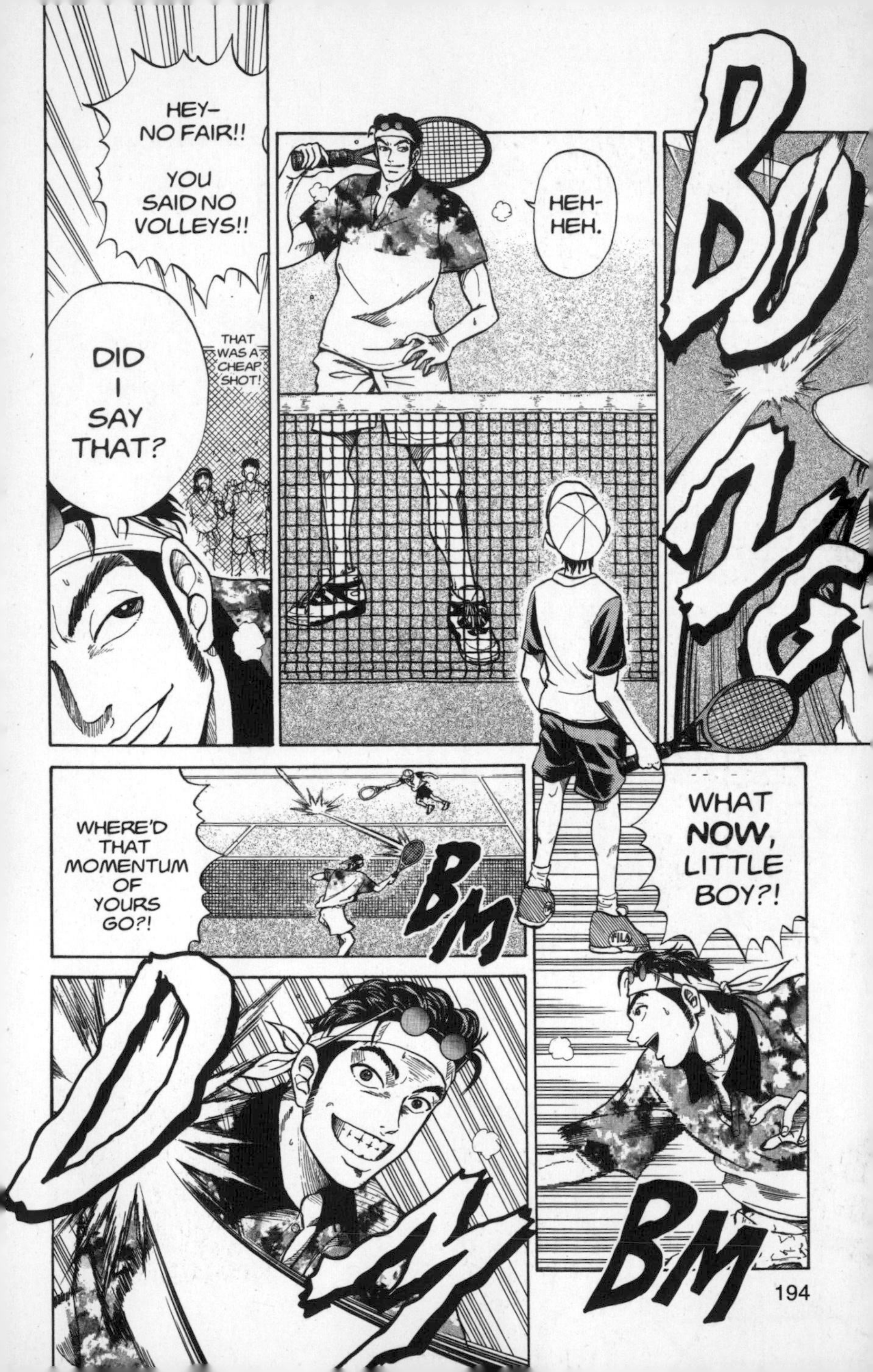
BOING
HEH-HEH.
HEY- NO FAIR!! YOU SAID NO VOLLEYS!!
THAT WAS A CHEAP SHOT!
DID I SAY THAT?
WHAT NOW, LITTLE BOY?!
BM
BM
WHERE'D THAT MOMENTUM OF YOURS GO?!

READ THIS WAY

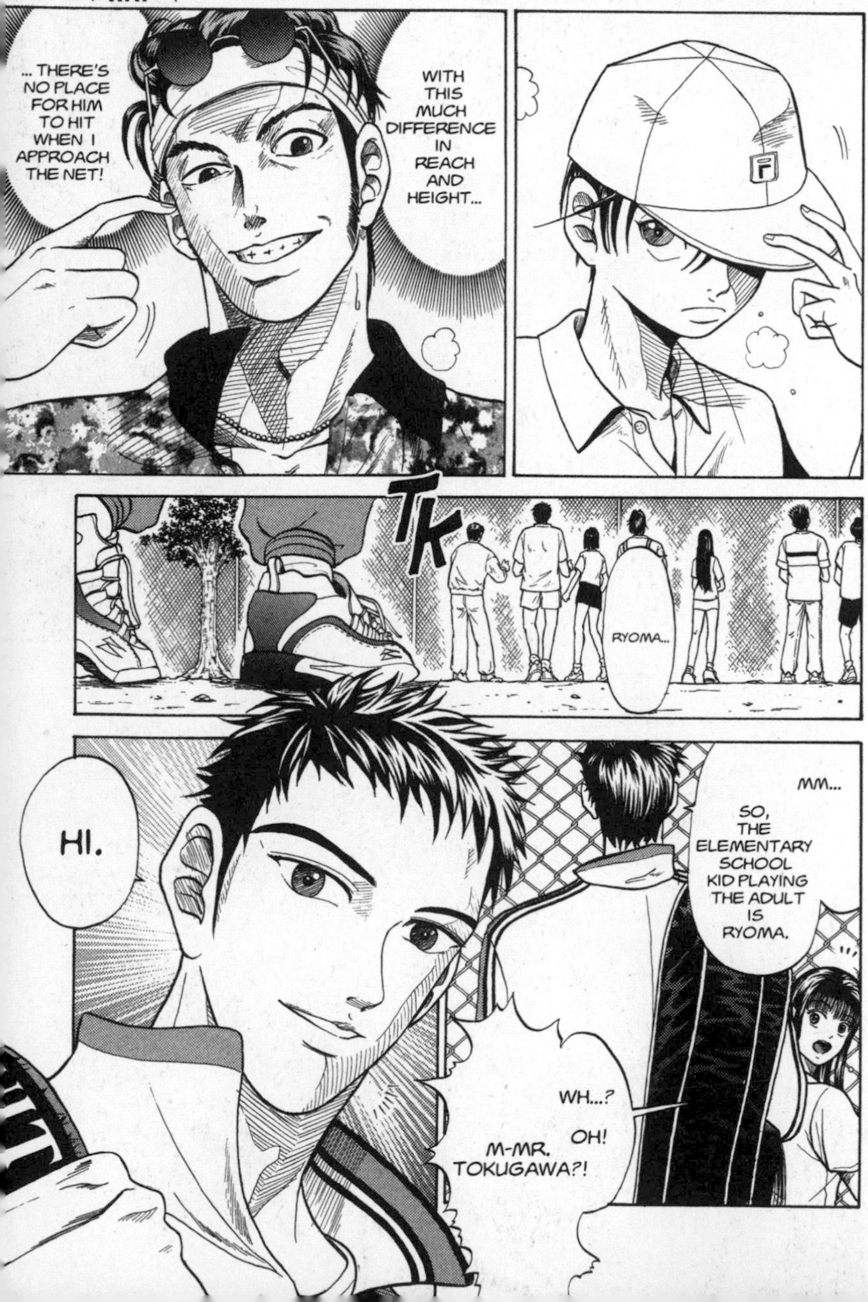

WITH THIS MUCH DIFFERENCE IN REACH AND HEIGHT...
... THERE'S NO PLACE FOR HIM TO HIT WHEN I APPROACH THE NET!
TK
RYOMA...
MM...
SO, THE ELEMENTARY SCHOOL KID PLAYING THE ADULT IS RYOMA.
WH...?
OH!
M-MR. TOKUGAWA?!
HI.

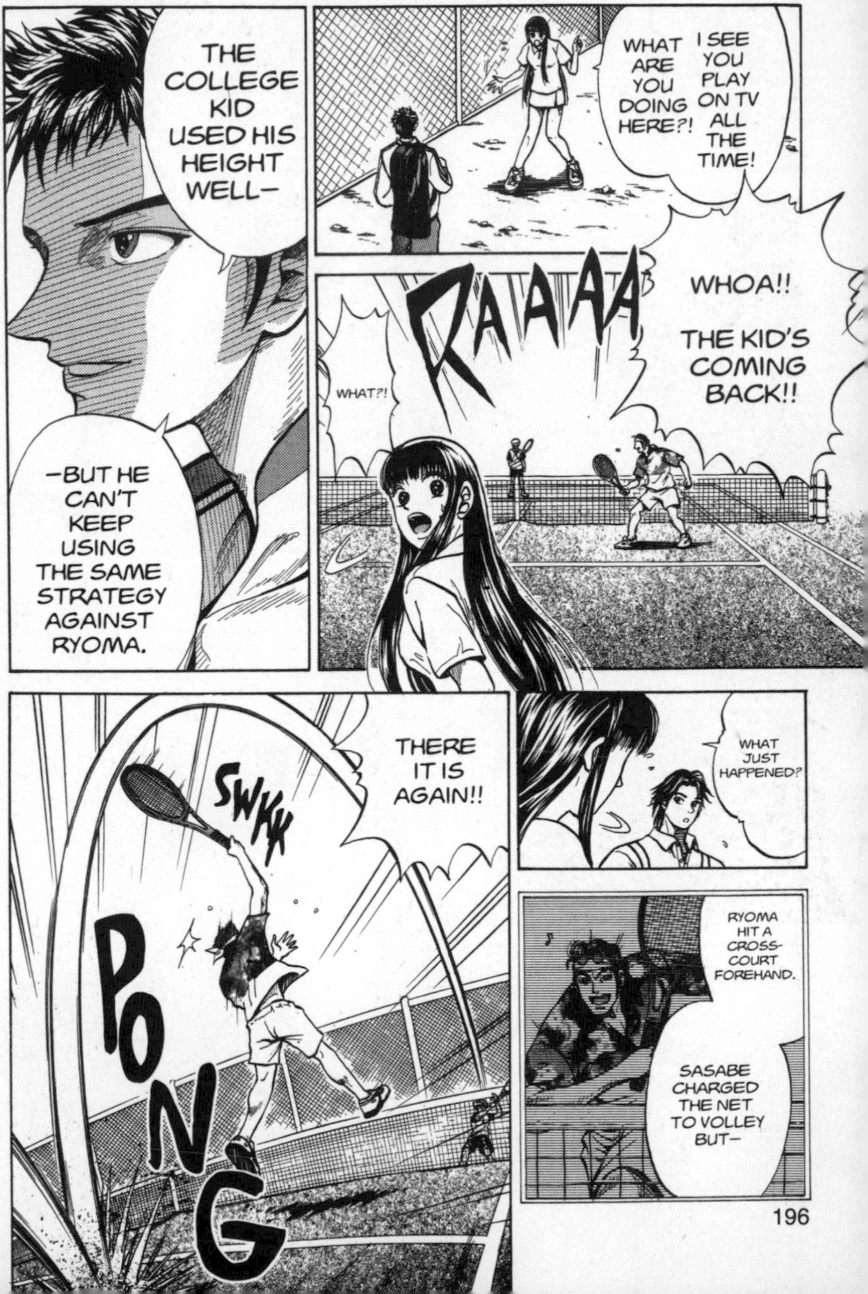
WHAT ARE YOU DOING HERE?!
I SEE YOU PLAY ON TV ALL THE TIME!
RAAAA
WHOA!!
THE KID'S COMING BACK!!
WHAT?!
THE COLLEGE KID USED HIS HEIGHT WELL—
—BUT HE CAN'T KEEP USING THE SAME STRATEGY AGAINST RYOMA.
WHAT JUST HAPPENED?
RYOMA HIT A CROSS-COURT FOREHAND.
SASABE CHARGED THE NET TO VOLLEY BUT—
SWKK
THERE IT IS AGAIN!!
PONG

READ THIS WAY

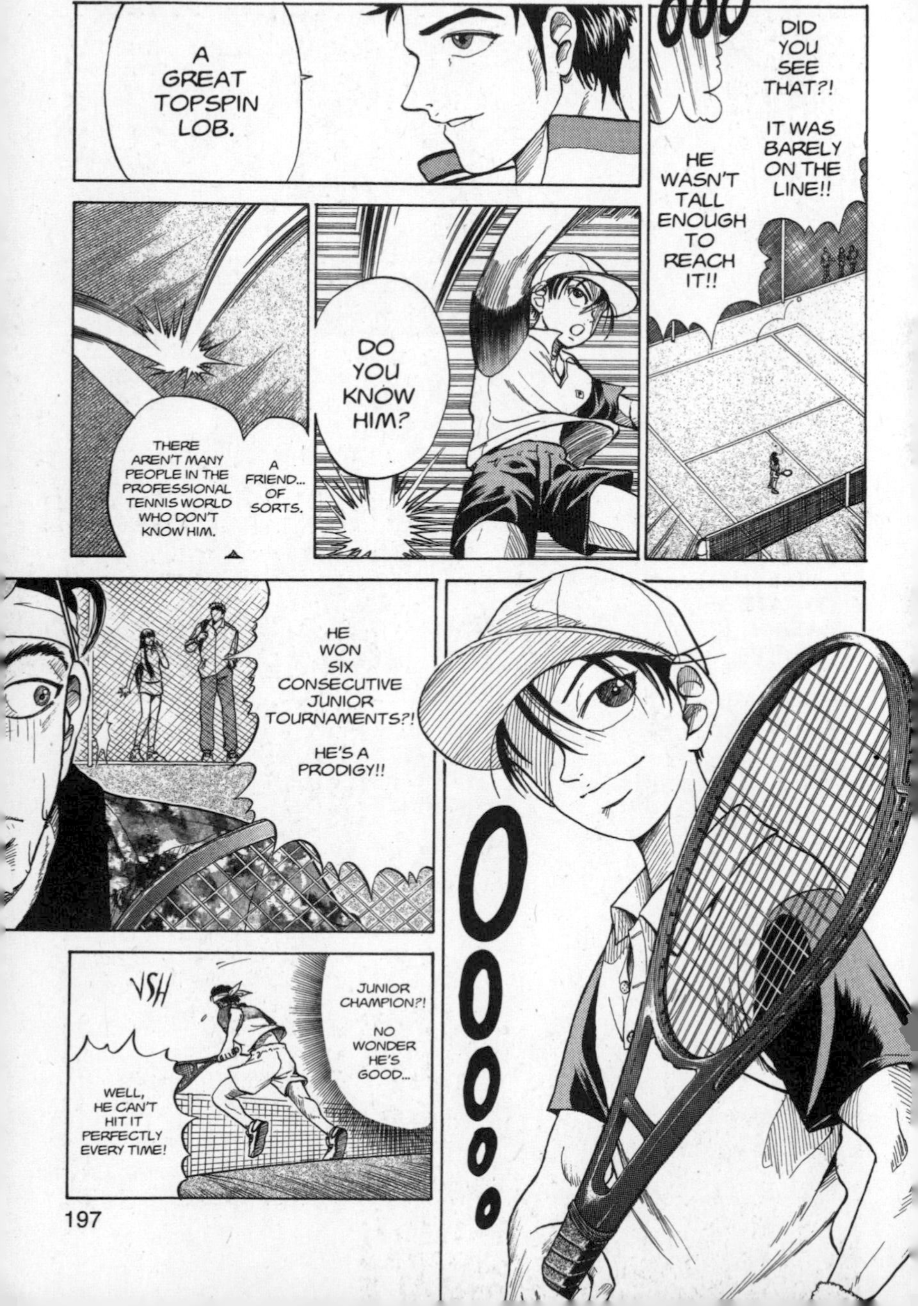
OOO
DID YOU SEE THAT?!
IT WAS BARELY ON THE LINE!!
HE WASN'T TALL ENOUGH TO REACH IT!!
A GREAT TOPSPIN LOB.
DO YOU KNOW HIM?
A FRIEND... OF SORTS.
THERE AREN'T MANY PEOPLE IN THE PROFESSIONAL TENNIS WORLD WHO DON'T KNOW HIM.
OOOOOOO
HE WON SIX CONSECUTIVE JUNIOR TOURNAMENTS?!
HE'S A PRODIGY!!
JUNIOR CHAMPION?!
NO WONDER HE'S GOOD...
VSH
WELL, HE CAN'T HIT IT PERFECTLY EVERY TIME!

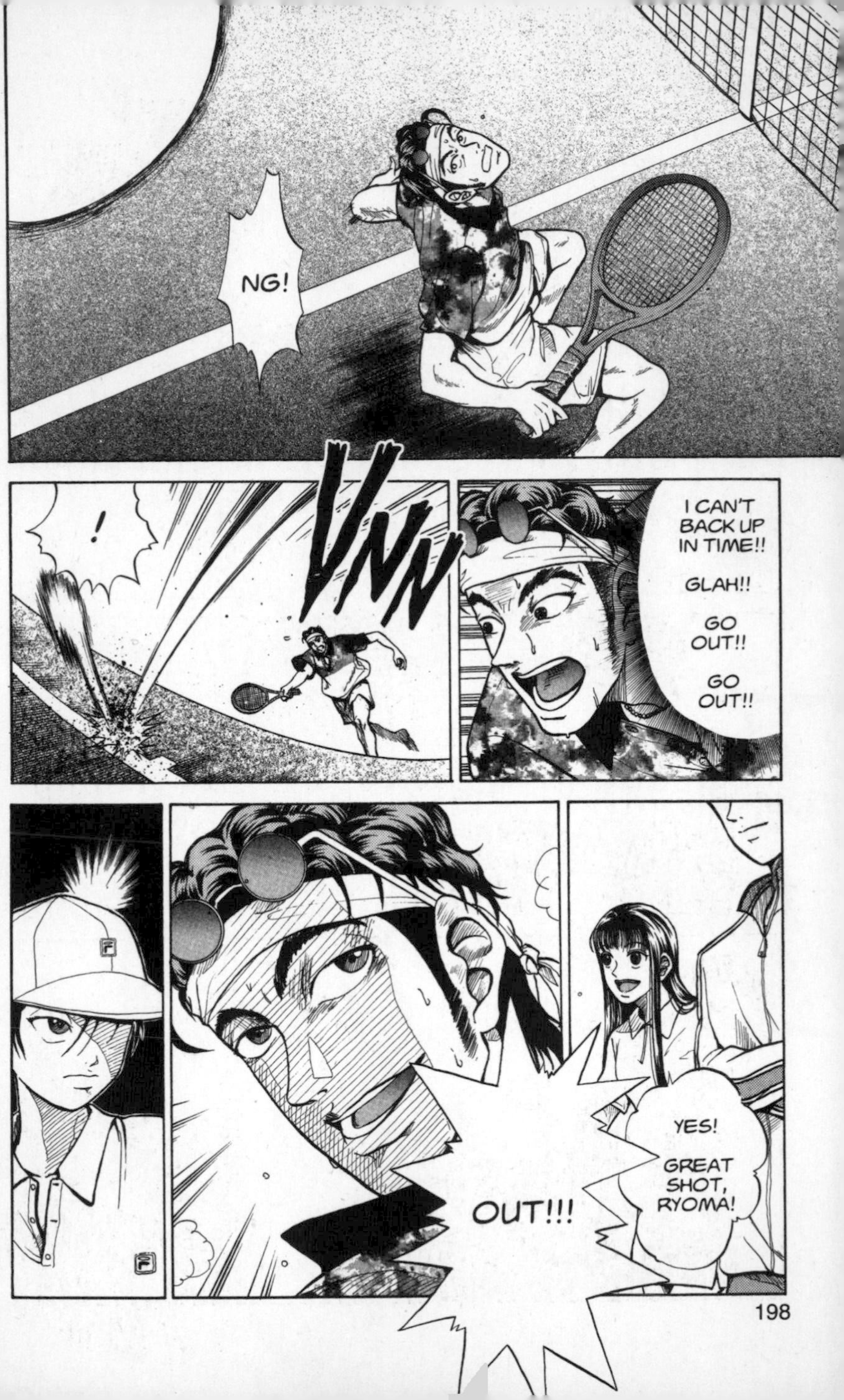
NG!
I CAN'T BACK UP IN TIME!!
GLAH!!
GO OUT!!
GO OUT!!
VNN
!
YES! GREAT SHOT, RYOMA!
OUT!!!

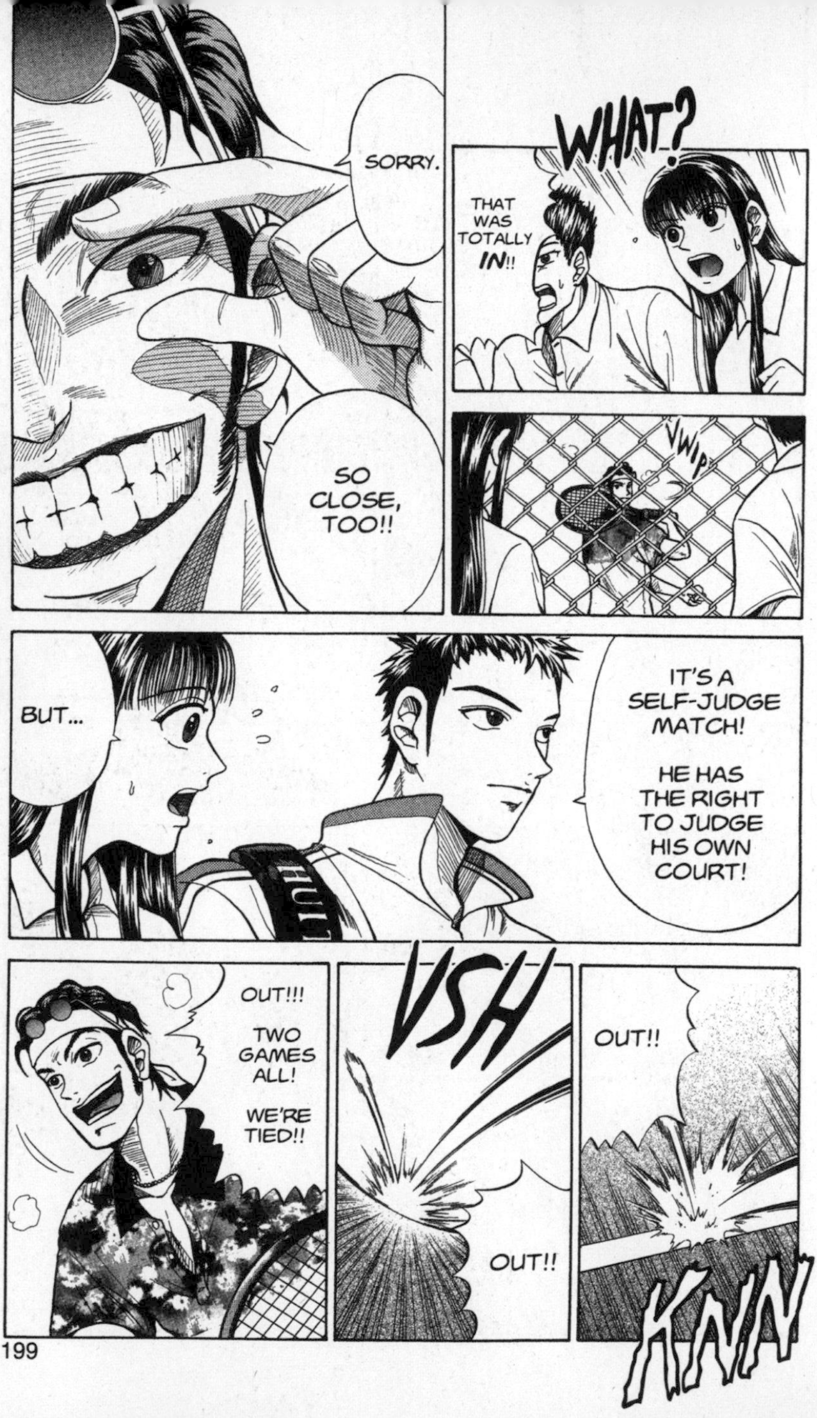
WHAT?
THAT WAS TOTALLY IN!!
VWIP
SORRY.
SO CLOSE, TOO!!
IT'S A SELF-JUDGE MATCH!
HE HAS THE RIGHT TO JUDGE HIS OWN COURT!
BUT...
OUT!!
KNN
VSH
OUT!!
OUT!!!
TWO GAMES ALL!
WE'RE TIED!!

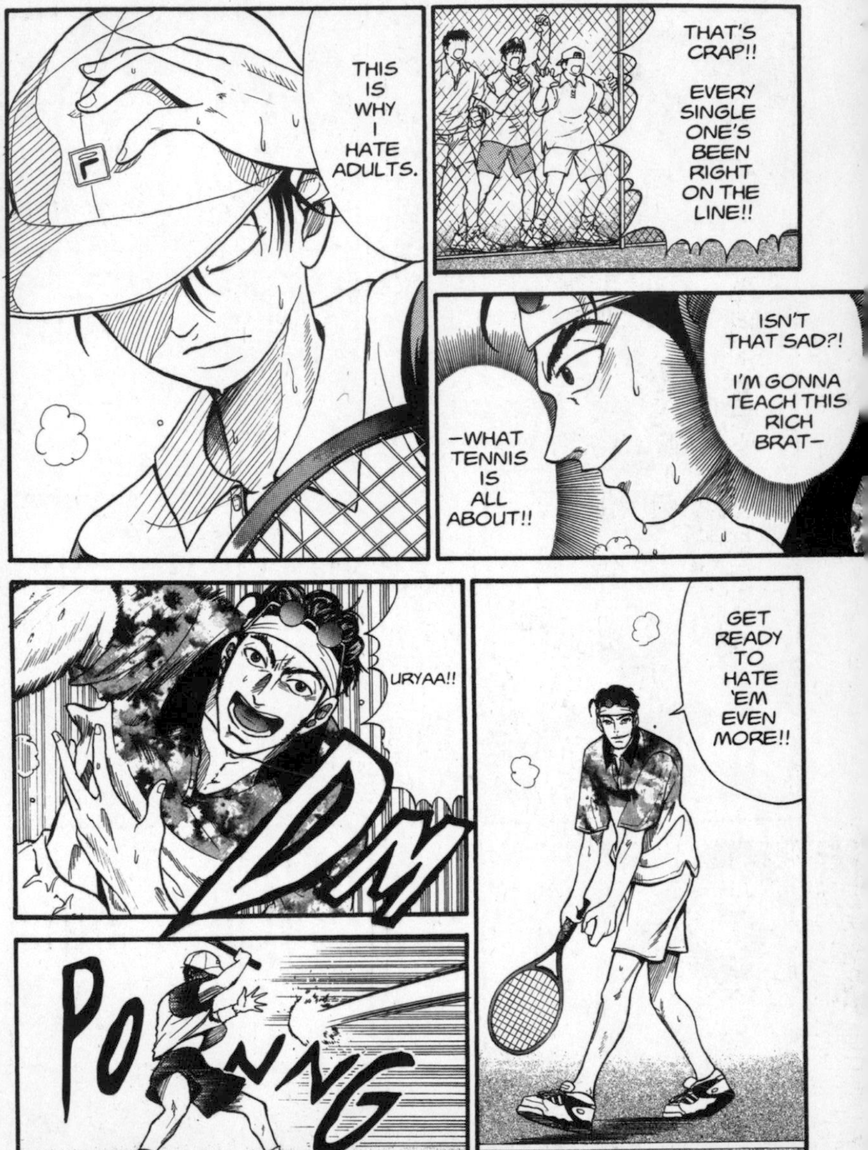
THAT'S CRAP!!
EVERY SINGLE ONE'S BEEN RIGHT ON THE LINE!!
ISN'T THAT SAD?!
I'M GONNA TEACH THIS RICH BRAT—
—WHAT TENNIS IS ALL ABOUT!!
THIS IS WHY I HATE ADULTS.
GET READY TO HATE 'EM EVEN MORE!!
URYAA!!
DM
PONNG

READ THIS WAY

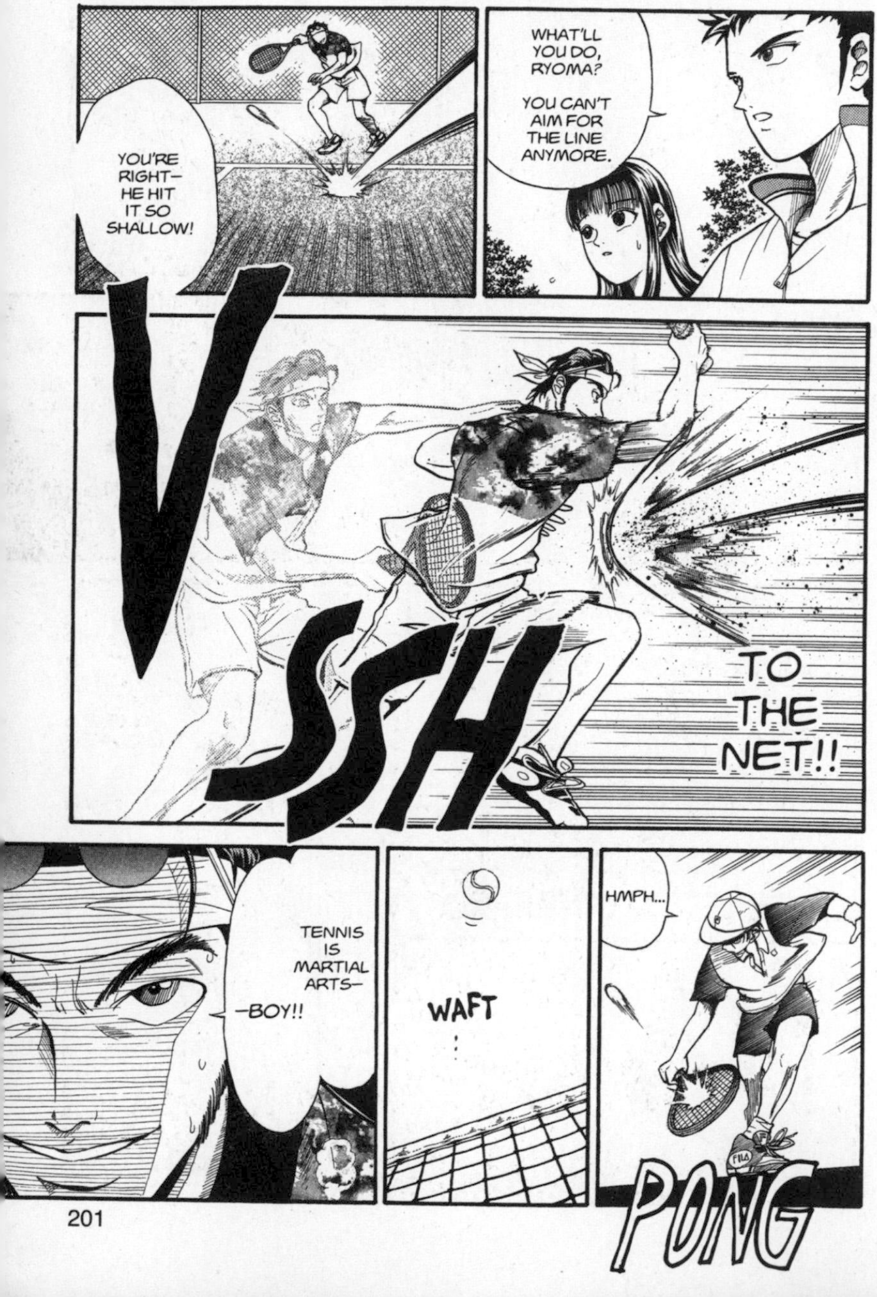

WHAT'LL YOU DO, RYOMA?
YOU CAN'T AIM FOR THE LINE ANYMORE.
YOU'RE RIGHT—HE HIT IT SO SHALLOW!
VSSH
TO THE NET!!
HMPH...
PONG
WAFT
TENNIS IS MARTIAL ARTS—
—BOY!!

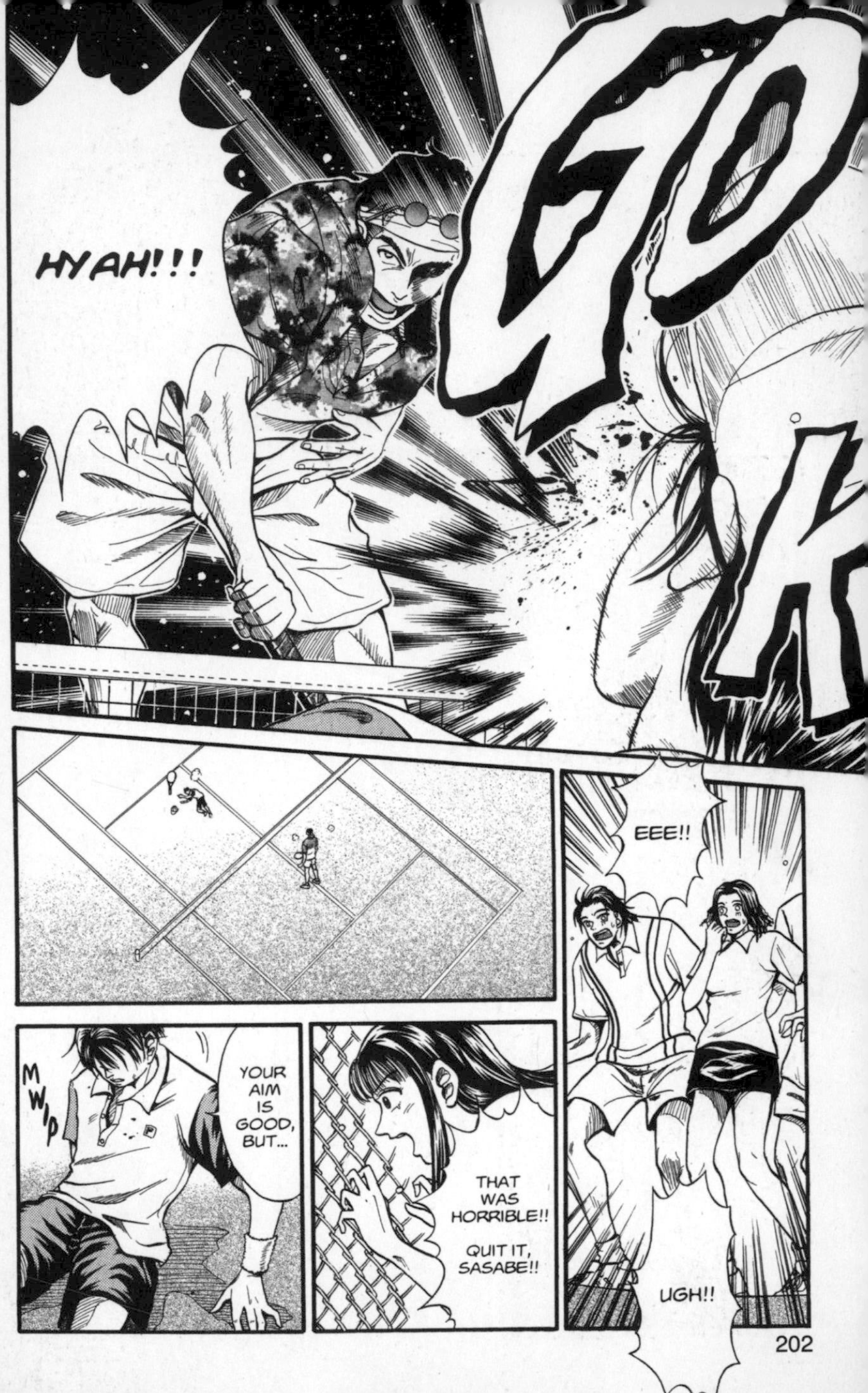
HYAH!!!
EEE!!
UGH!!
THAT WAS HORRIBLE!!
QUIT IT, SASABE!!
YOUR AIM IS GOOD, BUT...
MWIP

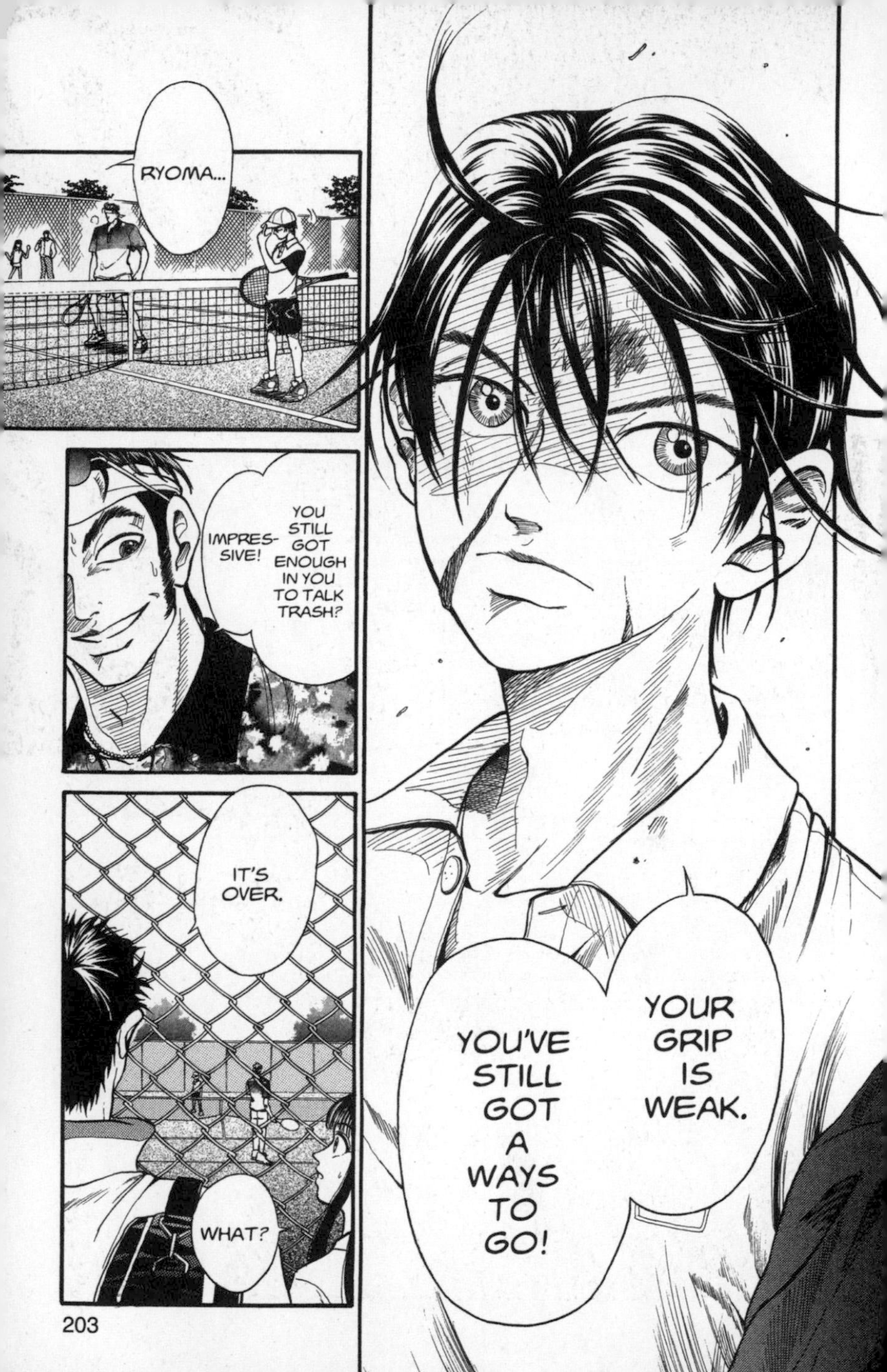
YOUR GRIP IS WEAK.
YOU'VE STILL GOT A WAYS TO GO!
RYOMA...
YOU STILL GOT ENOUGH IN YOU TO TALK TRASH?
IMPRES-SIVE!
IT'S OVER.
WHAT?

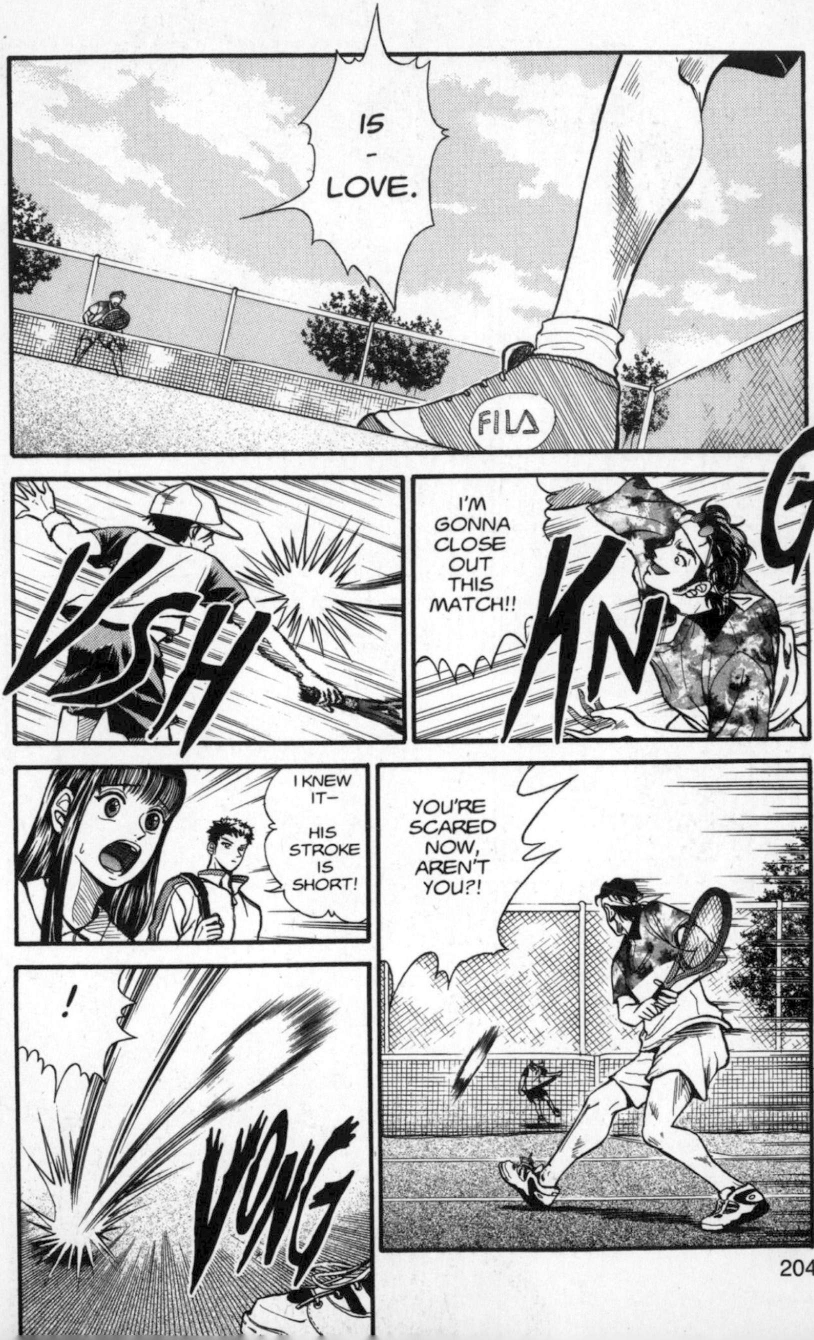
IS - LOVE.
I'M GONNA CLOSE OUT THIS MATCH!!
KNG
VSH
YOU'RE SCARED NOW, AREN'T YOU?!
I KNEW IT—
HIS STROKE IS SHORT!
!
VVONG

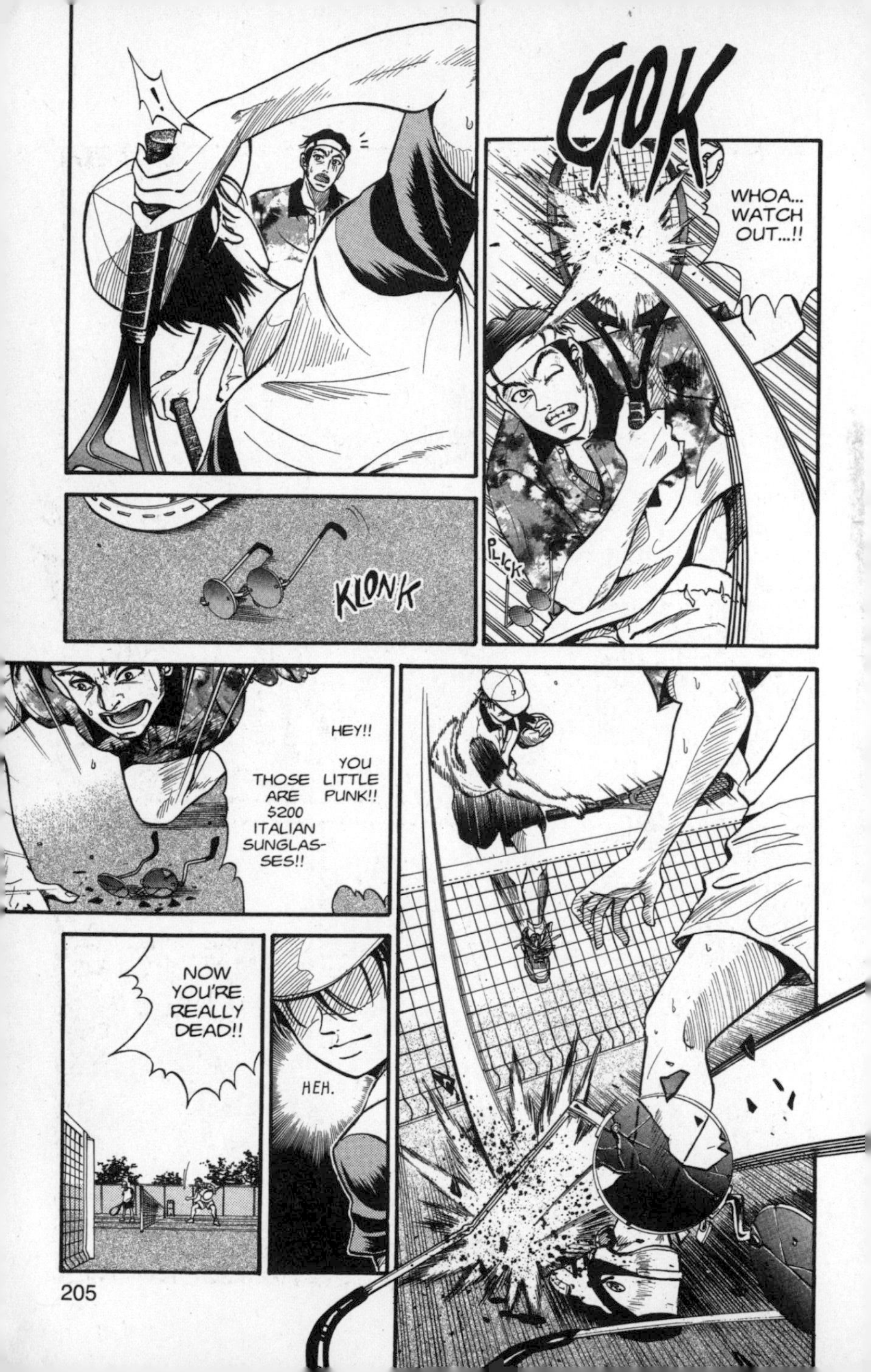
GOK
WHOA... WATCH OUT...!!
PLICK
!
KLONK
HEY!!
YOU LITTLE PUNK!!
THOSE ARE $200 ITALIAN SUNGLAS-SES!!
HEH.
NOW YOU'RE REALLY DEAD!!

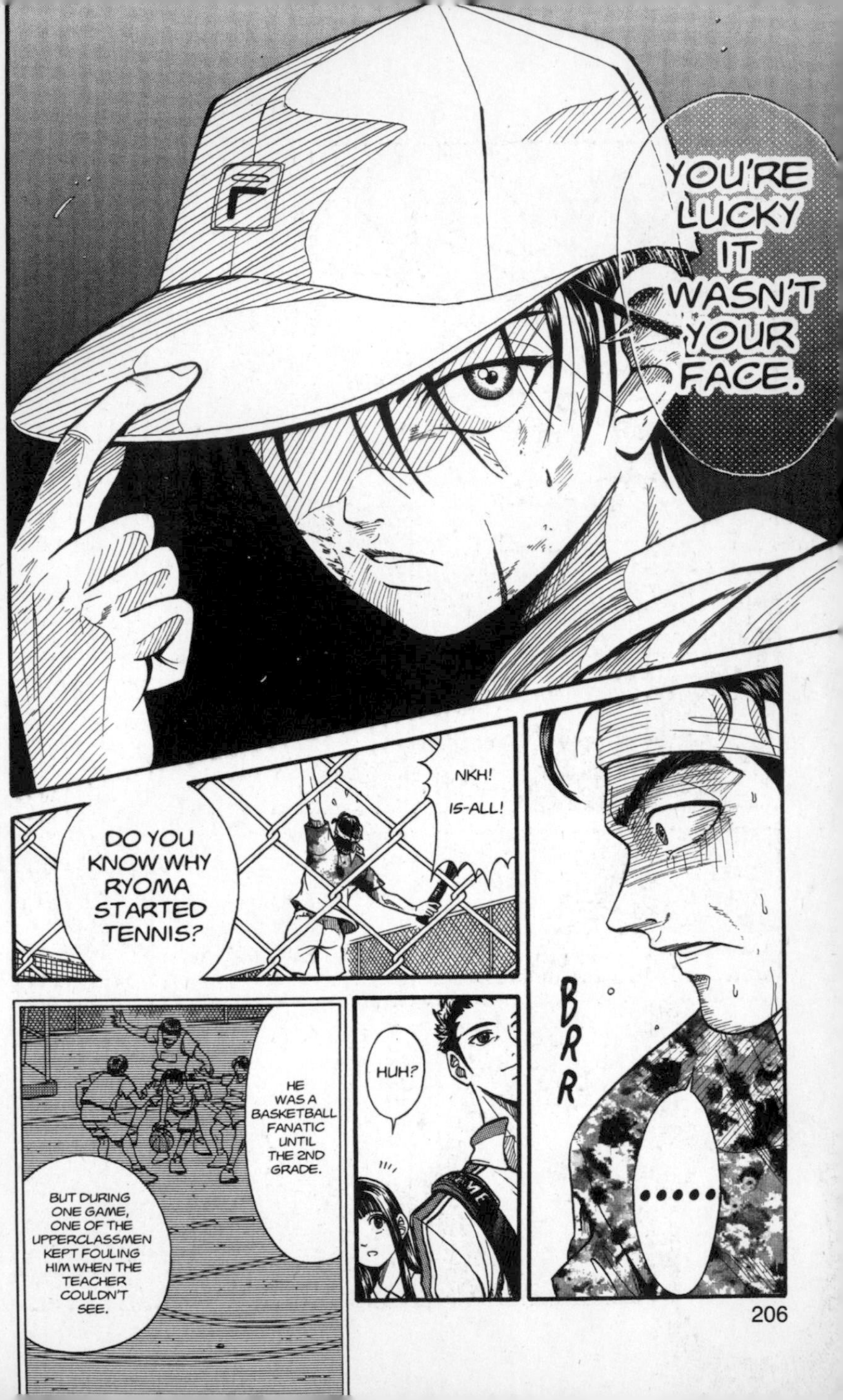
YOU'RE LUCKY IT WASN'T YOUR FACE.
BRR
.....
NKH!
IS-ALL!
DO YOU KNOW WHY RYOMA STARTED TENNIS?
HUH?
HE WAS A BASKETBALL FANATIC UNTIL THE 2ND GRADE.
BUT DURING ONE GAME, ONE OF THE UPPERCLASSMEN KEPT FOULING HIM WHEN THE TEACHER COULDN'T SEE.

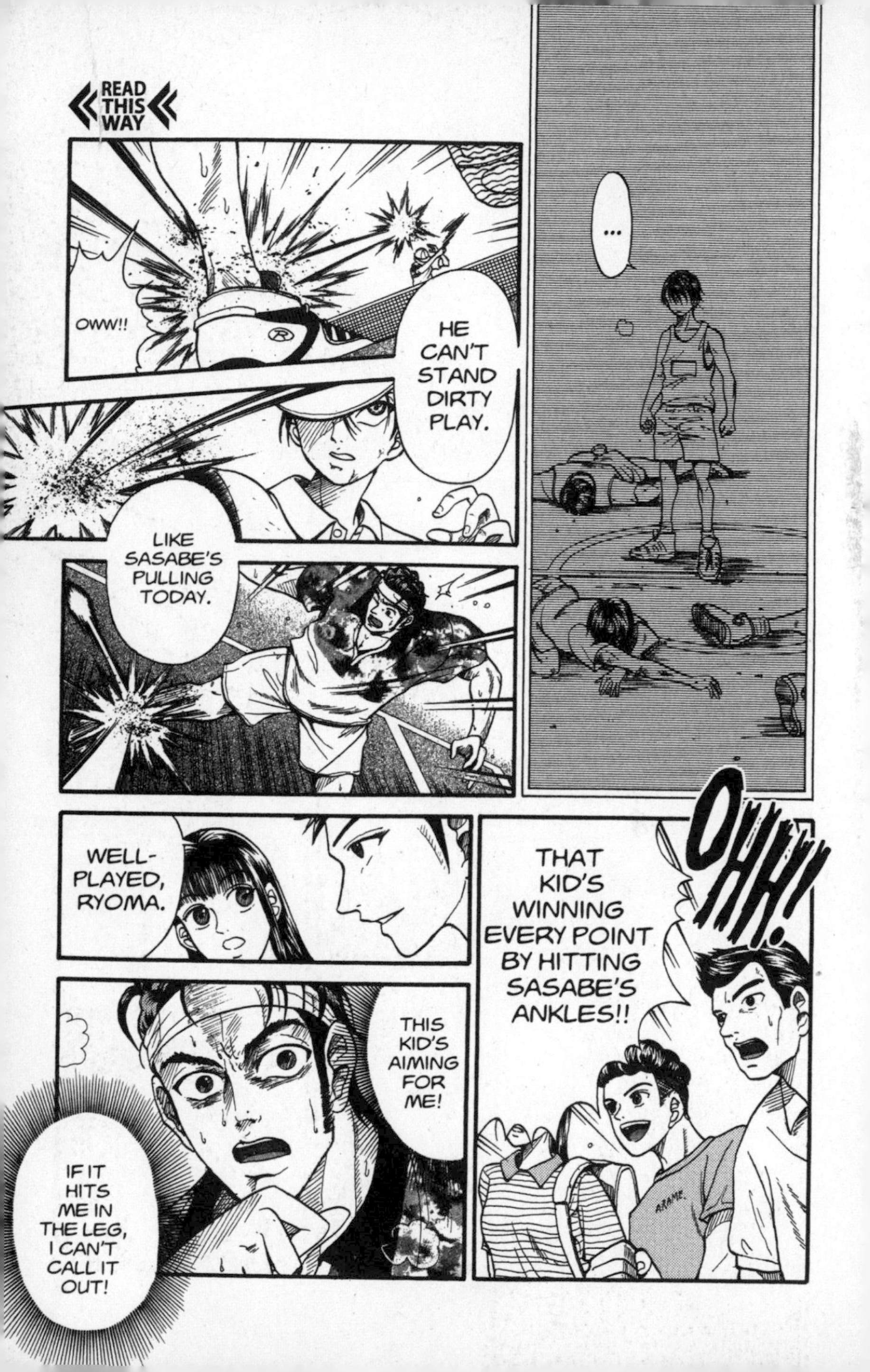
READ THIS WAY
...
OWW!!
HE CAN'T STAND DIRTY PLAY.
LIKE SASABE'S PULLING TODAY.
OHHH!
THAT KID'S WINNING EVERY POINT BY HITTING SASABE'S ANKLES!!
WELL-PLAYED, RYOMA.
THIS KID'S AIMING FOR ME!
IF IT HITS ME IN THE LEG, I CAN'T CALL IT OUT!

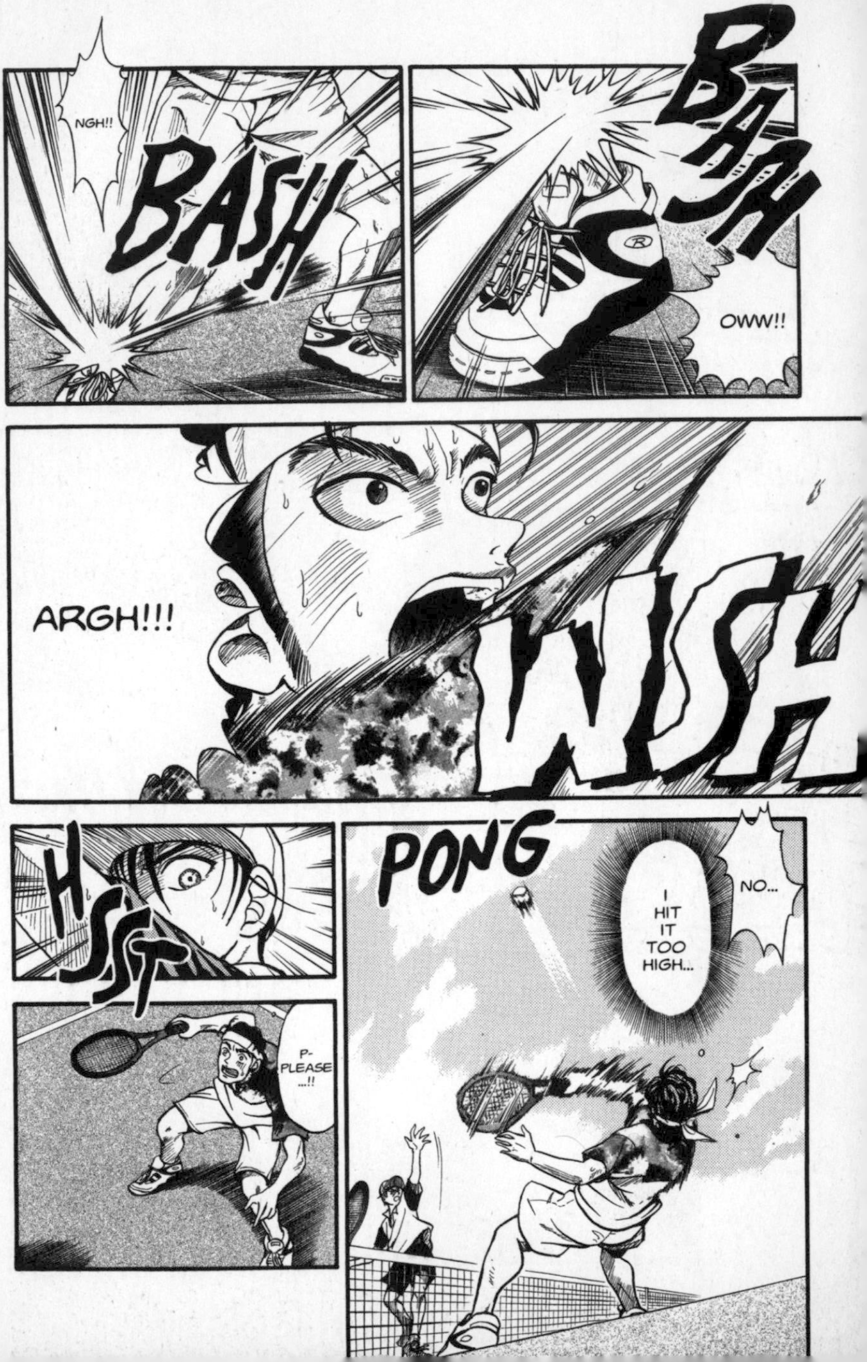
BAM
OWW!!
NGH!!
BASH
ARGH!!!
PONG
NO...
I HIT IT TOO HIGH...
HSST
P-PLEASE ...!!

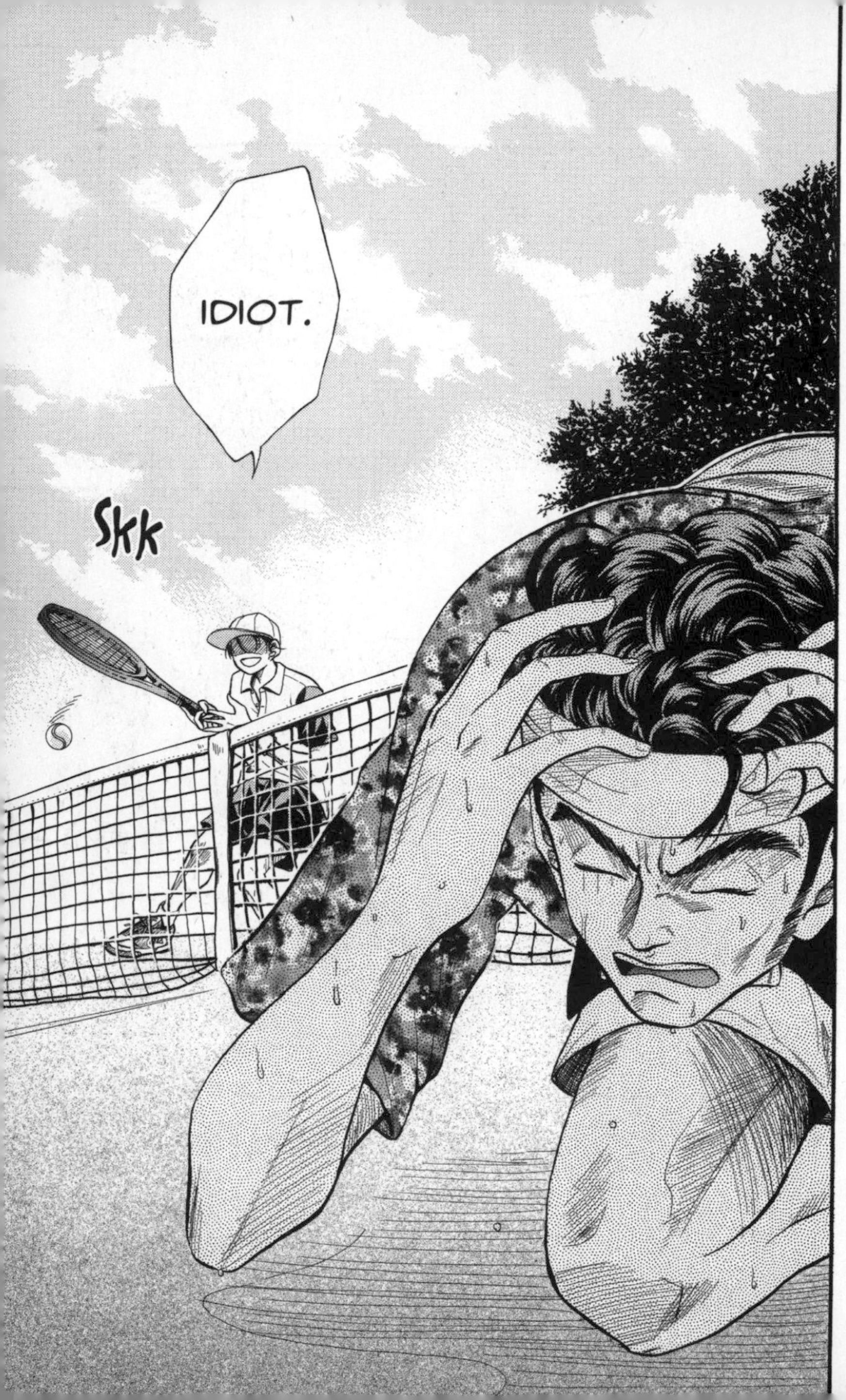
IDIOT.
SKK

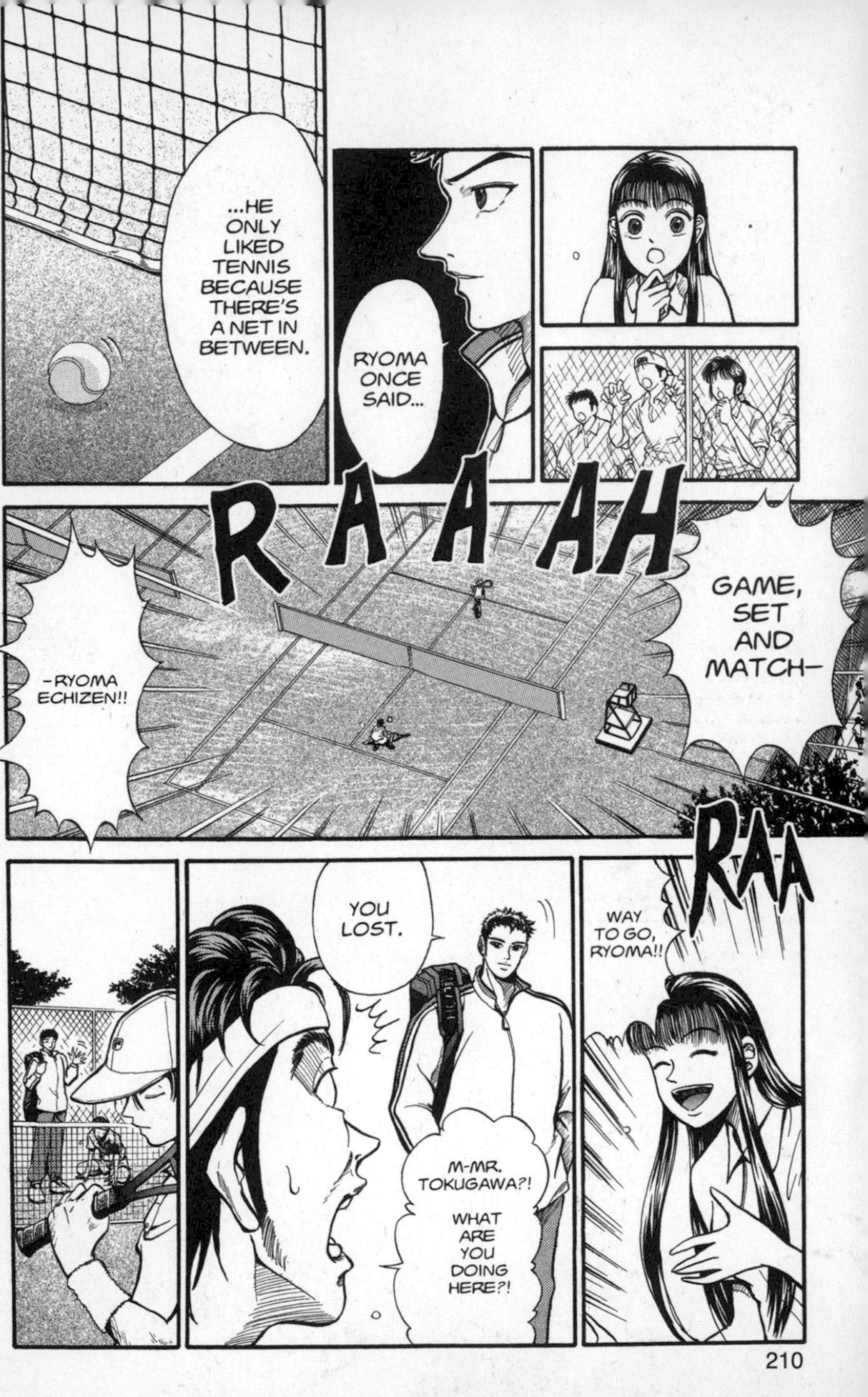
RYOMA ONCE SAID...
...HE ONLY LIKED TENNIS BECAUSE THERE'S A NET IN BETWEEN.
RAAAH
GAME, SET AND MATCH—
–RYOMA ECHIZEN!!
RAA
WAY TO GO, RYOMA!!
YOU LOST.
M-MR. TOKUGAWA?!
WHAT ARE YOU DOING HERE?!

READ THIS WAY

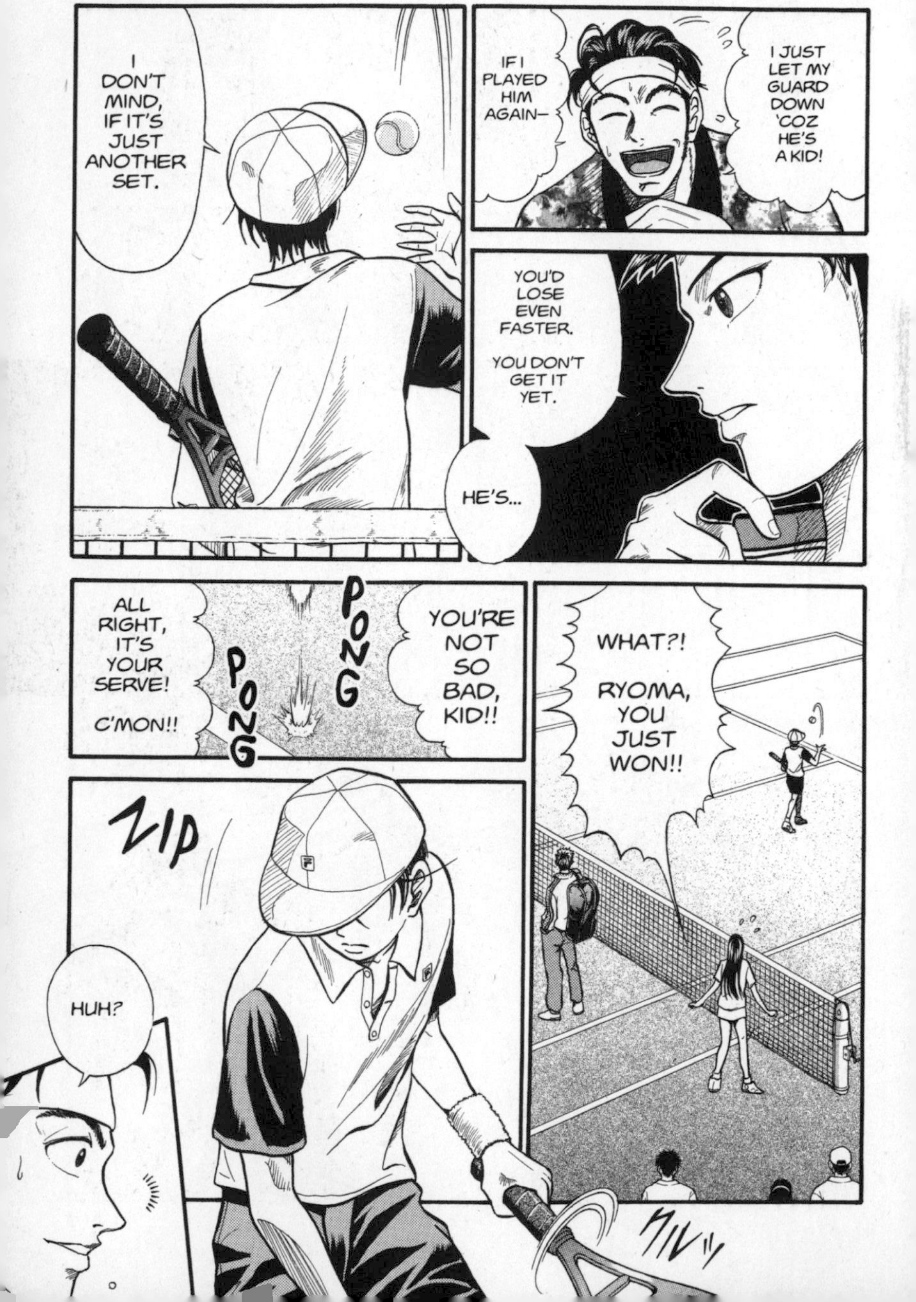
I JUST LET MY GUARD DOWN 'COZ HE'S A KID!
IF I PLAYED HIM AGAIN—
YOU'D LOSE EVEN FASTER.
YOU DON'T GET IT YET.
HE'S...
I DON'T MIND, IF IT'S JUST ANOTHER SET.
WHAT?!
RYOMA, YOU JUST WON!!
YOU'RE NOT SO BAD, KID!!
PONG
PONG
ALL RIGHT, IT'S YOUR SERVE!
C'MON!!
ZIP
HUH?

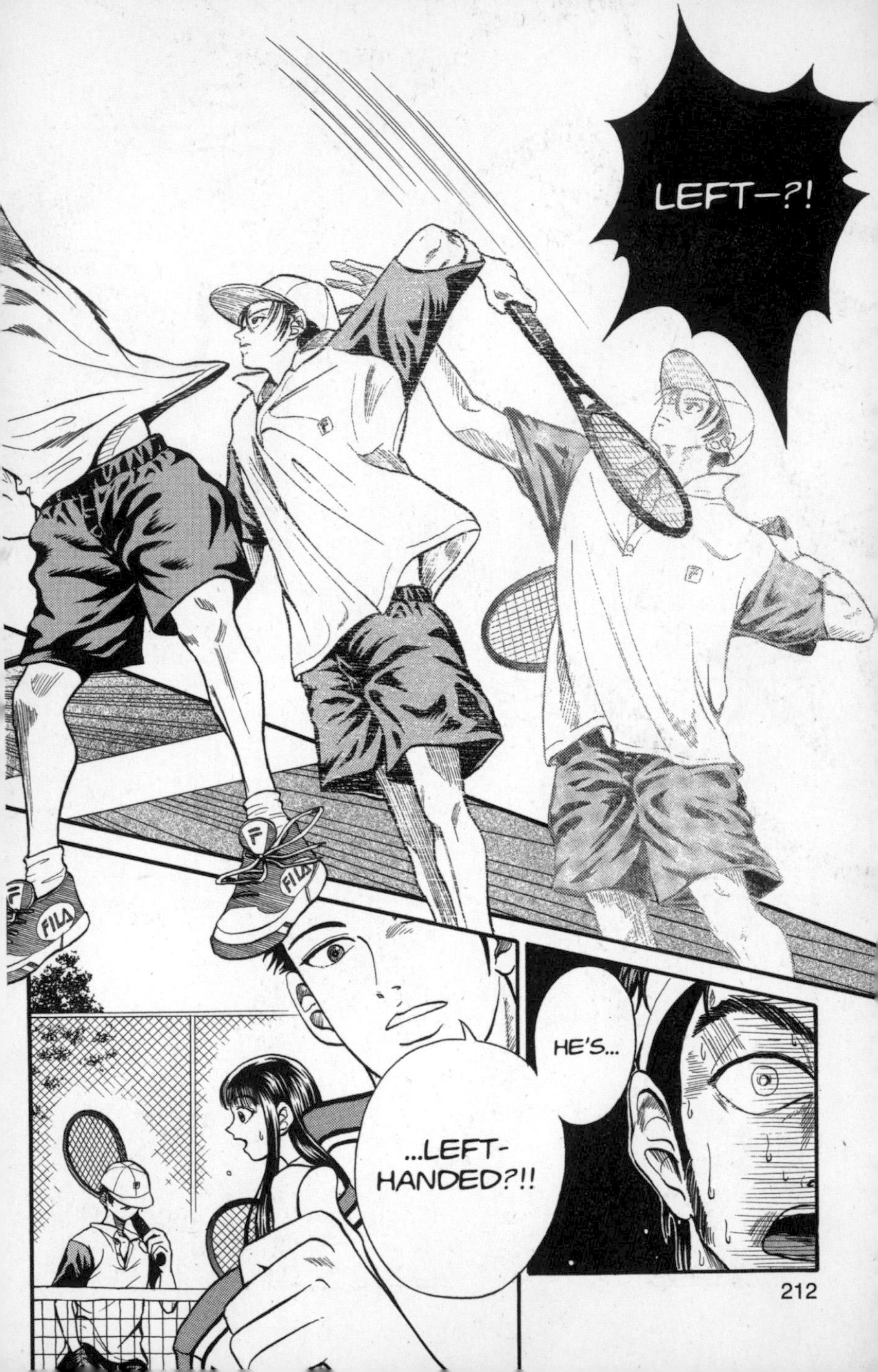
LEFT—?!
HE'S...
...LEFT-HANDED?!!

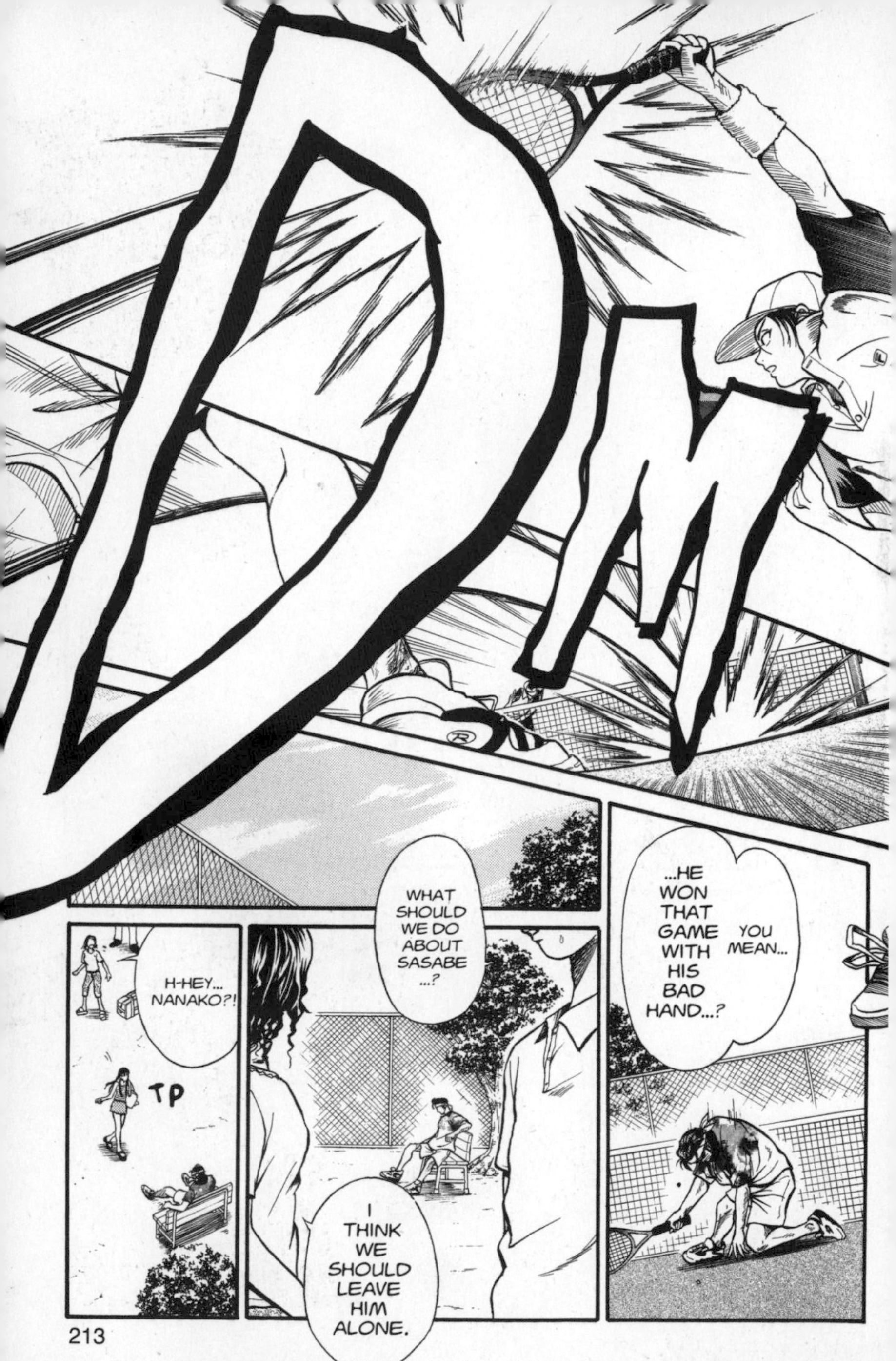
DM
YOU MEAN...
...HE WON THAT GAME WITH HIS BAD HAND...?
WHAT SHOULD WE DO ABOUT SASABE ...?
I THINK WE SHOULD LEAVE HIM ALONE.
H-HEY... NANAKO?!
TP

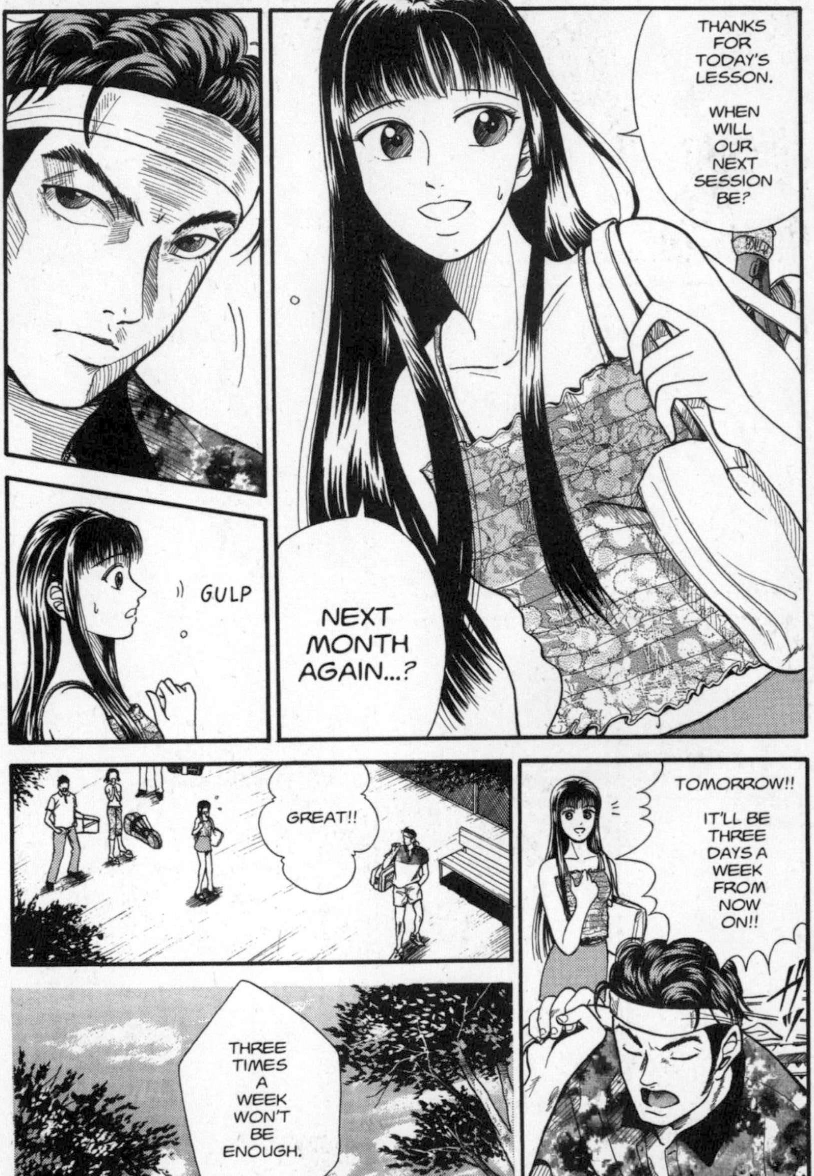
THANKS FOR TODAY'S LESSON.
WHEN WILL OUR NEXT SESSION BE?
NEXT MONTH AGAIN...?
GULP
TOMORROW!!
IT'LL BE THREE DAYS A WEEK FROM NOW ON!!
GREAT!!
THREE TIMES A WEEK WON'T BE ENOUGH.

READ THIS WAY

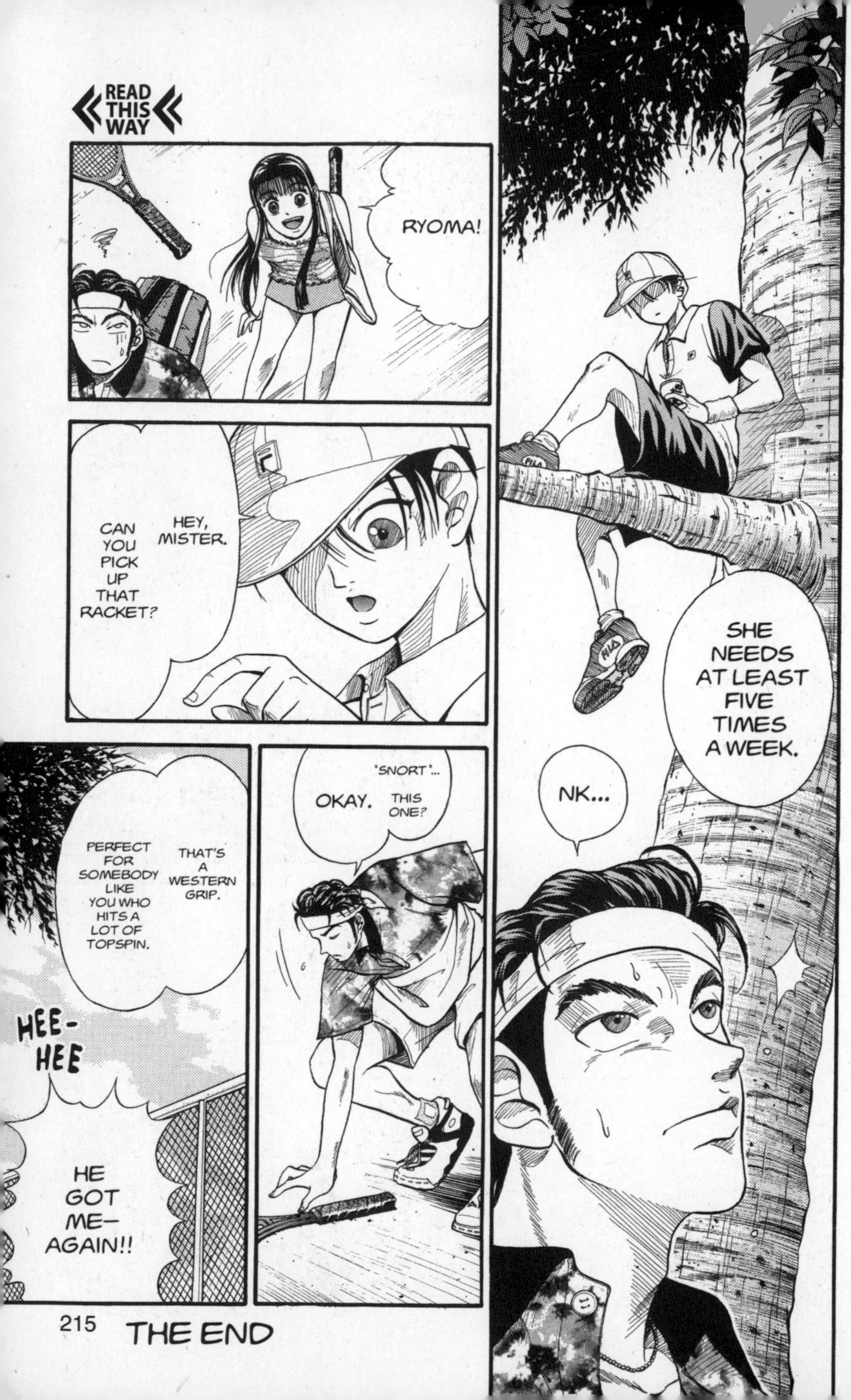

SHE NEEDS AT LEAST FIVE TIMES A WEEK.
NK...
RYOMA!
HEY, MISTER.
CAN YOU PICK UP THAT RACKET?
SNORT...
OKAY.
THIS ONE?
THAT'S A WESTERN GRIP.
PERFECT FOR SOMEBODY LIKE YOU WHO HITS A LOT OF TOPSPIN.
HEE-HEE
HE GOT ME—AGAIN!!

THE END

With Coach Ryuzaki's blessing, Team Captain Kunimitsu Tezuka challenges the Prince of Tennis Ryoma Echizen to a duel. Offended by Ryoma's cocky ways, Kunimitsu decides to settle the score once and for all. As the City Tournament approaches, Seishun encounters the slick maneuvers of Hajime Mizuki, St. Rudolph's manager and brilliant strategist.

Available Now!

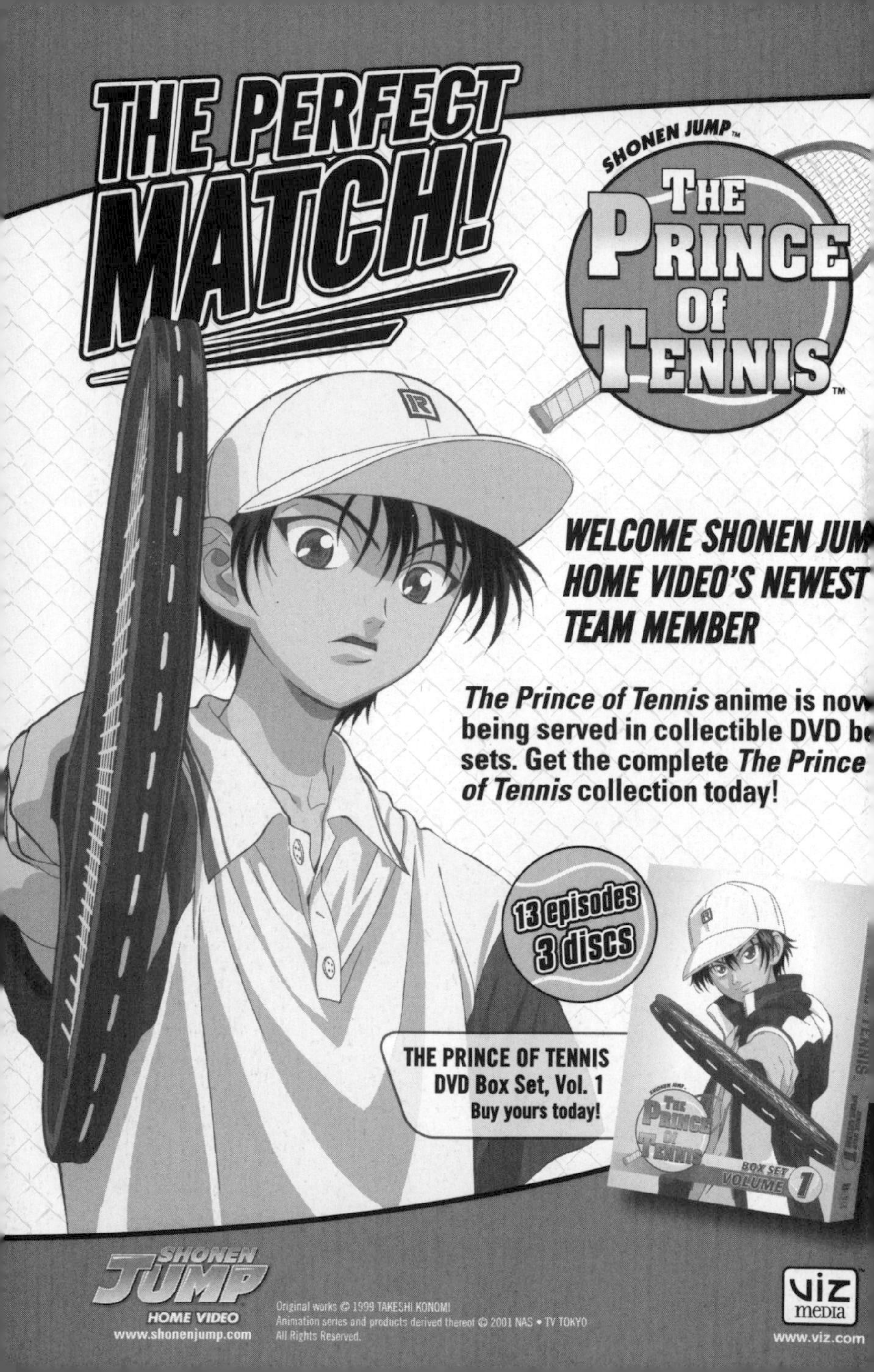
THE PERFECT MATCH!
SHONEN JUMP™
THE PRINCE OF TENNIS™
WELCOME SHONEN JU
HOME VIDEO'S NEWEST
TEAM MEMBER
The Prince of Tennis anime is no
being served in collectible DVD b
sets. Get the complete The Prince
of Tennis collection today!
13 episodes 3 discs
THE PRINCE OF TENNIS
DVD Box Set, Vol. 1
Buy yours today!
BOX SET VOLUME 1
SHONEN JUMP HOME VIDEO
www.shonenjump.com
Original works © 1999 TAKESHI KONOMI
Animation series and products derived thereof © 2001 NAS • TV TOKYO
All Rights Reserved.
viz media
www.viz.com

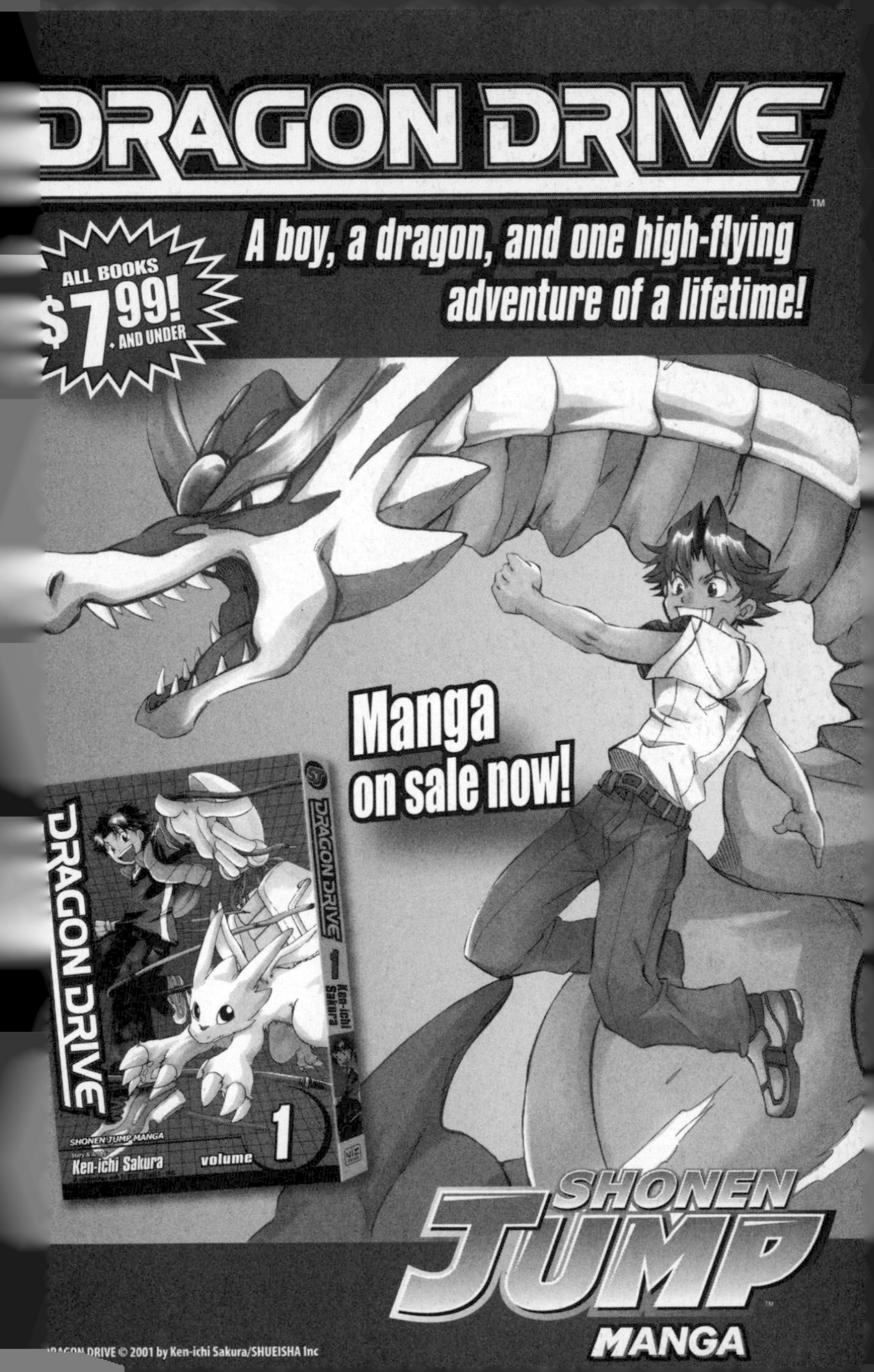
DRAGON DRIVE™
ALL BOOKS $7.99! AND UNDER
A boy, a dragon, and one high-flying adventure of a lifetime!
Manga on sale now!
DRAGON DRIVE
SHONEN JUMP MANGA
Ken-ichi Sakura
volume 1
SHONEN JUMP™ MANGA
RAGON DRIVE © 2001 by Ken-ichi Sakura/SHUEISHA Inc

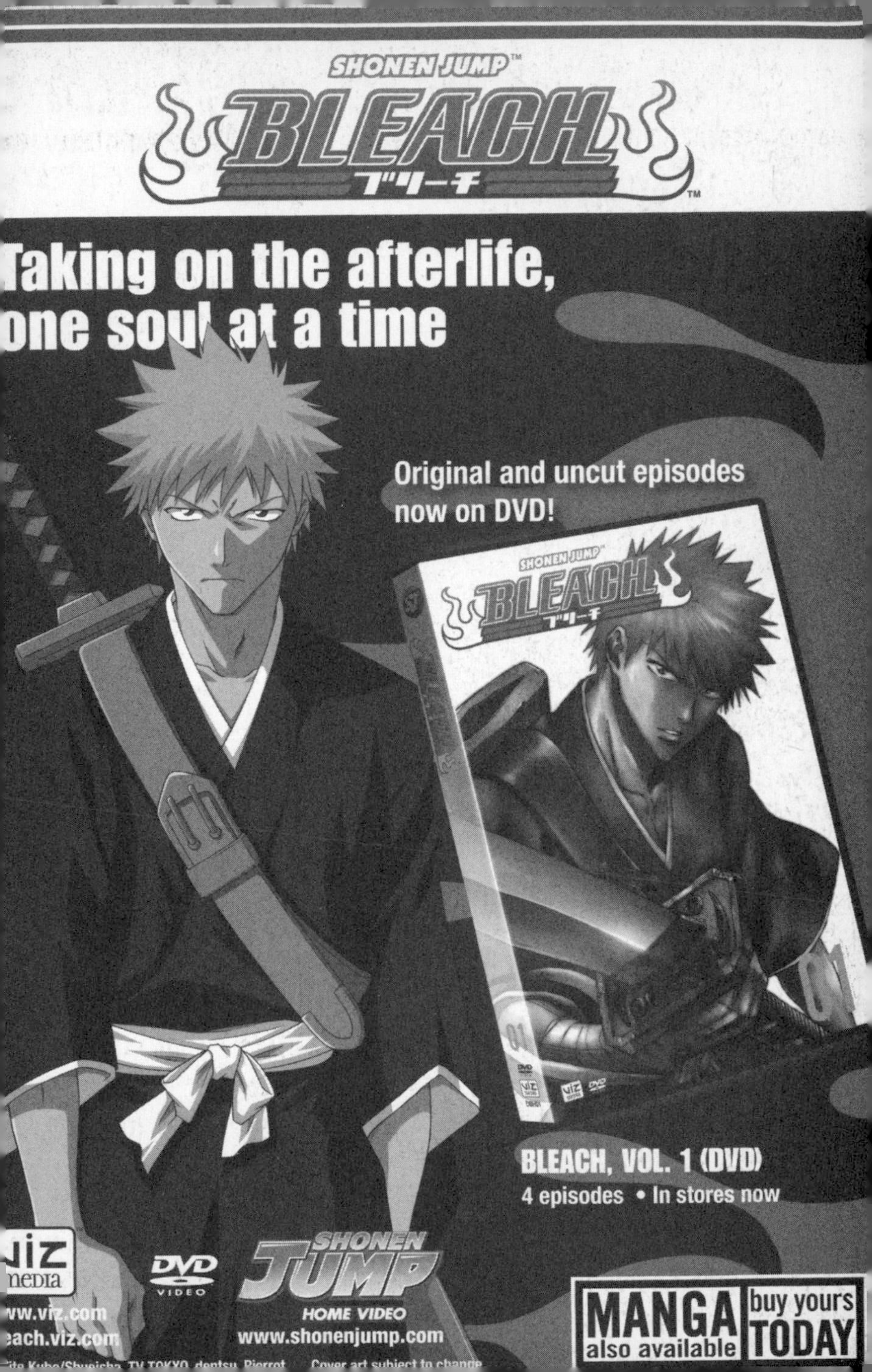
SHONEN JUMP™
BLEACH
ブリーチ
Taking on the afterlife,
one soul at a time
Original and uncut episodes
now on DVD!
BLEACH, VOL. 1 (DVD)
4 episodes • In stores now
SHONEN JUMP
HOME VIDEO
www.shonenjump.com
MANGA
also available
buy yours
TODAY

A BRUSH WITH THE AFTERLIFE

All Colour But The Black

THE ART OF BLEACH

By Tite Kubo, creator of *ZOMBIEPOWDER*.

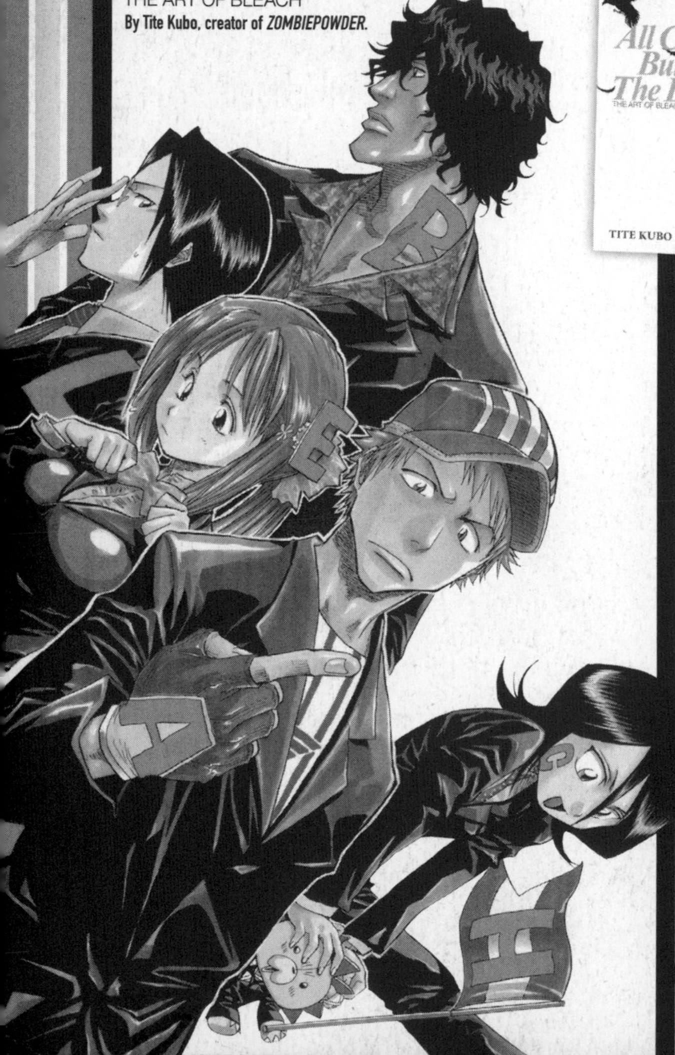

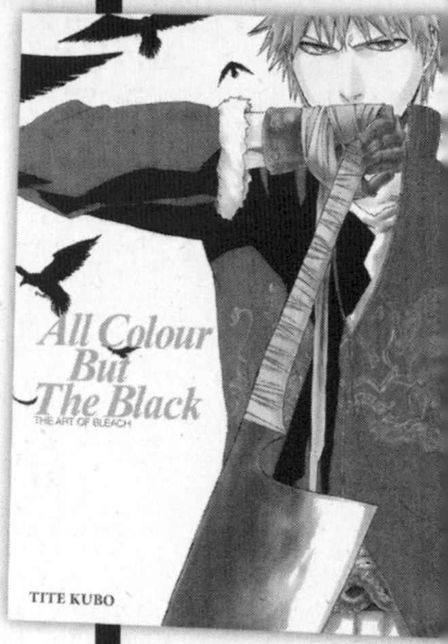
All Colour
But
The Black
THE ART OF BLEACH
TITE KUBO

EXPLORE THE WORLD OF *BLEACH* THROUGH THIS HIGH-QUALITY ART BOOK SHOWCASING ARTWORK FROM TITE KUBO'S POPULAR MANGA SERIES WHICH INCLUDES:

- Vibrant illustrations, including art from volumes 1-19
- An annotated art guide
- Extra character information

PLUS, AN EXCLUSIVE POSTER

COMPLETE YOUR *BLEACH* COLLECTION WITH *THE ART OF BLEACH*: *ALL COLOUR BUT THE BLACK*— GET YOURS TODAY!

On sale at
www.shonenjump.com
Also available at your local bookstore and comic store.

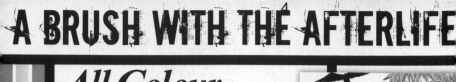

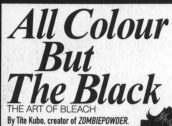

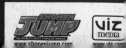

Tell us what you think about SHONEN JUMP manga!

Our survey is now available online.
Go to: www.SHONENJUMP.com/mangasurvey

Help us make our product offering better!

THE REAL ACTION
STARTS IN...

www.shonenjump.com

ADVANCED